Michele Wistisen

D0792869

Readings in Science Methods, K–8

An NSTA Press Journals Collection

Readings in Science Methods, K–8

An NSTA Press Journals Collection

Eric Brunsell, Editor

National Science Teachers Association

Arlington, Virginia

National Science Teachers Association

Claire Reinburg, Director
Jennifer Horak, Managing Editor, Books
Judy Cusick, Senior Editor
Andrew Cocke, Associate Editor
Betty Smith, Associate Editor

SCIENCE AND CHILDREN, Monica Zerry, Managing Editor
SCIENCE SCOPE, Kenneth Roberts, Managing Editor

ART AND DESIGN, Will Thomas, Director
    Tim French, Senior Graphic Designer, Cover

PRINTING AND PRODUCTION, Catherine Lorrain, Director
    Nguyet Tran, Assistant Production Manager
    Jack Parker, Electronic Prepress Technician

NATIONAL SCIENCE TEACHERS ASSOCIATION
Gerald F. Wheeler, Executive Director
David Beacom, Publisher

Copyright © 2008 by the National Science Teachers Association.
All rights reserved. Printed in the United States of America.
11 10 09 08 4 3 2 1

Library of Congress Cataloging-in-Publication Data

Readings in science methods, K-8 / Eric Brunsell, editor.
    p. cm.
 ISBN-13: 978-1-93353-138-0
 ISBN-10: 1-93353-138-X
 1. Science--Study and teaching (Elementary) 2. Science--Study and teaching (Secondary) 3. Teachers--Training
of. 4. College students--Training of. I. Brunsell, Eric.
 LB1585.R33 2008
 372.35'044--dc22
                        2008019265

NSTA is committed to publishing material that promotes the best in inquiry-based science education. However, conditions of actual use may vary, and the safety procedures and practices described in this book are intended to serve only as a guide. Additional precautionary measures may be required. NSTA and the authors do not warrant or represent that the procedures and practices in this book meet any safety code or standard of federal, state, or local regulations. NSTA and the authors disclaim any liability for personal injury or damage to property arising out of or relating to the use of this book, including any of the recommendations, instructions, or materials contained therein.

Permissions
You may photocopy, print, or e-mail up to five copies of an NSTA book chapter for personal use only; this does not include display or promotional use. Elementary, middle, and high school teachers *only* may reproduce a single NSTA book chapter for classroom or noncommercial, professional-development use only. For permission to photocopy or use material electronically from this NSTA Press book, please contact the Copyright Clearance Center (CCC) (*www.copyright.com*; 978-750-8400). Please access *www.nsta.org/permissions* for further information about NSTA's rights and permissions policies.

Contents

Section 2
Teaching Science 55

There's MORE to Teaching Science

By Doug Ronsberg

Doug Ronsberg is a special education paraprofessional for grades two and three at Castle Elementary in Oakdale, Minnesota.

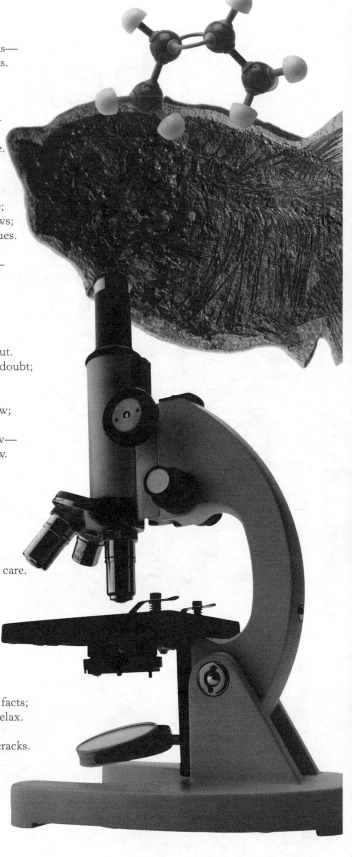

There's more to teaching science than stuffing kids with facts—
    'cause unconnected data flow like rain right off their backs.
    Help kids discover nature, stars and waves, and tracks,
    dinosaurs, and temperature, and killer bee attacks.

They have to learn to question, to observe, and to explore—
    to seek the basic causes, to measure, count, and more.
    So shelve that fault-line lecture; it'll bore them to the core.
    Active kid engagement is the key to learning's door.

Kids need to think like scientists, to sort and sift and muse;
    to evaluate the evidence—conclude what they should use;
    to see the laws of science through a range of different views;
    and find their way around the lab, to search for proper clues.

Encourage novel thinking, new approaches, different ways—
    creative problem solving fosters hope for future days.
    Emphasis on science terms and jargon doesn't pay;
    clarify their thinking and the elements will stay.

Don't be the only fossil that your students learn about;
    make your methods fit their needs and reassure throughout.
    Give lots of time with science tools to ease their fear and doubt;
    show women and minorities in science news you tout.

Cut down on competition and you'll help your students grow;
    use learning teams to multiply the science seeds you sow.
    Encourage interactions so they share the things they know—
    to reason and defend the things they think their data show.

The adage about "Rocket Science" shouldn't conjure fear;
    rocket science can be fun and you should make it clear—
    that everyone contributes to the learning of each peer,
    and they need not all aspire to "Rocket Engineer."

Don't preach on relativity—don't be an emcee square,
    'cause you're not Albert Einstein and they really couldn't care.
    Energize your classroom by getting kids to dare—
    to gather, sort and catalog, and theorize, and share.

History's a matter that requires your energy;
    a solid link between world and technology.
    Insist on clear expression, not gaseous lethargy;
    to make their learning liquid—and sound as it can be.

Yes, there's more to teaching science than stuffing kids with facts;
    you must make them feel comfortable and help them to relax.
    If the action just intimidates you know how they'll react;
    they'll lose their own inertia, and be forced between the cracks.

So be the supernova within their galaxy;
    encourage scientific minds and you will set them free—
    to love the world of science and almost guarantee—
    why not, one day they could become Nobel nominees!

Introduction

Quite often during the summer, my wife and I take our children on walks in the bluffs along the upper Mississippi River. They dart back and forth, flipping over rocks and branches, looking for salamanders, bugs, and snakes. Occasionally, they will slip an interesting rock into a pocket or find the perfect walking stick (more likely, a poke-your-sibling stick). The woods ring with the sound of laughter and a never-ending stream of questions. Usually, one of them has started a new question before we have a chance to answer the first. Children love exploring. The opening line of Doug Ronsberg's poem is the perfect way to begin this book: "There's more to teaching science than stuffing kids with facts...." Science is about questions and exploration. Teaching science is about helping students ask questions and explore and explain the world around them.

Ronsberg continues, "Encourage novel thinking, new approaches, different ways—/creative problem solving fosters hope for future days." Former NSTA President Harold Pratt recently wrote that good science teaching at the elementary level is critical to a child's future. Poorly presented science can deaden children's curiosity and lessen their wonder about the world around them. Students should be engaged "not only in the practice of science, but also the passion. Finding ways to ignite the curiosity and develop inquiring habits of mind is most important...." (2007). The purpose of this book is to provide a comprehensive compilation of practical examples and strategies for good science teaching, set in theoretical frameworks that support student learning. The book is divided into five sections that cover many aspects of teaching. Each section includes reflection questions and action steps that you can follow to deepen your understanding of the concepts presented.

Section 1 introduces you to how scientific knowledge is created. The section also describes a teaching approach—science inquiry—that provides a classroom model of how science is done. A selection of articles provides strategies to support student understanding of science and ability to conduct science inquiry.

Section 2 looks at teaching science through four lenses. The *learner-centered* lens focuses on student engagement and initial knowledge. A *knowledge-centered* lens focuses on what content students should learn and how they should learn it. An *assessment-centered* lens focuses on using assessment to inform instruction and enable learning instead of just summative assessment. A *community-centered* lens focuses on creating an environment that supports discussion and risk taking.

Section 3 describes teaching that supports learning by students from all backgrounds.

Section 4 provides a toolbox of strategies that are important to good teaching: supporting literacy, integrating other disciplines, integrating technology, and teaching preschool and kindergarten students.

Section 5 describes the content of science by providing an overview of the content standards from the National Science Education Standards.

For a matrix showing how the articles used in this book embody the content standards of the National Science Education Standards, turn to p. 341 where the articles are aligned with the pertinent Standard or Standards.

To kick off this book, I thought it would be appropriate to include the article "Inquiring Minds Do Want to Know" by Kaitlyn Hood and Jack A. Gerlovich. The article describes the experience of a preservice elementary teacher in an undergraduate science methods class as she engages fifth-grade students in scientific discovery. Hood describes the importance of this approach when she writes, "Perhaps more than anything else it changed the classroom atmosphere from presentation to discovery and application. I was no longer just a performer—I was someone who knew what the students could do and gave them a stage on which to perform."

My hope is that this compilation will help you to create a classroom that encourages creativity and promotes exploration, a classroom that rings with the sound of laughter and a never-ending stream of questions.

Eric Brunsell
Assistant Professor, Science Education
Department of Educational Studies
University of Wisconsin—La Crosse

Reference

Pratt, H. 2007. "Science education's 'overlooked ingredient': Why the path to global competitiveness begins in elementary school." *NSTA Express.* October 29, 2007. At *http://science.nsta.org/nstaexpress/nstaexpress_2007_10_29.htm*.

Inquiring Minds Do Want to Know

By Kaitlyn Hood and Jack A. Gerlovich

My first foray into inquiry science came a few years ago as part of an undergraduate science methods class at Drake University. In the class, groups of my colleagues were assigned to teach a four-to six-part lesson to students at various local elementary schools. The fifth-grade class to which my group was assigned was interested in tornadoes, so we decided to present a series of lessons that gave students a solid background for understanding how a tornado is formed. We visited the class six times, each time demonstrating a different aspect of tornados and how they affect people. (See Figure 1 for a day-by-day description of each visit's lesson plan.)

I chose to lead the group's fifth lesson. I wanted a lesson that went beyond the tornado in a bottle. I envisioned students making a tornado in the classroom so they could really see it working. I wanted the tornado to be close enough and safe enough for them to touch and perhaps even alter to make it taller, wider, or faster. Creating the tornado would be the students' experiment—not the teacher's. Although the idea was good, I

had struggled to put together a lesson plan and turned to my professor for help.

As I discussed what I wanted to do in the class, we wondered what would happen if I told the students, "We now know about the conditions necessary for a tornado to form; let's figure out how to make one in our classroom." This form of teaching—in which the teacher poses the question but lets the students decide how to answer the question—falls into the guided-inquiry approach (Martin-Hansen 2002). It was an approach I was eager to try.

Trying the Tornado

The idea to have students create a tornado in class made my mind race. Being a preservice teacher, I didn't have a lot of experience with students—and I did not see myself going into the classroom without knowing exactly what was going to happen. What would happen if students could not create the tornado? Would the students see us—their teachers—as failures? Or worse, would they think they themselves had failed? I knew enough about inquiry-based learning to know that some-

Figure 1.

Breakdown of tornado lessons

Day One: Informal Preassessment
This was a chance for the students to get to know their new teachers, as well as an opportunity for the teachers to find out what the students knew about tornadoes.

Day Two: Introduction to Tornadoes
The lesson started witph the students returning from "specials" to find their classroom hit by a tornado. As the class put the desks and other classroom materials back in order there was a discussion on how a tornado can affect someone very personally. We then read two short accounts of tornado victims to enforce the idea of tornadoes being amazing forces of nature but also something that can affect someone's life. We ended the class by introducing the idea of how tornadoes are formed by using bottle tornados as visual aids.

Day Three: Panel of Experts
We came into the classroom in costumes—we had a child who had lived through a tornado, a farmer, a tornado chaser, a weather forecaster, and a relief worker. We each gave the students a short talk on what we do when a tornado forms, and what kinds of things each expert finds really important. At the end of

this lesson we gave them a worksheet to review the main points of the lesson and to keep in their science journals for future reference.

Day Four: Science Safety
The class had already discussed the basic ideas of how to be a safe scientist, so we decided to focus more on having each student sign a safety contract. Two of us dressed up as Science Safety Agents and explained what we expected from them as scientists. At the end of class we told the students that we wanted them to try to make a tornado next time we came and compiled a list of materials they requested.

Day Five: Making a Tornado
We brought in the materials, divided into groups, and let the students work through their ideas twice. The only assistance we gave them was when we handled the dry ice.

Day Six: Assessment
The class was divided into two groups. Different tornado and science safety facts that had been discussed throughout our classes were the basis of the review game questions. Each team worked together to formulate their answers and really knew their material.

times the process is more important than the product. Wittrock and Barrow (2000) said that the teacher is more of a facilitator when teaching with inquiry, but, when I thought about that idea in a real-life scenario, it scared me to death. Still, I forged ahead and created a plan for the lesson by reviewing the research we had discussed in class and writing a rough time line. I tried to run through various scenarios and troubleshoot any roadblocks we might encounter.

Two days later I presented the challenge to

students in the classroom at our fifth visit. Students were primed for the challenge, because, at the conclusion of the fourth lesson, we had told students that we would be trying to create a tornado in the classroom on our next visit and we had brainstormed with them some materials we might need for this project: fans, spray bottles, bowls, and dry ice. Students chose fans to create wind and the spray bottles, because we had talked about humid air. They chose dry ice because it had been used recently in a school function, and the students knew that it formed fog, which they thought could be useful in trying to "see" the tornado they would create in the classroom.

When a teacher offers this kind of inquiry experience to a class, a lot of preplanning is needed, even if there is no predetermined path. The teacher should be aware of the potential hazards in the materials that are offered, make sure that the space and class sizes are appropriate, and discuss precautions with students. When student groups plan their own inquiry, they should think about their own safety plan and have it checked with the teacher. Before students handled any materials, we talked about safety procedures and established that the dry ice was to be handled only by teachers who would be wearing goggles and protective gloves. We also marked off a tornado "zone" so students could not reach the dry ice. In addition, we made sure water was kept away from the fan plugs and that the fans had screen finger guards.

When my colleagues and I arrived with the materials, I introduced the challenge. I explained how we (the teachers) wanted to show the class a tornado, but there was not a specific formula for creating one in a classroom setting. I told them that we had taught them a lot about how tornadoes are formed, and, if they used each other as resources, they would be able to try to create a tornado. Within minutes the kids were in groups formulating predictions and designing experiments.

Then, students started their experiments. We approved each one before they began but offered students no other help in the process except for handling the dry ice for safety purposes. When necessary, we asked guiding questions (What happened when you changed the position of the fan? Why did you make that decision?), referring them to their science journals so they could try each idea in an organized way. It was amazing to watch the students' faces as they saw each experiment begin to work in one aspect but fail in another. For example, one group had every fan pointed toward the bowl of dry ice to try to force the air up in a twister. Another group thought that they could create an upside-down twister by

having the dry ice on the top of a file cabinet and trying to move the "smoke" (what the children called the frozen water vapor) as it floated to the ground. Another group used the spray bottles to try to mix dry air with humid air.

I could see lightbulbs turning on in their minds. They spoke of the learning that had occurred earlier as they wrestled with their new challenge. They referred to parts of other experiments like fan placement and what kind of water created the most "smoke." They also took notes on what worked in their journals. They had to apply what they had learned about the atmospheric conditions from our weather forecaster lesson—air from two different directions has to combine—and what they had studied from using two-liter tornado bottle simulations—we put Monopoly houses in the bottles so the students could see in what direction the twisters were forming.

A Whirl of Learning

I wish I could say that students created a tornado, but they did not. They also did not realize that they "failed." In our wrap-up discussion that day, students admitted that they got close enough that they could now visualize the conditions necessary to simulate a tornado. We discovered that if you turn a box fan upside down the air will "pull the 'smoke' upward." To get it to spin, you need two fans pushing the air in opposite directions. The twister can reach only a few feet, but it does twist once you get the fans in the right position.

There was not a single child in that classroom who was not involved in that discussion.

Students were listening to what their peers were saying, because they had something to add to elaborate on the idea even more. We also took the conversation into what went wrong and how they were able to problem solve. They used the knowledge and processes of investigation—trial and error, problem solving—that we had guided them through and, by themselves, were able to come close to a product that was presented to them as nearly impossible.

Students were so excited about the process

they may not remember that they could not replicate a tornado. What they will likely remember is that they were given the opportunity to realize that science is truly a verb as well as a noun and that they loved the experience.

Keeping the Spark

Reflecting on the success of the tornado lesson, I tried to come up with a formula or a list of guidelines for myself for creating and maintaining this kind of spark in a classroom again. What I came up with was this: An inquiry-based lesson

- is more than the lesson idea or the proper equipment. It involves trusting your students to learn when you give them the time and responsibility to think on their own. Provide students the tools to know how to problem solve, give them guidelines on working with others, provide safety reminders, and let them explore. Our job as teachers is to circulate and guide students with questions as they discover the solutions.
- is the kind of activity in which everyone in the class can be involved; it may turn out that this is where a struggling student can really shine.
- can teach about more than just concepts. It gives students a process to use when they encounter other problems in and out of the classroom.
- allowed me to see the students use information to create something.

Perhaps more than anything else, the lesson changed the classroom atmosphere from presentation to discovery and application. I was no longer just a performer—I was someone who knew what the students could do and gave them a stage on which to perform. That is something that will be very hard for anyone who witnesses it to forget.

The tornado experience really surprised me. Not only did my group do something fantastic with a group of fifth graders that really sparked their interest, but the experience also sparked an interest in science in me and helped open my eyes to new opportunities. As a result of the lesson, I decided to intern at the Science Center of Iowa to teach inquiry-based projects to elementary students. I have continued to work with Drake students and the Science Center to promote inquiry in the classroom. I am in my second year of teaching and continue to incorporate inquiry-based learning in my classroom.

Three years ago, if someone had told me I would be excited by teaching with a science-based method I would have rolled my eyes, but this experience has changed me and my approach to almost everything in my classroom.

Kaitlyn Hood is in her second year of teaching for Des Moines Public Schools. Jack A. Gerlovich is a professor of science education at Drake University in Des Moines, Iowa.

Resources

Jesky-Smith, R. 2002. Me, teach science? *Science and Children* 39 (6): 26–30.

Kwan, T., and J. Texley. 2003. *Exploring safety: A guide for elementary teachers.* Arlington, VA: NSTA.

Martin-Hansen, L. 2002. Defining inquiry. *The Science Teacher* 69 (2): 34–37.

National Research Council (NRC). 1996. *National Science Education Standards.* Washington DC: National Academy Press.

Wittrock, C., and L. Barrow. 2000. Blow-by-blow inquiry. *Science and Children* 37 (5): 34–38.

Internet

Tornado Lesson Plan
www.educ.drake.edu/gerlovich/tornadoes

Connecting to the Standards

This article relates to the following National Science Education Standards (NRC 1996):

Teaching Standards

Standard A:
Teachers of science plan an inquiry-based science program for their students.

Section 1

The Nature of Science and Science Inquiry

The Nature of Science and Science Inquiry

What Is Science?

Science is a systematic process of learning about the natural world. Scientists attempt to understand the world by making careful observations and creating theories to explain those observations. They make observations in many settings and may observe phenomena passively, make collections, or actively probe the world. In some cases, scientists may control conditions through an experimental method (see p. 6). By focusing on the natural world, science precludes the use of the supernatural or magic as acceptable evidence or explanations. There are some questions that science simply cannot address. Science cannot investigate matters of religious faith, good versus evil, or beliefs such as astrology and supernatural hauntings. Because science is a human endeavor, the possibility of bias does exist. Through the process of examining evidence, however, bias is generally corrected over time.

A *theory* is a model of how a specific aspect of the world works. A theory becomes widely accepted as it becomes more precise and can be used to make predictions about the natural world. The big bang theory, for example, came about as scientists tried to explain observations that were consistent with an expanding universe. Among other predictions, the big bang theory predicted the ratio of hydrogen to helium in the universe and the background temperature of the universe. As scientific observations confirmed these predictions, the theory became widely accepted and alternative explanations were rejected. Like all models, theories are not absolute truth, but are approximations of the natural world. Because they are approximations of the natural world, they are subject to change: Although a theory may fit observations well, modifications to the theory or an alternate theory may lead to a better fit. Modification of ideas rather than outright rejection is the norm for theories that have become widely accepted.

What Should Science Look Like in the Classroom?

A knowledge-centered science classroom focuses on science concepts and processes. Social constructivism, pioneered by the Russian psychologist Lev Vygotsky (1987), views knowledge construction as a result of individuals interacting in social environments. The activity by which knowledge is developed is not separable from the learning that is taking place. This means that, if the classroom does not reflect the culture of science, students will not have a full appreciation of the science content presented in that classroom. If science is presented to students only as a body of facts to memorize, students will view science as a collection of facts rather than what it is: a way of understanding the natural world

In a knowledge-centered science classroom, students work to answer scientifically oriented questions by creating explanations based on evidence. This approach, called *science inquiry,* is how science is conducted. It creates a learning environment that reflects the culture of science. The National Research Council (1996) states that "inquiry into authentic questions generated from student experiences is the central strategy for teaching science." Inquiry teaching as described by the NRC has the following essential features:

1. The learner engages in scientifically oriented questions.
2. The learner gives priority to evidence in responding to questions.
3. The learner formulates explanations from evidence.
4. The learner connects explanations to scientific knowledge.
5. The learner communicates and justifies explanations.

Variations in inquiry strategies can be described on a continuum based on the amount of teacher intervention.
- *Open (or Full) Inquiry,* involves the least authoritative intervention by the teacher. Students generate questions and design and conduct their own investigations.
- *Guided Inquiry* involves more direction from the teacher and generally involves the teacher presenting students with the question to be investigated. Students then plan and conduct their own investigations to answer the question.
- In *Structured Inquiry,* teachers provide students with a series of questions and directions for investigations that students should complete. This is a more authoritative intervention: The teacher provides the problem and processes, but students are able to identify alternative outcomes.

Table 1 illustrates the variations in teacher control for each characteristic of science inquiry. Incorporating inquiry into your teaching requires that you strategically decide how much control to exercise over the inquiry process. Your decisions should support student learning and take into account your students' readiness to participate in inquiry.

In 2002, Chinn and Malhotra examined more than 400 activities found in nine commonly used middle school textbooks to determine how well they reflected characteristics of science inquiry. They found that nearly every activity failed to incorporate elements of science inquiry. To create a classroom environment focused on science inquiry, you will need to modify most of the activities that you use. The following list suggests simple modifications that you can make:

1. Have students create their own data tables.
2. Have students create their own procedures.
3. After completing the activity, ask students to pose questions for further research.
4. Focus students on providing evidence for every conclusion that they make.
5. Create "sentence strips" out of the procedures and have students properly sequence them.
6. Move the activity to the beginning of instruction. Have students complete the

Table 1.
Description of Various Levels of the Essential Features of Classroom Inquiry

Essential Feature	Variations			
	More ——— Amount of Learner Self-Direction ——— Less Less ——— Amount of Direction from Teacher or Material ——— More			
1. Learner engages in scientifically oriented questions	Learner poses a question	Learner selects among questions, poses new questions	Learner sharpens or clarifies question provided by teacher, materials, or other source	Learner engages in question provided by teacher, materials, or other source
2. Learner gives priority to evidence in responding to questions	Learner determines what constitutes evidence and collects it	Learner directed to collect certain data	Learner given data and asked to analyze	Learner given data and told how to analyze
3. Learner formulates explanations from evidence	Learner formulates explanation after summarizing evidence	Learner guided in process of formulating explanations from evidence	Learner given possible ways to use evidence to formulate explanation	Learner provided with evidence and how to use evidence to formulate explanation
4. Learner connects explanations to scientific knowledge	Learner independently examines other resources and forms the links to explanations	Learner directed toward areas and sources of scientific knowledge	Learner given possible connections	Learner provided with an explicit connection to scientific knowledge
5. Learner communicates and justifies explanations	Learner forms reasonable and logical argument to communicate explanations	Learner coached in development of communication	Learner provided broad guidelines to sharpen communication	Learner given steps and procedures for communication

Source: Data from National Research Council. 2000.

activity before they are introduced to the content.

7. Provide time for students to "mess about" with the materials before they begin their investigation.
8. Provide students with options of what or how they investigate.
9. Hold a "scientist meeting" prior to the activity to discuss possible questions for investigation or investigation procedures.
10. Hold a "scientist meeting" after the activity to discuss outcomes, conclusions and supporting evidence.

What Skills Do Students Need?

Students need to develop a variety of skills to fully participate in inquiry.

- Students should have frequent opportunities to *observe* objects and events. Good observations should include information gathered from multiple senses and may involve scientific instruments.
- Students should make educated guesses, or *inferences*, based on observations.
- Students should be able to *measure* using standard (including metric) and nonstandard tools.
- Students should be able to *classify* objects or events into categories based on criteria.
- Students should be able to use words, symbols and graphical representations of data to *communicate* ideas.
- Students should be able to *interpret* data by organizing data and identifying patterns.

Table 2 describes age-appropriate performances for each of these skills.

What Is the Experimental Method?

One process by which scientists create new knowledge is called the *experimental method*. It consists of a series of well-defined steps that test one aspect of a phenomenon while holding the others constant. Many K–12 textbooks call the experimental method the *scientific method,* This is not accurate, however, because the experimental method is only one of the processes that scientists use.

The experimental method involves the following steps:

1. Identifying a problem that can be investigated and determining the independent and dependent variables. Independent variables are those that can be easily changed or controlled. Dependent variables are those that are affected by the independent variables.
2. Stating a hypothesis. Experimenters should pick one independent variable and one dependent variable to test. They should then create a statement of how the independent variable will affect the dependent variable.
3. Testing a hypothesis. Experimenters design a "fair test" of their hypothesis. In a fair test, the independent variable is changed, the dependent variable is measured and the other variables are held constant.
4. Analyzing results. Students try to make sense of their data.
5. Communicating conclusions. Students compare their results to their initial hypothesis and communicate their results.

Table 3 describes age-appropriate experimentation.

Table 2.
Age-appropriate performances for science process skills

	Grades K–1	Grades 2–3	Grades 4–5	Grades 6–8
Observing	Students should be able to make basic observations using all five senses. Students should be able to make observations regarding color, size, and shape. Students should be able to use some basic scientific tools (e.g., hand lenses) to assist in making observations.	Students, with help, should be able to decide what observations are needed in order to provide useful data. Although most observations will be qualitative, students should begin making some quantitative observations. Students should be able to explain results or conclusions using observations.	By this age, observations using multiple senses should be natural for students. Students should be comfortable determining what observations are useful and identifying proper scientific tools to assist in making observations. Students should be able to make qualitative and quantitative observations. Student conclusions should be supported by their observations.	Students should be able to explain that scientific inquiry is not possible without accurate observations. Students should be able to describe how technological advances have helped scientists make more accurate and new observations that have lead to new scientific knowledge.
	IMPORTANT: Students should follow teacher directions for safe observing. Students should not use smell, taste, or touch when observing hazardous materials. The use of hazardous materials should be avoided in elementary grades.			
Inferring	Students should work with objects and activities that are relevant to them. They can make simple observations and make inferences as to why something happened, but with little background knowledge, based on their experiences.	Students have had more experiences, but not a lot yet. They are able to better analyze data to make simple inferences and predictions about their experiments.	Students are growing developmentally and at this stage can use scientific tools, equipment, logical reasoning, resources, and dichotomous keys as ways to help develop their inferences.	At this level, students are able to use the data they collected to support and explain their scientific inferences. They are also able to discuss ideas and results with peers, teachers, and other adults.
Classifying	Students should be able to sort objects into groups or categories based on common properties (color, size, shape, use). Students should be able to group objects by a single characteristic.	Students should be able to form groups that are subordinate to a larger group. Students should recognize that the same object may have more than one attribute or characteristic that can be used in classification.	Students should be able to form groups that are mutually exclusive. Students should also be able to abstract the general attributes of objects in a collection.	Students should be able to form hierarchical classification systems.

(Cont on p. 8)

NOTE: Contributed by University of Wisconsin–La Crosse science methods students during the fall 2007 semester.

(Cont from p. 7)

Communicating	Students should be able to share personal information (show and share), create basic graphs and read simple graphs and charts. Students should be able to describe objects, tell stories, and participate in playacting.	Students should be able to create and read graphs, charts and diagrams. Students should explore number sentences and participate in journaling and teacher conferencing.	Students should be able to complete group projects, communicate ideas through poster making, and use diagrams to explain information. Students should also be able to create more complicated graphs and charts.	Students should be able to deliver individual and group presentations and use mathematical equations and explanations to describe results.
Measuring	Students should be able to measure length and volume of simple objects using standard and nonstandard units. Students should be able to read a thermometer and clocks and be able to compare temperatures. At this age, student measurements should be to the nearest whole number.	Students should be able to measure intervals of time and compare weights. Students should become familiar with Fahrenheit and Celsius temperature scales.	Students should be able to estimate the distance between points, weigh and compare objects, and identify the freezing and boiling points of water. Measurements should be made using fractions.	Students should be able to determine volume by displacement and understand the difference between weight and mass. Students should be able to measure using the metric system.
Interpreting Data	Students should be able to report the results of science investigations to different audiences (friends, teachers, family) by using simple graphs, tables and illustrations. Students should be able to collect simple data from investigations.	Students should be able to use evidence to explain and justify results and conclusions. Students should recognize that there are multiple sources of information available to answer questions.	Students should be able to identify sources of data and be able to determine and explain which data are needed to answer a scientific question. Students should use data to support scientific conclusions. Students should routinely incorporate and discuss graphical representations of data.	Students should be able to use collected data to support and explain scientific inferences. Students should be able to critique experimental designs and procedures. Students should be able to use qualitative and qualitative data from multiple sources to develop and defend scientific conclusions.

Table 3.
Age-appropriate experimentation

Grades K–1	Grades 2–3	Grades 4–5	Grades 6-8
Students participate in simple investigations. • asking questions • making observations • identifying what variable may be causing another to change. • selecting equipment for and conducting simple investigations • collecting some data • reporting the results of the investigations to others by using simple graphs, tables, and illustrations	Students are able to conduct an investigation, interpret the results and modify questions accordingly: • planning a simple investigation • deciding what observations are needed to explain the results • acquiring the sense that there might be more than one variable that is causing a particular happening, and decide how they are going to investigate that. • predicting the results of the investigation • conducting simple investigations • using evidence collected to explain results • selecting relevant equipment to use during the investigations • identifying data relevant to their questions and investigations • interpreting data • developing additional questions that support new investigations on the original topic	Students are able to create their own experiments and all characteristics are appropriate for this age: • identifying questions that can be answered with available equipment • determining which equipment is most logical to answer each question • determining if the questions are testable • identifying sources of data • determining which data is needed to answer the question • explaining the results of an investigation to others using multiple forms of communication • verifying the results through other experimentation	Students are moving from the concrete stage to the abstract stage and are more able to be creative in planning experiments and analyzing results: • discussing the results and implications of an investigation • deciding if the results are logical and accurate • raising further questions after the experiment is done • collecting data and defending the validity of the experiment • developing alternative hypotheses for the question • designing and conducting investigations

NOTE: Contributed by Rachel Knutowski.

The Articles

This section contains seven articles that illustrate teaching that builds a learning environment conducive to student understanding of the nature of science and science inquiry.

Article: A Literature-Circles Approach to Understanding Science as a Human Endeavor
Key Ideas: This article describes an approach to help students gain an understanding of the nature of science by reading and discussing nonfiction.

Article: Light Students' Interest in the Nature of Science
Key Ideas: After students learn about electric circuits, they are challenged to explain how a "light up" shoe works. Students make observations and develop an explanatory theory for how the shoe works. This article describes connections between the activity and how scientific knowledge is created.

Article: Did You Really Prove It?
Key Ideas: This article describes four strategies for reinforcing the nature of science throughout the school year.

Article: An Inquiry Primer
Key Ideas: This article provides an overview of science inquiry by providing answers to questions commonly asked by teachers.

Article: Inquiry Made Easy
Key Ideas: This article describes a step-by-step process for introducing science inquiry into your teaching.

Article: Blow-by-Blow Inquiry
Key Ideas: This article describes the "Experimental Method" in progress. The authors also provide examples of how to scaffold students into inquiry.

Article: Why Do We Classify Things in Science?
Key Ideas: In this article, the author explains how scientists use classification to help them make sense of new things. The author explains why this skill is important in the classroom.

Action Steps

1. Read more about the Nature of Science at *http://evolution.berkeley.edu/evosite/nature/index.shtml*.
2. Read Chapter 1 of AAA's *Science for All Americans* at *www.project2061.org/publications/sfaa/online/chap1.htm*.
3. Watch NOVA's *Judgment Day: Intelligent Design on Trial* and describe how the show illustrates examples of the nature of science and examples of nonscientific thought at *www.pbs.org/wgbh/nova/id*.
4. Find a "cookbook" activity from the internet, a textbook, or an activity guide. Modify the activity so that it includes all of the characteristics of science inquiry. Try making modifications to create a guided-inquiry activity and an open-inquiry activity.

Reflection Questions

1. How is the popular use of the word *theory* different from the scientific use of the word?
2. What might a rubric for student understanding of the nature of science look like? What are the most basic ideas that students should master? What are the more complicated ideas?
3. Compare and contrast national or state standards for science inquiry for grades K–4 and 5–8. (Go to National Science Education Standards, Chapter 6 at *www.nap.edu/readingroom/books/nses/*)
4. Describe activities that you could use to introduce and reinforce the skills necessary to engage in science inquiry.

5. How do the selected articles exemplify the nature of science and the characteristics of science inquiry? If you were going to use these in the classroom, what changes would you make?

6. Under what circumstances would a high amount of teacher control in science inquiry be beneficial? A low amount of teacher control?

References

Chinn, C. A., and B. A. Malhotra 2002. Epistemologically authentic inquiry in schools: A theoretical framework for evaluating inquiry tasks. *Science Education* 86 (2): 175–218.

National Research Council (NRC). 2000. *Inquiry and the National Science Education Standards.* Washington D.: National Academy Press.

National Research Council (NRC). 1996. *National Science Education Standards.* Washington DC: National Academy Press.

Vygotsky, L. S. 1987. *The collected works of L. S. Vygotsky. Vol. I. Problems of general psychology,* eds. R. W. Rieber and A. S. Carton. N. Minick (trans.). New York: Plenum.

A Literature-Circles Approach to Understanding Science as a Human Endeavor

By William Straits

The National Science Education Standards suggest that middle school science teachers use "historical examples ... to help students see the scientific enterprise as more philosophical, social, and human" (NRC 1996). Fortunately for today's science teachers, science-related, historical nonfiction has become a popular literary genre. Teachers can select books on a wide range of topics to help learners of all ages explore the history and nature of science. (See Figure 1 for a list of titles appropriate for young adolescents.) The reading of these books alone, however, does not necessarily lead students to make personal connections to science or to understand science as a human endeavor interdependent with culture, society, and history. Teachers must structure students' reading to ensure that they consider specific aspects of science while reading and discussing books. One way for teachers to focus their students' attention on components of the nature of science is through the use of literature circles.

Literature Circles

Literature circles were initially developed for young adolescents' classroom reading (Daniels 1994) and have since grown to be a very popular choice for middle school language-arts teachers. Literature circles are "small, temporary discus-

Figure 1.

List of texts appropriate for middle school students' explorations of the history and nature of science. These books are suitable for long-term reading assignments.

Biographies of scientists	
Galileo: Astronomer and Physicist	R.S. Doak
The Wright Brothers: How They Invented the Airplane	R. Freedman
Curious Bones: Mary Anning and the Birth of Paleontology	T.W. Goodhue
Issac Newton	K. Krull
Always Inventing: A Photobiography of Alexander Graham Bell	T.L. Matthews
Something Out of Nothing: Marie Curie and Radium	C.K. McClafferty

Historical accounts of science	
Phineas Gage: A Gruesome but True Story About Brain Science	J. Fleischman
The Planet Hunters: The Search for Other Worlds	D.B. Fradin
Fossil Feud: The Rivalry of the First American Dinosaur	T. Holmes
An American Plague: The True and Terrifying Story of the Yellow Fever Epidemic of 1793	J. Murphy
Scientific Explorers: Travels in Search of Knowledge	R. Stefoff

sion groups" in which students are provided *prompts* or *roles* (Daniels 1994). The purpose of literature-circle roles is to guide students to develop understanding of particular concepts as they explore the text and meaningfully participate in small-group discussion. As students are reading, they perform specific roles and take notes that are used to support participation in small-group discussion. Several basic roles appropriate for the reading of most books have been offered by Daniels (1994) (see Figure 2). In addition to these all-purpose roles, others have been designed specifically with the goals of focusing students' attention to issues of the nature of science and promoting students' connection with science as they read historical nonfiction (Straits 2005; Straits 2007):

- Everyday life connector—Search the reading for events, ideas, characters, objects, and so on that remind you of everyday life. Pay particular attention to science concepts.

- Science skeptic—Analyze how science is done in the book. How does it compare to our inquiry investigations? Consider specific aspects of experimental design. For example, are scientists in the book controlling variables, repeating their tests, avoiding bias, and using a large enough sample size?

- Power investigator—Sometimes people with political, social, and/or economic power influence science. For example, they might determine who does science and who does not, or which ideas are investigated and which are not. Find out which group(s) have power and list a few ideas about how they are using their power to help or get in the way of scientists.

- Science translator—While reading, take note of science vocabulary and concepts in the book. Use the internet, textbook, and other sources to find out more information about these ideas.
- Historian—Scientific developments of the past are described in the book. Find out other things that happened at the same time (e.g., 1368–1644, Ming Dynasty; 1819, birth of Walt Whitman; 1908, Chicago Cubs win World Series)
- Science biographer—As you encounter different people doing science in the reading, use sources such as the textbook and the internet to locate interesting biographical information about each person, especially those connected to science.
- Nature-of-science investigator—Factors that accurately describe science include scientific knowledge is based on evidence; scientists can never know for certain that a conclusion is correct; scientific knowledge changes over time; there are multiple ways to solve problems in science; scientists are often very creative in their attempts to solve problems; and scientists are people, influenced by their own personal beliefs and by society. While reading, look for examples of these factors in the book.
- Science and culture connector—Science is greatly influenced by culture (the beliefs and values of particular societies at particular times in history). Consider ways science was influenced by culture in the past and ways that science is influenced by our culture today.

Group meetings are important times of learning as they provide a forum for active reflection that promotes the development and sharing of meaningful, personal connections to learning. During discussion in their small groups, students can use information gathered via their roles to help clarify meaning, draw parallels to other situations, articulate related personal experience,

Figure 2.

Generic literature-circle roles developed by Daniels (1994). These roles have become mainstays of the literature circles classroom and are appropriate for use with texts of nearly any topic.

- Questioner: Your job is to write down a few questions that you have about this part of the book.
- Literary luminary: Your job is to locate a few special sections or quotations in the text for your group to discuss.
- Illustrator: Your job is to draw some kind of picture related to the reading you have just done. It can be a sketch, cartoon, diagram, flowchart, or stick-figure scene.
- Summarizer: Your job is to prepare a brief summary of today's reading.
- Researcher: Your job is to dig up some background information on any topic related to your book.
- Word wizard: Your job is to be on the lookout for a few words that have special meaning, are puzzling or unfamiliar, or stand out in the reading.
- Scene setter: Your job is to carefully track where the action takes place during the daily reading. Describe each setting in detail.

offer additional information, critique and analyze the text, and connect the text to the nature of science and investigative skills learned in class. Although discussions are prompted and guided by literature-circle roles, conversations are far from limited to simply reporting information; roles should enrich conversations, not delineate them. It should be made explicit to students that "group meetings aim to be open, natural conversations about books, so personal connections, digressions, and open-ended questions are welcome" (Daniels 1994). In fact, it is these personal connections that are of particular value when discussing the interaction between science and social influences such as economics, history, culture, politics, and so on. For example, while discussing a book about inventions or discoveries of the past, students may talk about current events, their own family and personal experiences, as well as any number of topics ranging from professional athletes to today's environmental policies and concerns.

At the conclusion of each discussion, group members rotate roles and decide on a new section of text to be read. When the entire text has been completed, often after several group meetings along the way, group members create a presentation that represents their understanding of the topics/texts explored. These final presentations may take on any number of creative forms, such as impersonations of characters, an interview with the impersonated author(s), a news broadcast reporting events from the text, or a eulogy for a character (the preceding suggestions as well as many others are explained in Daniels 1994). Final presentations are valuable as they require students to organize information in unique ways, thereby demanding higher-level learning. The presentations serve as an opportunity for assessment and arouse the interest of other students in the topics/texts presented. If time allows, students can then choose new topics/texts, form new groups, and begin another round of literature circles.

Why Literature Circles Work

Readers may approach a book from an information-based or emotion-based stance, depending on their individual purposes for reading. The information-based, or *efferent*, stance accentuates the meaning readers take from the book, whereas the emotion-based, or *aesthetic*, stance prioritizes the previous experiences that readers bring to the text

(Rosenblatt 1978). As they are reading a book, readers may be oriented to any point along the continuum between efferent and aesthetic, based on textual clues and an individual's expectations and reasons for reading. For example, most fictional books orient readers toward the aesthetic. There is often, however, a great deal of information to be taken from these texts.

Consider Jack London's *To Build a Fire*, in which London visits a familiar theme, the folly of man's presumed superiority over nature. In this short story, a man and a dog take an ill-fated hike in the subfreezing temperatures of the Yukon Territory and the man's fear, panic, and ultimate acceptance of death are detailed as he freezes to death, unable to build a fire. Readers may bring with them fear of cold, hunger, and death, fears that surface in them as they read. However, they can also take from this story information about seasonality and the tilt of the Earth, the biotic and abiotic features of the taiga, and human physiology and thermoregulation. Similarly, students come prepositioned toward the efferent while reading most assigned science texts, including historical nonfiction. To identify with science and to see it truly as a human struggle, endeavor, passion, and need, students must be taken explicitly from their efferent stances and guided to view science reading from an aesthetic stance. Literature-circle roles are invaluable as they can guide learners toward both efferent and aesthetic interactions with text.

Final Considerations

Literature circles are an extremely flexible instructional strategy; there is no one right way to use them. But as you plan your instruction you may want to consider these lessons learned.

- Text selection—Success with literature circles depends on the text selected as well as the reading interests and abilities of students. In selecting books to use, it is beneficial if the topic(s) covered in the text parallel concepts taught in class. For example, classroom instruction about atomic theory, isotopes, and radioactive decay should be provided in concert with literature circles reading books that describe Marie Curie or the Manhattan Project. Your students are another important consideration in text selection. Ask colleagues or review student files to get a sense of individuals' reading abilities. Encourage students to select texts at their reading level. Finally, don't judge a book by its cover; be sure to read the books yourself before assigning them.

- Group size—Not all literature-circle roles need to be completed by each student or in preparation for each group meeting; group size is not dictated by the number of roles. Rather, group size should maximize the participation and learning of group members. Groups of three to five are generally preferred as they are large enough to allow for varying viewpoints and rich conversation and small enough to allow opportunities for members to contribute.

- Time—A basic premise of the circles is that the most meaningful learning comes not from the reading of text, but from the *discussion* of text. Optimally, students would meet in their discussion groups two or three times per week. However, more important than the number of meetings is the length of the meetings. As with most science instruction, longer intervals of time are ideal. Allot a minimum of 25 to 30 minutes per group meeting. If your schedule allows 60 minutes per week for discussion groups to meet, consider two longer meetings rather than three short ones. Whatever schedule you decide, stick to it! A recipe for disaster is to hold literature-circle meetings "if time permits." Depending on the frequency of

meetings and the length and difficulty of the texts, a single literature-circle cycle may last a few to several weeks. Whatever the duration, throughout the reading assignment remember that reading their texts and performing literature-circle roles represent a significant time demand for students—adjust other homework assignments appropriately.

- Assessment—Monitoring student discussion and roles can provide opportunities to give students feedback about their preparation for and participation during discussions. In addition to serving as formative assessment, monitoring student discussion will allow teachers to gather ideas for more formal assessments. Guided by roles, students will often ask extremely important discussion questions, compelling group members to explore personally meaningful connections to the text and the science presented within it. These very questions may be used later as individual summative assessments. Finally, group presentations provide opportunities for students to engage in higher-level learning as they synthesize a representation of their learning from the text and discussions and provide opportunities for you to assess each group's ultimate learning outcomes.

- Teacher's role—During discussions the teacher's role is one of facilitator. Productive and meaningful group discussion does not just happen; students will require support and prompting as they learn to discuss respectfully and productively. Taking time as a class to brainstorm the elements of productive discussions can be a valuable exercise. Also, as you read the texts in preparation for literature circles, it's helpful if you perform some of the roles yourself. These will provide you with questions, discussion topics, insights, and connections of your own to offer to groups that may need some prompting during their discussions. Finally, when all other groups are running smoothly, it is a great idea to join a literature circle as a group member. This participation has two key benefits. It will allow you to demonstrate for your students techniques for productive, respectful, and inclusive discussion and, most important, it will allow your students to see an adult's genuine enthusiasm for reading about the history of science.

William Straits is an assistant professor in the Department of Science Education at California State University, Long Beach, in Long Beach, California.

References

Daniels, H. 1994. *Literature circles: Voice and choice in book clubs and reading groups.* Portland, ME: Stenhouse Publishers.

National Research Council (NRC). 1996. *National Science Education Standards.* Washington, DC: National Academy Press.

Rosenblatt, L. M. 1978. *The reader, the text, the poem: The transactional theory of literary work.* Carbondale, IL: Southern Illinois University Press.

Straits, W. 2005. Pre-service teachers' representations of their developing nature of science understandings. Paper presented at the Qualitative Interest Group (QUIG) Conference on Interdisciplinary Qualitative Studies, Athens, GA.

Straits, W. 2007. Using historical non-fiction and literature circles to develop elementary teachers' nature of science understandings. *Journal of Science Teacher Education* 18 (6).

Light Students' Interest in the Nature of Science

By Joanne K. Olson

The nature of science is a vital part of students' educational experience. It includes understanding what science is and how it works, in accordance with Content Standard G of the *National Science Education Standards* (NRC 1996). Effective science instruction requires incorporation of science content, science processes, and the nature of science (Weinburgh 2003). Any one or two of these elements cannot effectively exist apart from the third. Portraying science accurately while teaching content and process is important to help students develop robust understanding. The issue is not whether we will teach the nature of science to our students, only what image of science will be conveyed (Clough 2000).

A few years ago, a colleague from Michigan shared an activity she used to help students apply their knowledge of electrical circuits. I have since used the activity with middle school students, and modified it so that science content, process, and the nature of science can be seamlessly incorporated together.

Lights On!

The activity involves the use of popular children's tennis shoes containing lights in the soles that flash when children walk in them. I use the activity at the end of an electricity unit, after students have spent significant time learning basic concepts about circuits such as the differences between series and parallel circuits, how switches and lightbulbs work, current, and resistance.

A typical unit on electricity may last between three to six weeks and involves relatively inexpensive equipment: D-cell batteries, pieces of insulated copper wire, small lightbulbs, masking tape, and inexpensive bulb holders found in science supply catalogs (see Figure 2). A wide variety of activities can be done during the unit and may vary depending on district curriculum requirements; the activities I use, however, are adapted from Stepans (1996).

My students begin the unit by predicting how to use a battery and wire to light a bulb, followed by testing their ideas. A full day may be required for students to determine what configurations are effective in lighting the bulb. Students are given the challenge to find as many ways as possible to make the bulb light. The teacher's role is critical during this process. Using open-ended questions such as, "What have you tried so far?" "How else do you think you could make that work?" and "What have you learned from the ones that didn't work?" is very important to prevent students from becoming frustrated if they do not have initial success. Students are asked to draw the successful configurations on notebook paper and describe what is needed to make the bulb light. Once students have completed a circuit, they are asked to complete additional explorations based on challenge questions (see Figure 1). After each exploration, the teacher needs to help students discuss their ideas and introduce terms as students need them, such as *circuit, switch,* and *resistance.* Rather than seeking right answers, asking questions that focus student thinking is critical. ("How did that change your thinking?" "What new ideas do you have?" "What could you do to test that?")

When students have completed each challenge activity, they are given two tasks that require them to build models. First, students build a flashlight using their materials and a cardboard toilet paper tube. (Some students request additional materials such as aluminum foil or foam cups.) This requires them to apply knowledge of circuits, particularly because they do not have a flashlight available to copy. A second task is to build a working model of the classroom lights—a formidable challenge as a classroom might have more than one light switch and a bulb or two that are burned out. Students work in groups of three or four to use available classroom materials to construct their models. Flashlights typically take one class session; classroom lights models may take two or more days to complete.

Figure 1.
Challenge questions

Put one challenge question at a time on the board for students. Students can work individually, in pairs, or in small groups. Discuss their findings as a class before you move on to the next challenge. If some students finish earlier than others, they can be provided with the next question.

1. Arrange a battery, bulb, and wire so that the bulb lights.
2. Using two batteries and two bulbs, make a circuit so that both bulbs light.
3. Using that circuit, add a bulb holder and describe how it works.
4. Using two batteries and two bulbs, make a circuit so that when you unscrew one bulb, the other one goes out.
5. Using two batteries and two bulbs, make a circuit so that when you unscrew one bulb, the other one stays lit.
6. Using the piece of equipment found in the box on the front table, place it into the circuit and determine what it does. (Note to teacher: Have a box containing knife switches available.)

Additional challenges can be created. For instance, if you plan to teach the direction of current, have students draw their ideas of how current may be moving in a circuit. Write all ideas on the board. Introduce students to *diodes,* describing briefly how current travels only in one direction. Have them use diodes to test which idea is consistent with their results.

Figure 2.
Materials list

This list will vary somewhat depending on the activities that are selected for the main part of the unit. This list is based on a class of 32 students.

- 32 D-cell batteries
- 64 pieces of insulated copper wire (about 15–20 cm each)
- 32 small lightbulbs
- 32 small lightbulb holders (available from science suppliers)
- 16 knife switches (available from science suppliers)
- 8 rolls of masking tape
- roll of aluminum foil
- 4 pairs of light-up shoes
- cardboard toilet paper tubes (or paper towel rolls cut in thirds)—1 per student
- miscellaneous supplies suggested by students (typically include paper clips, string, cups, and brass brads)

Walking Into the Nature of Science

At the end of the unit, when students have successfully completed their flashlights and classroom wiring models, I provide each group with a light-up tennis shoe. I am careful to select shoes that have an appropriate level of complexity. Some shoes have multiple bulbs that turn on at different intervals or have bulbs on both sides of the sole; these add additional complexity that can cause students to struggle. Shoes with a single bulb or multiple bulbs that light simultaneously are advantageous. Shoes are relatively inexpensive ($10–$15 per pair) and are available at most stores that sell children's shoes. When used in this activity, a single pair can last at least three or four years, and a class of 32 students requires only four pairs. Outgrown, but still working, shoes can also be donated from younger siblings.

Students are provided with another challenge question, "When does the shoe light?" Most students initially think pressure on the soles causes the bulbs to light, but this is not the case. The room quickly fills with excitement and wonder as students work to determine what conditions cause the shoes to light. (If students recommend cutting the shoes open, I set the guideline that they may not open the shoe.) I try to avoid providing many verbal directions or requiring predictions in advance of this activity because doing science often involves exploring a phenomenon and then pondering it after the experience.

After trying many things, students determine that motion is required, but that motion in certain directions doesn't work. The direction will depend on the brand of shoe. Some students conclude that if the shoe is moved at a steady speed, the lights do not stay on. Teacher patience is critical at this point! Although introducing the concept of acceleration is tempting, a second challenge question promotes further learning about motion while also building a foundation students will explore further when they reach high school physics. (Although middle school students do well with straight-line acceleration, they struggle to understand that something moving in a circle at a uniform speed is constantly accelerating. This concept is very difficult and can be memorized, but it won't be understood. It's best left for physics.) I ask the students how they could get the shoes to stay lit. Some students will inevitably shake the shoes up and down very quickly—a tiring process indeed! Over time, others find that holding the shoelaces and twirling the entire shoe causes the bulbs to stay lit. I don't formally use the concept of acceleration with this activity, even though some students use the term when moving the shoe quickly in a straight line. This activity provides a concrete experience, without the difficult vocabulary, that students can draw from later in high school.

Connecting to their previous work with circuits, students next tackle another challenge question: What might the inside look like? They are asked to draw a diagram of the inside and then attempt to re-create it by building a model, using their materials and other items I may have in the classroom. Model building may take several days. This task encourages the development of critical thinking, problem solving, communication, creativity, and the application of knowledge to real-world problems, while simultaneously promoting a deep understanding of science content. The activity is far from over, however. Although students have engaged in inquiry similar to that of the scientific community, students will likely not pick up on these similarities due to the pervasiveness of misconceptions about science and scientists. Teachers need to be very explicit when teaching the nature of science to address these misconceptions. An example of my process follows.

After student groups complete and test their models, they are asked to present their models to the class and describe their successes and frustrations. I do not grade their models or their presentations. The presentations are designed to provide a foundation for the nature-of-science concepts I wish to illustrate. Because of this, whole-class sharing is important, coupled with class discussion and a nonjudgmental teacher (scientists don't have an external authority who grades their work based on correctness; it is subjected to discussion with colleagues at conferences and in journals, and I want students to experience this process as closely as possible). After seeing several models, students inevitably want to know what is inside the shoe to determine which model is "correct." This is an ideal time to seamlessly address the nature of science. I inform the students that we cannot open the shoe; perhaps we don't have the

technology required to do this test, or we don't have the funding to replace the shoes (both are issues scientists face). Students groan, but I ask, "When scientists investigate something that has never been studied before, how do they know if they have the right answer?" I put all student responses on the board and we contact a local scientist by e-mail to settle any disagreements that may occur. (Scientists' e-mail addresses are available on university and government agency websites, and the scientists are usually very helpful.)

Most students are uncomfortable with the fact that nobody can tell scientists if they are correct. This addresses a pervasive misconception students possess: that science provides absolute truth. Be aware, however, that as a result of this revelation students may change their thinking to the opposite extreme and believe that scientists don't know anything at all. Refer students back to their models. Ask them what they know and how confident they are in their models. Students will find that they have greater confidence in some models than in others. Ask for their reasoning. Students typically use evidence from the shoes to support their viewpoints. Point out that scientists also reject ideas if they don't match the behavior of the phenomenon being studied. Pose another question: "What could you do to be more confident in your ideas?" Some students again suggest that you open the shoe, but others will propose additional tests, such as taking an x-ray of the shoe, building more models, using better materials, and determining if other people somewhere else came up with the same idea. Compare these ideas to how scientists work: "If scientists can't go to a book or someone else to see if they are right, how could they become more confident in their ideas?" Help students use their list to generate what a scientist would do: try different tests, build more models to see if any of them work better, try to get better materials, talk to other scientists, and share ideas.

Figure 3.
Sample Venn diagram

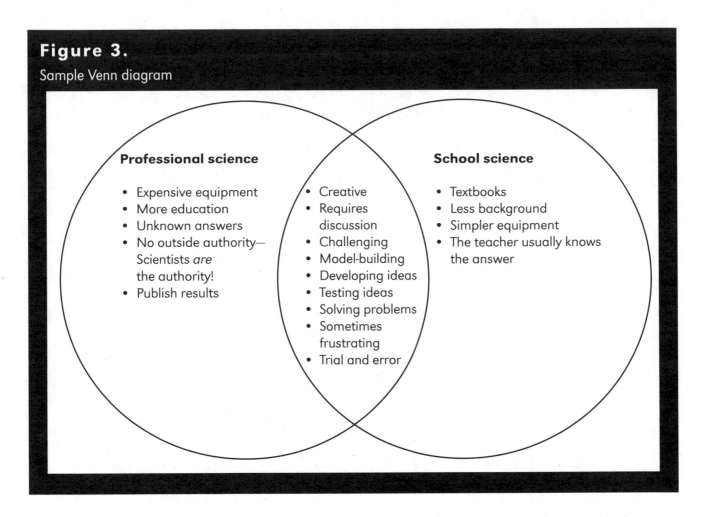

Additional Ideas

Other aspects of the nature of science can be introduced, depending on the classroom context and the amount of time available. The following are suggestions of additional nature-of-science ideas that can be taught using this activity.

- An important feature of science is model building. Ask students how they found out what was inside the shoe. Students will describe their tests and development of their model, but typically forget to include the influence other people had on their thinking. If this occurs, ask students how their model might be different if they built it without others in the room. Point out that scientists are also influenced by others' ideas, and discussions can change a person's thinking. Then ask how we can decide what the inside is like if we cannot

open the shoe. Students have to decide which model works the best. I continue my questioning further, "Suppose you decided that the model from Jenny's group was like the inside of the shoe. What would happen if later you developed an even better model?" Students might think the new model will easily replace the old one. I then ask, "How would you get the other scientists to change their ideas from the original model to your new one?" Scientists have to share their ideas with others, and sometimes scientists disagree. For example, Jenny might like her idea so much that she doesn't want to change it. I point out that the same thing occurs in "real" science.

- School science is similar to and different from what scientists do in some important ways. I draw a two-circle Venn diagram on chart paper or the board with "professional science" and "school science" in each circle (see Figure 3). I ask students to compare what scientists do to what they just did and record similarities in the intersecting area and differences in the respective circles. Student responses lead to fascinating discussions, and the chart can remain in the classroom for additions and changes throughout the year. This serves as a valuable formative assessment of students' understandings.

- Ask students to write their process of model development. Typically, students engaged in thinking, brainstorming, trial and error, and heated discussions. Read a textbook description of the scientific method. Have them compare the step-by-step scientific method to what they did. They will usually find that they didn't follow a scientific method in their investigation. Science isn't about following a single procedure; it is a creative process that requires imagination, interaction, testing ideas, and extensive thinking. This is important for students to know; research indicates many students opt out of science because they perceive science as uncreative (Tobias 1990).

Continuing the Thinking

This activity not only helps students apply their knowledge of electricity to a familiar context, but it can be used to teach aspects of the nature of science as well. The following nature-of-science ideas can be addressed:

- Scientists often cannot directly see what they are studying; they build models to help them understand.
- Scientists do not always agree; sometimes more than one idea can explain what they see.
- Data do not "tell" you anything; you have to come up with the idea to account for your data.

- Scientists share their ideas with each other, and are sometimes convinced that a new idea is better. (Some scientists are never convinced!)
- Science ideas can change as new ideas are developed.
- Not all ideas in science are simply discovered. Science ideas are often invented.
- Creativity is an important part of science.
- Scientists don't follow a single step-by-step scientific method.
- School science is different from what scientists do in important ways—we can compare our answers to scientists' answers. Scientists don't have an authority to go to; they must decide for themselves.

I never tell students what is inside the shoe; in fact, I don't even know. Many students pursue answers on their own and benefit from their attempts to find out. One student wrote to the shoe manufacturer and received a letter stating that it was "patent pending," and they would not reveal what was inside. Another student informed me that he had convinced his parents to cut open the soles of his outgrown shoes. To his dismay, several wires led from the bulbs to a small black box that he couldn't open. The shoe activity promotes important goals while addressing science content, process, and the nature of science. The beauty of this activity is that it models closely what "real" scientists do, and the thinking continues for months after the unit is over. A shoe remains on my desk throughout the year. Just when I think the activity is over, a student comes to class with yet another model and the inquiry begins again.

Joanne K. Olson is an assistant professor at Iowa State University in Ames, Iowa.

References

Clough, M. P. 2000. The nature of science: Understanding how the "game" of science is played. *The Clearing House* 74: 13–17.

National Research Council (NRC). 1996. *National Science Education Standards*. Washington DC: National Academy Press.

Rowell, J. A., and E. R. Cawthron 1982. Images of science: An empirical study. *European Journal of Science Education* 4: 79–94.

Stepans, J. 1996. *Targeting students' science misconceptions*. Riverview, FL: Idea Factory Inc.

Tobias, S. 1990. *They're not dumb, they're different: Stalking the second tier.* Tucson: Research Corporation.

Weinburgh, M. 2003. A leg (or three) to stand on. *Science and Children* 40: 28–30.

Did You Really Prove It?

By Carolyn Reeves and Debby Chessin

Ms. Washington located the assigned science fair projects on her judging sheets and noted the middle school students who were making last-minute inspections of their displays. The first student, Becky, spoke of her project with confidence, proudly concluding that her research had proven her hypothesis. "What makes you use the word 'proven'?" Ms. Washington asked.

"Well, I measured everything twice and I repeated my experiment, so my hypothesis has to be true."

Ms. Washington agreed that repeating her experiment made her results more reliable. But further probing questions failed to lead Becky to see that conclusions to scientific research are tentative explanations rather than proven facts.

Further down the line, Ms. Washington came to Eric, whose project was a construction of a working electric motor. Eric demonstrated his motor, which ran smoothly and efficiently. Ms. Washington asked Eric if he knew whether an electric motor was an example of science or technology. He remembered that technology was defined as applied science, so he concluded that an electric motor would fit into the science category. Ms. Washington suggested that this was technology because his focus was on

making the motor work well rather than on providing an explanation of how magnetic forces were used to produce motion. Eric smiled and agreed, but he still considered his motor to be a science project.

Near the end of the line, Mona had a neat colorful display, carefully organized into six easy-to-follow steps. Mona volunteered that if someone else carefully repeated these same six steps they would probably get the same results she had gotten, because repeatability is one of the characteristics of science. Ms. Washington complimented Mona on her understanding of how experimental scientific research is conducted. She then asked if all scientists always followed the same six steps Mona had used.

"I guess so. These are the steps in my science book about how scientists do research." Mona wasn't sure if scientists could use any other methods or not.

Ms. Washington also found that her students didn't realize that scientists were often ostracized by society because their new ideas did not fit the conventional thinking of the time. The students were surprised that many of the scientific ideas that we take for granted today took a long time to be accepted by other scientists and society.

Ms. Washington, like many other science teachers, recognizes that misconceptions about the nature of science abound among students. She also knows from personal experience that they are difficult to replace with realistic conceptions. This underscores the importance of finding effective strategies for teaching Content Standard G: The History and Nature of Science from the *National Science Education Standards* (NRC 1996).

Middle school students should develop and refine their understanding of the interrelationships among science, technology, and society while they are studying content. Several strategies to accomplish teaching the history and nature of science can easily be integrated into the science class with a little planning and research. Incorporating the history of science means including experiences in which students learn about the individuals from different cultures who have contributed to science and understand the difficulties they had for their ideas to be accepted during the time in which they lived. Through activities in science, students should also learn about the nature of science, meaning that scientists formulate and test hypotheses, and revise ideas based on new experimental evidence (NRC 1996).

Understanding the Nature of Science

As Ms. Washington reflected on her experience as a science fair judge, she tried to recall successful methods she and other teachers had used to teach Content Standard G. She already knew that combining concepts with the nature of science enhances students' understanding of both historical and scientific principles, so she devised a plan to help students better understand these notions. Ms. Washington chose several age-appropriate characteristics of the nature of science to incorporate into her teaching (Figure 1). To teach these principles, Ms. Washington decided to use four strategies in

her lessons to help students better understand the nature of science:

1. Reading and discussing historical stories that illustrate the characteristics of the nature of science,
2. Frequently reviewing concepts using a Question of the Day,
3. Critically analyzing and distinguishing between the methods used in scientific and technological studies, as reported in news articles, and
4. Ensuring that prelab activities include explicit instruction about why certain procedures are used, and postlab reports are analyzed by a checklist to identify misconceptions.

In addition to Content Standard G, incorporating these strategies supports the *National Science Education Standards*, Teaching Standard B, which states "teachers of science guide and facilitate learning...(and) encourage and model the skills of scientific inquiry, as well as the curiosity, openness to new ideas and data, and skepticism that characterize science" (NRC 1996).

The activities included here should be incorporated into the existing curriculum, so they should not take an entire class period. Rather, they can be implemented as mini lessons, preferably worked in at the beginning or the end of a lesson to enhance and extend student thinking.

Historical Stories

The first strategy involves using historical stories to teach and illustrate the six targeted characteristics of the nature of science. Historical stories provide a meaningful structure and concrete illustrations for the abstract ideas of what science is and how it works. Students find the biographies exciting ways to learn that science is done by a diverse group of persistent problem solvers! According to the National Science Education Standards, "The introduction

Figure 1.

Characteristics of the nature of science

- Scientists formulate and test their explanations of nature using observation, experiments, and theoretical and mathematical models.

- Scientific ideas are tentative and subject to change but, for most ideas in science, there is much experimental and observational confirmation.

- Scientists do and have changed their ideas about nature when they encounter new experimental evidence that does not match their existing explanations.

- It is normal for scientists to differ in their interpretation of the evidence or theory.

- It is part of scientific inquiry to evaluate the results of scientific investigations, experiments, observations, theoretical models, and the explanations proposed by other scientists who agree that questioning, response to criticism, and open communication are integral to the process of science.

- Many individuals have contributed to the traditions of science. Studying some of these individuals provides further understanding of scientific inquiry, science as a human endeavor, the nature of science, and the relationships between science and society.

- Science has been practiced by individuals in different cultures.

- Tracing the history of science can show how difficult it was for scientific innovators to break through the accepted ideas of their times to reach the conclusions we take for granted (NRC 1996).

of historical examples will help students see the scientific enterprise as more philosophical, social, and human" (NRC 1996).

Brief historical narratives of Marie Curie are published on the internet (see resources) and serve as a framework to study the characteristics of the nature of science. After reading the stories, the class discusses several questions that focus on the selected characteristics.

Students discuss concepts in relation to the story in small groups, share with the whole class, and record their ideas in their science notebooks or journals. Because this process usually takes no longer than 10 or 15 minutes, the class continues with the day's lesson. Questions from these discussions should be included on tests to check for understanding. Other historical stories can be read throughout the year to reinforce realistic concepts about the nature of science. Examples include the biographies of Nicholas Copernicus, Galileo, Johann Kepler, Alexander Fleming, Charles Darwin, Edward Jenner, Lise Meitner, George Washington Carver, and Rachel Carson, among many others.

Question of the Day

Ms. Washington's class begins with a question of the day, which is written on the board before students come into the room. Knowing that persistence is the key to correcting misconceptions, she continues to present realistic ideas about the nature of science throughout the year. Questions of the day are often selected as misconceptions and are identified by means of lab reports, discussions, written papers, or projects (Figure 2). The students write the question in their notebooks while roll is being taken. Ms. Washington allows up to 10 minutes for answering and, after a brief discussion, tells students the answer to the question before beginning the day's regular lesson. She makes the connection between the question and changing a misconception by pointing out examples from history, relating it to different discoveries, and then applying it to student work in the classroom.

Figure 2.

Question of the day suggestions

- Is the designing and building of rockets a part of science or a part of technology?
- Does a carefully conducted scientific experiment prove a hypothesis?
- What can a researcher do to make an experiment more reliable?
- Which is more correct: Science is a collection of proven facts or science is a collection of theories?
- Are theories based on evidence?
- Do scientific theories sometimes change?
- Are scientists considered mean and unfair when they criticize research done by another scientist?

Reading and Analyzing News Articles

A third strategy involves reading and analyzing news articles about various science or technology issues. Students are given one or more questions to answer about the article they read. These questions ask the students to critically analyze the articles. The analyses could include such things as predicting outcomes, analyzing research methods, challenging conclusions, or distinguishing between science and technology (Figure 3 is a sample). The questions are based on ideas about the history and nature of science that students have previously been taught.

Effective Laboratory Activities

Lab activities continue to be a big part of middle-level classes and are used as a means for teaching nature of science concepts. Lab activities enable students to experience some of the methods used by professional scientists and to think critically for themselves. Experience taught Ms. Washington that students often construct their own misconceptions about how science works

Figure 3.

Sample analysis of science in the news

In 1989, Dr. Pons and Dr. Fleischmann, professors of chemistry at the University of Utah and the University of Southampton respectively, made the incredible claim that they had created nuclear fusion in a beaker at room temperature. This was so important to society because, if it were true, cold fusion would be a clean new source of unlimited energy with no greenhouse gases. At the time, other scientists who studied hot fusion were unable to replicate the results, so the claims of Pons and Fleischmann were ridiculed and dismissed. Nevertheless, research continues, and a small but very active minority of scientists still believes in cold fusion.

Q: Were the other scientists wrong to be critical of the claims made by the team?

A: No. Critical peer review is a foundational part of science. Scientists usually publish their research, and this is an invitation for other scientists to contribute their own expertise to the research. They may have evidence that supports a published theory, which makes the theory stronger. They may have evidence that disagrees with the published theory or they may see a problem with how the research was done. This would make the theory weaker. Critical peer review is one of the main things that makes science work.

Q: Are the scientists who still believe in cold fusion wasting their time?

A: No. Understanding in science is constantly changing and new techniques, instruments, and perseverance may eventually uncover natural laws.

when teacher guidance is lacking. A checklist for final lab write-ups is used to help evaluate students' conceptions about the nature of science (Figure 4). Emphasis should be placed on the fact that the class is acting like a real scientific community by evaluating conclusions, identifying faulty reasoning, pointing out statements that go beyond the evidence, and suggesting alternative explanations for the evidence (NRC 1996). Address students' misconceptions by writing selected ones on the board and inviting the class to comment on whether the statement makes sense based on the data they collect in lab activities (evidence). Acting as a guide, the teacher helps to develop more realistic conceptions on closer examination of the data and invites students to rewrite the misconception to more closely reflect their data. To enhance students' understanding about the history of science, connect lab investigations with early scientists who did experiments in that area. This leads into a discussion about the connection between science and society through history and the interrelationships among science, technology, and society.

Don't Worry!

Teachers may be hesitant to incorporate Content Standard G into their lessons because they think it means adding a new unit to an already crowded curriculum. For the most part, the strategies outlined in this article are incorporated into existing units with little change in the length of the units. By using historical stories, lab activities, news accounts, and daily minireviews, the nature of science can be presented in an effective manner that students can understand and retain. Through these experiences, teachers help their students gain rich perspectives about the interrelationships among science, technology, and society both in the present and the past. Students gain an appreciation of the advances, as well as the limitations, in science and technology.

At the end of the school year, Ms. Washington wanted to know if her strategies changed

Figure 4.
Lab report checklist

____ 1. Did the student conclude that the results proved his or her hypothesis?
____ 2. Sometimes students are asked to identify sources of error. Did the student indicate that the experiment would have been proved if there had been no errors?
____ 3. Did the student indicate that more evidence would prove his/her hypothesis?
____ 4. Was the term *theory* incorrectly used to mean "hypothesis?"
____ 5. Did the student indicate that there was no ther possible explanation except the one he or she proposed?
____ 6. Did the student suggest ways to make his or her experiment more valid and reliable?

"Yes" answers to questions 1–3 indicate misconceptions about the tentative or developmental nature of science.

"Yes" answers to questions 4–5 indicate misconceptions about the correct use of the terms *hypothesis* and *theory* and the theory-building nature of science.

A "yes" answer to question 6 indicates a maturing approach to doing research.

some of her students' earlier misconceptions about the nature and history of science. As her students were working on a new laboratory investigation, she circulated with pencil, paper, and clipboard and wrote down what she heard the students saying: "When I look at the data, my conclusion is that I did support my hypothesis!"

"How did I get that answer—did I average the right numbers?" and "All of the other groups are getting different results from ours. Maybe we should repeat our experiment a few more times." She was very gratified to hear comments that reflected their new understanding of the nature and history of science.

Carolyn Reeves is an independent educational consultant, and Debby Chessin is an assistant professor of elementary education at the University of Mississippi.

Resources

World of Biography, Marie Curie—*scienceworld. wolfram.com/biography/CurieMarie.html*

Nobel e-Museum, Marie Curie—*www.nobel.se/physics/laureates/1903/marie-curie-bio.html*

Clough, M. P. 1997. Strategies and activities for initiating and maintaining pressure on students' naïve views concerning the nature of science. *Interchange* 28.

Lederman, N. B. 1999. Students' and teachers' conceptions of the nature of science: A review of the research. *Journal of Research in Science Teaching* 29 (4).

Rubba, P. A., J. K. Horner, and J. M. Smith. 1981. A study of two misconceptions about the nature of science among junior high school students. *School Science and Mathematics* 81 (3).

Weiss, P. 2002. Star in a jar? Hints of nuclear fusion found—maybe. *Science News* 161(10).

References

Holliday, W. G. 2001. Inquiry: critically considering inquiry teaching. *Science Scope* 24 (7) 54–57.

National Research Council (NRC). 1996. *National Science Education Standards.* Washington, DC: National Academy Press.

An Inquiry Primer

By Alan Colburn

The science education community has embraced no idea more widely than "inquiry," or "inquiry-based instruction." In fact, developing an inquiry-based science program is the central tenet of the *National Science Education Standards* (NRC 1996). Similarly, Project 2061's *Benchmarks for Science Literacy* discusses scientific inquiry throughout, and even devotes a section to the topic (1993).

If inquiry is so important, then why aren't more teachers using it in their classrooms? According to one study, the most common reasons include

- confusion about the meaning of inquiry,
- the belief that inquiry instruction only works well with high-ability students,
- teachers feeling inadequately prepared for inquiry-based instruction,
- inquiry being viewed as difficult to manage,
- an allegiance to teaching facts, and
- the purpose of a course being seen as preparing students for the next level (NRC 1996).

Let's address some of these issues and explain how you can create your own inquiry-based classroom.

What Is Inquiry?

Perhaps the most confusing thing about inquiry is its definition. The term is used to describe both teaching and doing science. The National Science Education Standards note this dichotomy:

Scientific inquiry refers to the diverse ways in which scientists study the natural world and propose explanations based on the evidence derived from their work. Inquiry also refers to the activities of students in which they develop knowledge and understanding of scientific ideas, as well as an understanding of how scientists study the natural world.

In this article, I will focus on inquiry as a teaching technique.

What Is Inquiry-Based Instruction?

My own definition of inquiry-based instruction is: the creation of a classroom where students are engaged in essentially open-ended, student-centered, hands-on activities. This definition embraces several different approaches to inquiry-based instruction, including

- *Structured inquiry*—The teacher provides students with a hands-on problem to investigate, as well as the procedures and materials, but does not inform them of expected outcomes. Students are to discover relationships between variables or otherwise generalize from data collected. Structured inquiry investigations are similar to those known as cookbook activities, although a cookbook activity generally includes more direction about what students are to observe and which data they are to collect.

- *Guided inquiry*—The teacher provides only the materials and problem to investigate. Students devise their own procedure to solve the problem.
- *Open inquiry*—This approach is similar to guided inquiry, with the addition that students also formulate their own problem to investigate. Open inquiry, in many ways, is analogous to doing science. Science fair activities are often examples of open inquiry.
- *Learning cycle*—Students are engaged in an activity that introduces a new concept. The teacher then provides the formal name for the concept. Students take ownership of the concept by applying it in a different context. (See Figure 1 for a comparison of these different approaches to inquiry-based activities as applied to a unit on electrical circuits.)

Is Inquiry Only for Bright Kids?

The short answer to this question is "No." The slightly longer answer is "Some inquiry activities probably are more effective for advanced kids." Read on, though, for a complete answer.

Over the last generation, many researchers examined learning from a Piagetian perspective. The researchers generally accepted these two conclusions:

1. Inquiry often requires hypothetical/deductive reasoning.
2. Concrete thinkers have a great deal of difficulty developing an understanding of abstract concepts.

Because most middle school students are concrete thinkers, they may have trouble using inquiry to explore abstract concepts. For example, inquiry-based instruction is great for showing students that chemical reaction rates depend on the concentrations of reactants. This is a concrete idea that students can

Figure 1.
Forms of inquiry

Structured inquiry—Students are given a step-by-step procedure, including diagrams for making various types of electrical circuits, including series and parallel. Questions prompt students to remove individual bulbs from each circuit and record their observations.

Guided inquiry—Students are given batteries, bulbs, wires, and other materials. Procedures instruct them to make a bulb light as many ways as they can using the supplies provided. Later, they are instructed to make two bulbs light, again using different combinations of materials. Finally, students are asked to note what happens when they remove individual bulbs from their circuits.

Open inquiry—Students are given batteries, bulbs, wires, and other materials. They are instructed to investigate how bulbs light in electrical circuits.

Learning cycle—Students follow guided inquiry procedures, then the teacher discusses their findings. Concepts such as series and parallel circuits are introduced at this time. Students have experienced the concepts before their introduction. They eventually return to the lab to apply what they have learned to a new situation. For example, they could be given additional equipment, such as ammeters or voltmeters, to quantitatively investigate current and voltage in circuits.

investigate. On the other hand, inquiry-based methods are less effective for helping students understand how scientists explain the phenomena through the kinetic-molecular theory. Similarly, students' understanding of the concept of chemical reaction will vary. Students currently unable to understand some abstract ideas in chemistry will not create a deep understanding of this concept.

The more familiar the activity, materials, and context of the investigation, the easier it is for students to learn through inquiry. To help all middle level students benefit from inquiry-based instruction, the science education research community recommends

- orienting activities toward concrete, observable concepts;
- centering activities around questions that students can answer directly via investigation (which goes a long way toward ensuring the activities are oriented toward concrete concepts);
- emphasizing activities using materials and situations familiar to students; and
- choosing activities suited to students' skills and knowledge to ensure success.

There is, however, a caveat to these recommendations. If the activities are too challenging, students will not learn content effectively. On the other hand, if the activities are too easy, students will not develop higher-level thinking skills. Maximum learning probably occurs when the activities are "just right"—cognitively challenging, but still doable. This implies, at least in theory, a classroom where students may not all be doing the same version of an activity at the same time.

What Does the Teacher Do in a Successful Inquiry-Based Classroom?

Successful inquiry-based instruction is more than curriculum materials. Instead, the teacher is the key element in a classroom. He or she must possess certain attitudes and skills to encourage student success in the inquiry-based classroom. First, the teacher must support inquiry-based instruction. He or she must believe in the value of students having some element of control over what they will do and how they will behave. In addition, to be really successful, the teacher needs formal operational thinking abilities, knowledge of the subject students are investigating, and some understanding of how students learn (to be able to respond effectively to student statements).

Research has also identified the following teacher behaviors that promote inquiry-based learning:

- Asking open-ended, or divergent, questions (such as "What are you doing?" "Tell me about what you're thinking?" and "What do you think would happen if…?");
- Waiting a few seconds after asking the questions, giving student time to think;
- Responding to students by repeating and paraphrasing what they have said without praising or criticizing (to encourage students to think for themselves and to stop looking to the teacher for validation);
- Avoiding telling students what to do, praising, evaluating, rejecting, or discouraging student ideas and behaviors; and
- Maintaining a disciplined classroom.

How Do You Prepare for and Manage an Inquiry-Based Classroom?

Inquiry-based instruction often creates a new and complex classroom situation. Both students and teachers alike need time to gradually make a transition from the more classical confirmation-type activities and lectures to open-ended activities characteristic of inquiry-based instruction. The key point is to make changes in your teaching *slowly*, not continuing with something new until both you and your students feel comfortable.

A good place to start is by tossing out any preconstructed data tables that accompany lab activities. Have students figure out for themselves what data to record and how to record it. Initial confusion will eventually give way to success. Many teachers have noted that students initially resist open-ended instruction, but after several weeks they grow to like it, or at least appreciate its value.

Once students are accustomed to recording their own data, you can make other modifications. For example, provide them with only some of the procedures. Or, have students attempt the activity before you lecture on the subject matter involved. These simple changes eventually lead to true inquiry.

Can Students Learn Facts in an Inquiry-Based Classroom?

Most studies state that inquiry-based instruction is equal or superior to other instructional modes and results in higher scores on content achievement tests. However, some of these studies focused on students who were studying concrete content, which is the strength of inquiry-based instruction.

Perhaps this is one source of confusion about inquiry-based instruction being only for "advanced" students. This, of course, is a misconception. After all, elementary students learn

quite effectively using hands-on, inquiry-based materials in the hands of a skillful teacher.

Still, research seems to support the idea that students can discover concrete concepts that lend themselves to direct observation through inquiry-based instruction. Students will be even more successful if you guide them toward understanding by implementing the kinds of teacher behaviors mentioned earlier in the article. However, there's no such thing as a teacher-proof curriculum, and there are lots of times when inquiry-based instruction is less advantageous than other methods. It's up to you to find the right mix of inquiry and non-inquiry methods that engages your students in the learning of science.

Alan Colburn is a professor in the Department of Science Education at California State University Long Beach in Long Beach, California.

References

National Research Council (NRC). 1996. *National Science Education Standards.* Washington, DC: National Academy Press.

Project 2061. 1993. *Benchmarks for science literacy.* New York: Oxford University Press.

Suchman, J. R. 1964. The Illinois studies in inquiry training. *Journal of Research in Science Teaching* 2: 230–232.

Welch, W. W., L. E. Klopfer, G. S. Aikenhead, and J. T. Robinson. 1981. The role of inquiry in science education: Analysis and recommendations. *Science Education* 65: 33–50.

Inquiry Made Easy

By Wendy Pierce

According to the National Science Education Standards, all children should have the ability to do scientific inquiry by fourth grade (NRC 1996). They should be able to ask questions, plan and conduct simple investigations, employ simple equipment and tools to gather data, use data to construct reasonable explanations, and communicate investigations and explorations.

Several years ago, I attended the Exploratorium Institute of Inquiry through the Keystone Science and Technology Grant (a National Science Foundation local systemic change grant based in Montana). In this workshop, teachers experienced inquiry and the underlying structure involved in using inquiry in the classroom. I became convinced that using inquiry as a teaching method was valuable and that content as well as inquiry could be taught in this manner.

"Doable" Inquiry

During the 1999–2000 school year, I was a teacher on special assignment with the Keystone Grant. One of the grant's goals was to help teachers model inquiry techniques using science kits. Participating teachers had attended summer workshops that emphasized inquiry, but many were hesitant to teach an actual inquiry unit. In

conversations with teachers I found their hesitancy centered around issues such as

- inquiry takes too much time,
- when students develop their own questions, the questions don't relate to the required curriculum,
- teachers are uncomfortable sorting questions (Harlen 1997), and
- teachers feel unprepared to help students with difficult questions, due to a lack of background knowledge.

In general, I found that teachers were looking for more structure than an entirely open-ended inquiry. In "How to Make Lab Activities More Open Ended" (Colburn 1997), Colburn writes about varying levels of openness in instruction ranging from a level 0 (the problem, instructions, and answer are all given) to a level 3 (the problem, instructions, and answers are all open). Although I believe students should have the opportunity to experience open-ended inquiries, I understand the complexities of teaching. Approaching new teaching strategies slowly will likely create lasting science reform.

While working with classroom teachers, we developed a "doable" format for inquiry. This format emphasizes using a question wheel (Figure 1) as a tool to help students identify independent and dependent variables that drive the underlying structure in inquiry. The format is not entirely open ended, but it allows students to ask questions driven by their own curiosity, make predictions, develop procedures, participate in experiments, collect data, and make conclusions based on evidence. This format worked particularly well in first- through fifth-grade classrooms; with a few adjustments, it can work well in middle school classrooms.

Steps to Inquiry

Each step takes between 45 and 60 minutes in a classroom. The example used throughout this article relates to a chromatography experiment, though the format can be easily adapted to suit your students' needs.

Day One: Developing Questions

1. Brainstorm independent and dependent variables on the board to help students generate two lists:

   - The factors that we can change—the *independent variable*, such as types of markers, type of paper, and type of liquid
   - The factors that we can count, measure, or observe—the *dependent variable,* such as types of colors, length of colors, and pattern of colors

2. Use question wheels to help students devise inquiry questions. To make one, cut

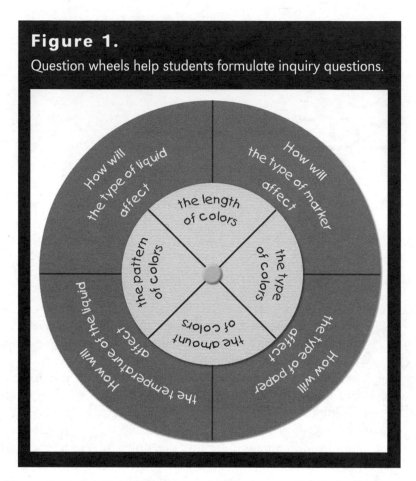

Figure 1.
Question wheels help students formulate inquiry questions.

out two circles, one 12.5 cm in idameter and one 7.5 cm, from two different-colored pieces of paper. The large (outer) circle represents the independent variable. The smaller (inner) circle represents the dependent variable. With lines, divide both circles into quarters, thirds, or halves (depending on the age and abilities of your class and the number of variables you are working with). On the outer circle, write the phrase, "How will _____ affect _____ ?" in each divided section of the circle. Leave the inner wheel blank. Attach the circles together with a brad in the middle. Then, using the items generated on the lists, students can

- fill in the independent variable on the outer wheel,
- fill in the dependent variable on the inner wheel.

3. Next, using the wheel, have students choose two questions and write them on a sentence strip. On a wall, hang questions by category: types of markers, type of paper, and type of liquid.

4. Have a "question walk." Students walk around the room and read all the questions. Once they have read the questions, students go to the category that interests them and choose a question from the wall. Make sure to emphasize that scientists choose questions because they are interested in the questions.

Continued Learning

Day Two or Three: Develop a Prediction and Make a Data Sheet

Depending on your class and topic, students can begin the inquiry investigation either by developing a prediction or by making a data sheet.

Prediction
- Using the inquiry activity sheet as a guide (Figure 2), the students write down their questions. The students should examine their question and then underline the independent variable and circle the dependent variable—as in how will the type of paper affect the length of colors?
- The students fill in their prediction and circle what they are keeping the same for their experiment (everything except the variable with which they are working).
- Students can illustrate what they think will happen if they change one variable and keep the rest of the variables the same.

Data Sheet
Sometimes it works for students to create a data sheet (Figure 3) before recording their predictions so they can focus on what they are trying

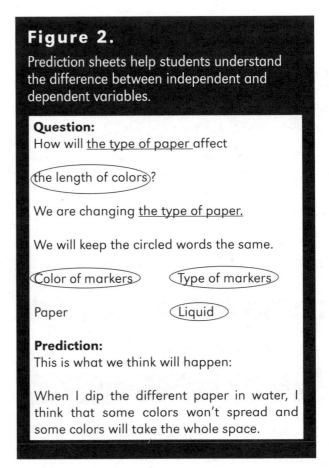

Figure 2.
Prediction sheets help students understand the difference between independent and dependent variables.

Question:
How will <u>the type of paper</u> affect (the length of colors)?

We are changing <u>the type of paper.</u>

We will keep the circled words the same.

(Color of markers)   (Type of markers)

Paper   (Liquid)

Prediction:
This is what we think will happen:

When I dip the different paper in water, I think that some colors won't spread and some colors will take the whole space.

to measure, count, or observe. The students use the data sheet to

- write down their question(s);
- look at their question(s) and underline the independent variable and circle the dependent variable;
- record (on the top of the data sheet) the variable that they have circled (the dependent variable); and
- record (on the side of the data sheet) the variable that they have underlined (the independent variable).

I usually model creating a data sheet on the board or an overhead, discussing at this time the idea of multiple trials. Also, I discuss how many ways they might want to change their variable

Figure 3.
Inquiry Data Sheet

Length of Color

Type of Paper	Trial 1	Trial 2	Trial 3	Average
copy paper	0 cm	0 cm	0 cm	0 cm
white construction paper	3.5 cm	4 cm	5 cm	4 cm
newsprint	4 cm	4 cm	4.5 cm	4.25 cm
coffee filter	5.5 cm	5 cm	6 cm	5.5 cm

This is what we discovered:
The marker spread more on the coffee filter than on any other paper.

Figure 4.
Sample chromatography investigation
Materials and planning sheet

Materials we will need:
1. different types of paper
2. water
3. container
4. purple markers, rubber bands, paper clips

Plan:
1. Put the water in the container.
2. Put the rubber bands on the container.
3. Put the color on different papers.
4. Put different papers with color on it in the water.
5. Measure the length of the color.

and how many spaces they will need on their data sheet. Typically, I model a few experiment scenarios and then walk around the room to answer questions as students create data sheets for their own experiments.

Experimenting and Beyond
Day Four: Plans and Materials
During this period, have the students do quiet work while you talk with individual students about their questions. Review each student's question and discuss what materials will be needed for the experiment. Help students learn how to write a plan so anyone could follow it just as scientists do.

Figure 4 is an example of one student's plan for a chromatography experiment investigating the question, "How will the type of paper affect the length of colors?"

Day Five: Experiment Day
On this day, the children should be ready to perform their experiments. Walk around the classroom and question the children about their experiments and help them solve their problems.

Day Five or Six: Scientific Conference
Depending on how long the experiments take, a scientific conference can be held the same day or at a later date, but the children should always share what they've discovered. This is what scientists do.

The Structure of Inquiry
Teachers who used this format and adapted it to fit their classroom experiences found it very useful. The questions were controlled enough that the teachers felt comfortable helping the children, and the inquiries had a definite timeframe in which teachers could work.

My hope is that as teachers use this format, they will become comfortable with content and the structure of inquiry. As students become more experienced with using inquiry, they will ask richer, higher-level, more meaningful questions and become independent science learners. That is the goal!

Wendy Pierce is a science teacher at Chief Joseph Middle School in Bozeman, Montana.

Resources

Colburn, A. 1997. How to make lab activities more open ended. *California Science Teachers Association Journal* (fall): 4–6.

Harlen, W. 1997. *The teaching of science in primary schools.* London: David Fulton.

National Research Council (NRC). 1996. *National Science Education Standards.* Washington, DC: National Academy Press.

Blow-by-Blow Inquiry

By Cathy A. Wittrock and Lloyd H. Barrow

The National Science Education Standards were developed to provide K–12 science teachers with information about what students should know and be able to do, what science teachers need to know and be able to do to facilitate students' learning, how to assess students' understandings and abilities, and how school programs and systems should promote high-quality science opportunities for all students (NRC 1996). Science as Inquiry is one of eight categories of the content standards published in the *National Science Education Standards*. Inquiry is the process by which students learn to think and act in ways that promote critical thinking by asking questions, planning and conducting investigations using appropriate tools to answer questions, and presenting their results to others (NRC 1996, p. 122).

Bybee (1997) considers inquiry an essential component for all science programs, and the *Standards* recommends that all students be involved in their own learning. The view of science teaching at the beginning of the 21st century is different from the way science was taught in the past. The *Standards* reflects an image of science education where the emphasis is on learning and identifies three types of learning outcomes from students doing inquiry:

science subject knowledge, abilities necessary to do scientific inquiry, and understandings about scientific inquiry (NRC 1996, p. 121–122).

Hurd (1995) says that this is a knowledge-intensive society and that the emphasis needed for students is "learning to learn or life-long learning ... including how to find sources of reliable information, how to access new knowledge, and how to use it" (p. 97). The spirit of the *Standards* moves toward those goals by requiring teachers to shift from their dependence on textbooks to using them simply as references to support hands-on, minds-on learning. This transformation is facilitated through the proper use of inquiry—in which the teacher is the facilitator rather than disseminator of knowledge.

A teacher might face a number of challenges when starting an inquiry. My challenge was preparing the school's third-grade students for the new state science assessments while encouraging increased enthusiasm and participation in the school's newly revised science fair. My answer was to issue a challenge to students, all of whom were enthralled in the home run–hitting race between professional baseball players Mark McGwire and Sammy Sosa. Capitalizing on this interest, I encouraged my third-grade students to challenge the first-grade students to a contest, not of hitting home runs but of blowing cotton balls. This inquiry activity is designed for five 30 to 40 minute blocks of classroom time (Figure 1).

Figure 1.
Schedule for the Huff 'n Puff activity

Day 1
- Complete prior knowledge chart
- "Think Like a Scientist" poster presentation
- Ask question and make prediction
- Discuss experiment (fair test)
- Compose procedure as a class

Day 2
- Do experiment
- Record data in chart format

Day 3
- Discuss raw data and look for patterns
- Complete a bar graph using data

Days 4 and 5
- Write conclusions (see Figures 4, 5, and 6 for suggestions)
- Class discussion to share ideas

The Huff 'n Puff inquiry addresses the following Standards:

- Science as inquiry: "All students should develop abilities necessary to do scientific inquiry and understanding about scientific inquiry."
- Physical Science: "All students should develop an understanding of properties of objects and materials [and] position and motion of objects" (NRC 1996).

My first step involved assessing students' prior knowledge of force and motion through a series of questions and discussions. How can you make an object move? What kinds of objects can humans move? How do objects act when they move? Recording students' responses on a classroom chart motivated participation, validated the importance of students' responses, encouraged the sharing of ideas, and provided a point of reference for later conclusions and writing exercises. This discussion concluded with the introduction of the four-step inquiry process called "Think Like a Scientist" (Figure 2) and a brief explanation of each step. The process was presented to students as a teacher-made poster. As each step was explained, students drew the images from the poster in their science journals. Throughout the year, students referred back to the poster and journal drawings to determine whether they were thinking like scientists.

The following inquiry questions were posed: Do you think a third-grade student can blow a cotton ball farther than a first-grade student can? How could you find out? After a brief discussion, each third-grade student made a prediction. "I predict that a third-grade student can/cannot blow a cotton ball farther because _____." Their ideas varied greatly, so all students were encouraged to share their statements with the class. This sharing was a very important aspect of the inquiry because each student was able to hear other students' approaches and reasoning.

Next, students generated a list of questions they would need to answer to have a fair test of blowing ability.

- Where will we blow the cotton balls: on the floor, outside, on a table? (on a table)
- Will we stand up or sit down? (stand up)
- Will we blow directly on the cotton ball or through a straw? (through a straw)
- If we use straws, how will we protect against germs? (Each student will each use his or her own straw.)

Figure 2.

Think Like a Scientist teacher-prepared poster

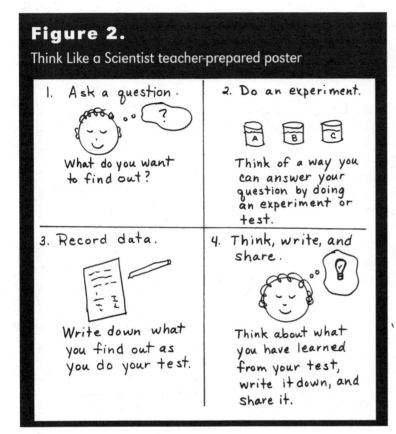

1. Ask a question.
What do you want to find out?

2. Do an experiment.
Think of a way you can answer your question by doing an experiment or test.

3. Record data.
Write down what you find out as you do your test.

4. Think, write, and share.
Think about what you have learned from your test, write it down, and share it.

- How will we hold the straws? (with a mechanism designed to hold the straw)
- Will we use the same cotton ball for every trial? (yes)
- How will we measure accurately? (using metersticks along the side of the blowing surface)
- How many times will each person blow? (three)
- What if the cotton ball falls off the table? (The student gets to blow it again.)
- Where will the cotton ball be placed to start? (at the same place for every student)

Students' overall concern was fairness—one aspect of the inquiry process that primary students can easily understand. Of course, they were actually determining the constant variables that would make the experiment and their data reliable.

The materials and a sample procedure are listed in Figure 3, as are steps the teacher should follow to prepare for the Huff 'n Puff activity and a diagram of the setup. Finally, students conducted the activity, and the third-grade students were encouraged to help the first-grade students in measuring and recording data. Throughout this activity, there was a healthy spirit of competition between the grades.

Following this activity was a third-grade lesson on analyzing data using a graph. Before analyzing the data, the students reviewed the criteria they had established to ensure a fair test (constant variables) such as using the same starting point, the same type of straw, and the same cotton ball for every trial. Students also identified those factors that were changed on purpose (independent variables: the age and grade level of the blower) and the factor that changed by itself each time (dependent variable: the distance the cotton ball traveled). Teams of students prepared bar graphs comparing the average distance (determined by the teacher) that each grade level blew the cotton ball. It has been my experience that the concept of averaging is introduced to students in late third grade or early fourth grade. For this exercise, I prefer to allow students to concentrate on analyzing the raw data tables for patterns, so I define "average" for them as what happened most of the time with the most students.

To conclude this inquiry, the students wrote about what they learned. They described what their bar graph showed (that the first-grade students blew the cotton ball an average of 105 cm and the third-grade students blew it an average of 108 cm) and decided whether the data supported or did not support their predictions. Most third-grade students predicted

Figure 3.
Setting up the activity

Materials:
- a long, flat surface at least 2 m long, such as a tile floor or table top
- 2 metersticks
- 1 cotton ball
- 1 clear plastic drinking cup with two holes punched 1 cm below the rim on opposite sides (this will serve as the straw holder), see diagram
- straight plastic drinking straws of uniform size, 1 for each student
- masking tape

Setup (to be done in advance by the teacher):
1. Tape the clear plastic cup upside down at the edge of the surface with holes lined up to face the edge of the surface (see diagram).
2. Tape down the metersticks end to end along the side of the surface. This will allow students to measure the distance the cotton ball travels.
3. Mark the starting point for the cotton ball with a dot of masking tape. Make this point even with the end of the first meterstick.
4. Prepare a data chart for students to record their measurements.
5. Invite a classroom of first-grade students to do the activity also. The third-grade students can help the younger students by measuring and recording their data on separate charts.

Procedure:
1. Put the cotton ball on the starting dot.
2. Put a clean straw into the straw holder.
3. Line up end of straw 2 cm away from the cotton ball.
4. Each student stands at the end of the table and blows once through the straw.
5. Use the metersticks along the side of the surface to measure the distance the cotton ball moved.
6. Record this distance on the data chart.
7. Put in a new straw for the next student, and repeat all the steps.

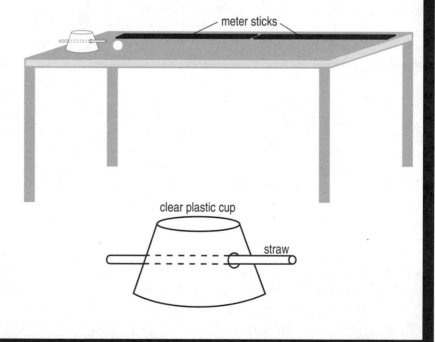

meter sticks

clear plastic cup

straw

that they would be able to blow the cotton ball farther than the younger students, though one student predicted no difference between the grade levels. Students' original predictions that the third-grade students would "win" were based on reasons such as third-grade students have bigger lungs, have had more practice, and will try harder (so they will do better). Some students thought the first-grade students would "win" because the younger students have had more recent experience with blowing while the older students had outgrown making blowing noises all the time.

Each student explained in his or her own words why the third-grade students were able to blow the cotton ball 3 cm farther. Most students concluded that the difference was due to larger lungs (based on research they had done using health books), but they were disappointed that the difference was so small. When directed to reflect on what they would do differently the next time and what else about motion or force they would like to study, students asked to repeat the experiment with other grade levels. They were ready to call in high school and pre-school siblings to test a wide range of subjects. Many suggested comparing different methods of blowing the cotton ball, such as with the straw and without the straw.

Most primary students will need a fill-in-the-blank model or a sentence starter to begin their writing exercise (Figures 4 and 5). Another option for beginning science writing is to pair verbally weak students with stronger ones or to allow groups of students to discuss ideas and then write those ideas onto a classroom chart before writing in their journals. Special-needs students might be encouraged to draw and label pictures rather than write sentences (Figure 6) or to use a tape recorder to share their learning. The important element in science writing is guiding children to express their learning in their own words. When the writing is completed, allow ample time for students to share orally and revise their work after they hear others' ideas.

Figure 4.

Science writing prompts for primary or novice writers

On our data chart, the longest distance that a first-grade student blew the cotton ball was _____ cm. The shortest distance was _____ cm. The longest distance for a third-grade student was _____ cm, and the shortest distance was _____ cm.

Our bar graph shows that the average first-grade student could blow the cotton ball _____ cm. The average third-grade student could blow the cotton ball _____ cm.

My prediction was *(copy from student's journal)*. The data *does/does not* support my prediction. The average distance for third-grade students *was greater than/was less than/was equal to* the average distance for first-grade students.

I think this happened because *(expressed in student's words after discussion)*. I learned that *(expressed in student's words)*.

What Was Learned

Students benefit from inquiry-based science instruction because it is interest driven. Instead of reading a textbook unit and doing an activity that "proves" the textbook is correct, students discover concepts and relationships through their own questions that are reinforced by textbook resources. The third-grade students involved in the Huff 'n Puff inquiry learned how to use inquiry to gain an understanding of force and motion and practiced science-process skills such as measuring and graphing. Later, they analyzed their data to determine if they had indeed answered their question. As is often the case with real scientists, they could not agree! Most students concluded—after a fierce debate—that the 3 cm difference in blowing

Figure 5.

Science writing prompts for advanced or intermediate writers

1. What was the range of data for each group (first- and third-grade students)?

2. What does your bar graph show about the average distance for each group?

3. Did the data support or not support your hypothesis? Why or why not?

4. What did you learn from this experiment?

5. What would you change about the experiment if you did it again?

6. What else would you like to study about force?

Figure 6.

Science writing prompts for special-needs students

Draw a first-grade student here:

1. The longest distance was _____ cm.

2. The shortest distance was _____ cm.

3. The average distance was _____ cm.

Draw a third-grade student here:

4. The longest distance was _____ cm.

5. The shortest distance was _____ cm.

6. The average distance was _____ cm.

Who has the bigger number in average distance?

Now draw a circle around the picture that shows who could blow the cotton ball farther.

ability between the age groups was not very important. They had discovered, on an elementary level, the concept of statistical significance.

When teachers are encouraged to work from students' prior knowledge, interests, and questions and move to student-designed inquiries, much perceived risk for the teacher is removed. Many primary teachers we spoke with confess feeling afraid of science because of bad luck with textbook activities, unrealistic and overwhelming curricular demands, and their own inadequate science background. With inquiry, teachers and students can discover the answers to their questions and can use other resources to expand their knowledge base at the same time. In this inquiry sequence, third-grade students designed a fair test to answer a class question, then used their resulting data to answer that question—and create additional questions.

This inquiry enabled students to practice being scientists while gaining knowledge.

As with any new skill, students must crawl before they walk and walk before they run. Therefore, primary teachers must direct, guide, and model elements of the inquiry process and provide ample opportunities for students to practice their new skills. The inquiry described here and others like it can be used as springboards for entire units of science instruction. Motivation for learning is enhanced when inquiry is used as the vehicle to guide instruction, rather than the caboose that ends it.

Cathy A. Wittrock is a third-grade teacher at Cedar Springs Elementary in House Springs, Missouri. Lloyd H. Barrow is a professor of science education at the University of Missouri—Southwestern Bell Science Education Center in Columbia.

Resources

Bybee, R. 1997. *Achieving scientific literacy: From purpose to practices.* Portsmouth, NH: Heinemann.

Bybee, R., and J. McInerney, eds. 1995. *Redesigning the science curriculum.* Colorado Springs, CO: Biological Sciences Curriculum Study.

Howe, A. 1998. Turning activities into inquiry lessons. *Science Activities* 34(4): 3–4.

Hurd, P. 1995. Reinventing the science curriculum: Historical reflections and new directions. In *Redesigning the science curriculum,* eds. R. W. Bybee and J. D. McInerney, 1–11. Colorado Springs, CO: BSCS.

National Research Council (NRC). 1996. *National Science Education Standards.* Washington, DC: National Academy Press.

Why Do We Classify Things in Science?

By Bill Robertson

Each year, in thousands of classrooms across the country, students classify animals, rocks, and other things as part of their science studies. Each year, thousands of students no doubt ask, "Why in the heck are we doing this?" Classifying things according to their properties and characteristics is a big part of science, but what's the purpose? Why do it in science class, and why do scientists do it as part of their work?

Careful Observation

An activity that's been around a long time is giving a group of students a handful of peanuts. Each student chooses a peanut and writes a detailed description of the peanut. The students put the peanuts back in the original pile and then trade descriptions with other students. Then the students match the description they have with one of the peanuts in the pile. This activity helps students learn the skills of observation and communication, skills that are important when doing science. Also, it's just plain fun to

do. Unfortunately, though, much of science instruction doesn't get beyond observing, communicating, and classifying. For example, it's common for students in Earth science classes to classify rocks according to their luster, hardness, and other characteristics and then move on to other subjects. A first step in chemistry often is for the students to memorize the location of elements on the periodic table. And, of course, biology students know the pain of memorizing the kingdoms and phyla of lots of different organisms. Do we do these things in the classroom because they're inherently interesting? Unlikely. At any rate, the peanut activity I refer to here has been around awhile, which is why I used it as an example. If you would like to try this activity with students, make sure none of your students are allergic to peanuts.

Classifying for a Purpose

In her first week of chemistry, my daughter came home and asked me to help her by identifying the line on the periodic table between metals and nonmetals. I asked her what the difference was between metals and nonmetals, and of course she didn't know. We were even, because I didn't know offhand where that line was between metals and nonmetals.

Historically, chemists classified different elements and came up with the beginnings of the periodic table before they had an understanding of the underlying structure of elements. The organization of the periodic table was important, however, as a prelude to this understanding, which we call atomic theory. Once you know something about the way in which protons, neutrons, and electrons come together to form atoms, the periodic table has a whole new meaning. I'll discuss what this implies for teaching kids about chemistry in a bit. For now, we can look at other ways that classifying has helped scientists develop a deeper understanding of the world.

When physicists took on the entertaining task of smashing different particles into one another, they found that they produced a whole bucket load of new subatomic particles. What caused the production of these new particles, and how did they fit into our theory of atoms? As a first step toward answering these questions, physicists began classifying the new subatomic particles according to properties they could observe, such as *charge, mass, charm,* and *strangeness* (Yes, these are actual properties—who says scientists aren't whimsical?). With the classification schemes, they were able to develop a theory of "quarks," and later "strings," which can explain the original classification and give us new insights into the structure of matter.

On to Earth science. As with the previous examples, geologists classify rocks to further their understanding. Knowing what kinds of rocks are found at different locations of the Earth, one can determine the processes that might have formed the rocks and thus piece together a history of the formation of the Earth's features. Engineers also use the classification of rocks and soils to predict the behavior of these rocks and soils when you begin moving them around and using them for various structures.

In the Classroom

As I said in the beginning, classification for the sake of classification can be fun and useful, but I wouldn't recommend it as a steady diet. It always helps to have a reason for doing the classification. Let's take taxonomy in life sciences as an example. Suppose you have students memorize the kingdoms and phyla of various organisms simply because that's what you do in life science. Suppose also that, after this memorization, you move on to studying ecosystems. Does knowing the aforementioned taxonomy help you understand ecosystems? Not much. It would be better to classify organisms as herbivores, carnivores, and omnivores prior to studying ecosystems. That way, construction of food chains as an understanding of the energy flow in ecosystems makes a lot more sense.

In chemistry, should you have students memorize the periodic table, or portions thereof, before investigating the structure of atoms? Yes, if your purpose is to help the students understand the historical development of chemistry. No, if your purpose is to have the students use the periodic table to predict what happens when different elements come together. Once students know how electrons fill energy levels, the periodic table becomes a convenient method for viewing what different atoms look like and knowing what they are likely to do when they encounter other atoms. Why memorize the table before knowing the atomic structure that underlies the overall organization? For that matter, why memorize the table at all?

To close, here are a few simple guidelines for the use of classification in science classrooms. Classification for the purpose of building observation and communication skills is okay, but on a limited basis. Be wary of using classification simply because it's what scientists do. Classification in the classroom should lead toward the understanding of concepts, or at least should be done with an eye toward the ultimate purpose, such as the classification of rocks leading toward an understanding of the formation of geologic features. Finally, even though classification might have historically preceded understanding, as with the periodic table, the historical approach might not be the best way for students to understand important concepts.

And with those recommendations, I'll file this column under "the nature of science." Or should I file it under "interdisciplinary science?" How about according to "date created"? Or maybe according to how close I was to missing the deadline.

Bill Robertson is the author of the NSTA Press book series, Stop Faking It! Finally Understanding Science So You Can Teach It.

Section 2

Teaching Science

Teaching Science

As you read in Doug Ronsberg's poem in the preface, "there's more to teaching science than stuffing kids with facts … ." This section will look at that kind of science teaching through four lenses. The lenses, *learner-centered, knowledge-centered, assessment-centered,* and *community-centered,* are based in research into how students best learn, not just science, but all subjects (Donovan and Bransford 2005).

- The learner-centered lens emphasizes understanding the ideas students bring to the classroom and engaging the students in activities that build on what they know.
- The knowledge-centered lens focuses on understanding the content that students should learn and how they learn the content.
- The assessment-centered lens emphasizes the need to "assess for learning" instead of only conducting assessments of learning.
- The community-centered lens encourages questioning, respect, and risk taking.

Learner-Centered Lens

A learner-centered teacher realizes that students do not enter the classroom with empty heads. Instead, the teacher pays close attention to students' ideas, knowledge, and attitudes. Vygotsky (1987) describes these initial ideas as spontaneous knowledge that is generated primarily through observations made in everyday, nonschool situations. A learner-centered teacher begins instruction by engaging students with their initial ideas and providing concrete opportunities for them to explore those ideas. A learner-centered teacher also pays careful attention to his or her students' cultural background and abilities (discussed in section 3).

We build explanations for our observations of the world that are often inconsistent with scientific knowledge. Posner et al. (1982) established a theory of conceptual change in an attempt to explain how a person's initial conceptions change from one set of concepts to another set that is incompatible with the first. For the initial conception to be changed to a new conception, four conditions must be present:

- First, students must identify and become dissatisfied with their current conception.
- Second, the new conception must be understandable, or intelligible.
- Third, the new conception must appear to be initially plausible; it must resolve the student dissatisfaction with their initial conception.
- Fourth, the new conception must be fruitful; it must show the possibility of being able to solve current and future problems.

According to Posner et al. (1982), if these conditions are met, a student may undergo conceptual change.

Knowledge-Centered Lens

A teacher looking at instruction through a knowledge-centered lens will focus on what is important for students to know and be able to do. This involves identifying the core concepts of a subject through analysis of national, state, or local science standards documents. While looking through the knowledge-centered lens, connections between science content and the students' "real world" should also be identified. Determining the appropriate way for students to build concepts is also important. Section 1 explained that science should be taught in a manner that reflects how scientific knowledge is created. Therefore, the knowledge-centered lens also needs to identify opportunities for student inquiry and the development of knowledge claims supported by evidence. Section 5 provides examples of teaching specific science concepts.

The BSCS 5E model is a powerful instructional model that can help connect process and content.

- Instruction using this model begins by engaging students with a task that stimulates prior knowledge and promotes curiosity (*Engage*).

- Students then explore their current ideas through a set of common explorations (*Explore*). Next, students are introduced to specific content and skills (*Explain*).
- Students deepen their understanding by applying what they have learned in new activities (*Elaborate*).
- Finally, students show how they have progressed towards meeting the educational objectives (*Evaluate*).

Appendix 1 illustrates how to use the 5E model for unit planning.

Assessment-Centered Lens

The assessment-centered lens supports the learner-centered and knowledge-centered classroom. Initial assessments identify students' existing ideas, skills, and attitudes. An assessment-centered teacher understands what he or she expects students to learn and uses ongoing (formative) assessments to monitor student progress throughout instruction. The assessment-centered teacher uses these formative assessments to modify instruction to promote student mastery.

An assessment-centered teacher also provides students with opportunities for metacognition. Metacognition involves students understanding not just what they are learning, but also how and why they are learning. Students ask questions such as, "Why is this important?" "Why did I choose to accomplish this task in this manner?" and "How is this different from what I understood before this task?"

Georghiades (2000) contends that student self-reflection using their own words leads to deeper understanding, and therefore the new conceptions will be more durable and the students will be better able to transfer the new conceptions to different settings. His study involved 68 fifth-grade students divided into two groups. Both groups received identical instruction except for the infusion of brief "metacognitive instances" at selected points in the instruction for the experimental group.

Table 1.
Metacognitive instances

Activity Type	Example
Questions/ Discussions	Before having this lesson, what was your belief regarding (X...)? Have you changed your views? If so, why? Explain to your friend the way you solved that problem. Can you name two reasons why we are learning these things? How can they be useful in everyday life?
Keeping a Diary	Write down three things you learned in today's lesson and any points that might not be very clear. (This was also done in the form of an anonymous Question Box.)
Annotated Drawing	Draw any tool you want that can safely be used by an electrician, indicating the material(s) from which it is made.
Concept Mapping	Create a concept map as either a whole-class or individual activity.

Source: Georghiades, 2000, p. 131.

These metacognitive instances included discussion, pair activities and thinking, writing, and drawing tasks. The brief time spent on these activities helped to hold student interest and participation. Table 1 provides examples of the types of activities that students were asked to complete. Students involved with metacognition activities were more engaged in discussions and remembered more of the material when compared to the control group. Additionally, interviews and testing were conducted one week, two months, and eight months after instruction. In each case, the experimental group outperformed the control group. The researchers also noted that metacognitive instances conducted in small groups were more effective than those conducted in large groups. Students seemed more comfortable revealing their thoughts in smaller groups, had more effective discussions, and received more personalized feedback.

Community-Centered Lens
The community-centered lens focuses on the interpersonal relationships in the classroom culture. The classroom culture should encourage the expression of ideas, respect differences in ideas, encourage questioning and collaboration, promote risk taking, and celebrate discovery. One of the primary aspects of promoting this type of classroom culture is fostering dialogue.

Newton et al. (1999) investigated the opportunities provided to students during 34 science lessons for discussion and social construction of knowledge. They found that the highest percentage of student time was spent passively listening. The lesson observations showed that opportunities for discussion that lasted for more than 10 minutes were offered in only two of the 34 cases. The dominant form of interaction in the classroom was teacher talk. Even when opportunities were provided for student talk through teacher questioning, they invariably led to students "guessing what is in the teacher's mind," instead of developing understanding through students' contributing their emerging understandings. The researchers concluded that lessons should be organized so that students participate actively in thinking through issues and developing their own arguments. Students need to be given a greater voice in lessons.

Mason and Santi investigated the changes of conceptions about the greenhouse effect and global warming due to interaction developed in small- and large-group discussions among fifth-grade students. The students had small-group discussions focused on specific aspects of the greenhouse effect and global warming. Students then developed larger themes and issues. The teacher facilitated discussion by posing initial questions and explicitly drawing out evidence and justifications. Mason and Santi found that these interactions improved student learning. The researchers concluded that discourse can be used as a cognitive tool for structuring and restructuring knowledge:

> Discourse is not a mere vehicle to transmit disciplinary information, used by the teacher in order to give answers to never raised questions, but rather as a way to express personal ideas, sharing with other thinkers the understanding of examined phenomena by confronting different conceptions and reflecting on them. It can be stated that a classroom discussion, as a learning environment which encourages questioning, criticizing, evaluating and produces dissatisfaction with the existing state of knowledge, can act as a fruitful breeding ground for conceptual change (1998, p. 83).

Teachers can foster meaningful discourse by asking probing questions and exploring incorrect, naïve, or alternative answers. Through practice, the purposeful use of different types of questions should become natural. Teachers also need to encourage student "cross-talk."

The Articles

This section contains 23 articles that provide classroom examples of learner-centered,

knowledge-centered, assessment-centered, and community-centered classrooms. Although the articles are categorized into the different lenses, many provide illustrations of aspects of more than one lens.

Learner-Centered Lens

Article: Teaching Space Science for Conceptual Change

Key Ideas: This article examines the difficulty of teaching to change students' incorrect ideas. The article uses a Moon-phase activity as an example of how to help students create and resolve cognitive conflict by exploring alternative explanations for why we see different phases.

Article: Egg Bungee Jump

Key Ideas: This article describes an engaging activity that gives students the opportunity to identify and explore their initial ideas related to force and energy. The article illustrates the learner-centered lens by engaging students in a concrete and familiar activity while providing opportunities to identify students' initial ideas. The article then provides suggestions for how to use the activity to introduce specific content.

Article: Science Homework Overhaul

Key Ideas: A learner-centered classroom focuses on students interacting with relevant and familiar materials and ideas. This article explains how to create engaging and meaningful homework that supports classroom learning.

Article: Investigating Students' Ideas About Plate Tectonics

Key Ideas: In this article, the authors present common student misconceptions about plate tectonics. The authors also describe the assessment process that they used to uncover these misconceptions.

Article: More Than Just a Day Away From School

Key Ideas: This article provides guidelines for conducting field trips that encourage learning while making science relevant to students. The authors describe different purposes for field trips and ideas for focusing students on important components of the experience.

Knowledge-Centered Lens

Article: Explaining Science

Key Ideas: This brief article examines the use of evidence-based explanations in teaching science. One aspect of a knowledge-centered classroom is a focus on helping students learn science content in a manner similar to how scientists create knowledge. As we saw in Section 1, science uses evidence to create explanations for phenomena.

Article: The Stations Approach: How to Teach With Limited Resources

Key Ideas: A knowledge-centered teacher clearly identifies the learning outcomes for a unit and plans instruction to meet these outcomes. The approach described in this article begins with identifying what students should know, understand and be able to do at the end of the unit. Then, multiple activities are chosen to help students move toward these outcomes. The author faces large class sizes and limited resources, so uses a station approach where groups of students are working on different activities at the same time. The article also reinforces the learner-centered and community-centered aspects by differentiating instruction to multiple modalities and encouraging small-group discourse.

Article: How Do You Know That?

Key Ideas: In this article the authors describe how to use science inquiry to help kindergarten students create evidence-based explanations for their observations of organisms.

Article: Plants and Pollution

Key Ideas: This article illustrates how to use a long-term investigation to improve students' inquiry skills and increase the relevancy of content.

Students investigated the effects of different pollutants on the growth of plants as they learned about the parts of plants and life cycles.

Article: Rock Solid Science

Key Ideas: This article provides an example of using the 5E instructional model. The authors use children's books to engage students in exploring rocks.

Article: "Inquirize" Your Teaching

Key Ideas: This article explains how to create an instructional sequence using the 5E model. The author begins by identifying the concept and a possible exploration activity. Next, the author describes how to make an "explore" activity more inquiry based. Once you have an appropriate exploration activity you can identify activities or tasks for the *engage, explain, extend* and apply *(elaborate)* and *evaluate* phases.

Article: Embracing Controversy in the Classroom

Key Ideas: In a knowledge-centered classroom, students should be exposed to important contemporary science concepts. Occasionally, these concepts may be controversial. The authors explain how to approach controversial concepts in a respectful manner while maintaining scientific integrity.

Assessment-Centered Lens

Article: Embed Assessment in Your Teaching

Key Ideas: This article describes how to create and use an embedded assessment cycle to monitor student learning throughout instruction. Embedded assessment refers to activities or other tasks that provide teachers with learning data without using obvious assessments (like quizzes).

Article: Seamless Assessment

Key Ideas: This article applies the ideas of embedded assessment to the 5E model. The authors discuss the reasons for assessing and provide strategies for assessing in each phase of the 5E model.

Article: Using Interactive Science Notebooks for Inquiry-Based Science
Key Ideas: The author describes how he uses science notebooks to monitor student learning throughout instruction. The notebook helps students organize classroom handouts, notes, and work. Additionally, the notebooks provide an efficient way for the teacher to provide feedback on student learning.

Article: Formative Assessment Probes
Key Ideas: This article describes the creation and use of formative assessment probes to identify student understanding of concepts. Formative assessment probes are very useful for identifying students' initial ideas about a topic. They can also be used throughout instruction to monitor conceptual understanding.

Article: Assessing Scientific Inquiry
Key Ideas: This article describes how to assess both process and knowledge during scientific inquiry. The article provides multiple strategies for assessing students' abilities to participate in scientific inquiry.

Article: Cartoons—An Alternative Learning Assessment
Key Ideas: This article describes multiple strategies for using cartoons to assess student understanding of concepts.

Community-Centered Lens

Article: Making Time for Science Talk
Key Ideas: This article introduces characteristics of meaningful science conversations. The authors contrast "science talk" with the normal classroom discourse pattern and suggest ways to promote "science talk" in the classroom.

Article: Evidence Helps the KWL Get a KLEW

Key Ideas: The approach described in this article fosters student collaborative investigations and discussion. KLEW is a modification of the popular KWL (Know-Wonder-Learned) process that emphasizes the use of evidence to support learning claims.

Article: Questioning Cycle
Key Ideas: This article describes a cycle of questioning and provides examples of questions that can be used to elicit different types of responses. Additionally, the authors describe the importance of appropriate feedback for questions.

Article: Thinking About Students' Questions
Key Ideas: In this article the author identifies different types of questions and discusses how to help students identify questions and improve their questioning skills.

Article: The Eight-Step Method to Great Group Work
Key Ideas: A community-centered classroom engages students socially. Students collaborate in small and large groups. This article identifies strategies that lead to positive and productive group interactions.

Action Steps
Learner-Centered Lens

1. Use national or state science standards documents to identify a topic. Either create and administer a formative assessment probe or conduct interviews with a small group of students to determine their initial understanding of the topic.
2. Identify a topic that is commonly taught in either elementary or middle school. Determine connections between the topic and experiences relevant to students in your community.

Knowledge-Centered Lens

3. Explore either the national or your state

science standards for physical science, life science and Earth/space science. Create a poster that visually represents the concepts that are included in a single grade or grade band.

4. Explore either the national or your state science standards. What categories are included? Write a two-sentence summary for each category in each grade band.

Assessment-Centered Lens

5. Use the embedded assessment and seamless assessment articles to create an assessment plan for a unit.

Community-Centered Lens

6. Observe a classroom, and identify strategies that are used to foster a sense of community. Also, describe how the layout of the room encourages (or discourages) a sense of community.

7. Research strategies for promoting cooperative learning in your classroom.

Reflection Questions

1. Identify a misconception that you held. Reflect on what happened to help you change your ideas.

2. How do the national or state standards documents balance traditional content (life, physical, Earth/space) with other important concepts needed for science literacy?

3. Create an analogy for the relationship between instruction and assessment. For example, *Assessment* is to *instruction* as *sonar* is to a *submarine*—You can sail a submarine without sonar, but you wouldn't have a clue as to where you were going!

4. Reflect on an experience in your educational career (as a teacher or student) where you felt a real sense of community. How was that culture created?

5. Review the example electric circuits unit in Appendix 1. Describe how the unit reflects the four lenses described in this section. What changes or improvements would you make?

6. This section describes effective science teaching through four lenses. How do these lenses describe good teaching in other disciplines?

7. Synthesize the strategies described in this section to create a personal blueprint for creating a classroom that is learner centered, knowledge centered, assessment centered, and community centered.

References

Anderson, L. W., and D. R. Krathwohl, eds. 2001. *A taxonomy of learning, teaching, and assessment: A revision of Bloom's taxonomy of educational objectives.* New York: Longman.

Donovan, M. S., and J. D. Bransford, eds. 2005 *How students learn: History, mathematics, and science in the classroom.* Washington, DC: The National Academies Press

Georghiades, P. 2000. Beyond conceptual change learning in science education: focusing on transfer, durability and metacognition. *Educational Research* 42 (2): 119–139.

Mason, L. and M. Santi. 1998. Discussing the greenhouse effect: Children's collaborative discourse reasoning and conceptual change. *Environmental Education Research* 4(1).

Newton, P., R. Driver, and J. Osborne. 1999. The place of argumentation in the pedagogy of school science. *International Journal of Science Education* 21 (5): 553–576.

Posner, G. J., K. A. Strike, P. W. Hewson, and W. A. Gertzog. 1982. Accommodation of a scientific conception: Towards a theory of conceptual change. *Science Education* 66: 211–227.

Vygotsky, L. S. 1987. *The collected works of L. S. Vygotsky. Vol. I. Problems of general psychology.* Eds. R. W. Rieber and A. S. Carton. N. Minick (Trans.). New York: Plenum.

Teaching for Conceptual Change in Space Science

by Eric Brunsell and Jason Marcks

The Harvard-Smithsonian Center for Astrophysics' video *A Private Universe* dramatically depicts the difficulties Harvard graduates have answering questions related to space-science concepts commonly taught in elementary and middle school. The video continues by examining high school students' misconceptions of the reasons for the seasons and phases of the Moon and how these misconceptions persist even after classroom instruction on the subject. Nearly 20 years after the release of this video, much research has been done about students' understanding of space-science concepts and how to effectively change these ideas. Student difficulties with basic space-science concepts still persist however. This article describes some of the common student misconceptions related to phases of the Moon, introduces a conceptual-change teaching approach, and provides an example of an activity that can be used to address common misconceptions.

What Are They Thinking?

To get a better idea of what students were thinking about the Earth-Moon-Sun system, we asked some of our colleagues to survey their students. We received surveys from 52 sixth-grade students, 83 eighth-grade students, and 47 tenth- and eleventh-grade students. The survey asked the following questions:

1. What causes the phases of the Moon?
2. If the Earth were the size of a quarter [circle provided], draw how big the Moon would be.
3. Based on the scale in question 2, about how far apart would the Earth and Moon be?

Figure 1.

Student responses to a survey regarding the Earth/Moon system

Question	Sixth grade	Eighth grade	Tenth, Eleventh grades
Moon size compared to the Earth			
Correct	12%	14%	33%
Too big	35%	71%	8%
Too small	53%	14%	58%
Moon–Earth distance			
Correct	15%	9%	25%
Too far	40%	68%	17%
Too close	45%	23%	58%
Moon phases			
Correct	4%	5%	19%
Shadows	47%	40%	44%
Different amounts of Moon lit by Sun	13%	10%	19%
Clouds/weather	20%	35%	6%
Other	16%	10%	13%

The variety of student misconceptions related to these questions was similar to that found in a review of astronomy-education research conducted by Bailey and Slater (2004). Our results are shown in Figure 1.

Teaching for Conceptual Change

Students do not enter the classroom with empty heads. Instead, they have ideas about how the natural world works based on a rich tapestry of prior experiences and understandings. Explanations are often contradictory to science or scientific knowledge but make sense to students. They are therefore persistent and highly resistant to change. Strike and Posner describe these misconceptions as "embedded in a conceptual context" and immediately add that "students will have to alter other concepts as well … conceptions often come with their own support group" (1992).

One goal of science education is to move students' naïve understandings of the world toward those that are more scientific. To do that, Posner et al. explain that educators should use a situation, such as anomalous data or a discrepant event, to create dissonance, or dissatisfaction, with students' initial conceptions (1982). For example, it is quite common for students to believe that the different seasons are caused by Earth's distance from the Sun. In this misconception, students in the Northern Hemisphere believe that the Earth is closer to the Sun in the summer and therefore that is when they experience warmer temperatures. However, the Earth is closest to the Sun in January. This data should cause dissonance with students' initial ideas and open the door for learning a more scientific explanation.

Unfortunately, the introduction of anomalous data or a discrepant event by itself often does not lead to conceptual change. Mason explains that students often react to anomalous situations by either ignoring the event or subconsciously changing their perception of the data instead of becoming dissatisfied with their initial ideas (2001). The likelihood that students will become dissatisfied with their initial ideas is increased by having students identify and commit to their initial ideas and discuss each others' conflicting ideas and evidence.

After students become dissatisfied with their initial ideas, Posner et al. describe three additional conditions that are necessary for conceptual change to occur (1982). First, students must be able to understand the new idea (intelligible), understand how it can be used to resolve the dissatisfaction (plausible), and see how the new idea can be used in other situations (fruitful).

Applications in Space Science

Conceptual-change teaching can be used to help students understand many topics in space science. For example, a very common demonstration of the reason for Moon phases involves using a bright light, a ball, and your head. Place a bright light at approximately eye level and use your head to model the Earth. When you are looking directly at the light, it is noon. When you are looking directly away from the

light, it is midnight. A ball held at arm's length represents the Moon. If you turn in circles, keeping the ball in front of your face, but out of your head's shadow, you can recreate all of the Moon's phases. This is a very simple demonstration that can prove to students that the phases are caused as we see different portions of the lit half of the Moon. As we discussed earlier, however, simply introducing a correct model often is not enough to make students change their minds. The following activity uses a conceptual-change approach.

First, students should focus on the topic by determining the pattern of Moon phases by looking at a Moon-phase calendar (see Resources). Next, each student should individually write down his or her explanation for why we see different phases of the Moon. Then, students should discuss their ideas in small groups. During this discussion, move among groups and write down on chart paper different ideas that are discussed. Explain to students that they are going to test these different ideas. Because one of the most common misconceptions for explaining phases is that the Moon enters Earth's shadow, instruct students to recreate the pattern of Moon phases by casting a shadow of one ball onto another when using a central bright light (a floor lamp works best). If students do not already know, explain that it takes about one month for the Moon to orbit the Earth. Give students enough time to become frustrated with testing. It is possible to recreate some of the phases, so some student groups may claim success. If they do, challenge them by asking how their pattern compares to the monthly pattern that they observed earlier. Soon, students will realize that their model would mean that all of the phases would occur over a few days, while we would have a full Moon for the majority of the month. Additionally, many students will realize that it is impossible to recreate the gibbous phase. We have achieved cognitive conflict! As necessary, discuss and model other alternative ideas (clouds, different amounts lit, and so on).

Next, introduce the scientific explanation by having students model the demonstration described at the beginning of this section. This demonstration will make the scientific idea intelligible and plausible. As an extension, you can introduce how lunar eclipses occur to show what the shadow of the Earth does. A possible assessment for this activity is shown in Figure 2.

Conclusion

Many students come to our classes with naïve views of the solar system that may make sense to them, but are not scientific. A conceptual change-based instructional approach encourages students to identify and commit to their ideas, become dissatisfied with those ideas, and then introduces a more scientific explanation. This approach provides students with the opportunity to gain a deeper understanding of the world around them.

Eric Brunsell is an assistant professor of science education at the university of Wisonsin-LaCrosse. Jason Marcks is executive director of Space Education Initiatives.

Figure 2.

Moon-phase assessment

You are helping two of your friends prepare for a test on the phases of the Moon. Here is how they explain the cause of the phases.

Friend #1: "It depends on how much of the Moon is in the Earth's shadow."
Friend #2: "Sunlight hits the Moon at different angles, lighting different amounts."

- Do you agree with either student?
  If so, explain which one you agree with and why. Also, explain why the other is not right. If not, explain why you do not agree with either student. Then, write how you would explain the cause of phases of the Moon to your friends.

- Draw the position of the Moon for each situation.

 Full Moon   New Moon

 Waning gibbous   Waxing crescent

- Did you change your view of phases of the Moon after this lesson? If so, how? If you answered yes, why did your view change?

References

Bailey, J. M., and T. F. Slater. 2004. A review of astronomy education research. *The Astronomy Education Review* 2 (2): 20–45.

Mason, L. 2001. Responses to anomalous data on controversial topics and theory change. *Learning and Instruction* 11 (6): 453–83.

Posner, G. J., K. A. Strike, P. W. Hewson, and W. A. Gertzon. 1982. Accommodation of a scientific conception: Towards a theory of conceptual change. *Science Education* 66 (2): 211–27.

Strike, K. A., and G. J. Posner. 1992. *A revisionist theory of conceptual change.* In *Philosophy of science, cognitive psychology, and educational theory and practice,* eds. R. A. Duschl and R. J. Hamilton, 147–76. Albany, NY: State University of New York Press.

Resource

Moon-phase calendar
http://stardate.org/nightsky/moon/index.php.

Egg Bungee Jump

By Thomas Tretter

In the spirit of the *National Science Education Standards* (NRC 1996), many teachers attempt to have their students experience science in a constructivist, inquiry-oriented manner. The egg bungee jump activity will certainly support that mode of teaching and has the added benefit of providing a concrete context within which students can explore rather abstract concepts of force, motion, and energy transformations.

Activity

To introduce the egg bungee jump activity to the class, set up the apparatus (Figure 1) on the demonstration table in the front of the room. Inform students that they will be gathering data on a raw egg bungee jump using rubber bands for a bungee cord. The goal of the lab is to have the egg bungee jump from 2 m and get as close as possible to the floor without hitting it. It is the students' job to determine how many rubber bands should be used to create the bungee cord. Discuss the safe use of rubber bands with students. You may want to ask students to wear eye protection, even though no projectiles are involved.

To prepare for the 2 m jump, students first measure how far the egg will drop using bungee cords made from one rubber band, two bands, three bands, and four bands. Students then use the data collected to determine how many rubber bands they'd like to use for the 2 m jump.

Students work in teams of four. One member is responsible for keeping the ring stand from toppling off the table when the egg is dropped and holding the meterstick vertically with the zero at the bottom of the hook. A 1 m stick is usually sufficient for data collection because students are going to measure only up to 4 rubber bands—it typically takes about 10 or 11 rubber bands to reach 2 m. If students are using extra-large rubber bands and need more than 1 m to measure the jump with 4 rubber bands, I suggest students tape together two 1 m sticks to get the needed length. Another team member lines up the bottom of the egg with the bottom of the hook (see Figure 2), drops the egg straight down, and holds a finger over the rubber band on the hook so that it doesn't jump off during the egg's rebound. The third member is the "egg protector" and keeps the egg from swinging, pendulumlike, into the side of the lab bench after it rebounds from its lowest point on the initial drop. Protection of the egg is best done by cupping both hands and letting the egg fall to rest in the cupped hands at the top of its bounce after rebounding from the lowest point or cupping the egg on its way up after the lowest point; this technique avoids allowing the egg to bounce around multiple times. If the egg should break, most of the mess will likely be contained in the sack it is in. If any raw egg should leak out, instruct students to put on rubber gloves to avoid any possibility

Figure 1. Laboratory equipment

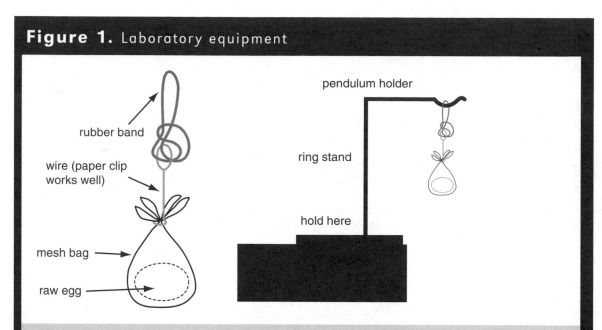

rubber band

wire (paper clip works well)

mesh bag

raw egg

pendulum holder

ring stand

hold here

Notes:
1. A mesh bag created from cutting a sports ball carry bag into squares about 20 cm x 20 cm works well, but cloth bags cut from clothing scraps work too. Alternative materials are possible, such as mesh bags used to package some fruits or onions. The sack is created by bringing all four edges together at the top of the egg.
2. Be sure to have the wire tightly wound (maybe using pliers) around the top of the mesh bag to avoid the bag slipping through the wire and spilling the raw egg during the experiments. A large paper clip works well for the wire, but a long twist tie may also work if it can be securely tightened.
3. Make the length of the wire significantly shorter (approximately half works well) than the length of the unstretched rubber band so that the bottom of the egg can be lifted to be even with the hook for the first drop.
4. If no pendulum holder is available, any clamp that attaches to the ring stand (e.g., a test tube clamp) will work if a rubber band can be looped over some part of the clamp and a student's finger can hold the rubber band securely. If no ring stands are available, this activity could be done by extending any long, narrow, and straight object (e.g., a broom handle) over the side of the lab bench (or table) and suspending the rubber bands from the end of the extension, from which the egg will bungee jump.
5. List of materials needed per lab group:
   - 1 egg (plus a few backups for the class in case of breakage)
   - 1 egg sack
   - 1 wire (a large paper clip works well, or a long twist tie may work)
   - access to many rubber bands (approximately two dozen or more per lab group—I usually have available a large box or two for the whole class). To provide students options, a teacher may wish to have available rubber bands of different widths, thicknesses, and lengths—almost any sizes will work as long as they aren't so weak that they break with the force exerted by the falling egg or they aren't so strong that they hardly stretch from the force exerted by the falling egg.
   - 1 meterstick (or 2 metersticks taped together if extra long rubber bands are used)
   - 1 ring stand (or alternative—see note 4 above)
   - 1 pendulum holder (or alternative—see note 4 above)

of salmonella poisoning and use paper towels to mop up the egg. It may be necessary to follow up the initial wiping using wet and soapy paper towels so that the floor isn't slippery. The fourth member of the group crouches down to determine the lowest falling point of the egg by referring to the adjacent meter stick.

You can either instruct students how to use the data to determine the number of rubber bands needed for a 2 m jump (as suggested in the sample student lab sheet), or you can allow students to devise their own methods of using the data. The amount of data analysis guidance given to students should be based on their abilities and your pedagogical goals.

Pedagogical Benefits and Alternatives

There are a number of science skills, process skills, and social skills that could be addressed with this activity (Figure 3). Students spend a lot of time working together in inquiry-oriented science classes, and an activity such as this can increase their comfort with working together. This activity is also beneficial for creating cooperative teamwork because the nature of the activity requires four people to be involved and does not permit one or two team members to take a purely passive role.

Although this bungee activity could be done with other objects such as a golf ball, the possibility of making a mess with raw eggs increases interest. The open-ended nature of the details of carrying out the activity encourages students to think about lab techniques. Some students comment that because not all the rubber bands in the boxes provided are the same, their results could be adversely affected.

Figure 2.

Drop position of the egg for each trial

Figure 3.

Sampling of skills that could be addressed with the egg bungee jump activity

Science skills	Process skills	Social skills
Data collection	Careful lab techniques	Active involvement with group
Creating line graphs	Replicability of results	Sharing responsibility
Writing and interpreting equations	Identifying and minimizing sources of error	Collaborating on data analysis
Force, motion, and energy concepts addressed		

A teacher could reply with something like, "How will you prevent that from becoming a problem?" In this way, students are encouraged to take the initiative with developing the details of their lab procedures. Likewise, some teams may decide to repeat each drop several times and average them to get a better value. Some students may comment that, after a number of drops, the rubber bands may become "tired" and that in future drops the distance will be greater than what they've measured. Others may not be careful to always release the egg from exactly the same height, creating a potential source of error. Some of the students reading the drop distance may not have their eyes horizontal with the lowest position of the egg, causing parallax to affect the accuracy of the distances they measure. These and other possibilities for affecting accuracy provide a rich source of postlab discussion of sources of error in lab measurements. The teacher may wish to create postlab worksheets with questions on this aspect of the lab or any other they'd like to reinforce.

When analyzing the data, you may choose to explicitly instruct students on how to perform the analysis (as is done in item number 5 in the sample student lab sheet), or you may allow students free rein to devise ways to analyze the data themselves. Alternatives to creating a graph and linearly extrapolating to 2 m (as suggested by item number 5) are: identifying how many additional centimeters each rubber band adds (on average) to the drop and computing how many rubber bands are needed to reach 2 m; graphing the data, writing the equation of the best-fit line (if students have had algebra), and solving that equation for the desired y-value; and making a table of number of rubber bands and fallen distance for rubber bands one through four and extending that table until the distance fallen reaches 2 m.

Students can retain their data from this activity to return to after they have learned how to write equations in slope-intercept form. These data provide a nice context for such equations, with the large benefit of both the slope and the y-intercept being readily interpretable as opposed to merely abstract numbers. The slope of this line represents the additional falling distance per added rubber band, while the y-intercept represents the combined length of the wire and the egg in the mesh bag hanging down from the hook with no rubber band.

Assessment

For the activity itself, I recommend assessing in a manner that is easy on the teacher, exciting for the students, and that almost invariably results in a good lab grade for students. Each student must provide the accompanying data tables and graphs in order to earn the grade. The grade is computed from 100 minus the number of centimeters off the ground for the 2 m egg bungee jump. Students can be allowed three trials so that they have a chance to correct problems, without penalty, on the first or second try if needed. An advantage of this policy is that it encourages students to go back to the data to reanalyze the results when determining how many additional rubber bands to add for trials 2 and 3. Another possibility is to establish a minimum score of 80 no matter how their egg performs, as long as they've completed the lab data and graphs as required. With the multiple trials, most teams earn a score of at least 90, and best of all, this activity is easy for the teacher to grade.

Energy, Force, and Motion Concepts

This egg bungee jump activity can be used to teach or reinforce a number of concepts revolving around the topics of energy, force, and motion. Once students have completed the initial activity and come to appreciate the predictability of this system, they can then delve more deeply into various underlying science concepts. Possible concepts to be addressed include transformations between potential energy and kinetic energy, analysis of balanced and unbalanced forces and sources of those forces, and analysis of the acceleration and velocity of the egg at various points in its fall. A detailed analysis of this motion can be rather complex for middle school students because of the multitude of forces and the nonconstancy of the acceleration due to stretching rubber bands, but the analysis can be simplified to be accessible to middle school students.

A way to simplify the analysis for middle school students and still address some important force, motion, and energy concepts is to focus attention only on the starting and end-

ing points of the egg drop and eliminate the detailed analysis of what happens during the fall. Students should be able to explain that at the moment before beginning the fall, the egg possessed only gravitational potential energy (GPE) and no kinetic energy (KE). They can identify the weight of the egg as the only force acting on it at this point, and that its velocity was zero before being dropped.

At the end of the drop, the egg-and-rubber-band system now possesses the least GPE, no KE (it is not moving), and lots of elastic potential energy (PE) due to the stretched rubber bands. Thus students could express knowledge of the

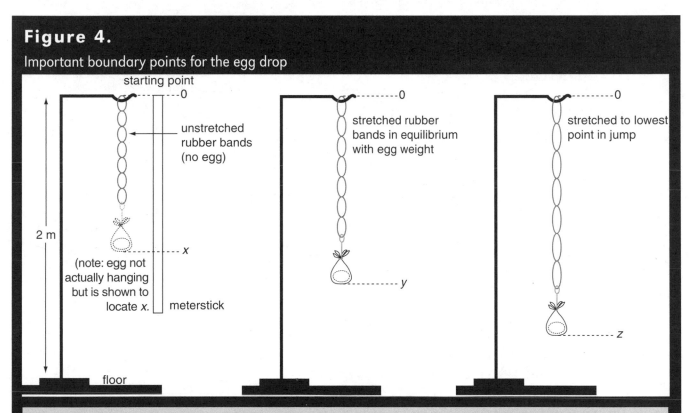

Figure 4.
Important boundary points for the egg drop

0 = The starting point of the bottom of the egg. This establishes a reference point for this experiment.

x = The length of the unstretched rubber band chain plus egg sack without the egg hanging on it. Note that x must still take into account the length of the egg sack for consistency even though the egg sack isn't attached to the rubber bands for this measurement.

y = The length of the rubber band chain plus egg sack with the egg hanging on it in equilibrium.

z = The length of the rubber band chain plus egg sack at the lowest point in the drop.

Law of Conservation of Energy by stating that all of the initial GPE of the egg went into elastic PE at the bottom of its fall. Additionally, they could identify that at the bottom of the fall, there are two forces acting on the egg—the upward pull of the rubber bands and the downward weight of the egg. Because the upward force is greater, the egg accelerates in an upward direction, beginning its rebound. Students may also be able to describe when the forces (weight of egg and stretch of the rubber bands) are again balanced by recognizing that after the egg settles down from bouncing back and forth and is just hanging there, the acceleration is zero and hence the net force at this equilibrium point (the point where the system comes to rest) is zero.

Energy Transformations and Conservation

You could focus only on analysis of the beginning and ending points or could expand the analysis to include significant intermediate points during the fall. Initially, the egg has only GPE as it is held at the top of the 2 m fall. As it falls down to distance x shown in Figure 4, this GPE is being reduced and there is a corresponding increase in KE as the egg gains speed (Figure 5). After the egg passes point x, the rubber bands begin to stretch, thus storing elastic potential energy in the rubber bands. Once the egg reaches its lowest point at z (see Figure 5), it is no longer moving and so all of the initial GPE at the top has now been transformed into elastic PE of the rubber bands. Figure 5 includes statements about energy transformations at various points throughout the fall, but a teacher may choose to explore these ideas with students (described below) or restrict the analysis to only the beginning and ending points.

Forces and Motion

The forces acting upon the egg can be analyzed next, with connections to its motion simultaneously made. The analysis described below will include significant points throughout the egg's fall, but you may choose to restrict discussion with your students to only the beginning and ending points and not explore the details in the middle of the egg's fall. For the discussion of motion, students need to know the relationship (encapsulated in Newton's second law of motion) that a net force results in an acceleration of an object ($F = ma$). Additionally, they should be familiar with the concept that an acceleration is a change in velocity. For simplicity, the following discussion will ignore relatively minor forces such as air resistance.

When the egg is dropped initially, the only force acting on it is its own weight. Thus, the egg begins to free-fall until point x (see Figure 4). Since there is a net force acting downward, the egg will accelerate downward, which the students might also describe as gaining speed in a downward direction. Since the egg is in free fall, this downward acceleration is simply the acceleration due to gravity, 9.8m/s^2. This corresponds nicely with the energy graphic that shows the egg gaining KE (gaining speed) in the portion of the fall before point x (Figure 5).

At point x, the rubber bands begin to stretch, providing an upward force that begins to counteract the egg's weight. However, that upward rubber band force doesn't balance out the weight until the egg reaches point y because that is the point at which the weight of the egg hangs in equilibrium with the stretched rubber bands (Figure 4). Thus, between points x and y, the downward weight of the egg is still more than the upward force of the rubber bands, resulting in a net downward force in this section of the drop. This net downward force is smaller than the full weight of the egg. Although there is still a downward acceleration of the egg between points x and y, that acceleration continually grows smaller and smaller as the egg approaches point y. In terms of speed, this means that the egg continues to gain downward speed between x and y, but it gains that speed at a slower and slower rate. This analysis permits students to answer the energy question (posed in Figure 5 as "losing KE somewhere in here") about when the KE of the egg begins to decrease. Between points x and y, the egg continues to gain speed (but at a slower rate), thus the egg continues to gain KE (but at a slower rate than before).

At point y, the downward weight of the egg is balanced by the upward force of the rubber bands because that is the hanging equilibrium point. Thus, the net force at this point is zero, which means the acceleration is zero. Alternatively, students could describe point y as the place at which the egg ceases to gain speed. After point y, the upward force of the rubber bands is greater than the downward weight of the egg,

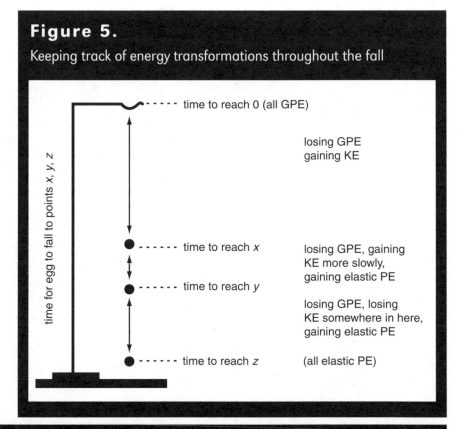

Figure 5.

Keeping track of energy transformations throughout the fall

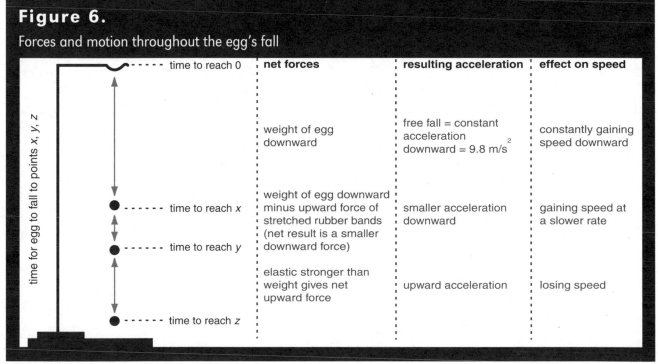

Figure 6.

Forces and motion throughout the egg's fall

resulting in a net upward force. This net force causes an upward-directed acceleration that opposes the ongoing motion of the egg, resulting in a slowing of the egg's downward speed. This means that the maximum speed of the egg was at point y (see Figure 6), hence the KE begins to be reduced after point y but not before, a result that can be used to update the energy graphic in Figure 5 to answer the question of when the loss of KE begins to happen. The upward force of the rubber bands continues to strengthen as the egg is falling past y, resulting in an ever-increasing acceleration upward that slows the egg's downward fall more and more quickly until the egg comes to a momentary stop at the bottom of its drop at point z. Verbally describing or reading about these various changes in forces and motion in text form can be a bit confusing, so I recommend teachers provide their students with a graphic similar to Figure 6 (and also an energy graphic similar to Figure 5) so that students can record the various transformations throughout the fall as the class discussion progresses. These graphics (Figures 5 and 6) provide a concise, understandable form to arrange all of these relationships.

An analysis of the energy, forces, and motion of the egg during its bungee jump provides students opportunities to encounter a variety of situations encompassed within one experiment they are able to perform relatively easily. When students have completed this analysis and fully understand the underlying science behind the egg jump, they will have a reasonably sophisticated conceptual knowledge of some topics that are often quite abstract and difficult for them to apply in typical situations.

Making a Lasting Impression

With this activity, students enhance their understanding that science is a process of active exploration involving mutual collaboration with classmates, that it is full of opportunities to try out ideas without risk of penalties, and that it combines interesting activities with complex concepts. Students are challenged to develop laboratory procedures; to conduct experiments with care; to generate, process, and interpret data; and to do so in an atmosphere of respect for others' ideas.

An important benefit of this activity is that it combines very concrete, hands-on experiences and measurements with an analysis of concepts that are often abstract for students. The ease of implementation of the egg bungee jump permits students serious mental engagement with the fundamental physical science concepts of energy, force, and motion. In spite of the relative ease of implementation, sophisticated science laboratory skills and analysis skills can be addressed, and an added bonus is that students tend to enjoy the challenge of keeping their egg safe during its dangerous leap.

Thomas Tretter is an assistant professor of science education at the University of Louisville in Louisville, Kentucky.

Reference

National Research Council (NRC). 1996. *National Science Education Standards*. Washington, DC: National Academy Press.

Science Homework Overhaul

By Michelle Trueworthy

D o your students groan when you an-nounce a homework assignment? Do they have so much math and language arts homework that they just don't have time for science homework? Does the homework you give help students to better understand key science concepts? These are some of the questions that led me to reevaluate the science homework I was giving my sixth graders.

In many elementary schools across the coun-try, science instruction often gets pushed aside in favor of math or reading instruction. In my school, sixth graders move to different classes for math, science, and social studies. Although I am fortunate to have time each day to teach science, I found my students didn't have much time available after language arts and math homework to focus on science homework. When I did give science homework, a typical assignment was to answer questions or review science vocabulary or concepts. Although most students would do the homework, they didn't seem to be spending much time thinking about

science concepts or how these ideas relate to their own lives. I started talking to students about homework to identify which factors made for effective science homework. I share what I found out here.

Reflect Real Science

Teaching the nature of science to students means allowing them to work as scientists and reflect on the processes real scientists use. I had been talking about the nature of science during class time with students but hadn't really carried that over to homework assignments. Our National Science Education Standards call for students to be engaged in activities that allow them to "do" science (NRC 1996). Again, this is some-thing I do during class but rarely carried over to homework. I decided to try giving a homework assignment that allowed students to act like sci-entists at home. So, after studying energy roles in ecosystems, rather than have students answer the end-of-chapter questions, I gave them the following homework assignment:

Part I, Directions: Choose four days to walk around your yard. If you do not have a yard, observe any small space that has vegetation growing—such as the edges of a sidewalk—or do your observations in a nearby park or in our schoolyard.

On your walk, make a list of the living organisms you discover. Be sure to look closely at the ground, trees, etc. Make a chart to organize your information. You should record the organisms you find. You may borrow identification guides. If you do not know the name of an organism, do your best to describe it and give its identifying features. Also record what energy role each organism fills (producer, consumer, or decomposer), how many organisms you counted, and any other information you feel is important. If the organism is a consumer, specify whether it is a carnivore, herbivore, or omnivore.

Safety reminder: Before going outside, be sure to let a family member know where you will be. Remember some organisms can be poisonous, sting, or bite. Do not touch anything that you are unfamiliar with. Remember you are there to observe. Do not disturb any organism or its habitat.

Incorporate Student Choice

It occurred to me that, if I wanted my students to learn to work like scientists and understand the nature of science, then I needed to give them more choices in how they worked. I decided that for the second part of the homework assignment, in which I wanted students to show their understanding of how energy flows through an ecosystem, I would do just that. I offered several suggestions for activities or told students to choose their own way of demonstrating what they knew:

Part II, Directions: Choose one of the following:

- Make a food web that shows how the organisms on your property are connected.

You may draw, photograph, or print pictures from the internet to represent the organisms you find.
- Make a food chain that represents a meal you have eaten recently.
- Find a story or movie that demonstrates how energy flows in an ecosystem. Write an explanation of your choice.
- Write your own story or comic strip that shows your knowledge of how energy flows in an ecosystem.
- Create your own homework assignment that demonstrates what you know about how energy moves through an ecosystem.

One interesting thing that I noticed after giving this assignment was that most students were excited about having choices. Some of the usual high achievers, however, were a little unsettled about having to make their own decisions. They wanted me to tell them what to do. After seeing how other students were tackling this assignment, they eventually made their own decisions and moved forward with confidence. Without specific directions, they were forced to do their own thinking and tap into their own creativity.

Having a choice in how they completed this assignment energized my students. They came up with creative ways to show what they knew that I would never have thought to assign.

For example, one student made her own puppets and performed a puppet show that demonstrated a food chain. Another student wrote a song and insisted the rest of the class sing it back to her with enthusiasm. The tune of the song was so catchy I heard students humming it later in the day. One boy produced his own video tour of his backyard habitat. Students truly used their own talents and incorporated the science content in ways that were meaningful to them and entertaining for the rest of the class.

One aspect of the nature of science is creativity. These assignments allowed students to incorporate their own creativity into their science work.

Family Involvement

Another factor I thought a lot about was family involvement. I wanted the homework to get my students talking and thinking about science with their families. I did not want parents taking over and doing too much for their child, but I wanted to engage their family members too. So, I asked students to interview their families about this homework assignment:

Directions: Show a family member your homework assignment sheet. Read through it and explain which assignment you chose and how you plan to complete it. Show your family member the chart of the organisms you found on your property and discuss it together. Write their comments here.

The purpose of this interview was to get families involved in science discussion. I wanted students to be using the vocabulary in a way that was meaningful. After the assignment was due, student shared the comments their families made. The families' comments demonstrated that families were involved in meaningful discussions:

- "I didn't know we had such a variety of plants on our property."
- "We planted that tree when you were born. It's been fun to watch it grow as you grow."
- "I didn't know we had so many ants. Maybe it's time to call an exterminator."
- "I think the deer have been chewing on our bushes."
- "I would like to have more flowers in our yard, but we need to find plants that do well in our shady yard."
- "Bats are good to have in our yard. They eat the mosquitoes."

Time Frame

Before revamping my science homework, I would give students a day or two to complete a homework assignment. This assignment, however, included going outside and finding time to involve a family member, so I knew students would need more time. I gave students the assignment on a Monday, and it was due the following Monday so that they would have a weekend to work. The longer time allowed students time to do the science homework while also completing homework in other subjects.

Inspired Results

The week my students were working on this assignment was filled with excitement. So many students wanted to talk about what they were doing that I set aside 10 minutes each day during class so students could talk to each other about the homework. Students came into school asking to borrow field guides to identify the plants and animals they were finding. They also asked to borrow materials, such as magnifying glasses and bug boxes.

Having choices was the most motivating factor for my sixth graders. Many students put more effort into this homework assignment than any other I'd seen all year.

All but two of my 67 students passed the assignment in on time. One student who rarely did homework not only completed the assignment, but he also typed it and made it neat. It was clear he was proud of the work he had done. The following comments made by students show how positive they felt about this homework assignment:

- "This was more fun than most other homework."
- "I was reminded of important facts to know on my test."
- "I liked this assignment because it let you choose and you could do whatever you are good at like drawing or writing."
- "In other homework assignments, I was just to use ideas right out of the book but with this assignment I had the opportunity to really look around and figure things out for myself."

- "I got to walk around my yard and actually see some producers, consumers, and decomposers."
- "This homework assignment helped me to understand my science vocabulary in a whole new way."

As a class, students looked at each other's results and discussed similarities and differences among the information and how the information was presented. This naturally led to a discussion about the nature of science and how real scientists work.

I asked students to talk about how the ways they worked on this project were similar to or different from the way real scientists work, and I also asked them to think about whether any one student's project gave the best or most correct information about the organisms that lived in our community. After some heated discussion, students decided that all of the information was valuable even though it was presented differently. They agreed that real scientists sometimes come up with different results and share their results in different ways. They talked about the importance of following a scientific procedure to gather accurate results. We also discussed that, although students gave results of their observations, they might change their conclusions after further study. Students identified that this was something scientists do as they learn more information.

This assignment also allowed students to practice doing science independently. As they weren't being guided by a teacher, they had more freedom and had to rely on their own thinking and decision-making skills.

Outcomes

This assignment was completed during the second chapter of a new book we were using in science class. Students previously had had a great deal of trouble on the Unit 1 test. I think they had never had a program that was so rich in vocabulary and covered so many concepts.

After completing this assignment just before

the Chapter 2 test was given, the average test score for each of my science classes went up significantly. I felt like improvement was because the students were using the vocabulary and concepts in a way that was meaningful to their own lives.

As I reflect about this experiment with homework, it occurs to me that the answer is really quite simple. The same factors that make science class engaging and meaningful to students are what make for successful science homework, too. The best change is now instead of groaning and complaining about homework my students are asking for homework!

Michelle Trueworthy is a sixth-grade teacher at Burr District Elementary School in Higganum, Connecticut.

Resources

Cooper, H. 2003. *Homework for all in moderation.* Reston, VA: Association for Supervision and Curriculum Development.

Lederman, N. G., and J. S. Lederman. 2004. Revising instruction to teach nature of science. *The Science Teacher* 71 (9): 36–39.

National Research Council (NRC). 1996. *National science education standards.* Washington, DC: National Academy Press.

Van Voorhis, F .L. 2001. Interactive science homework: An experiment in home and school connections. *National Association of Secondary School Principals Bulletin* 85 (627): 20–32.

Connecting to the Standards

This article addresses the following National Science Education Standards (NRC 1996):

Content Standards Grades 5–8

Content Standard C: Life Science
Populations and ecosystems

Content Standard G: History and Nature of Science
Science as a human endeavor

Investigating Students' Ideas About Plate Tectonics

By Brent Ford and Melanie Taylor

There is a good deal of evidence that learning is enhanced when teachers pay attention to the knowledge and beliefs that learners bring to a learning task, use this knowledge as a starting point for new instruction, and monitor students' changing conceptions as instruction proceeds (Bransford et al. 2000).

Giant exploding volcanoes…asteroids crashing into Earth…continents floating across the oceans…massive pools of lava…violent earthquakes splitting continents—middle school students hold a variety of ideas about Earth, how it has changed over time, and what caused these changes. For example:

- "Pangaea broke apart a long time ago. Now the continents are coming back together on the other side of Earth. That's

what causes earthquakes—the continents bumping into each other."
- "A giant meteor hit Earth, back when the dinosaurs were around. That killed off the dinosaurs and caused Pangaea to break up."
- "There are more plates in the Pacific than the Atlantic. That's why earthquakes and volcanoes are more common in the Pacific."
- "A volcano is just a mountain with the top cut off so that the lava can come out. Any mountain could become a volcano."

Listening to students talk about how the world works is fascinating. Some students describe ideas that are essentially correct, while others reflect familiarity with the content but their understanding is incomplete or includes inaccuracies. Still others have little understanding of the content but imagine dramatic scenes of destruction when questioned about earthquakes, volcanoes, and plate tectonics. Beyond just listening, uncovering students' initial ideas and attending to how those ideas change over a unit of instruction are important to ensuring that students learn scientifically correct ideas.

Eliciting Students' Ideas About Plate Tectonics

As part of a project designed to develop, among other tools, an assessment for measuring middle school student understanding in plate tectonics, researchers from Horizon Research, Inc. (HRI)—a research firm specializing in science and mathematics education—interviewed middle school students about their ideas in plate tectonics and processes that shape Earth. The purpose of the interviews was to uncover common, incorrect student ideas that could serve as distractors for the multiple-choice test being developed. Prior to conducting the interviews or writing any test questions, HRI researchers, working from Benchmarks for Science Literacy and the National Science Education Standards, defined the boundaries for the content of the assessments as follows: "The outer portion of Earth—including both the continents and the seafloor beneath the oceans—consists of huge plates of solid rock. The plates move very slowly (a few centimeters per year). Plate movement causes abutting plates to interact with one another. Interactions between plates result in events and features that are observable on Earth's surface (such as earthquakes, volcanoes, and mountain ranges); these typically occur along boundaries between plates." This learning goal includes a number of more narrowly defined sub-ideas (see Figure 1).

Next, a series of open-ended questions was crafted to elicit students' ideas about these concepts. Questions covered the whole range of ideas within the learning goal; a few are included here.

Figure 1.
Defining and clarifying the content

The learning goal: The outer portion of Earth—including both the continents and the seafloor beneath the oceans—consists of huge plates of solid rock. The plates move very slowly (a few centimeters per year). Plate movement causes abutting plates to interact with one another. Interactions between plates result in events and features that are observable on Earth's surface (such as earthquakes, volcanoes, and mountain ranges); these typically occur along boundaries between plates.

Helping students achieve an understanding of this learning goal involves attending to each of several subideas within the larger idea above. These subideas include the following, although they could be broken apart even further:

- Earth's surface is made up of plates (including characteristics of plates, plates abut one another, number of plates, how continents and ocean floor relate to plates).
- Earth's plates move around, and because plates abut other plates, they interact with one another along their boundaries.
- Plate interactions result in interesting and observable geological features and events (including earthquakes, volcanoes, deep sea trenches, mid-ocean ridges, mountain ranges).
- Plate material is recycled (including: new plate material is added in some places, some plate material is removed from Earth's surface in other places).

- "Scientists have found that earthquakes occur more often in some places than others. Do you think there is a reason for this or does it just happen by chance? Why do you think that?"
- [Students were shown a world map and asked to look at Africa and South America.] "Do you see how the west coast of Africa and the east coast of South America look like they might fit together like a jigsaw puzzle? Do you think there is a reason for this or did it just happen by chance? Why do you think that?"
- "You seem to know something about Earth's plates. Will you draw a side-view picture of what a plate looks like? What's underneath the plate?"
- "If you wanted to go and touch a plate, where would you have to go?"

Twenty-six middle school students were individually interviewed for about an hour. Some students had already received instruction in plate tectonics, while others had not. Students were asked to answer each question as best they could and, in some cases, to draw pictures to describe their ideas. The analysis of the interviews focused on identifying incorrect student ideas that were likely to be seen as plausible distractors for the multiple-choice questions being written.

Results

Preliminary lists of ideas were developed from a literature search and from the experiences of the research team in teaching Earth science. Although many of the ideas included on this preliminary list in fact showed up in interviews, a number of additional ideas surfaced as well. Some students seem to think that there are large gaps or spaces between Earth's plates. For example, a number of students thought that, as plates move away from each other, large gaps filled with magma or lava are created; others thought that plates come crashing together

much like cars in an automobile accident—envisioning that the plates are apart, then close a gap as the plates crash together. (Several students thought that these collisions were the cause of earthquakes; the bigger the "crash," the bigger the earthquake.) Students were also apt to think of continents and plates as the same thing, although other students thought plates were far down in Earth and had no relationship to Earth's surface. For example, one student described *platelets* as being well below Earth's surface. His "platelets" were very energetic, zooming all around, crashing into one another and bouncing off in other directions.

Figure 2 includes many other examples of incorrect student ideas about plate tectonics, either identified or confirmed through interviews, which could be used to formulate distractors. Students offered other incorrect ideas that, although some were not included in the list if they did not seem to be plausible distractors for the test questions. For example, in one interview, a middle school student suggested that plates move away from one another because, "Like family, you sometimes get tired of being around each other."

Making Sense of Results

An interesting aspect of the interviews was that students rarely said "I don't know," instead offering some type of explanation in response to the question. Further, it was clear that students drew from their own knowledge base to construct logical answers, although in some cases from unexpected sources.

Over the last few years, the terms *misconception, prior conception, naïve conception,* and others have come in and out of favor in education circles. Although there has not been universal agreement on what these terms mean or their relative importance in teaching and learning, there is agreement that students come to science class not as empty vessels, but with their own ideas about the world. There is also agreement that some incorrect ideas that students have are

Figure 2.

Misconceptions related to plate textonics

Plates

- Plates stack like dinner plates in a kitchen cabinet.
- A continent is a plate; plates are the same shape as the continents.
- The plates are somehow "down there"—not really related to Earth's surface.
- Continents have no relationship to the plates.
- The plates are under the oceans, but do not include the continents.

Plate movement and plate interactions

- Continents move by somehow floating across oceans.
- The continents float around on something—molten rock or water—like very large ships.
- All plates move in the same direction and at the same speed.
- Plate motion cannot be measured because it is so slow.
- If plates are moving apart two centimeters per year, that distance is so insignificant that it could never be noticed.
- Since the super continent Pangaea split up 200 million years ago, the continents have remained in essentially the same positions.
- Earthquakes caused Pangaea to break apart.
- The fact that the east coast of South America and west coast of Africa have shapes that would fit together like a jigsaw puzzle is just a coincidence.
- Continents (and plates) can never join together.
- Continents (and plates) cannot split and become smaller.
- It is impossible for the continents to have been parts of one large continent in the past.
- Plates are the same size and shape now as they've always been.
- When plates move toward one another, they fill a gap that once existed between the two plates.
- When plates move away from one another, a space between the two is created.
- Continents do not move.
- After Pangaea broke apart, the continents moved around to the other side of Earth and will bump back into one another. (This bumping will lead to earthquakes.)

Plate interactions resulting in events and features

- The plates move, but they have no effect on one another.
- There is no way to determine the location of boundaries between plates.
- The plates move so slowly that their interactions are insignificant.
- Erosion is the only process that alters the appearance of Earth.
- All changes to Earth's surface occur suddenly and rapidly.
- All events that affect Earth are gradual or slow.
- All Earth processes operate at the same rate (on the same time-scale).
- All changes to Earth occur so slowly that they cannot be detected during a human lifetime.
- Earthquakes, volcanoes, and mountain formations usually occur in the same general areas, but there is no explanation for this.
- Volcanoes and earthquakes always occur at or near plate boundaries. They cannot occur in the interior of plates.
- When two plates come together, nonvolcanic mountains always form.
- Earthquakes are caused by plates crashing into each other. The bigger the crash, the bigger the earthquake.
- Mountains form when earthquakes push the ground up.
- Earthquakes occur most frequently along coastlines, without regard to the location of plate boundaries.
- Earthquakes cause all volcanic eruptions.
- Volcanic eruptions cause all earthquakes.

Recycling of plate material

- "New" rock is created when a large rock is broken into smaller pieces—the smaller pieces are the "new" rock.
- All rock on Earth is the same age.
- New rock is added to plates only from the top when volcanoes spew out molten rock that solidifies into new rock on the surface of the plate.
- The subduction of plates means that Earth is becoming smaller.
- The continual formation of new rocks that are under the ocean (ocean floor) means that Earth must be getting larger.

strongly held and quite resistant to instruction. Even with instruction, it is often difficult for students to let go of these incorrect ideas and internalize the correct understanding of the situation (Bransford et al. 2000). In other cases, however, students' incorrect ideas about a topic may not be strongly held or resistant to instruction. For example, many interviewed students seemed to understand that Earth is much hotter at its center than at its surface. That correct understanding coupled with television images showing erupting volcanoes spewing out molten lava may give rise to the notion that huge pools of magma are underneath all of Earth's plates, an incorrect idea held by many interviewed students. Students, however, typically do not have direct experience with volcanoes or Earth's interior, so getting them to let go of this incorrect idea in favor of the correct one may not be as difficult as tackling other incorrect ideas that are reinforced by everyday experiences.

Implications for Instruction

Regardless of whether students have deeply held misconceptions or simply have naïve ideas about a particular topic, it is important that they be provided with opportunities to express their ideas (Bransford et al. 2000; Minstrell 2003). Accordingly, various learning-cycle approaches to teaching include time for students to talk about and share their ideas. In addition to helping students directly, this approach also gives teachers a chance to learn what students are thinking. In cases where basic research on student conceptions has already been done, for example in the area of force and motion, students may confirm that their ideas are very much aligned with the research. In the case of plate tectonics, informal research of the kind described in this article may provide teachers with insights into what students might be thinking about plate tectonics and processes that shape Earth. In many other topic areas, however, even informal research on student thinking has not yet been done, making

it more difficult for teachers to recognize the ideas they are trying to elicit from students.

Eliciting students' ideas and then responding in ways that promote student learning are at the heart of teaching, but are by no means easy tasks. Part of the problem lies in difficulties associated with constructing elicitation activities and questions that draw out student thinking. But even more difficult is the task of attending to student misconceptions that have surfaced. The best approach to address those misconceptions is not always clear, and research in this area is limited. It does seem to be clear, however, that teachers, in a sensitive way, need to find situations that engage students in cognitive conflict and then discuss the conflicting viewpoints (Bransford et al. 2000). Figure 3 offers three different examples in plate tectonics of how a teacher may go about eliciting and analyzing students' ideas, as well as possible strategies for moving students forward in their thinking about those ideas. (For similar prompts in other areas of science, check out NSTA's *Uncovering Student Ideas in Science: 25 Formative Assessment Probes,* available at *http://store.nsta.org.*)

Beyond eliciting students' initial ideas, it is also important for teachers to use formative assessment strategies to continue to monitor the development of students' ideas throughout a unit and make instructional adjustments when required (Boston 2002; Shepard 2000). For example, having students respond to prompts such as "Today I learned _____, but I'm not clear on ___," or having students make drawings of their ideas provides opportunities for teachers to quickly assess student thinking.

Finally, it is important that teachers be aware of how language, visual representations (such as diagrams in textbooks or computer simulations), and models can influence students' thinking (Michael et al. 1999). With respect to language, teachers have the difficult task of talking with students using words and language that students understand, although such language may actually reinforce the wrong ideas (Veiga

Figure 3.
Moving beyond misconceptions

Targeted concepts	Elicitation	Possible student response
The outer portion of Earth consists of huge plates of solid rock that abut one another on all sides. The upper portions of some of Earth's plates contain the continents and the seafloor beneath the oceans. Since the continents are a part of the plates, they move in the exact same way as the plate moves.	Show students a world map and say: *Look at this map. Do you see that the west coast of Africa and the east coast of South America look like they might fit together like a jigsaw puzzle? Do you think there is a reason for that? Why?*	"Yes, the continents used to be connected a long time ago. But then a bunch of really big earthquakes broke them apart and they moved to where they are now."
Earth's plates move and, because they abut other plates, they interact with one another along their boundaries. Plate interactions result in observable geological features and events (earthquakes, volcanoes, etc.).	*What happens when Earth's plates move?*	"Earth's plates move so slowly that nothing really happens."
Earth's plates move and, because they abut other plates, they interact with one another along their boundaries. When plates move away from each other, the following geological features and events are typically evident—earthquakes, volcanic activity, mid-ocean ridges, rift valleys, for example.	*What happens at a plate boundary where two plates are moving away from each other? Draw a picture—a side view—to show me your answer.*	

Analysis of student thinking	Strategies to move student thinking forward
Students seem to correctly recognize that Africa and South America were once joined. Two aspects of students' responses, however, deserve further attention:	To address the first concern, students need to understand what an earthquake is (vibrations caused by breaking rock) and that earthquakes result from plate motion, not the other way around. An activity, computer simulation, or discussion targeted specifically at what an earthquake is would likely prove helpful.
1. Students seem to think that earthquakes are responsible for continental breakup; and	To address the second concern, it is probably important that the teacher first try to determine more about what students are thinking. So additional questions (Did the earthquakes cause the breakup only or the movement too?) would likely prove helpful in gaining a better understanding of what students are thinking.
2. Students are not clear about how the continents moved to their current positions.	
The teacher may also want to attend to whether students think that continents and plates are the same things.	If students say something that indicates a belief that plates and continents are the same thing, the teacher needs to help students understand that Earth's plates cover the entire surface of Earth. One approach to address this situation is to show students a world map that includes plate boundaries and diagrams or computer simulations that show a cross-section of a plate and then to engage them in a discussion of their ideas relative to what is depicted in these visuals.
There are aspects of students' responses that suggest students have some correct ideas, but others that suggest students may also have an incorrect idea about the question.	There seem to be at least two different issues that may be individually or jointly responsible for students' misunderstanding.
Correct: 1. Earth has plates. 2. Earth's plates move very slowly.	1. The problem may be the result of students not thinking about change over VERY long periods of time—recognizing that even very small change adds up over millions of years, resulting in big changes. In this case, activities, computer simulations, or discussions targeted specifically at change over time would likely be helpful.
Incorrect: 1. Earth's plates move too slowly for anything to happen.	2. Another problem may be that students don't recognize that geologic activity occurs when plates interact. One way to provide evidence of such is to have students plot earthquake and volcanic activity onto a world map that shows plate boundaries. Locations of earthquakes and volcanoes will cluster along plate boundaries providing evidence that something is happening.
There are aspects of this drawing that are correct and others that are incorrect or unclear.	
Correct: 1. The plates are shown as moving *away* from one another. 2. The plates are shown as thick slabs of solid rock.	Before trying to move students' thinking forward, the teacher should probably try to get a better understanding of what students are actually thinking. Additional questions could prove helpful, such as: Does the ocean that you've drawn extend under the plates? What is under the plates you've drawn?
Incorrect: 1. The plates are not touching. 2. No features/events are shown other than "moving away."	As described in the first example above, if students say something that indicates a belief that plates and continents are the same thing, the teacher needs to help students understand that Earth's plates cover the entire surface of Earth. One approach to address this situation is to show students a world map that includes plate boundaries and diagrams or computer simulations that show a cross-section of a plate and then to engage them in a discussion of their ideas relative to what is depicted in these visuals.
Unclear: 1. Are the plates floating on the ocean? 2. Is there a plate under the ocean too? 3. Does the student think that continents and plates are the same thing?	

et al. 1989). For example, describing two plates as "moving apart" may convey the idea that a gap between the plates is created and then grows; two continents "crashing" together may imply fast speeds, as in cars crashing together. Similarly, visual representations and models may sometimes interfere with student learning of the correct ideas. For example, in textbook diagrams Earth's interior is often depicted in varying shades of red to show the different layers. It seems reasonable to expect that such representations may introduce or reinforce students' ideas that much of Earth's interior is molten or that Earth's plates float around on large pools of magma. Having students use their hands to model relative plate motion may also reinforce the wrong idea that gaps are created between plates as they move in opposite directions.

The implications for classroom practice are not, however, the wholesale removal of simplistic language, visuals, or models from teaching. Instead, teachers need to be aware of how these aspects of their teaching can affect students' understanding, to be prepared to monitor student understanding, and to adjust instruction if problems arise. As middle school teachers prepare for and teach units on plate tectonics and processes that shape Earth, it is important that they tune in to students' thinking about the way the world works. Undoubtedly students will come to class with a variety of ideas—correct, incorrect, and partially correct—about the topic. It is important that teachers pay attention to students' ideas and monitor their development throughout the unit to ensure that students develop the correct ideas. It is also important that teachers consider how language, visual representation, and models can positively, and negatively, affect student learning. Employing these approaches is likely to improve student learning, a goal of all teachers.

Brent Ford and Melanie Taylor are research associates at Horizon Research, Inc. in Chapel Hill, North Carolina.

Acknowledgment

This project is funded by the National Science Foundation (NSF) under grant no. EHR-0335328. Any opinions, findings, and conclusions or recommendations expressed in this material are those of the author and do not necessarily reflect the views of NSF.

References

American Association for the Advancement of Science/Project 2061. 1993. *Benchmarks for science literacy.* New York: Oxford University Press.

Boston, C. 2002. The concept of formative assessment. *Practical Assessment, Research and Evaluation* 8 (9). *http://PAREonline.net/getvn.asp?v=8&n=9*

Bransford, J. D., A. L. Brown, and R. R. Cocking. 2000. *How people learn: Brain, mind, experience, and school.* Washington, DC: National Academy Press.

Michael, J. A., D. Richardson, A. Rovick, H. Modell, D. Bruce, B. Horwitz, M. Hudson, D. Silverthorn, S. Whitescarver, and S. Williams. 1999. Undergraduate students' misconceptions about respiratory physiology. *Advances in Physiology Education* 22 (1): 127–135.

Minstrell, J. 2003. Helping teachers attend to student thinking. Essay on TE-MAT *www.te-mat.org/minstrell.aspx.*

National Research Council (NRC). 1996. *National Science Education Standards.* Washington, DC: National Academy Press.

Shepard, L.A. 2000. The role of assessment in a learning culture. *Educational Researcher* 29: 4–14.

Veiga, M., D. Cost Pereira, and R. Maskill. 1989. Teachers' language and pupils' ideas in science lessons: Can teachers avoid reinforcing wrong ideas? *International Journal of Science Education* 11 (4): 465–479.

More Than Just a Day Away From School

By Michelle Scribner-MacLean and Lesley Kennedy

With all the things that middle school science teachers have to juggle during the year, designing a science field trip can seem like a daunting task. Fortunately, there are many strategies teachers can use to help ensure that field trips are more than just a day away from school—that they are instead a truly meaningful learning experience.

Some middle school science teachers have had students do scavenger hunts around museums and science centers. These experiences do not always engage student minds, however, or connect well to the science that students are learning at school or at home. Instead of simply handing students worksheets of things to locate in a science center, many teachers have found that, with a clear goal and some help from the staff at the field-trip site, they can plan science field trips that support their classroom teaching and get students excited about learning science.

What Research Has Taught Us About Field Trips

Researchers have been examining the elements of effective science field trips for decades. Wolins, Jensen, and Ulzheimer (1992) found that students tended to remember trips in which they had high involvement (mental engagement and actual physical engagement with exhibits and objects). Another factor in the success of field trips was whether or not the teacher built links into the curriculum. Researchers concluded that the strength of the field-trip experience was clearly affected by whether or not the teacher was able to create a context for the field trip.

Set Clear Goals

As with any successful learning experience, you should decide what the goals are for your science field-trip experience and communicate these goals to your students. Are you hoping that they will visit an exhibit that will reinforce

Figure 1.

Science field-trip planning questions

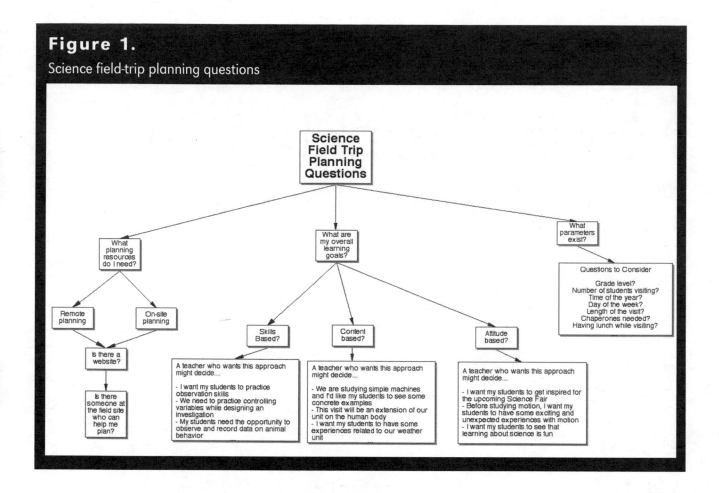

the content you've been teaching in class in an in-depth manner? Are you hoping that they practice science-process skills in a variety of exhibits? Do you want them to gain an understanding of how technology can be integrated with science and engineering? In addition to content or skills-based goals, you might consider goals such as having students develop a positive attitude about science. Getting students excited about science is something that museums can do very well. Regardless of the goals for your trip, a clear focus will help you build the experience you want students to have while out of the classroom.

Before the field trip, you should plan to visit the site to become familiar with offerings and to help establish goals (Koran and Baker 1978). Many science museums offer pretrip planning meetings to allow teachers to get an advanced peek at exhibits and resources available for students. Museum educators can often help

teachers tailor their field-trip experience to the needs of their students. If a pretrip visit is not possible, many institutions will help teachers with remote planning through e-mail or phone conversations. In addition, there are several museums across the country with excellent websites for field-trip planning (see Resources). These resources can be used by teachers who are in rural areas, whose classes cannot afford the expense of a trip, or where taking students out of school would be disruptive to other teachers' classes. Figure 1 outlines some important questions a teacher should consider when planning a science field trip.

Science Field-Trip Models: What Will Your Approach Be?

Museums provide many resources to help plan your science field-trip experience. Wolins, Jensen, and Ulzheimer (1992) found that teach-

Figure 2.

Field-trip types and examples

Field-trip type	Elements of this type of field trip	Examples
Open-ended experiences	• Addresses broad goals • These experiences can directly support developing a positive attitude about science and an excitement about learning science • Adaptable to many situations • Students can work individually or in groups • Can be created to ensure a highly interactive experience • Encourages students to make their own connections to the learning experiences	• Teacher-prepared trip sheets can be open-ended to guide inquiry and incorporate drawing, role-playing, and writing (Wolins, Jensen, and Ulzheimer 1992). • Free choice: Give groups of students the opportunity to self-direct their science field-trip experience (Wolins, Jensen, and Ulzheimer 1992).
Focused experiences	• Addresses content or skill-specific goals • Asks students to concentrate on collecting specific type of data, but can also be adaptable to many situations • Students can work individually or in groups • Can be created to ensure highly interactive experience	• Lecture tours by museum educators • Teacher-prepared trip sheets use questions and hints that are completed by students during trip (Wolins, Jensen, and Ulzheimer 1992). See example in sidebar. • Participatory lessons and presentations: In many science museums, teachers can choose from a set menu of classes that feature a variety of topics for different grade levels, which students attend as part of their field-trip visit.

ers choose a variety of formats to structure student visits to museums. Some may find that they want students to have a more open-ended experience during their field trip, while others might choose for their students to have a more focused experience. Figure 2 explores the elements of these different field-trip types. Field-trip planners may intentionally incorporate some aspects of each type.

More tools

In addition to the tools mentioned in this article, you might also decide to provide your students with digital cameras, clipboards, or digital video recorders to have them document what they learned. Regardless of your approach, with clear goals and some easy tools, science teachers can plan a meaningful and interesting science field-trip experience that can easily extend back into the classroom.

Focusing your science field trip

Having a clear focus for your trip can have a positive impact on the experience for students (Bailey 1999). If you're trying to build a science field-trip experience that looks beyond the traditional scavenger hunt, you may want to design focus sheets for your middle school science students. A focus sheet looks dramatically different from the classic text-based scavenger hunt with 50 or so fill-in-the-blank questions, whose answers require little thought.

Here are some criteria to consider when designing your focus sheet:
- Be clear about your learning objective for the field trip.
- Articulate the trip goals to students.
- Create open-ended types of questions that require participants to interact with an exhibit or an exhibit component in pursuit of a response.
- Ask students to complete tasks that are appropriate for the learner's age and developmental level. Devise tasks that can realistically be accomplished in the busy museum setting.

Some things to keep in mind:
- Worksheets do not necessarily have to be completed by each individual. It can work well to have a group collectively respond to a challenge on one worksheet.
- Although worksheets can help students understand what is expected of them during the field trip, they may also limit free-choice learning opportunities unique to the science field-trip setting.
- Worksheets that require students to use one specific exhibit component may be difficult to complete because on any given day that component may be in high demand, under repair, or removed from the floor.
- Worksheets designed in any given year, based on specific exhibits, should always be revised because the exhibit halls change dramatically season to season and year to year.

Sample Focused Field-Trip Activities

Everyone's a Critic
This approach can be used by individuals or groups. The objective is for learners to experience an exhibit. The teacher may assign a given exhibit or involve students in choosing an exhibit.

Focus sheet
- At the field-trip site: Imagine that you have been sent by your local newspaper to review the exhibit.
- On a piece of paper: Write at least six comments about the exhibit (positive or negative) that will be the basis for your written review.
- Back in the classroom: Write a review of the exhibit. What was it about? What did you like or dislike? Who might be a good audience for this exhibit? What did you learn?

Animal observation
This activity can also be used by individual students or by a group. Although this particular example focuses on an observation of a tamarin, this activity could be modified to help students focus on the behavior of a variety of animals.

Tamarin observation sheet
- Observe all the tamarins for three to four minutes *before* collecting data. Be certain you understand each target behavior.

Choose one tamarin to follow for five minutes. Note the behaviors on your sheet (see Figure 3).

Michelle Scribner-MacLean is a visiting assistant professor at the University of Massachusetts Lowell Graduate School of Education in Lowell, Massachusetts. Lesley Kennedy is a teacher educator at the Museum of Science, Boston, with more than 20 years of experience helping teachers plan field trips.

Figure 3.

Tamarin observation

Target behavior	Minute 1	Minute 2	Minute 3	Minute 4	Minute 5
Chasing					
Scent marking					
Eating (left or right hand?)					
Grooming (self or other)					
Additional behaviors noted					

References

Bailey, E. 1999. *School group visits to museums.* Available at *www.astc.org/resource/education/bailey.htm*

Koran, J., and S. Baker. 1978. Evaluating the effectiveness of field experiences. In *What research says to the science teacher, Vol. 2*, ed. M. Rowe, 50–64. Washington, DC: National Science Teachers Association.

Wolins, I., N. Jensen, and R. Ulzheimer. 1992. Children's memories of museum field trips: A qualitative study. *Journal of Museum Education* 17 (2): 17–27.

Resources

Boston Museum of Science
www.mos.org/educators
This website provides a wide variety of teacher tools for field-trip planning, including exhibits and programs mapped to curriculum frameworks and national standards.

Exploratorium
www.exploratorium.edu/educate/index.html

Fort Worth Museum of Science and History
www.fwmuseum.org/educate/field_trips_omni.html

Monterey Bay Aquarium
www.mbayaq.org/lc/teachers_place/fieldtrip.asp

Explaining Science

By Mark J. Gagnon and Sandra K. Abell

The National Science Education Standards state that there should be less emphasis on "science as exploration and experimentation" and more emphasis on "science as argument and explanation." Can my students do this? Can I?

What Is Explanation and Why Is It Important in Science?

We often think of science as exploration and experiment. Classrooms that portray only this view of science, however, fail to capture an essential feature of science—evidence-based explanation. When scientists encounter patterns in the world, they construct theories to explain them. What does it mean to explain in science? Explanation is more than summarizing the data that have been collected. Explanations tell why phenomena occur. They involve a leap of imagination. Scientists explain by building and testing models of how the world works. Scientific explanations emphasize evidence and employ accepted scientific principles. For example, different states of matter are explained by the arrangement and movement of molecules. The best explanations are the simplest and take into account the most evidence. The central role of explanation in science should be part of science classrooms. According to the National Academies Committee on Science Learning, Kindergarten through Eighth Grade (Duschl et al. 2007), elementary science should be aimed

at helping students "know, use, and interpret scientific explanations … [and] generate and evaluate scientific evidence and explanations" (p. 36). But can elementary students generate viable explanations using scientific evidence?

Can Children Generate and Evaluate Explanations From Evidence?

To what extent is it reasonable to ask elementary students to generate scientific explanations? Several educational psychologists have explored this question in clinical settings. Sodian et al. (1991) presented first and second graders with two conflicting hypotheses and asked them to choose a test to decide between them. Seventy-five percent of the first graders and all of the second graders were able to choose a conclusive test. Samarapungavan (1992) interviewed first, third, and fifth graders to find out what criteria they used for choosing among alternate explanations about the relative shapes, positions, and movements of heavenly bodies. She found that even the youngest children could use logic to choose the best explanation based on evidence. Ruffman and colleagues (1993) used a set of interview tasks in the form of stories with four- to seven-year-olds to investigate how children understood the relation of evidence and explanation. They found that by age six, most children recognized how the characters in the stories might form correct or incorrect explanations based on the evidence. These studies demonstrate the potential of young children to think scientifically in psychology laboratories. However, how do students perform in classroom settings?

What Do Classrooms Focused on Explanation and Evidence Look Like?

Several studies about students' ability to construct scientific explanations have taken place in elementary classrooms with classroom teachers as part of the research team. The researchers have found that students at various grade levels can be successful in generating scientific explanations from evidence. Kawasaki et al. (2004) examined the evolution of students' explanation building and modeling in a unit on sinking and floating. They found that students initially did not offer explanations but merely described the phenomenon. With time and prompting by the teacher, students began to discuss relations among variables and eventually used model-based reasoning, where they realized that explanations might need to change in light of new evidence. In Taiwan, Wu and Hsieh (2006) studied how sixth graders constructed explanations about force and motion and electricity. Like Kawasaki and her colleagues, they found that, although at first students did not include data as evidence in their discussions or presentations, with more experience they were able to support their explanations with data. Abell and Roth (1995) found that fifth graders could generate their own models of energy flow from plants to herbivores to predators through an ecosystem that took into account evidence from their classroom terraria, but the students had difficulty understanding the standard scientific model of the energy pyramid. In a study of third graders' reasoning about principles of sound, Abell et al. (2000) found that students used evidence to support their explanations and

to select among explanations. Not all students, however, ended the sound unit agreeing about how sound is produced. What these classroom-based studies tell us is that learning to generate and use scientific explanations is a reasonable expectation in elementary science classrooms, but it does not happen automatically without specific scaffolds provided by the teacher.

How Can Teachers Build a Classroom Atmosphere for Developing Explanations?

We can learn ways to support students as they generate explanations in science by reading how other teachers have accomplished this in their classrooms. Gallas (1995) conducted numerous "science talks" with first- through fourth-grade students. She described the anatomy of a science talk, including the role of the teacher in helping students uncover children's questions and explanations. Her examples are useful models. Folsom and her partners (2007) helped kindergartners develop evidence-based explanations about animals. They described specific techniques—asking students to write evidence-based explanations and defend them, probing students for evidence when they offer an explanation ("What makes you think that?"), asking guiding questions about how students might figure something out, and holding students "scientifically accountable" for their explanations (versus merely correcting their ideas). In the examples of classroom-based research presented above, the role of the teacher is clear. Teachers helped students compare and think through their developing explanations during scientist meetings, gave students opportunities to argue and explain their ideas, and listened to their explanations to understand their thinking. In classrooms where scientific explanations are the focus, the student becomes the center of sense making while the teacher carefully structures and directs the work from the side.

Mark J. Gagnon has taught elementary and middle school science and worked with teachers in science professional development settings. He is a doctoral student in science education at the University of Missouri-Columbia (MU). Sandra K. Abell, a former elementary science teacher, is Curators' Professor of Science Education at the University of Missouri, where she directs the MU Science Education Center

References

Abell, S. K., G. Anderson, and J. Chezem. 2000. Science as argument and explanation: Inquiring into concepts of sound in third grade. In *Inquiring into inquiry learning and teaching in science,* eds. J. Minstrell and E. van Zee, 65–79. Washington, DC: American Association for the Advancement of Science.

Abell, S. K., and M. Roth. 1995. Reflections on a fifth-grade life science lesson: Making sense of children's understanding of scientific models. *International Journal of Science Education* 17 (1): 59–74.

Duschl, R. A., H. A. Schweingruber, and A. W. Shouse. 2007. *Taking science to school: Learning and teaching science in grades K–8*. Washington, DC: The National Academies Press.

Folsom, J., C. Hunt, M. Cavicchio, A. Schoenemann, and M. D'Amato. 2007. How do you know that? Guiding early elementary students to develop evidence-based explanations about animals. *Science and Children* 44 (5): 20–25.

Gallas, K. 1995. *Talking their way into science: Hearing children's questions and theories, responding with curricula.* New York: Teachers College Press.

Kawasaki, K., L .R. Herrenkohl, and S. A. Yeary. 2004. Theory building and modeling in a sinking and floating unit: A case study of third- and fourth-grade students' developing epistemologies of science. *International Journal of Science Education* 26 (11): 1299–1324.

National Research Council (NRC). 1996. *National Science Education Standards*. Washington, DC: National Academy Press

Ruffman, T., J. Perner, D. R. Olson, and M. Doherty. 1993. Reflecting on scientific thinking: Children's understanding of the hypothesis-evidence relation. *Child Development* 64 (6): 1617–1636.

Samarapungavan, A. 1992. Children's judgments in theory choice tasks: Scientific rationality in childhood. *Cognition* 45 (1): 1–32.

Sodian, B., D. Zaitchik, and S. Carey. 1991. Young children's differentiation of hypothetical beliefs from evidence. *Child Development* 62 (4): 753–766.

Wu, H-K., and C-E. Hsieh. 2006. Developing sixth graders' inquiry skills to construct explanations in inquiry-based learning environments. *International Journal of Science Education* 28 (11): 1289–1313.

The Station Approach: How to Teach With Limited Resources

by Denise Jaques Jones

Several years ago, my middle school experienced a huge growth spurt. Before I knew it, my classroom was bulging with many more students than resources. I was determined not to let my now-stretched resources keep me from my favorite labs and computer activities.

My colleague Sarah Harashe and I were able to do this by designing a strategy we call the "Station Approach." We thought this would achieve our purpose, but what we discovered really surprised us. Students loved the stations and continually asked when they would get to do them again. It increased students' interest in the topic, kept them motivated, and eliminated many behavior problems.

What Is the Station Approach?

The Station Approach is a method of instruction in which small groups of students move through a series of learning centers, or stations, allowing teachers with limited resources to differentiate instruction by incorporating students' needs, interests, and learning styles. The Station Approach supports teaching abstract concepts as well as concepts that need a great deal of repetition. Stations can cover a single topic, such as density, or several independent topics such as reviewing the scientific instruments. Stations can last one class period or several.

The Station Approach is actually an adaptation of the reading groups used in elementary school classrooms. The difference, however, is that in the elementary school model students rotate only to those stations that meet their specific learning needs, while in our approach every student rotates through each station and performs all the activities. Perhaps the greatest strength of the Station Approach is that it incorporates many concepts used for differentiated instruction.

Designing Stations and Setting Up the Classroom

Two to four stations are optimum for most activities. More stations can be designed when introducing or reviewing multiple concepts or if class sizes are large. Stations should be independent of other stations and can be completed in random order. When working with large classes, or when using a small number of stations, consider setting up multiples of the same activities and divide your class into two or more rotating groups. Student groups should consist of no more than four to six members. Larger groups have a tendency to become loud and disruptive to other stations.

Design stations so that only one requires the teacher's continued presence. The remaining stations should be self-explanatory or require only limited instructions, which can be posted at each station.

Strive for activities that last approximately the same amount of time at each station. Choose your main activity, and modify the remaining activities to take about the same amount of time to complete. The amount of time for each station can vary anywhere from 20 minutes to an entire class period if the content requires several class periods to complete. Designing stations in this way allows for smoother transitions, reducing student frustration at either leaving work incomplete or having to wait idle for other stations to complete their work.

Design stations so that they vary based on students' different learning styles, interests, and/or levels of readiness. Each station should require students to look at the concept in a different way. This can be accomplished by

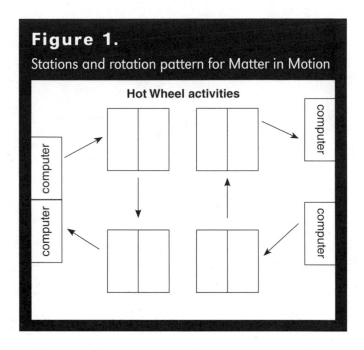

Figure 1.
Stations and rotation pattern for Matter in Motion

Hot Wheel activities

computer

computer

computer

computer

thinking of each station as a specific learning style. One station would be your hands-on or kinesthetic station. Here students would complete labs or build models. Another could be the visual station, where students would quietly read, complete computer research, or explore concepts visually. Another station could be an auditory station, where students could have discussions or listen to information on tape.

When setting up the classroom, make use of all available resources—books, computers, and lab equipment. Look around your classroom; something as simple as a lab counter, rug, bookcase, or teacher's desk can become a station. With the Station Approach, even a single computer can become a viable station.

Divide the classroom into discrete areas or stations (see Figure 1). Stations should be flexible and easily accessible by students and the teacher. Stations are not designed to be permanent. They should be easily set up and then removed. Be creative. A bookcase or small rolling cart can change a space into a workable station. Remember to place computers and equipment so that you can easily observe students working. Consider the traffic pattern when setting up your stations. Visualize how students will move from one station to another. Think of your room as a rectangular clock and have students move clockwise around the room. Check with your building custodian or supervisor regarding fire and other safety codes. It is important that you carefully examine all stations for any safety risks. Never block exits, leave extension cords lying where students can trip, or leave objects such as hot plates where they can be knocked over.

Possible Stations

Lab area—A table or tables where students perform hands-on activities.

Quiet work area—Set aside a place in the room, such as a corner, with chairs or a rug. Students sit and quietly complete higher-level thinking questions, peer edit, read supplemental materials, and practice math and process skills. A quiet work area can include televisions or tape players with earphones or books on CD.

Figure 2.
Rules during station work

1. Do not disturb the teacher when he or she is working with other groups.

2. Do not leave your station without permission. The only students with permission to leave their group are the supply person and the information person.

3. If you have a question:
   a. Reread the data sheet.
   b. Ask someone in your group.
   c. Quietly ask someone who has already been to that station.
   d. Write your question on a piece of paper and continue to work (if you can't continue, begin a sponge activity) until you see that your teacher is no longer working with another group and is free to help you.

Figure 3.
Posted job assignments, station rules, and station rotations (color-code). Velcro makes changng jobs and stations easy.

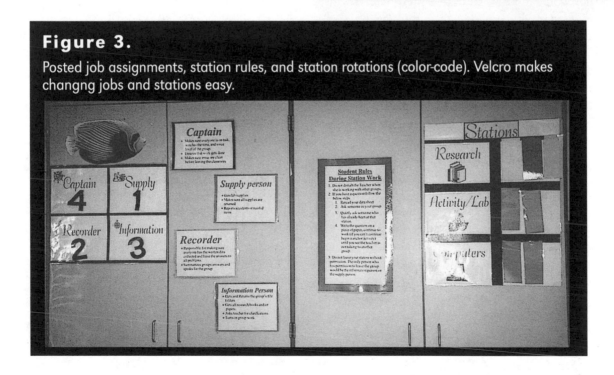

Computer—Students conduct research, design presentations, complete web quests, or use probeware.

Teacher-directed area—Small-group remediation, acceleration, or a place where students discuss assignments and projects with their teacher. This can take place at the teacher's desk, or by grouping several student desks together in an easily accessible area of the room.

Production area—A section of a lab counter or a table with markers and poster board for easy use by students. If you have audiovisual equipment available, section off a corner of your room and place a video camera, VCR, television, and a computer there. Students can record weather reports or perform skits and present them to the class. Solicit parent volunteers or teacher assistance to help students videotape and edit their presentations.

Managing the Classroom

When we designed our first stations, we believed they would increase student achievement because we were teaching a concept in multiple ways and addressing students' unique learning styles. In addition, stations allowed us to differentiate instruction by grouping students based on pretests. This allowed us to remediate certain students while accelerating others. What we had not anticipated was the reduction in behavior problems that we observed using the Station Approach.

We concluded that this was due to several factors. First, students weren't required to remain at a task for too long. Rotating students through stations that varied between quiet, mental tasks and active, verbal ones kept them interested and reduced off-task behaviors. Students seemed better able to stay quiet and focused when necessary, knowing that they would move soon to a more-active station. For some students, the transitions between stations gave them a quick mental break, and they exhibited renewed energy and focus.

With this in mind, I have outlined some key points that will help with managing the movement around the room and reduce behavior problems.

Student preparation—Before you use stations in your classroom, it is important to teach students how the process will work. Make sure students understand that all of them will complete each activity no matter where they begin. Be sure to explain how they will move through the series of stations. This will reduce student confusion when it is time to rotate. Let students know ahead of time how long they will be at each station. Purchasing a large egg timer will help everyone keep track of time. This helps students adjust their pace and frees you from constantly watching the clock.

Rules and procedures—Display a list of rules and procedures for students to follow. You can post this in the front of the classroom or at each station. Review these rules before the activity (Figure 2).

Coded stations—Design a rotation strategy that can be displayed in front of the classroom for easy reference. Color coding or naming areas reduces student confusion (Figure 3). Poster board with Velcro numbers and colors makes rotations easy to manage.

Student jobs—When stations have cooperative activities, groups of four work best. Assign each student in the group a job. This will give each student a reason to stay focused and a sense of purpose. Jobs could include recorder, information person, supply person, and group captain (Figure 4).

Handouts and paperwork—When determining how to handle student paperwork, you may want to consider the following options:

- Place copies of all work sheets and directions at each station. Depending on the type of station, you may require a single work sheet for the group to complete, or have each student complete his or her own work sheet. No matter what format you choose, make extra copies in case of the inevitable lost or messed-up work sheet.

- Copy all necessary work sheets and directions in the form of a packet and hand out to students at the beginning of the activity. The benefit to this strategy is that it is neat and organized. The only problem is that, if a student loses his or her packet, then all of the work is gone, not just the work from a single activity. Designating a crate in which students store their packets can minimize the risk of this occurring.

- Create student contracts, which allow you to differentiate instruction. After pretesting, students' work can be modified based on their current level of understanding. A contract is a way of making an individual educational plan for each student based on his or her pretest scores. Stations can then be written at multiple levels of difficulty, allowing all students to experience success.

Figure 4.
Job assignments

Captain
Your responsibilities include

- making sure everyone is on task,
- watching the time and voice level of group members,
- making sure that the groups' work is completed, and
- supervising the clean up of stations prior to rotating to the next station.

Recorder
Your responsibilities include

- completing all worksheets while groups are completing cooperative activities,
- summarizing for the group the decisions or findings that were reached by consensus, and
- speaking for the group when the group is called upon.

Supply person
Your responsibilities include

- getting supplies for the group,
- returning all supplies when finished, and
- reporting accidents or needed items to the teacher.

Information person
Your responsibilities include

- getting and returning the team's file folders,
- getting all research books and/or papers,
- asking the teacher for clarifications, and
- turning in group and team's individual work.

Sponge activities—A *sponge* is any activity designed to fill the extra time when students complete their station early or for some reason cannot continue working at their station (see Figure 2). To discourage students from rushing through their work, sponges can include self-checking completed work. This can be accomplished by keeping an answer key in a folder students can obtain after work is completed. Students check their work and correct existing errors. Make sure students show that their work is completed in detail before getting the answer key. Another sponge activity is allowing students to peer edit. Independent activities such as Sudoku or logic puzzles can also be made available. Again, students must demonstrate

Figure 5.

KUD chart for Matter in Motion

At the end of this unit students will

Know

- Vocabulary: motion, reference points, speed, velocity, acceleration, force, net force, balanced force, unbalanced force, gravity, mass, weight, friction, and types of friction (sliding, rolling, fluid, and static)
- Newton's three laws of motion

Understand (generalizations)

- We measure the motion of an object in relationship to a point of reference.
- Distance, time, and direction are used to measure motion.
- Unbalanced forces change the motion of an object; balanced forces do not change the motion of an object.
- Friction is a force that opposes motion.
- The gravitational forces of the Earth affect motion.
- The forces of gravity increase as mass increases, and decrease as distance increases.

Be able to do

- Identify the relationship between motion and a reference point.
- Identify the two factors on which speed depends.
- Describe the difference between speed and velocity.
- Analyze the relationship between velocity and acceleration.
- Interpret a graph of acceleration.
- Give examples of different kinds of forces.
- Determine the net force on an object.
- Compare balanced and unbalanced forces.
- Explain why friction occurs.
- List the types of friction and give examples of each.
- Explain how friction can be both helpful and harmful.
- Explain the law of universal gravity.
- Describe the difference between mass and weight.
- Carry out an investigation using scientific process skills.

that they have completed the assignment prior to doing these activities.

Designing Station Activities

There are many ways to determine which lessons you turn into stations. For the Matter in Motion unit, students stay at each station for 30 to 45 minutes, two sets of three stations are used, and students are grouped (four per group) based on pretest scores on simple speed problems.

Step 1. When beginning to design your stations, first complete a KUD chart. This is a simple unit outline identifying what you want students to **k**now, **u**nderstand, and be able to **d**o (see Figure 5).

Step 2. Using your KUD chart, determine which concepts you think will give students the most difficulty. From experience, these concepts are usually those that involve mathematical equations and those that require higher-level thinking skills. Star these on your KUD chart. The starred items become the focus of the station. In the Matter in Motion unit, I knew students would struggle with the speed, momentum, and acceleration problems.

Step 3. Brainstorm all of your potential resources: lab activities, web quests, books, AV equipment and other media, and computers. Make sure to take advantage of resources available through your school library. Think of labs and activities you have done in the past and those you couldn't do because there wasn't enough equipment for all students. Brainstorming the concept *speed*, I wanted to work speed problems using real-life applications. I determined that planning a trip using different modes of transportation might interest students. We also wanted students to race Hot Wheel cars, despite having a limited number of ramps and stopwatches. These ideas became the foundation for our Matter in Motion stations.

Step 4. Once you determine what is available, decide which activities you want to turn into stations. Look at all of your choices, and pick those that address your topic in multiple ways. Remember that only one station should require a teacher's continued presence. The remaining ones should be designed so that students can complete them independently or with a minimum of instruction. You may need to modify these activities so students can complete them in approximately the same amount of time. After determining our foundation activities, we decided to have two sets of three stations. Twelve students in groups of four would rotate through one set of three stations and the remaining 12 students would travel through the second set of stations. The three stations were (1) Hot Wheel car races, (2) computer-aided trip comparions, and (3) teacher-assisted math problems related to speed.

Step 5. Write station directions, making them as simple and clear as possible. To reduce the amount of paper used, you may want to laminate directions and place them at the station. This is an opportunity to differentiate instruction by level of difficulty, student interest, or learning style. We decided to use pretest scores as a basis for differentiating our speed problem station. We did this by modifying our speed work sheets so students completed the same number of problems, but at different levels of difficulty.

Step 6. Divide students into groups, determined randomly, using pretests for readiness or by using interest surveys. Group sizes will ultimately depend on the availability of equipment and class size. If you have three computers available, placing students in groups of six, two to a computer, works well. Based on pretests, we grouped students according to their level of readiness with mathematical computations.

Assessing Student Work

Assessing stations can be tricky, especially when differentiating subject matter. When we designed these activities, we decided that we would give percentage grades. Each assignment was graded and the percentages were used to record a letter grade. Safety and work ethic were also included in the grade. Consider how you would grade these assignments individually.

Conclusion

Once you have set up stations, you may find that they work for many activities. I have used the same basic stations from the Matter in Motion unit when working with density and with atoms. In the atom unit, I substituted building models at the laboratory station.

If all of this sounds daunting, try this quick and easy rotation: Group student desks into pods and arrange them in a row across the room. For a class of 32, two sets of four pods, with four students at each station works well. Place an instrument with an object to measure at each group of desks. Give students a work sheet so they can record their measurements. Groups spend 20 minutes at each station. This is a quick-and-easy verision of the Station Approach to try.

Using stations allows you to teach with limited resources, add variety to your teaching, and lets you do all those lessons you know will help students learn and be successful.

Denise Jaques Jones is a teacher at LaSalle Spring Middle School in Wildwood, Missouri.

Acknowledgments

I would like to thank Sarah Harashe, whose organized and forthright style helped make this idea a reality. I would also like to thank Robin Jaques and Michael Jones, who made sure this article made sense.

Resources

Tomlinson, C. 1999. *The differentiated classroom: Responding to the needs of all learners.* Alexandria, VA: ASCD Publications.

Winebrenner, S., and P. Espeland. 2000. *Teaching the gifted student in the regular classroom: Strategies and techniques every teacher can use to meet the academic needs of the gifted and talented.* Minneapolis, MN: Free Spirit Press.

How Do You Know That?

By Jennifer Folsom, Catherine Hunt, Maria Cavicchio, Anne Schoenemann, and Matthew D'Amato

The purpose of many animal studies at early grades is to build observation skills, develop a knowledge base, and practice age-appropriate science skills such as comparing, describing, and drawing. Although these are important learning experiences, the National Science Education Standards also recommend that students engage in scientific inquiry (NRC 2000). Our team of educators, curriculum developers, district administrators, and scientists believes it is possible and beneficial for even the youngest students to participate in a rigorous scientific inquiry that builds a conceptual understanding of animals and the nature of studying animals.

To test this idea, we created an inquiry-based unit on animals, implemented it in kindergarten classrooms, and observed the students' responses. Our unit focused on guiding students to formulate explanations about animals based on scientific evidence.

We wanted students to use direct observations of animals as the primary source of evidence for their explanations about animals' needs, structures, behaviors, and relationships with the environment.

Choosing appropriate animals was critical because we also wanted the animals to serve as a venue to learn about the process of science inquiry. The animals needed to be safe for students to handle and easy to maintain in the classroom. See "Animals in the Classroom" box for tips. Students were going to do more than just look at an animal and even more than just make and record observations. They were going to ask questions and conduct investigations with these animals to help explain what animals need and how those needs are met in their environment. With these considerations in mind, our team determined that the students would study humans, snails, guppies, and isopods.

Animal Explorations

To begin the unit, we read storybooks and discussed personal experiences with animals to develop an explanation about what animals need to survive. We began by creating a class chart of all the things the animals did in the stories. Next, we circled all of the things on our list that real animals do and discussed why real animals do those things. We guided students to the idea that animals do these things because of their need to survive. Finally, we grouped the ideas into categories of how they help animals

Animals in the Classroom

Safety Precautions:

When allowing students to handle any animal in the classroom, it is important that you have made them understand what steps they must take to keep themselves and the animals safe at all times. We developed class statements with the students that reflected what behavior they thought was appropriate for "scientists in training." For example:

• "Good scientists always wash their hands with soap and rinse them all the way before and after touching the animals or their homes."

• "Good scientists do not put anything into their mouths, ears, or noses while studying animals."

• "Good scientists make sure that the animals they are studying are kept safe from being dropped or from stuff dropping on them."

• "Good scientists check on their animals at least once a day to see if they might need something to stay healthy."

Maintenance:

Keeping the animals alive and healthy in a kindergarten classroom required a few adjustments to daily routines. The aquatic animals, about four guppies and four snails, lived in one 6 L plastic container. Students stirred the water each day to incorporate air or used an aerator. We changed out one-third to one-half the dechlorinated water each week, and used a turkey baster to remove debris from the bottom of the tanks without disturbing student investigations set up inside the tanks. Aquariums contained live Elodea, and we added fresh vegetables and fruits for the snails and fish food for the guppies.

The terrestrial animals, about 10 isopods, lived in a 6 L plastic container. Moist soil and damp paper towels provided the moisture isopods needed to breathe. Bark, dead leaves, and vegetables were used for food and protection.

survive, such as to keep from being eaten, to get food, to get water, to get air, and to find a home.

Next, we compared the results of our discussion with a scientific list of animals' basic needs—energy, water, air, and protection. The students analyzed how their terms compared to how scientists described animal needs and determined that the scientific list was just worded differently from their own. For example, the scientific term *protection* encompassed many phrases they used like "to keep from being eaten," "to find a home," and "to stay out of the wind." Students were amazed that just one new vocabulary word could describe so much of their thinking.

Once the students had explained what animals need and evaluated those needs against a scientific list, they were ready to begin investigating how animals meet those basic needs. We used an animal data chart to begin this process (Figure 1). We made sure students understood that the chart was a place for accurate data. When they presented us with data and explained how they knew that data to be true, we added it to the chart, using either words or pictures.

Humans and Prior Knowledge

The first animals studied were humans. One full lesson period was devoted to students measuring, observing, and sharing prior knowledge about human structures and behaviors and using this as evidence to complete the Human Row on the Animal Data Chart. Together we discussed the labels for each column of the chart and came to a consensus about what should be written in each box.

Students constructed evidence-based written explanations for how humans meet their basic needs of food, water, air, and protection. Students easily developed these explanations and quickly identified evidence to support their ideas when prompted. When students suggested an explanation but did not include evidence, we asked them, "How do you know that?" or

Figure 1.
Animal data chart

What kind of ANIMAL is it?	What SIZE is it?	What SHAPE is it?	What does it EAT?	How does it MOVE?	Where does it LIVE?
Human	40 cm to 200 cm		fruit vegetables pizza	walk crawl swim	house apartment
Snail	2 cm to 4 cm		lettuce	slide	in water on rocks
Guppy	3 cm to 8 cm		shrimp fish food	swim wiggle	in water behind plants
Isopod	2 cm		potatoes apples cucumbers	walk run some curl	in moist soil under leaves

"What makes you think that way?" Then, we paraphrased what they said and introduced key terms that we expect them to use in science, like *evidence*. For example, "I heard Josie say that humans get protection from wearing clothes, and she knew that because one time she went out in the sun without long sleeves and got sunburned. She is doing a good job of behaving like a scientist because she had an idea [that clothes are a kind of protection] and she supported her idea with evidence [firsthand knowledge that long sleeves keep her from being sunburned]. Who else has an idea that they can support with evidence?" They shared explanations such as, "Humans get food by lifting a fork with their hand and putting the food into their mouths. Then, they chew and swallow. We know this because we do it, we have seen other people do it, and we have read about it in books."

We explained that this process of using evidence to develop explanations would be re-peated for each animal they were going to study. They were excited to fill out the next row on the Animal Data Chart (Figure 1).

Snails and Evidence

When students began collecting data on snails (simple qualitative and quantitative measurements of length, overall shape, and patterns of behavior regarding eating and moving), their initial efforts were much different from their work with humans. Students presented things as facts that they never observed. They developed spontaneous explanations about how snails meet their basic needs that had no supporting evidence. They said things like, "The snails sucked their food into their shell and ate it inside." As students made assertions that reflected their preconceptions about animals, we probed them with "How do you know that?" and variations on that question. We continued to direct students back to using their observations as a source of evidence.

Figure 2.
Student depictions of isopod habitats

Note the isopods found on the tree trunk and near the fallen leaf at the bottom-center of the picture.

Note the isopods in the tunnel, near the dead leaf, underground.

The following teacher-student interaction was typical of how we began to hold students more scientifically accountable for their explanations without simply correcting their ideas.

Teacher: How do you know that snail is a daddy snail?

Student: Because it's the biggest one in the tank.

T: Do you think that boys are always bigger than girls?

S: Yes.

T: I am a girl and you're a boy and I am bigger than you.

S: Yeah, but you're old.

T: Do you think that your big snail could just be older than your other snail?

S: Probably, but it might be a boy, right?

T: It might be. Do you think that explains why it's bigger?

S: No, some girls are bigger. How can I tell if it's a boy? They all look the same.

T: You're right. I read in my teachers' guide that boy and girl snails look the same on the outside.

S: Okay then, I'll give it a different name, "Giant." That could be for a boy or a girl.

As we questioned the students' ideas, they came to realize that the assertion of the snail being a "daddy" did not have enough support. The students understood that to make this claim they needed another piece of evidence—how to tell boy and girl snails apart—something they had been unsuccessful in observing. We gave the students information when they expressed their need to know and not before. It was not a correction of the students' initial claim. Instead, it became an additional piece of evidence for the students to use in developing their own revised explanation.

Guppies and Guiding Questions
Observations and measurements of guppies followed, similarly to those of the snails (length,

shape, habits). In addition, the focus on guppies became an emphasis not only on what the students were observing but also on how they were to problem solve a question they had based on those observations—an emphasis on the next stage of inquiry.

One important feature of our unit was to guide students in using direct observations of these animals as evidence for explanations. To facilitate this, we used a simple questioning strategy. When students did not know something, we asked them how they were going to figure it out. The following teacher-student conversation provides a good general example of the questioning strategy.

Several baby guppies had appeared in a tank after our lunch break, and we were attempting to develop an evidence-based explanation for their appearance.

T: You said that our babies came from eggs. Did you see the babies hatch from eggs?

S: No.

T: What makes you think they came from eggs?

S: Fish lay eggs. When the bluegills lay eggs, you can't try to catch them.

T: You are right about bluegills, but do you know for sure that these babies came from eggs? Did you see eggs in your tank before lunch?

S: No, their eggs are too small to see.

T: But right after lunch you saw baby guppies that are half a paperclip long. Does it make sense that a baby that big came out of an egg that was too small to see before lunch?

S: No. You must have given them to us as a treat!

T: No, I didn't. Where else do you know of that babies come from?

S: My brother came out of my mom's belly.

T: If this is what happened with the guppies what would you expect our mother guppy to look like?

S: Skinny! Her belly would be gone.

T: And, if the guppies hatched out of eggs, what might we find in the tank if we look closely?

S: Empty eggshells. Can we go look now?

Changing Conceptions

These early lessons were challenging for both students and teachers. We were changing the way we responded to student assertions that lacked support, and the students were struggling to find evidence to substantiate their claims. As the unit progressed, students adjusted to this new expectation of using evidence-based answers during science time. They began to think about the validity of their ideas before making claims. The impulsiveness of student answers lessened. There were many instances of students taking cues from the teacher and probing each other with "How do you know that" types of questions. This is not to say that all student explanations were substantially supported by evidence, but students were beginning to understand if they made a claim like, "I think snails can swim," they needed to follow that claim with a reason like, "because I saw them floating on top of the water without hanging on to anything. How else could they have gotten there?"

As students provided reasons for their explanations, we were able to assess their level of understanding about animals. Because we knew what they thought and why, we could design experiences to clarify any misconceptions and build a more conceptual understanding of animals. For example, when some students thought snails could swim, we set up an experiment and pulled some off the side of the tank and floated them in the water. After observing that they did not move on their own and did not appear to have fins like other fish, students more readily accepted the scientific answers.

In addition to the questioning strategies, we also assessed student understanding using an embedded performance task. Groups of students were challenged to build their own aquariums for snails and guppies using their knowledge of animals' basic needs, structures, and behaviors as evidence for determining what should be in their aquarium. We dispensed supplies to students only after they had justified the reason for needing the supply. For example, a group of students explained that the aquarium should have protection for snails because it was one of the snail's basic needs. The students thought that snails would prefer to be on a pile of rocks instead of out in open water. We provided them with two colors of rocks, which prompted the following teacher-student interaction:

T: You said that you wanted to put in the green rocks. What makes you choose the green ones instead of the black ones?

S: The green ones are prettier.

T: Does that make them better for the snails?

S: No, the black ones are better. They're the same color as the snails. They could blend in.

S: No, the green ones are better because they're smoother. The snails can slide on them. The black ones are too rough.

T: How can you figure out which ones the snails prefer?

S: Give them both and let them pick!

T: Okay, where should the rocks go in the tank?

S: In a big pile over there.

S: No! If you put them in a big pile you won't know that they don't like the black ones. They might be on a black one just to get to a green one. You have to space them out.

S: Black ones over there; green ones over here. If the snails go over there, those will be the better rocks.

T: Sounds like you have a good reason to put both colors of rocks in and a plan for testing your ideas. Here are your rocks.

The process of handing over the reins and allowing students to develop their own aquariums with very little direction was a challenge for us. We were initially unsure that something we had done year after year could be turned over to students with a successful outcome. We found it enlightening that students could design aquatic environments that met the basic needs of the animals they were studying and provided a venue for them to conduct simple tests to gather more data about their animals. We discovered that we only needed to ask thoughtful guiding questions and challenge student claims that lacked evidence. The students did the rest, and they did it with a level of engagement and ownership in their learning we had not seen before. During this process, the students began to see observations and simple tests as critical tools for answering scientific questions. If they wanted to know if snails preferred to eat lettuce or apples, they did not just ask for the answer. They asked if it was okay for them to set up the test in their aquariums so they could figure it out.

Student Success

Following the aquarium assessment, our goal with the last animals, isopods, was for students to demonstrate their ability to progress through an entire cycle of inquiry at an age-appropriate level. First, we modeled a simple isopod preference test to determine if isopods preferred dry or moist soil. Then, the class conducted multiple trials of another preference test, such as preference for soil type, humidity, or food. Finally, each student team designed and conducted its own preference test. Some examples of these include comparing fresh wet leaves and dead wet leaves or moist soil and dry soil. They also drew isopod habitats that demonstrated their understanding (Figure 2).

As students worked together—sharing their results and rigorously debating the explanations they developed from their data—we felt a thrill of pride. It was one of those moments when we remembered why we had become teachers. We had succeeded in using scientific inquiry to guide our students to their own understanding about animals, and, in turn, they succeeded in showing us how capable they were of rigorous learning through inquiry.

Jennifer Folsom and Matthew D'Amato are Associate Outreach Specialists with the System-wide Change for All Learners and Educators (SCALE) Partnership at the University of Wisconsin-Madison in Madison, Wisconsin. Catherine Hunt and Maria Cavicchio are kindergarten teachers at Mendota Elementary and Lowell Elementary schools, respectively, in the Madison Metropolitan School District, Madison, Wisconsin. Anne Schoenemann is a district elementary science instructional resource teacher in the Madison Metropolitan School District.

Resources

American Association for the Advancement of Science (AAAS). 1993. *Benchmarks for science literacy.* New York: Oxford University Press.

Jacobs, D. 1999. *What do scientists do?* New York: Newbridge Educational Publishing.

National Research Council (NRC). 2000. *Inquiry and the National Science Education Standards.* Washington, DC: National Academy Press.

——. 1996. *National Science Education Standards.* Washington, DC: National Academy Press.

Plants and Pollution

By Eric Brunsell and J. William Hug

Investigations with Wisconsin Fast Plants can make the subject matter come alive ... or dead, depending on the experimental treatment. This became apparent when a university-based teacher educator and a fifth-grade teacher collaborated on a professional development experience aimed at increasing understanding of how science inquiry could be used effectively in diverse classrooms. This professional development experience centered on cocreating a unit for fifth-grade students as a part of a study of plant and animal cycles. Although the unit included numerous activities (Figures 1 and 2 show the "activity calendar" for the entire unit), this article focuses on the inquiry portion of the study, as students investigated how pollutants might affect plants.

Unit Planning

After reviewing the district's standards and learning targets for fifth grade, the teacher knew he wanted to focus his unit on plants and plant life cycles. One of our goals for this professional development experience was to create units using a context that was interesting to students. Because his students came from an urban setting and had expressed an interest in pollution previously in the year, the teacher felt that studying the effect of pollution on plants could help relate the topics of plant needs and their life cycles to his students' lives.

As a starting point for unit planning, the teacher and one of his colleagues collaborated to develop a pretest, which the teacher then implemented. The pretest consisted of a series of open-ended questions:

1. Draw a plant and label its parts.
2. List the things that a plant needs to survive.
3. What could cause the leaves of a houseplant to turn brown?
4. Draw and label the life cycle of a plant.
5. Why are bees good for plants?
6. What might make trees sick in the summer?

The results from the pretest indicated his students had some general knowledge of plants and of pollution but very little understanding of how pollution affects plants. Only three students identified pollution as a reason for plants or trees getting sick in pretest questions. Additionally, students had almost no under-

Figure 1.
Unit activity calendar, days 1–10

Day 1. What Do You Know?

- Students were asked to "think, pair, share," focusing on what they know about plants, pollution, and the effects of pollution on plants.
- Class responses were recorded on chart paper.

Day 2. Benchmark—What Is Pollution?

- Students read, outlined, and discussed a chapter in a general science resource book that focused on pollution. The discussion focused on garbage, air pollution, water pollution, and disposal methods.

Day 3. Benchmark—What Is Pollution? and Inquiry—Why Is It Important That I Learn How Pollution Affects Plants?

- Students were told that they were going to individually respond to the question, "Why is it important that I learn about the effects of pollution on plants?" after viewing Bill Nye's *Biodiversity* video.
- Students viewed the video.
- Students shared their responses to the question. No "passes."

Day 4. Inquiry—Develop Questions and Plant Wisconsin Fast Plants

- The whole class brainstormed different kinds of pollution that we could test on plants. Students engaged in some discussion of where the pollution is found and how it might get on plants.
- Students were divided into teacher-selected groups, and groups selected a pollutant to test.
- Students recorded their question and predictions in their science journals.
- With teacher guidance and written directions, groups planted the Wisconsin Fast Plant seeds.

Day 5. Benchmark—Measuring Length Using Millimeters and Centimeters

- As part of a math lesson students reviewed the relationship between milimeters and centimeters.
- Students practiced measuring in centimeters and milimeters using a teacher developed worksheet. Feedback on student progress was immediate.
- All students were asked to show their competency by accurately measuring the last few items without assistance.

Day 6. Benchmark—Recording Data

- Students discussed what types of data would be useful in investigating the effects of pollution on plants.
- Class ideas were incorporated into a data collection format that all groups would use throughout the investigation.
- The terms *control* group and *treatment* group were introduced by the teacher.
- Students practiced recording data by copying data from pretend control and treatment plants.

Day 7. Inquiry—Record Observations/Data (Initial)

- Students worked in groups to record their initial data set.
- Students applied the first treatment to plants after deciding how much to put on the plants.

Days 8, 9, 10. Inquiry—Record Observations/Data (Continuing)

- Students recorded their observations in science journals.

Figure 2.
Unit activity calendar, days 11–16

Day 11. Benchmark and Inquiry—Parts of a Plant	Day 12. Benchmark—Preparing to Report Results of Investigation
• Students read about vascular plants in their science book and completed the vocabulary and review exercises. • Students viewed Bill Nye's video, *Plants*. • Students examined, drew, and labeled parts of plant specimens mounted by third-grade teachers and students. • Students viewed plant cells using microscopes.	• Students worked in groups to prepare their presentations. Teacher acted as a resource and provided encouragement.
Day 13. Inquiry—Communicating Results of Group Investigations	Day 14. Benchmark—Human Progress Can Sometimes Lead to Unintended Consequences.
• Groups communicated their results to small groups of third graders, who had also been studying plants. • Each group presented to at least five third-grade groups. • Teachers circulated asking questions and encouraging presenters.	• Students viewed the Dr. Seuss video, *The Lorax*. • Students discussed the relevance of the video.
Day 15. Benchmark—Parts of a Flower and Plant Reproduction	Day 16. Inquiry—Pollination of Wisconsin Fast Plants
• Students drew and labeled the parts of a flower with guidance from the teacher and a large flower model. • Using a model and diagrams, a teacher explained how plants reproduce.	• Students pollinated Wisconsin Fast Plant flowers using a dead bee at the end of a toothpick (dead bees purchased from Carolina Biological).

standing of the life cycle of plants and how plants reproduce.

Armed with this understanding of students' initial conceptions, the teacher developed an inquiry-based unit based on a central investigation exploring how pollution affects plants. By the end of the unit's activities, he expected that students would be able to describe some sources of pollution and their potential effect on plants. Additionally, he expected that students would be able to describe the reproductive parts of a plant and the life cycle of a plant.

Because Wisconsin Fast Plants have a very short life cycle (approximately six weeks), the teacher chose to have his students investigate the effect of pollution on plants using these plants (see Internet Resources). The teacher planned a series of benchmark activities that would be woven into the student investigations. These benchmark activities would introduce and reinforce specific content objectives, including identifying plant parts, pollination, and the life cycle of plants. Additionally, the benchmark activities would help students build skills that they need to conduct inquiry, such as observation, measure-

Figure 3.

A student journal entry for the plant unit

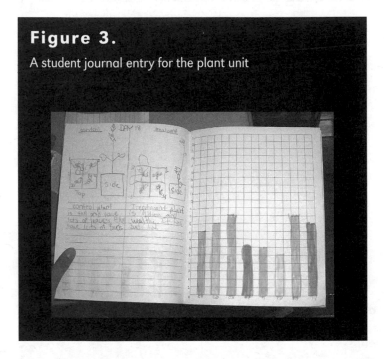

ment, identifying and controlling variables, and using evidence to support conclusions.

Conducting the Investigations

The teacher began the student investigations by having students brainstorm a list of pollutants that could be tested on plants. Students suggested a diverse list of pollutants, including road salt, acid rain, laundry detergent, gasoline, antifreeze, and motor oil, all of which students felt could adversely affect plants in their neighborhood. Students realized that some pollutants were not safe to test in the classroom, so we brainstormed alternatives—like vinegar for acid rain and cooking oil for motor oil.

First, each group selected a pollutant (road salt [dissolved to saturation in warm water before being given to the students], vinegar, laundry detergent, or cooking oil) to test on their plants. There are safety steps to take for this activity. Make sure your students wear safety goggles and gloves for this activity. Instruct students not to touch the pollutant or the soil after the pollutant has been added. Provide all chemicals in highly dilute conditions (<1%)

in very small labeled containers (up to 5 ml). Keep MSDS sheets for all substances used in the classroom (*www.hazard.com*).

Next, students wrote their investigation question and predictions in their science journals and planted their Wisconsin Fast Plant seeds. The class discussed what types of data would be useful in investigating the effects of pollution on plants. Students suggested that the health of the plants could be measured by recording the height, color, and number of leaves. They also said they could measure the temperature of the room, the amount of water the plant receives, and the amount of light that each plant receives.

At this point, the teacher introduced students to the idea of a *control* group and a *treatment* group. To begin, he asked students how they would be able to tell that the pollutant affected the plant. Initially, students responded, "They will get sick." He asked, "How would you know that the behavior is not normal for the plant or caused by something besides the pollutant?" The students quickly provided the idea that they should also grow some plants that they did not put pollution on, and the teacher explained that these plants are called the *control* group and the plants that get pollutants added to them are called the *treatment* plants.

Once the plants germinated (in about three days), students began collecting height and color data for their control plants and their treatment plants. After the plants had begun growing, the students were ready to apply their chosen pollutant to the treatment plants. The teacher provided 5 ml of the chosen pollutant to each group. After the pollutant was applied, students continued to collect data from their control and treatment plants for four more days. Students were highly engaged and often stopped by the room before school to check on their plants. Many of the students were dismayed that their treatment plants grew sick and died within days after applying the treatment.

Throughout the unit, students maintained

a science journal. This journal contained observational data about the health of the plants, drawings of the plants, and measurements of the control and treatment plant heights. Figure 3 shows an example entry from one student's journal. Students prepared presentations using their journal data on how their selected pollutant affected their plants. The presentations included a statement of their experimental question, a conclusion about the effect of their pollutant on the growth of their plant, and the evidence from their data that supported their conclusion. For example, the "Road Salt" group said that their plants began to wilt and turn yellow the day after the treatment was applied. All of the students concluded that the pollutants were very harmful to their plants.

Assessment and Learning Gains

Our observations indicated that students were engaged and thinking about ideas beyond that of textbook knowledge. The teacher rarely had to refocus his students during the unit. Students felt ownership over the investigation and their plants. Students frequently gave unsolicited suggestions as to why some plants died quickly after the pollutant treatment. Even though all students followed similar plant care procedures, including the amount of water, some students suggested that the plants might not have received the same amount of water. Other students said that the seedlings might be more fragile than older plants. Additionally, students were noticing things without being prompted. For example, one group of students suggested that the plants were small and the results might be different if they were testing larger plants. During the presentations, one group of students said that they wondered what happens to all of the chemicals that they use when they do chores. They were interested in finding out where they go and if chemicals would affect plants. That question would never have been asked if it were not for this style of inquiry.

The plant investigation was the core of this

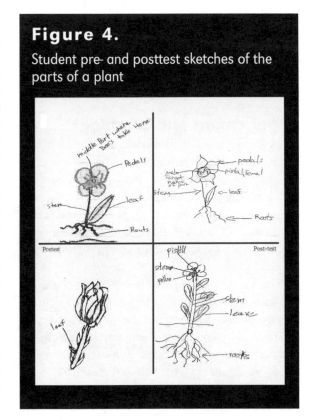

Figure 4.

Student pre- and posttest sketches of the parts of a plant

unit, but the overall goal was for students to learn more about the needs and life cycle of plants. Students were assessed in multiple ways. The teacher assessed the investigation portion of the unit through the presentations and science notebooks. In the notebooks, the teacher looked for evidence that students were diligent in recording their observations and measurements. Because the teacher understood that his students, many of whom were English language learners, were not comfortable presenting to large groups, he had the students prepare scripts. These scripts were assessed for evidence of students' inclusion of the question and the use of evidence to support their conclusion.

Finally, at the end of the unit, students retook the pretest. A comparison of student responses on the pre- and posttests showed considerable gains (Figure 4). Compared to the pretest, students were able to label more plant parts correctly and to describe more causes for unhealthy plants. Before the unit, no students drew or labeled the pistil or stamen. After the unit, 10 of 21 did so. Before the unit, only one student accurately described the life cycle of a plant. After the unit, 14 of 21 students did so.

Engagement and Learning

Developing science inquiry units can be a difficult and time-consuming process. However, the payoff is increased student engagement and learning. In this unit, the students learned inquiry, organizational, presentation, and teamwork skills. They also learned about plants and got a sense of the role humans play in the fate of our planet.

The classroom teacher concluded, "I am really enthusiastic about what we accomplished; it was interesting seeing the growth in kids' learning. It gave me a push and renewed my interest in how we educate our students in science." The success of this collaboration only confirms our belief in the value of partnerships between teachers and teacher educators for the benefit of student learning.

Eric Brunsell is an assistant professor of science education at the University of Wisconsin–La Crosse. J. William Hug is an educational consultant specializing in science teaching methods, experiential education, and place-based education.

Acknowledgment

This research was supported by The Center for Learning and Teaching in the West (NSF Award #0119786), Montana State University, and Space Education Initiatives *(www.spaceed.org)*. Opinions expressed in this article are those of the authors and not necessarily the position or policies of the National Science Foundation. As this was part of a research project, the school district requires that we protect the privacy of the participating teacher and students.

Resources

National Research Council (NRC) 1996. *National Science Education Standards*. Washington, DC: National Academy Press.

Internet

Wisconsin Fast Plants
  www.fastplants.org

Rock Solid Science

By Karen Ansberry and Emily Morgan

Children are naturally curious about the world around them, including the rocks beneath their feet. By observing, describing, and sorting a variety of rocks, students can discover that rocks have certain physical properties by which they can be classified. This article takes a fun approach to learning about the properties, uses, and formation of rocks. Students in grades K–3 explore the properties and uses of their own "pet rock," while students in grades 4–6 investigate "rock stories."

For Grades K–3: Pet Rocks

The National Science Education Standards state that students in grades K–4 should understand that earth materials include solid rocks and soils, and that these materials have different physical and chemical properties that make them useful in different ways. The Standards also suggest that young children be encouraged to closely observe the objects and materials in their environment, note their properties, and distinguish them from one another.

Following these suggestions, the K–3 lesson focuses primarily on recognizing properties of rocks, such as shape, size, color, texture, and luster; understanding how properties of rocks can be used to sort them; and exploring how a rock's properties and its uses are related. The Standards advise that for grades K–4, the study of rocks not be extended to the changes in the solid earth known as the *rock*

Trade Books

If You Find a Rock
By Peggy Christian.
Harcourt. 2000.
ISBN 97801523933907.
Grades K–4

Synopsis
Poetic text and soft, hand-tinted photographs combine to explore the variety of rocks that can be found, including skipping rocks, chalk rocks, and splashing rocks.

Rocks: Hard, Soft, Smooth, and Rough
By Natalie M. Rosinsky.
Picture Window Books. 2003.
ISBN 9781404800151.
Grades K–4

Synopsis
Simple text and cartoon-like illustrations provide information about igneous, sedimentary, and metamorphic rocks.

cycle, because this concept has little meaning to young children. The Standards do suggest that students in grades 5–8 develop an understanding of the process by which old rocks at the Earth's surface weather, forming sediments that are buried, then compacted, heated, and often recrystallized into new rock. Eventually, those new rocks may be brought to the surface and the rock cycle continues. The 4–6 lesson is based on the idea that every rock has a "story" that can be uncovered through observation and research. Students observe different rock samples, discover that rocks are composed of minerals, and learn that rocks can be classified as igneous, sedimentary, or metamorphic, depending upon how they are formed. They form "rock groups" to do research on a particular rock and then create a picture book to tell the story of that rock.

For Grades K–3: Pet Rocks

Engage: Introduce the book *If You Find a Rock.* Build connections to the author by telling students that the author is a "rock hound," a person who loves to collect rocks, and ask if any of them would consider themselves to be a rock hound. Explain that, while you are reading the book aloud, you want them to think about what some of the rocks are used for and what properties, or characteristics, make them suited for that use. After reading, discuss the various uses and properties of the rocks in *If You Find a Rock.* For example, a skipping rock is used for skipping across water. The properties that make it suited for that purpose are its flat and rounded shape and its small size. Shape and size are properties of rocks. A chalk rock is used to make pictures on the pavement. The properties that make it suited for that purpose are its white color and its soft, dusty texture. Color and texture are also properties of rocks. Another property of rocks is luster, or how the minerals in rocks reflect light. Words that describe a rock's luster include *shiny, dull,* and *sparkly.*

Explore/Explain: Ask students if they have ever heard of a "Pet Rock." Explain that way back in 1975, a businessman in California came up with the idea of selling rocks as pets. The Pet Rock became a huge hit. Tell students that they are going to be rock hounds on the hunt for their own pet rock. They can go home and search for a rock with adult supervision or select a rock from their own collection. Discuss these rules: Your pet rock must be smaller than a tennis ball, and you are not allowed to throw your pet rock. The next day, give students rulers and hand lenses to observe their pet rock's properties, including shape, size, color, texture, and luster. Discuss how observations such as big or small are not scientific observations because they are not exact. Using measurements to describe the size of a rock is more scientific. Demonstrate how to determine the length of a rock by measuring its longest side in centimeters. Have students choose three properties of their rock and write each property on a separate sticky note. Next, make a properties chart on the board with six columns labeled, Shape, Size, Color, Texture, Luster, and Other. Model how to use the chart by having one student share a sticky-note observation and then place it in the appropriate column on the chart—smooth, for instance, goes in the texture column). Then have small groups of students take turns placing all of their sticky notes in the appropriate columns on the chart. Some students may need help in determining which observations go in which column.

Elaborate: Have all the students stand, holding their pet rocks. Choose one sticky-note observation from the Properties Chart, such as "smooth." Students will then determine whether or not their rocks are smooth and form two groups in the room: "smooth" and "not smooth." Have them compare their rock to the others within their group and then let them switch groups if they wish. Repeat this sorting and classifying process using several more observations from the Properties Chart. Explain that scientists use properties like color and texture to help them classify rocks.

Evaluate: Younger primary students can draw a detailed picture of their rock, listing as many properties as they can. For older primary students, explain that the original Pet Rock was packaged in a box that looked like a pet carrying case. The Pet Rock inventor used creative advertisement to help sell his product.

Have students create advertisements for their pet rocks. The ads should show what they have learned about properties of rocks, including the following:

- A description of the rock's shape, size (including measurements), color, texture, luster, and any other properties
- Suggested uses for the rock based upon its properties
- A labeled drawing of the rock highlighting its unique features

For fun, ads can also include the following:

- A drawing of the rock's packaging — a crate, box, or bag, for insance
- Training tips for the pet rock
- Commercials, slogans, or jingles

Afterward, have students share their advertisements with the rest of the class.

For Grades 4–6: Rock Stories

Engage: With a rock hidden in your hand, announce that you are holding something that is older than them, older than the school building, even older than you … something that could even be millions of years old. Have students guess what it is. Reveal the rock, and then tell students that a rock is probably the oldest thing that they will ever touch. Explain that every rock has a story that they can uncover through careful observation and research—a story about how it formed, what it is made of, and how it can be used.

Explore/Explain: Give each student a hand lens, centimeter ruler, and one of the following rocks: obsidian, granite, sandstone, limestone, or marble. Tell them that, to uncover their rock's story, they can begin by observing physical properties including shape, size, color, texture, and luster. Model how to make good qualitative and quantitative observations of a rock's properties, such as: My rock is irregular in shape, has a mass of 56 g, and is 8 cm long. It is reddish brown, with a dull luster and rough texture. It has grains the size of sand. They should measure their rock in as many ways as they can, such as length, circumference, and mass. Have students create a table to record their rock's properties and then share their observations with others.

Next, tell students that the picture book *Rocks: Hard, Soft, Smooth, and Rough* can give them more clues about their rock's story. Each one of the rocks they have been observing is described in the book. Have them signal when they hear a description that matches their rock as you read the book aloud. After reading, discuss why properties such as color, texture, and luster might be better ways to identify rocks than size or shape. Then have students use hand lenses to look for specks, crystals, grains, or stripes in their rock samples. These are the minerals that make up their rocks. Some rocks are made of a single mineral, but most are made of several minerals.

Elaborate/Evaluate: After all students have identified their rocks, have them form rock groups with other students who have the same rock. These groups can use books and websites to research their rock's story in order to create a picture book. The book should include the name of the rock, its properties, the minerals it is composed of, the rock group to which it belongs (igneous, metamorphic, or sedimentary), an explanation of how it formed, and some possible uses. For fun, they can even write a "rock song." Have each group share their picture book with the rest of the class or with younger students.

Karen Ansberry is the elementary science curriculum leader at Mason City Schools in Mason, Ohio. Emily Morgan is the science consultant at the Hamilton County Educational Service Center in Cincinnati, Ohio. They are the authors of Picture-Perfect Science Lessons: Using Children's Books to Guide Inquiry, *available from NSTA Press.*

Connecting to the Standards

This article relates to the following National Science Education Standards (NRC 1996):

Content Standards

Standard D: Earth and Space Science
- Properties of earth materials (K–4)
- Structure of the earth system (5–8)

Resource

National Research Council (NRC). 1996. *National Science Education Standards*. Washington, DC: National Academy Press.

"Inquirize" Your Teaching

By Susan Everett and Richard Moyer

Consider the following classroom scenario: After reading about cloud formation, students are given a glass jar with a small amount of hot tap water in it and ice sealed in a plastic baggie. The teacher drops a lit match into each group's jar, creating particulates in the air on which the water can condense. Students quickly place the baggie of ice over the opening—creating a temperature gradient—and observe the formation of a cloud in the jar. Students are asked to write how the cloud in the jar is like the clouds they read about in their text.

Now consider this scenario: The teacher conducts the cloud demonstration and initiates a discussion about what the students have observed. Students are encouraged to focus on the factors that they think may affect the formation of the cloud in their jars. Students then investigate a factor of their choice and discuss results with the class before reading their text.

The difference between these two scenarios is not trivial. While both are hands-on activities, they are not both inquiry activities. In the first example, students are following a procedure but are not involved in answering a question for themselves—a key element in inquiry. In contrast, the children in the second example are actively investigating a question to which they do not know the answer.

The first activity is probably like many you will find in textbooks, websites, activity books, as well as some of your old favorites that have been around for many years. These activities, while hands-on, are primarily demonstrations that verify some science concept. It is usually possible to adapt these kinds of activities into inquiry investigations that answer questions for students, as in the second scenario. It has been *inquirized*—turned into an inquiry investigation.

The *National Science Education Standards* (NRC 1996) note that the basic elements of inquiry include: ask a question, conduct an investigation, make observations and collect data, use data to develop an explanation, and communicate results. We've found the 5E learning cycle model useful for designing lessons that include the above inquiry abilities. The learning cycle includes five phases: *engage* focuses students on a question; *explore* in which that question is investigated; *explain* in which the data from the investigation are analyzed and interpreted; *extend* and *apply* in which concepts are connected

125

Figure 1.

Ten steps for inquirizing activities

Preplanning
1. Consider your concept and objective.
2. Identify a possible activity that teaches your concept.

Explore Phase
3. Determine whether the activity answers an explorable question.
4. Alter the activity into an investigation that does answer a question for the students. Formulate an explorable question or questions. Consider safety of the original activity and of your modifications.

Engage Phase
5. Now you can write the engage portion of your lesson. Its main purpose is to focus students on the explorable question(s) and how they will try to answer it.
6. Demonstrations, real-world contexts, discussions, discrepant events, photos, and the like are all possible methods to be used in the engage phase.

Explain Phase
7. Begin the explain phase of the lesson with a discussion of the students' results. Students typically discover what happens but are likely to need help understanding why it happened.
8. This is an appropriate time for students to read and be introduced to any necessary vocabulary.

Extend and Apply Phase
9. Consider how the new understandings relate to other concepts and applications to the real world.

Evaluate Phase
10. If possible, use performance assessment in your evaluation.

Source: Moyer, Hackett, and Everett 2007.

to other concepts as well as to the real world; and finally, *evaluate* in which the understandings are assessed.

In this article, we describe how to inquirize a demonstration activity with steps that can be applied to any activity (Figure 1).

Explore Phase

You need to begin with an explorable question, one that can be answered for students by means of a simple hands-on activity. Check to see if the activity actually answers a question for the students, as this is critical to inquiry. If it does not, it must be altered so that it does. Consider the cloud in the jar demonstration in the first scenario above. At first glance it seems that this activity answers the question "How do clouds form?" However, the first cloud activity demonstrates what components form a cloud but does not offer an explanation of how the components interact to form the cloud. It simply shows that they do. Therefore, we need to alter the activity so that it does answer a question. We can do this by having students change one of the variables to see how it affects the formation of the cloud. For example, students could manipulate the temperature of the water and note the effect on the cloud. Now, the explorable question becomes "What effect does water temperature have on cloud formation in the jar?" Or, students could vary the size of the jar, number of matches, the amount of ice, the amount of water, and so on. To make the investigation more student-centered, you could use the explorable question, "What factors affect cloud formation in the jar?" In that way, the students could investigate a variable of their own choosing.

There are safety precautions: Be sure you tightly control matches at all times whether this activity is used as a demonstration or as a student inquiry in which teachers add the matches. Before planning this activity, check to make sure matches are allowed in your classroom. Teacher and students should wear goggles when working with matches.

Engage Phase

Next, plan how you will engage the students. Note that we are suggesting that you plan the engage phase after you plan the explore phase. The reason for this is that the purpose of the engage phase is to set up the explorable question. In practice, the engage phase will occur first, but you cannot set up a question before you determine what it is.

The most important function of the engage phase is to focus students on the explorable question and how the investigation will attempt to provide answers. Consider your students' prior knowledge and understandings in designing the engage phase. In the first scenario, students were introduced to the activity by reading their textbook. In this case, students were not asked to use their prior knowledge of clouds, express their ideas about cloud formation, or make predictions about what might occur in the activity. In the second case, they observed the perhaps-unexpected formation of the cloud and were asked to speculate on the variables involved. These students were asked to consider what they already know in light of the demonstration and to use some of these ideas in the investigation. To determine if you have adequately focused students, you might ask them to describe what they are going to do in the exploration. They should be able to tell you how their actions are helping them answer the explorable question and not merely that they are on step number three of a procedure.

Explain Phase

The explain phase should always begin with a discussion of the students' results. For example, students may find that denser clouds were formed when they used warmer water. Students may deduce that this is due to increased evaporation. The teacher's role is to help students make these connections by asking questions and guiding students to consider prior knowledge.

Note also that in the inquiry scenario, students read their text after they have explored thoroughly. The exploring gives students a reason to read their text. It provides both a motivation and a conceptual foundation for the reading. Thus, the reading is set up by the exploration and its analysis, resulting in the reading being more meaningful.

Extend and Apply Phase

Many of your old favorite activities will not have any useable suggestions for extension and application of the concept. Because learning is thought of as assimilating new information into prior knowledge, it is helpful to make this an explicit part of your teaching pedagogy. The purpose of the extend and apply phase is to relate the newly learned concept to similar concepts as well as real-world applications. For example, in the cloud activity, you can make connections to the condensation in a bathroom after a hot shower, foggy conditions, or condensation on a cold glass of ice water.

Connecting to the Standards

This article relates to the following National Science Education Standards (NRC 1996):

**Content Standards
Grades 5–8**

Standard A: Science as Inquiry
- The abilities necessary to do scientific inquiry
- Understandings about science inquiry

Standard D: Earth and Space Science
- Structure of the Earth System

Teaching Standards

Standard A: Teachers of science plan an inquiry-based science program for their students.

Figure 2.

"Inquirized" cloud lesson (for Grades 4–8)

Engage Phase

Demonstrate the formation of a cloud in a jar and initiate a discussion. Ask students about their prior understandings of cloud formation. Lead them to a consideration of the factors that might affect the cloud formation. Discuss how students might proceed to investigate one or more of these factors (e.g., water temperature, amount of water, amount and location of ice). For example, if students select water temperature, they might determine the effect on the formation of the cloud when they use ice cold water, room temperature water, and warm tap water. Be sure students are aware of the explorable question: "What factors affect cloud formation in the jar?" To focus students on their questions, you might write them on the board, have students record them in a journal, and as you interact with each group, ask them to tell you what question they are trying to answer with their investigation.

Explore Phase

Have students select a factor to investigate and develop a procedure to answer the explorable question. Students should have their procedures approved before they begin by individually sharing their plans with the teacher. At the time of this discussion, help students determine what data

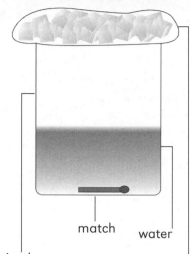

match   water

air where the cloud will form

plastic baggie with ice cubes

to collect and how it might be organized. In this case, the results for the dependent variable (cloud formation) will be qualitative—students will write descriptions of their clouds and whether they formed or not.

Explain Phase

Have students share their results for the factors they tested as they attempted to answer the explorable question. Using these results as a springboard, help students understand that three components are necessary for cloud formation: sufficient water vapor, a change in temperature (temperature gradient), and particulates in the air on which the water can condense (condensation nuclei). You may help students draw these inferences by asking them to refer to their observations and note what factors are always

present when a cloud forms in the jar. Or, have students consider the conditions under which no cloud formed in the jar. This is an appropriate time for the students to read their texts.

Extend and Apply Phase

Relate cloud formation to students' experiences with hot showers and "foggy" bathrooms. In addition to seeing the cloudy atmosphere of the bathroom, they will recall seeing condensation on mirrors and other surfaces. In this case, the water molecules are condensing on a surface instead of a particulate in the air. Other examples include dew on the grass and seeing your breath when it is cold outside.

Evaluate Phase

Present students with a glass of ice water and have them observe the formation of condensation on the outside of the glass. Have them investigate what factors lead to its formation in much the same way they investigated the cloud formation. Ask students to explain how the formation of the condensation is similar to cloud formation—both require moist air, a temperature gradient, and a surface on which the water molecules can condense. (Note that in dry climates it is very difficult to get any condensation on a glass of ice water.)

Evaluate Phase

Again, most of the demonstration ideas you may find will not include assessment ideas. Many of the ideas you considered for your real-world contexts or applications can serve as useful performance assessments. In the cloud lesson here, you could present students with a glass of ice water and have them investigate factors that result in condensation forming on the glass. They would then be asked to explain how this process is similar to the cloud formation.

Inquirized Investigations

The lesson outlined in Figure 2 shows how the above steps lead to a complete 5E learning cycle lesson. Following the above process, you can inquirize all of your old favorite activities.

Susan Everett is an assistant professor of science education at the University of Michigan-Dearborn. Richard Moyer is a professor of science education and natural sciences, also at the University of Michigan-Dearborn.

References

Moyer, R., J. Hackett, and S. Everett. 2007. *Teaching science as investigations: Modeling inquiry through learning cycle lessons*. Upper Saddle River, NJ: Pearson Merrill Prentice Hall.

National Research Council (NRC). 1996. *National Science Education Standards*. Washington, DC: National Academy Press.

Embracing Controversy in the Classroom

By Kelly Cannard

"The world might become overpopulated because fewer people would be dying. We'd use a lot more resources. We'd have to use solar powered cars."

"People would be able to do much more. Like, take the perspective of a scientist who has been researching something his whole life, and if he could live longer, he might make a gigantic breakthrough and help the entire world."

"When you get old, it's not just your bones and muscles that are dying, sometimes it's your brain. Can stem cells curb that?"

—Middle grade students' thoughts on how stem cell research might affect their lives in the future.

Discussing controversial topics such as stem cell research is a great way for students to build scientific understanding, enhance communication skills, and develop an appreciation for civic decision making. Tackling a topic such as stem cells at the middle level, however, can be a challenge because most young adolescents see the world in black-and-white terms. Instead of shying away from this challenge, I developed a five-tiered approach that

allows students to delve into the gray areas that surround controversial issues and makes them great topics for discussion.

To promote in-depth discussion of controversial topics, students should be provided with

- solid background information,
- multiple perspectives,
- guidelines for discussing issues as a group,

- substantive discussion questions, and
- strong follow-up.

Solid Background Information

To find good information on current controversial issues in science, explore the websites of reputable science museums, research institutions, newspapers, and public television and radio stations. Most have a link from their main page to community education resources for educators and students.

Preview the basic information provided on a site, looking for clear, descriptive language presented in manageable chunks, preferably with useful graphics. The information should avoid loaded language. When an opinion is shared, alternative positions should also be mentioned respectfully.

To adequately prepare students for a fruitful discussion, it is essential to go beyond providing an introductory lecture or assigning independent reading of an article. Present the material in two or three different ways and verify that students have a strong grasp of the topic before commencing with discussion on a controversy.

Multiple Perspectives

Familiarizing students with various perspectives on a controversial topic prepares them to be active participants in a discussion. To learn how others feel about a specific issue, I have students interview people to gather at least

Figure 1.

Stem cell research perspectives

You are collecting informed opinions on stem cell research. Your goal is to find as wide a variety of perspectives as possible. Find at least three individuals with three different perspectives on stem cell research and, for each, record his or her name, opinion, factors that influenced his or her opinion, and what role he or she has in the community. You are encouraged to talk with members of your family and community and read reputable newspaper or internet articles on the topic.

Name of person and opinion on stem cell research	What factors shape his or her opinion?	What role does he or she have in the community? Whom might he or she influence?

three different perspectives on an issue. Asking for three different perspectives reinforces the notion that we don't live in a black-and-white world. Not all students succeed at this initially, but, by later pooling their responses in groups, they generally achieve a good level of diversity. Students can gather the opinions from a variety of sources. I strongly encourage them to interview family and other adults in the community, such as religious leaders, physicians, teachers, and so forth. Having students interview people they know personalizes the issue, and immerses them in the controversy. Figure 1 is a chart my students use when gathering their perspectives.

Additionally, I post several relevant websites with interviews from many sides of the issue. (Figure 2 is a collection of websites I post for stem cell research.) For students who lack the resources to complete the assignment, I offer to print out some of the internet interviews for them to read, or I encourage them to find adults

Figure2.

Sample resources for student research on stem cells

- **Human embryonic stem cells, an animated introduction to stem cells** *www.sumanasinc.com/webcontent/anisamples/stemcells.html.*
- **National Institutes of Health** *http://stemcells.nih.gov/index.asp.* This page contains several informative pieces on stem cell basics. Clicking on the Other Online Resources link will lead to Educational Resources, including the animated stem cell presentation and the Genetic Science Learning Center.
- **PBS Online NewsHour** *www.pbs.org/newshour/health/stemcells. html.* This site includes interviews with individuals with diverse viewpoints and updated reports on the embryonic stem cell debate.
- **Stem cells in the spotlight, University of Utah's Genetic Science Learning Center** *http://gslc.genetics.utah.edu/units/stemcells.* In addition to excellent background information for students and teachers, this site addresses the ethical, legal, and social questions surrounding use of embryonic stem cells.

influence their outlook. In addition, students indicate whom they think each person might influence, prompting them to think about who should and who does influence policy decisions. For example, would an individual influence family and friends, a religious congregation, or the public at the local, state, or national level? Identifying these influences helps prepare students for the group discussion. Ultimately, I hope examining ethical and political issues of stem cell research will encourage students to examine their own opinions more deeply and realize how they might persuade others of their positions.

Protocols for Group Interaction

Because discussing controversial topics differs from talking about the points of a lab procedure or other typical science class activities, it is imperative to establish group interaction protocols. Posted on the wall are group work expectations:

- Be on task
- Cooperate and participate
- Respect others and their ideas
- Use a conversational voice and avoid extraneous noise

Keeping the noise level in check while heatedly discussing a topic can be a challenge, so I sometimes stand a digital sound meter on the overhead for all to see and establish a decibel level for the class to maintain. To encourage respect for one another's opinions, I post a grayscale graphic (a large poster of gradations of gray from white to black) next to the group expectations. It's a visual reminder that not everything is a black-and-white issue.

There are also protocols for the teacher. Show value in the activity by interacting with each of the groups. Position yourself so you can keep an eye on the other groups, and then find an opportunity to clarify any misconceptions that arise or probe the group to delve deeper in their thinking by posing a related question. Excellent

around the school at lunch. Scheduling the computer lab for a class session is another excellent method for giving students the opportunity to gather perspectives. Giving students a few days to collect this information leads to better results and is worth the time investment.

At the same time as students gather various perspectives on stem cell research, I ask them to find out what factors shape each individual's opinion. Students begin to understand how having a particular disease or religious belief might

discussions require the participants to apply their knowledge and thinking and to explore new possibilities. Instead of asking students to immediately share their personal opinions on a controversial topic, I like to have them imagine how others might feel about the topic. Figure 3 describes the roles I ask students to assume for our stem cell research discussion.

Students can also assume the role of presidential advisers to offer their opinions on a topic. Playing an "expert" increases student motivation and participation. Figure 3 also includes sample questions presidential advisers must address to help the president set policy on stem cell research.

Figure 3.

Sample substantive stem cell discussion questions

1. Imagine that you are each of the people listed below. With your group, decide what you think your position on stem cell research would be. What types of stem cell research would you be against or for? What encouragement or cautions would you give the public?

- A 17-year-old who suffers from cystic fibrosis. Your doctor says you have about five years to live, but researchers are working toward successfully implanting healthy lung cells into humans and coaxing them to divide and replace unhealthy ones.
- A religious leader who believes life starts at the moment two gametes (egg and sperm) join. You are interested in protecting human life.
- An elected official. Your constituency is split on the topic of stem cell research.

2. Imagine that you have been selected as an advisory group to the president. Discuss each of these questions and list some additional questions that would arise from this issue.

- If you were in charge of creating a bioethics committee on stem cell research, how would you organize it and who would you want to be on it? (Think about positions, such as a scientist or a religious leader, not particular individuals.)
- How might society and the environment change if people were able to live to be 125 or 150 years old?

Source: Adapted from *What Are Some Issues in Stem Cell Research?*, produced by the Genetic Science Learning Center at the Eccles Center of Human Genetics, University of Utah, *http://gslc.genetics.utah.edu/units/stemcells/scissues.*

Strong Follow-Up

There are numerous ways to follow up on a controversial discussion. Students can

- write a letter to the president, their congressional leaders, or the editor of the local paper;
- hold a formal debate;
- write a traditional persuasive essay; or
- hold a town meeting.

All of these follow-up activities require students to demonstrate their understanding of the debates surrounding stem cell research, providing the teacher with a meaningful assessment of their learning. I focus my assessment on four factors:

1. Success in understanding different perspectives: Look for students' ability to communicate the salient arguments and underlying assumptions of different perspectives, such as "human life starts when a zygote is formed" or "using embryos that will be discarded from fertility clinics is resourceful."
2. Discussing collaboratively: Students should volunteer ideas in a group, building on what others have said and not merely agreeing with others. Students should demonstrate their listening skills with appropriate body language and without interrupting. When students

disagree, they should talk about their own position and present evidence from their preparatory reading and interviews. Students with differing opinions should ask each other clarifying questions to understand their different perspectives more deeply.

3. Communicating understanding of the underlying issues: Students should be able to articulate the primary barriers to universal agreement on an issue, such as specific beliefs held by a significant proportion of society or reasonable projected outcomes of a public decision.

4. Presenting one's own educated perspective: Evaluate students' ability to take a stand (making it clear this does not have to be a permanent opinion), present solid arguments with evidence from experts, and deal with the major arguments in opposition to theirs.

I generally gather evidence of the first two factors through informal monitoring of small group discussions and students' written records of their discussions. Often, I have students complete a short self-evaluation of their participation in a group discussion. The latter two factors can be evaluated through one of the follow-up activities listed previously.

Why Invite Controversy?

So often in science, I can anticipate the results of an inquiry or an activity. When we discuss a controversial topic, however, students always surprise me with the variety of their thinking. I take pleasure in observing students develop their thinking about meaningful, real-life issues. They, in turn, relish the chance to exchange their opinions with others. In an era when society has numerous ethical decisions to make regarding science, it is imperative to teach our students how to think critically and converse persuasively and respectfully with others. Get your students thinking by introducing a little controversy in your science classroom.

Kelly Cannard is a science teacher at Jason Lee Middle School in Vancouver, Washington.

Embed Assessment in Your Teaching

By David F. Treagust, Roberta Jacobowitz, James J. Gallagher, and Joyce Parker

Understanding can be improved when teachers use curricular and instructional strategies that allow for frequent and ongoing assessment. When teachers use information from ongoing assessment about their students' ideas and reasoning and make adjustments in their teaching, students learn and understand more science (Black and Wiliam 1998, Champagne et al. 1990, Duschl and Gitomer 1997, Simpson 1993, Wiggins 1998, Shepard 2000).

Ongoing assessment, however, is not part of the common model of teaching. Assessment in middle school science classes often involves teaching a topic followed by testing students in order to assign grades on their mastery of the content. Moreover, teachers do not often alter their instructional plans based on what they learn from an assessment tool (Gallagher 1993). The National Science Education Standards recommend that teachers need to probe for students' understanding, reasoning, and the utilization of knowledge, rather than check whether students have memorized certain items of information (NRC 1996).

But what should this alternative assessment look like and how will it help? Assessment that matches best-teaching practices is called *embedded assessment*, or *formative assessment*, because the assessment is an integral part of teaching. Embedded assessment is defined as an ongoing, cyclical process in which teachers gather information on their students' understanding and reasoning about any particular content knowledge in science, make sense of that information, and use it to make adjustments for teaching in response to students' learning needs.

Embedded assessment tends to be informal but well organized. As part of their normal teaching, effective teachers observe and listen to students engaged in a task, talk with them, ask probing questions, involve students in whole-class discussions, and examine written and graphic work (VEA 1992). According to the Standards, when teachers use these approaches, they will plan more effective curricula and lessons, develop self-directed learners, report students' progress, and become more reflective about their teaching practices. Taken together, these changes result in improved teaching effectiveness.

The change from the common assessment practices to those just described requires substantial changes in teaching and learning from a testing culture to an assessment culture (Wolf et al. 1991). Broadly defined, embedded assessment using performance tasks requires students to write, read, and solve problems in genuine, rather than artificial, ways. This systemic change in teaching requires a change in thinking by teachers, educational institutions, testing agencies, and parents.

Putting Embedded Assessment to Work

Embedded assessment blurs the lines between teaching and assessment. Many assessment activities become effective teaching activities, and many effective teaching activities also are very useful sources of assessment data. This interrelationship between teaching and assessment is shown in Figure 1. Ideally, one type of assessment task is used for different activities, such as when students read from a variety of sources, view laser disks and video clips, use simple equipment to explore various phenomena, collect data from experiments, or explain phenomena orally, in writing, or with diagrams and pictures. A variety of embedded approaches, with examples of specific tasks given during the topic of sound, are shown in Figure 2. The following are some effective strategies for implementing embedded assessment:

- **Use pretests** consisting of at least five open-ended questions at the beginning of the topic to identify students' personal conceptions, misconceptions, and problems in understanding the topic. In this case, the pretest ascertained students' knowledge and understanding and application of the basic concepts of sound.
- **Ask questions to elicit students' ideas**

Figure 1.

Embedded assessment

- How can I obtain information on students' ideas and reasoning on the topic of instruction?

- What does this information tell me about students' understanding and how they make sense of this topic?

- What action should I take to help students advance their understanding?

and reasoning throughout each lesson to engage students and deepen their understanding about the underlying scientific principles. Acknowledge each student's answers by recording them on the board or by asking other students to comment on the answers. These questions can guide the development of students' understanding as well as keep them on task.

- **Conduct experiments and activities** to enable students to engage in direct experiences so that they can challenge their own ideas and write down their findings, which they can share with their peers.
- **Use individual writing tasks** to provide opportunities for each student to expand his or her personal ideas and reasoning and reconcile them with accepted scientific concepts and processes. The writing tasks can capture students' understanding so the teacher can assess their progress.
- **Use group writing tasks,** such as the production of a booklet describing the main experiments and how these inform the group about the topic of study. In this way, students work together to illustrate each other's understanding of the main concepts on the various parts of the topic. The teacher is then able to make judg-

ments about which students need further directions for study before entering into summative assessments. The quality of the written reports provides the teacher with evidence of students' reconciliation of their personal ideas and the accepted scientific concepts as well as students' initial conceptions about sound and its properties.

- **Have students draw diagrams or create models** that demonstrate their understanding and ability to make sense of scientific principles. These tasks can be done with students working individually or in groups.

How Effective Is Embedded Assessment?

A teaching style focusing on continuous, embedded assessment of students' understanding of key concepts of sound enables them to be involved in fruitful discussions with the teacher and their peers and to be able to write both abbreviated summaries and detailed descriptions about what they have learned. They engage in laboratory activities and view video material that enriches their understanding of concepts and investigative procedures. They have opportunities to respond to questions from, and prepared by, the teacher in a variety of formats, which encourage them to learn and be perceptive about what they had learned.

The culture of this eighth-grade class was that of assessment, as opposed to testing, a culture in which ideas could be explored, discussed, reflected upon, debated, and reflected upon further. Students were guided in developing their understanding of scientific ideas and in reconciling them with their personal experiences. Students were able to find a niche for their contributions to the group, allowing some students to be active in one or more modes of interaction and to be passive in others. As a result, students increased their understanding

of the scientific ideas they were learning, and their motivation, self-esteem, and confidence were enhanced. Teachers became confident about using embedded assessment to improve their teaching. For example, one middle school teacher who worked with us for a few months stated that, since she started using embedded assessment, her students were more motivated, better behaved in class, and achieved higher grades.

The classroom culture supported all students' learning for understanding and application of science (NRC 1996, Rutherford and Ahlgren 1990). National and state goals are manifested in the local school district by concerns for grades on report cards and scores on external tests. Low levels of achievement on the Michigan Educational Assessment Program (MEAP) for the eighth-grade science test by students in this school district ensured that grading was an important end result of the semester's or topic's work. The approach of embedded assessment achieved positive results quickly. For example, 25 percent of students in the class taught by one of the authors were rated "proficient" on the MEAP Science Test compared to 8% of other eighth-grade classes in the school. On this test, students performance was rated as proficient, novice, or not yet novice. These results provide support for the efficacy of including continuous embedded assessment as an integral part of teaching and learning.

The implications from this middle school science classroom study are that it is possible to develop an assessment culture, as opposed to a testing culture, in which the teacher can guide both the design and delivery of instruction using information obtained from a variety of assessment strategies. When students are given the opportunity to express their understanding and reconcile their personal ideas with scientifically accepted ideas, meaningful learning occurs. Moreover, students become more engaged in learning when their teacher gives attention to

Figure 2.
Examples of embedded assessment in the topic of sound

Assessment approach	Examples of embedded assessment tasks	Interpretations of data by the teacher	Next actions by the teacher
Pretests	How does sound travel from one place to another? Explain how your ear helps you hear. What is an echo? How can you make an echo? Can sound travel through anything else except air?	If students give inaccurate or incomplete responses to pretest items it probably indicates incomplete or erroneous understanding of the topic.	Plan instructional activities to help students develop the desired understandings—e.g., have students perform experiments to measure conduction of sound through water, glass, and metal.
Ask questions of students during instruction	What causes sounds to have different pitch?	If students are not able to state or show that frequency of vibration determines pitch, then they have not comprehended an important concept.	Have students work with and report to classmates about vibrating objects such as tuning forks—e.g. clamp a meterstick to a table so that various lengths will vibrate at different frequencies and show different pitch.
Conduct experiments and activities	Make sounds with rubber bands on a sounding board. Make sounds by blowing across bottles with different amounts of water. Write down what you observe and try to explain it.	If students are not able to report observations accurately, and formulate valid explanations using pictures, written sentences and oral descriptions, they probably do not understand fundamental principles of sound-generation.	Have students review hands-on activities and describe observations orally, in writing, and with diagrams. Present anonymous samples of students' work for discussion of quality and correctness of different answers.
Individual writing tasks	Have students write answers to questions such as "Describe three ways that you can change the pitch of a vibrating string."	If students do not relate pitch to length, tension, and size of the string, then they do not understand the relationship.	Give students an additional hands-on experience to measure influences on pitch and then have them summarize their experiences in a written form with accompanying diagrams.
Group writing tasks	How can you demonstrate that sound needs a medium in which to travel?	If students cannot illustrate how an echo occurs, they do not understood the essential concept of reflection of sound.	Have students carry out experiments similar to those described in the pretests.
Drawing diagrams or making models	Draw a diagram to explain how an echo occurs.		Give students opportunities to draw diagrams and make models of sound concepts such as sound propagation, echos, and how the ear functions.

students' ideas and learning and adjusts teaching to nurture their development.

David F. Treagust is a professor of science education at he Curtin University of Technology in Perth, Australia. Roberta Jacobowitz is a teacher at Otto Middle School in Lansing, Michigan. James J. Gallagher is a professor of science education and Joyce Parker is an instructor at Michigan State University in East Lansing, Michigan.

References

Black, P., and D. Wiliam. 1998. Assessment and classroom learning. *Assessment in Education: Principles, Policy and Practice 5* (Special Issue) 1–44.

Champagne, A. B., B. E. Lovitts, and B. J. Calinger, eds. 1990. *Assessment in the service of instruction.* Washington, DC: American Association for the Advancement of Science.

Duschl, R. A., and D. H. Gitomer. 1997. Strategies and challenges to changing the focus of assessment and instruction in science classrooms. *Educational Assessment* 4 (1): 37–73.

Gallagher, J. J. 1993. Secondary science teachers and constructivist practice. In *The practice of constructivism in science education,* ed. K. Tobin, 181–191. Washington, DC: American Association for the Advancement of Science.

National Research Council 1996 (NRC). *National Science Education Standards.* Washington, DC: National Academy Press

Rutherford, J., and A. Ahlgren. 1990. *Science for all Americans.* New York: Oxford University Press.

Shepard, L. A. 2000. The role of assessment in a learning culture. *Educational Researcher* 29 (7): 4–14.

Simpson, M. 1993. Diagnostic assessment and its contribution to pupils' learning. In *Teaching, learning and assessment in science education*, eds. D. Edwards and E. Scanlon. London: Paul Chapman, the Open University.

Virginia Education Association 1992. *Alternative assessment in mathematics and science.* Washington, DC: Office of Educational Research and Innovation.

Wiggins, G. 1998. *Educative assessment.* San Francisco: Jossey-Bass.

Wolf, D., J. Bixby, J. Glenn III, and H. Gardner. 1991. To use their minds well: Investigating new forms of student assessment. In *Review of Research in Education*, ed. G. Grant, 31–74. Washington, DC: American Educational Research Association.

Seamless Assessment

By Mark J. Volkmann and Sandra K. Abell

We all want to know whether our students have learned, but if we wait until the end of a unit to assess understanding, then we lose valuable instructional impact. In this article, we demonstrate how assessment can function throughout an instructional sequence to provide important information about student learning. Using Bybee's (1997, 2002) *5E* model—*Engage, Explore, Explain, Elaborate,* and *Evaluate*—we describe a variety of purposes and strategies for assessing student learning.

This article describes how we link these strategies to each stage of the 5E sequence when teaching preservice teachers a unit about phases of the Moon. Although we taught this unit to preservice teachers, the unit is identical to many units for upper elementary students, so our experiences are applicable to inservice teachers as well.

Embedding Assessment

The 5E model defines a sequence of inquiry-based science instruction that helps students focus on evidence and explanation, both essential features of inquiry (NRC 2000). Each stage implies a unique purpose for assessment:

diagnosing students' incoming ideas, collecting information about students' formative understanding, determining if students can apply their understanding to a new problem, and providing data for summative evaluation. Figure 1 describes the 5E stages and assessment purposes associated with each stage.

Our experience teaching preservice teachers illustrates how assessment can occur throughout a unit of instruction. In our classes, we typically use the Moon investigation to help future teachers think about themselves as science learners and develop their ideas about science teaching. By studying the Moon in depth, preservice teachers gain confidence in their ability to inquire into and understand concepts they will teach to their students. One of the main goals of the unit is for them to understand phases of the Moon in terms of the relative positions of the Earth, the Moon, and the Sun.

Using the 5E instructional approach

- we engage students in studying the Moon;
- students explore by observing the Moon and recording their observations over four weeks;

Figure 1.

A comparison of the 5E model of science instruction (Bybee 2002; National Academy of Sciences 1998) and assessment purposes

Model Phase/Description	Assessment Purpose
Engage • Initiates the learning task • Introduces the major ideas of science in problem situations • Makes connections between past and present learning experiences • Focuses student thinking on the learning outcomes of the upcoming activities • Mentally engages students in the concept to be explored	• To identify students' existing science ideas
Explore • Provides opportunities for students to test their ideas against new experiences and compare with the ideas of their peers and teacher • Provides a common base of experiences in which students actively explore their environment or manipulate materials	• To determine how students are building conceptual understandings
Explain • Provides opportunities for students to develop explanations • Introduces formal language, scientific terms, and content information to make students' previous experiences easier to describe and explain	• For students to demonstrate their current understanding
Elaborate • Applies or extends students' developing concepts in new contexts • Students develop deeper and broader understanding	• For students to demonstrate their ability to apply/transfer their understanding to new contexts
Evaluate • Encourages students to assess their understanding as they apply it to solve problems	• To determine what students learned from the lessons • For students to be metacognitive about their learning

- we help students explain their observations by developing models of the Moon; and
- students elaborate and evaluate their understanding by solving new problems related to the phases of the Moon.

We use assessment throughout the unit to find out what ideas students bring into the investigation, to see how their ideas are developing, and to determine their understanding at the end of the unit. Figure 2 describes the assessment strategies we use throughout the Moon unit. Below, we describe each of these strategies in turn.

Figure 2.
Assessment strategies for the Moon investigation.

5E Phase	Assessment Strategies
Engage	• Moon Explanations Questionnaire
Explore	• Moon Observation Journal • Moon Puzzlers
Explain	• Moon Models
Elaborate	• Thought Experiments • Evaluating Children's Books • Individual Moon Investigation Plans
Evaluate	• Moon Explanations Essay • Moon Investigation Poster Presentation

Incoming Ideas

The phases of the Moon is a difficult concept to understand and misconceptions abound. To determine our students' incoming ideas, we developed a questionnaire based on the most common alternative conceptions about the Moon's phases (see Driver et al. 1994)—that phases of the Moon are caused

- when planets cast a shadow on the Moon;
- when clouds cover part of the Moon;
- when the shadow of the Earth falls on the Moon; or
- when the shadow of the Sun falls on the Moon.

We present these alternatives, as well as the scientifically accurate answer—that the relative positions of the Earth, the Moon, and the Sun create the phases—and ask students to select the explanations that seem most reasonable to them. We also ask them to explain why they think the Moon's appearance changes over time.

We have found that our students enter the Moon investigation with the same set of common misconceptions as found in the research. Few have a solid understanding of the Moon's phases. With knowledge of their incoming ideas in hand, we're ready to move on to the next phase of instruction—guiding students as they form new ideas.

Forming New Ideas

Throughout the Moon study, students keep a journal in which they record their observations (Brandou 1997). We also ask them to describe the patterns they have noticed, make predictions, ask questions, and posit tentative explanations for their observations. When we periodically collect these journals, we learn how students are developing their ideas and where they are having difficulties. The journals suggest next steps in our instruction that will challenge students to think in new ways.

In response to students' formative ideas, we have developed a series of "Moon Puzzlers" (Abell et al. 2002). Moon Puzzlers make explicit what students are struggling to understand by posing thought-provoking questions. We insert the puzzlers into instruction when we judge our students are ready for them.

For example, early in the Moon investigation, students often fail to see the Moon and get frustrated. Moon Puzzler #1 helps them use this experience to think more about their observations: "OK, this is crazy. I go out every night and look for the Moon, but I don't see it. I see the stars, but I don't see the Moon. What suggestions could you give me so that I would be successful in seeing the Moon?"

Typically, students generate such suggestions as

- look at a different place in the sky;
- look at a different time of day; and
- look from a different location.

We help the class plan new observations around these suggestions. Later in the Moon investigation, as students have collected and shared more observations, they are ready for a more difficult puzzler.

Discrepancies often arise as students share their data. Moon Puzzler #2 helps students sort out data that is reasonable and data that is unreasonable:

"1. Someone in my class saw the Moon last night at midnight in the southwest sky. I saw it at 6 p.m., and I swear it was in the southeast. Who is right?

"2. Someone in my class saw the Moon on Sunday and said it was full. I saw the Moon on Monday and it was half full. Could that be? What do you think?"

When students analyze their own data and class data, they typically recognize that Part 1 of the puzzler is possible, but Part 2 could never happen. These puzzlers not only provide information about student thinking, they also help students form new ideas. As student facility with puzzlers increases, they demonstrate they are ready for the next phase.

Demonstrating Understanding

After students have been observing the Moon for several weeks, we ask them to explain the patterns they have seen using a model-building activity (for example, Foster 1996). Students make models of the Earth–Moon–Sun system, act out various phases of the Moon, and discuss their explanations in small groups. Our assessment at this phase of the instructional sequence is structured to find out to what degree students understand the scientific explanation for the Moon's phases.

After they have made and discussed the models, we ask individuals to replicate several Moon phases (for example, full, new, first quarter, waning gibbous) by drawing two-dimensional representations. For each phase, students draw the relative positions of the Earth, the Moon, and the Sun as if they're viewing it looking down on Earth's north pole. In addition, they indicate the direction of the Moon's motion and provide a written description of their drawing.

These drawings and writings provide assessment information about the quality of students' current understanding. These activities also help students clarify their thinking about the Earth–Moon–Sun system. However, at this stage, students are still constructing complete explanations and our instruction and assessment continue.

Applying Knowledge

In the Elaborate phase of the instructional sequence, we change our assessment objective from finding out what students know to seeing how they apply their current understanding to new problems. One way we do this is through thought experiments reminiscent of great scientists such as Galileo and Einstein. Thought experiments—essentially thought-provoking questions for students to explore using the models—enable preservice teachers to think more deeply about the models and test out their applicability in various situations. Students respond to our thought experiments individually or in small groups.

For example, typically, we ask students to use their Earth–Moon–Sun model to explain why lunar and solar eclipses do not appear during each lunar cycle. (Lunar eclipses occur when the Earth blocks sunlight from reaching the Moon—when the Moon is full. Solar eclipses occur when the Moon blocks sunlight from reaching the Earth—when the Moon is new. Because the Moon's orbit is slightly inclined with respect to the plane of the Earth's orbit, we experience full Moons and new Moons regularly, but lunar and solar eclipses rarely.)

Or, we ask students to imagine what the first- and third-quarter Moons would look like in Australia. (The Moon's apparent shape during each phase—except full—appears the opposite to Australians because an observer in the Southern Hemisphere is facing north during viewing the Moon while an observer in the Northern Hemisphere is facing south.)

More Applications

Another application assessment we have used involves evaluating representations of the Moon in children's picture books, which we have often found to be inaccurate. For example, in Crockett Johnson's *Harold and the Purple Crayon* (1981), a young boy named Harold gets lost and searches for his way home. Then he remembers something. "He remembered where his bedroom window was, when there was a moon. It was always right around the Moon."

Preservice teachers who have been studying the Moon for almost a month realize that this cannot be true. They feel confident enough in their own Moon understanding to question that of the author. This in turn helps them feel more prepared to teach the phases of the Moon to their own students someday.

Another way we assess students' application of their current understanding is through asking them to plan individual investigations. Each student chooses to investigate a question that

emerges from observations and discussions. These questions have a special appeal, because they arise out of the student's own curiosity. Examples of questions that students have pursued in the past include the following:

- Does the full Moon decrease in size as it rises from the horizon?
- Does the Moon always set at the same position on the horizon?
- How much time passes from one moonrise to the next?

Our assessment involves examining the quality of their investigation questions (Do the questions require further observation and not merely library study?) and the quality of their investigation plan (Will their plan help them answer their question?).

Determining Learning

Toward the end of the instructional sequence, we need to assess student understanding in a summative manner. This assessment helps both instructors and students see how far their understanding has progressed. Two summative assessment strategies we have used in the Moon investigation are the Moon Explanations Essay and the individual Moon Investigation Poster Presentation.

Students complete these assignments individually and we evaluate their products using a scoring rubric. The rubric for the explanations essay defines levels of understanding about phases of the Moon. The rubric for the poster includes categories for the quality of the question, the methods, the findings, and the presentation.

The Moon Explanations Essay requires students to write a synthesis of what they have learned. Using a series of prompts, we ask students to draw their current understanding of the Earth–Moon–Sun system and explain at least three phases of the Moon using that model. We encourage them to include diagrams

Connecting to the Standards

This article relates to the following National Science Education Standards (NRC 1996):

Assessment Standards
Standard A: Assessments must be consistent with the decisions they are designed to inform.
- Assessments are deliberately designed.
- Assessments have explicitly stated purposes.

Standard C: The technical quality of the data collected is well matched to the decisions and actions taken on the basis of their interpretation.
- Assessment tasks are authentic.
- Students have adequate opportunity to demonstrate their achievements.

Content Standards
Grades K–4
Standard D: Earth and Space Science
- Objects in the sky
- Changes in Earth and sky

Grades 5–8

Standard D: Earth and Space Science
- Earth in the solar system

the question they investigated, data gathered, and an explanation based on the evidence. With the posters exhibited in the classroom, we invite other faculty and students to view them and speak to the investigators. Students receive feedback about their work and recognize that they have become experts about one facet of the Moon.

Deeper Understanding

Assessment should take place at every phase of an instructional unit, serving various purposes across the unit. The mark of a good assessment is that it not only provides information about what students know but also challenges students to develop deeper understanding.

Each of the assessment tools we used to monitor preservice teachers' understanding about the phases of the Moon meets these criteria. We believe that, with a few adjustments, these assessment strategies could be applied to any science content area at any grade level.

Mark J. Volkmann is an associate professor of science education, and Sandra K. Abell is a professor of science education and Director of the Southwestern Bell Science Education Center, both at the University of Missouri—Columbia.

and data from class observations to clarify their explanations. In the essay, we also ask students to compare their incoming explanations on the Moon Explanations Questionnaire to their final explanations. This demonstrates to them—and to us—just how far they have come in their thinking.

We use the poster presentation as a summative assessment of the individual investigations that students undertook during the Elaborate phase. The students design posters to display

Resources

Abell, S., M. George, and M. Martini. 2002. The Moon investigation: Instructional strategies for elementary science methods. *Journal of Science Teacher Education* 13: 85–100.

Brandou, B. 1997. Observing Moon phases. *Science and Children* 34 (8): 19–21, 48.

Bybee, R. W. 1997. *Achieving scientific literacy: From purposes to practices*. Portsmouth, NH: Heinemann.

Bybee, R. W. 2002. Scientific inquiry, student learning, and the science curriculum. In *Learning science and the science of learning*, ed. R.W. Bybee, 25–35. Arlington, VA: NSTA Press.

Driver, R., A. Squire, P. Rushworth, and V. Wood-Robinson. 1994. *Making sense of secondary science: Research into children's ideas*. New York: Routledge.

Foster, G.W. 1996. Look to the Moon. *Science and Children* 34 (3): 30–33.

Johnson, C. 1981. *Harold and the purple crayon.* New York: HarperCollins.

National Academy of Sciences (Working Group on Teaching Evolution). 1998. *Teaching about evolution and the nature of science.* Washington, DC: National Academy Press.

National Research Council (NRC). 1996. *National Science Education Standards.* Washington, DC: National Academy Press.

National Research Council (NRC). 2000. *Inquiry and the National Science Education Standards.* Washington, DC: National Academy Press.

Using Interactive Science Notebooks for Inquiry-Based Science

By Robert Chesbro

Educators know that there is nothing so personally and professionally degrading as the sight of the garbage cans overflowing with discarded student work on the last day of school. I have often asked myself whether we are doing all we can as professional educators to ensure that our students get the most of their education. A garbage can full of tangible examples of student learning seems to do nothing but suggest otherwise.

In my first six years of teaching middle school science I often asked myself questions such as what exactly do my students remember from my science class? How can I get my students to be better learners in general? How can I get students to see the inherent link between emotion, personal connections, and learning? How can I better differentiate assignments to meet the unique developmental needs of a wider base of my middle school science students? How can I get away with using less paper? The answer to my questions came at the beginning of my seventh year when I was introduced to Jocelyn Young's article "Science Interactive Notebooks in the Classroom" (2003). I interpreted her methodology and tailored the notebook concept and setup to my own teaching style and the inquiry-based Carolina *Science and Technology Concepts for Middle Schools* (NSRC 2000) modules used by my district. These modules emphasize the process of focusing, exploring, reflecting, and then applying as a systematic means of students conducting inquiry-based learning, and the interactive science notebook is an excellent way of promoting that model.

Using Interactive Science Notebooks in the Classroom

The interactive science notebook is a perfect opportunity for science educators to encapsulate and promote the most cutting-edge constructivist teaching strategies while simultaneously addressing standards, differentiation of instruction, literacy development, and the maintenance of an organized notebook similar to that of laboratory and field scientists. Students then have a packaged notebook representing all of their learning throughout the year.

The notebook used in my eighth-grade classroom is a bound 200-page composition journal that students purchase at the beginning of the school year. (They also buy separate notebooks for the chemistry and physics portions of the school year.) The notebook is small enough to fit in the pocket of a three-ring binder and is therefore less likely to be lost or misplaced. Moreover, it remains essentially intact, whereas spiral-bound notebooks typically become inaccessible once the spirals are crushed or unraveled. I've found that the notebooks with plastic covers are the most durable and tend not to come apart as easily as the cardboard ones.

Students are asked to bring in a roll of clear tape during the first week of school, and this tends to be enough to use in the classroom throughout the school year. The tape is placed in a plastic box on their classroom tables along with the colored markers, pencils, and sticky notes that I provide. I discourage the use of glue because it can make the pages stick together. Total cost for one box of supplies for a group of four runs on the order of $12 to $15. Having the box in such an accessible place for students allows them to efficiently fold and tape any handouts to the appropriate notebook pages.

When setting up the notebook, students are required to label and date each page based on the assignment or lesson. Handouts can be cut and taped to pages, or taped so they flip up as pages of a clipboard notebook might. Students skip the first page of the notebook so that I can use it to indicate scores for notebook assessments. At the end of the year, a student generates a condensed foldout table of contents and tapes it to that front page. Students cut and tape an assessment rubric (see Figure 1) to the inside cover of the notebook for quick and easy reference for both the student and teacher. The rubric is used for assessments throughout the year, and each point is assessed with a different color marker to show trends in performance from one notebook check to another. I collect the notebooks at the end of each marking period for a 60-point score, and then again as a finished product for a 120-point score. Minor notebook checks along the way may span a few pages and amount to 10-point grades.

The interactive science notebook is broken down into a right-side and left-side page technique in which students create "input" on the right-side pages (lecture notes, lab data, and reading notes, for example) and then process that input in a meaningful and personalized manner on the left-side pages in the form of "output" (Young 2003). Left-side output ranges from the creative arrangement of input information into predesigned or original graphic organizers for visual and spatially adept students (see examples of student output) to acrostics and the 3-2-1 Review, or other countless written summary exercises for language-oriented students. For an acrostic exercise students are encouraged to write a statement about the content of study that starts with the first letter of a word or statement (if the phrase were "Atoms are tiny," then a student might start with "atoms are the building blocks of matter and are indivisible"). I encourage students to use online abbreviations, such as *lol, omg,* and *ttyl,*

Figure 1.
Assessment rubric

Category	10—Poorly done and fragmented	15—Needs improvement	24—Proficient	30—Advanced proficient
Left side: Personal connections	• Does not yet meet proper requirements • Blank pages Red Alert!	• Some processing and personalization • Personalization should be much deeper or more related to concepts • Personalization hard to understand	• Shows basic processing of info • Shows basic personalization of learning • Shows basic personal connections • Personal connections a little hard to understand	• Shows in-depth processing of info • Shows deep personal connections to learning concepts • YOU come through in the personalization!
Category	8—Poorly done and fragmented	12—Needs improvement	16—Proficient	20—Advanced proficient
Right side: Detail of input	• Does not yet show proper requirements • Blank pages Red Alert!	• Right side somewhat detailed • Care and attention to concepts shown with frequent gaps • Some improvement still needed in presentation of data and tables	• Right side fairly detailed • Shows some care and attention with minor gaps • Minor improvement needed in presentation of data and tables	• Right side very detailed • Shows care and attention to concepts • Data are clearly set up in properly constructed data tables
Category	4—Poorly done and fragmented	6—Needs improvement	8—Proficient	10—Advanced proficient
Interactive science notebook-standards: Page numbers, dates, proper placement of work, neatness	Many errors or omissions in the standards (8 or more)	A few errors or omissions in the standards (4–7)	Only minor errors or omissions in the standards (1–3)	• All pages are numbered and dated • All items are taped in their proper place • Work is neat, organized, and legible

Figure 2.
Student handout detailing input and output

Left Side—Output	**Right Side—Input**
This is where you personally connect with the information on the attached right side page	This is where you put incoming information: notes, data, and so on.

On the left side you will:

Date, label, and number each page

Do output exercises, such as:

- Summary techniques
- Word splat
- Alphabet review
- CD label
- 321 reviews
- The thing about…
- First letter first word (acrostic)
- One word/one image summaries
- Synectics
- Graphic organizers
- Tables/graphs
- Flow charts
- Word webs
- Mind maps
- Concept maps
- Diagrams
- Venn diagrams
- Creative stuff
- Pictures/drawings
- Brainstorming/brain dumps
- Poems/limericks/raps/quotes/songs/ cartoons
- Weird and bizarre thoughts/ideas/images
- Outcome sentences
  - I learned…
  - I am surprised…
  - I wonder…
  - I now understand…
  - I rediscovered…
  - I like…
  - I don't like…
  - The important thing about…

On the right side you will:

Date, label, and number each page

Write down information from:

- lectures
- readings
- presentations
- videos
- labs

Resource note: For online graphic organizers try *www.eduplace.com/graphicorganizer.* Print them out and tape them in.

Figure 3.

Student input and output on the topic Development of the Atomic Theory

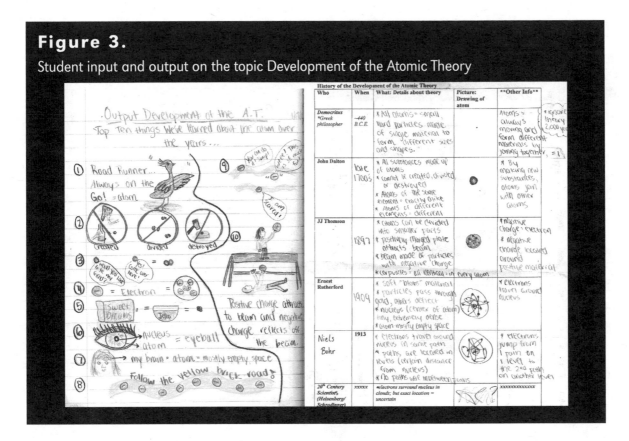

as well as Yoda talk (backward), as long as the statement is scientifically accurate. For a 3-2-1 Review, I might ask students to "list three things you learned, two things you wonder, and one symbol that captures the essence of the topic of study"—for example, density, solubility, or the metric system. Another strategy to the 3-2-1 Review approach is to ask students to invent and respond to their own categories.

In essence, any summary activity that promotes higher-order thinking can be considered an output activity. Students are free to invent their own form of output with teacher approval. Figure 2 is the document my students receive at the beginning of the year that shows the difference between the right side and the left side and shows possible output activities, including a graphic organizer link from which students may print graphic organizer templates.

Figure 3 shows an example of graphically organized input notes on the right-side page on the topic of atomic theory development. Students then generate a Top 10 List for homework output. The output shows personalization of the information read about in class.

Once an inquiry has been completed, students are asked to write a paragraph explaining both the results and possible flaws in the experiment, and then to invent and explain a symbol that represents a relevant concept (Figure 4). Labs are kept in the notebook, with data on the pages or accompanying handouts. All student work is kept in chronological order. With the online version of this article (at *www.nsta.org*) you will find examples of

- input data collected by students for an inquiry investigating the solubility of various substances;
- a teacher-generated graphic template that

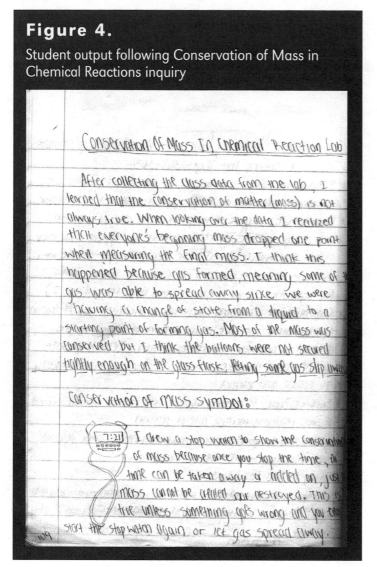

Figure 4.

Student output following Conservation of Mass in Chemical Reactions inquiry

guides students to create output by interpreting the graph and then placing various personalized touches in the additional bubbles;

- a student-generated graphic of output for the topic of States of Matter and Their Characteristics; and
- a double-sided inquiry handout used as input that contains introductory concepts, a student-generated procedure, and all lab data.

One particularly popular form of output that my students enjoy is the CD label. Students read information or collect class notes as input and then create a CD label reflecting what they've learned, inventing the name of a band, album title, and track titles based on the topic.

Whatever the form of output, students are required to show that they "get" the content of the lab or assignment in a way that works for them. This allows students to make deep and resonating connections and allows me to get to know them through their writing when I assess their notebook. I recommend that teachers consistently model student work that accurately shows personalization of content.

Assessing the Interactive Student Notebook

Assessment should vary depending on the style of the teacher. My approach comes in two forms, and I use the rubric for both (Figure 1). Although there is no single way to assess the notebook, it is essential that teachers assess and provide feedback on a regular basis. The first mode of assessment is the periodic notebook check mentioned, in which I will briefly check notebooks in class or collect a class set of notebooks overnight. The periodic notebook check is designed to offer consistent feedback to ensure that students are keeping a tidy notebook with dates and labels, organized notes, and in-depth personalization.

The second mode of assessment is a more holistic student self-evaluation used at the end of the year. Students evaluate and explain the effectiveness of the interactive science notebook as a valid learning tool based on their own notebooks; the final score must then be approved by me. Scores typically fall very close to the score I would assign. For those teachers hesitant to allow self reflection in their classroom, don't worry. Students are typically very honest critics of themselves, and they are the only ones who know the degree to which the interactive science notebook has worked for them.

There are the occasional students who neglect the interactive notebook, usually due to laziness. These students receive the consequent low grades on the notebook checks and are encouraged to stay after school with a student to help get caught up. The notebook is a useful indication to the parents of unmotivated students as it shows the degree to which the student is not performing compared to another student's notebook. Students who struggle with the notebook are offered copies of class notes and an ongoing table of contents. The notebook amounts to about 15% to 20% of the marking period grade. One particularly tricky issue is what to do when students lose a notebook. I ask students to label the cover "If lost, please return to Mr. Chesbro's room: E104" to avoid disaster, but this is not foolproof. Students who do lose theirs are asked to start a new notebook. I have to gauge an appropriate consequence for the student depending on the scenario surrounding the loss.

Conclusion

True to the nature of the interactive science notebook, teachers should practice what they preach and personalize ways in which they implement the notebook as a learning tool in their classrooms. They should treat the recommendations stated here as merely one teacher's approach to a multifaceted classroom tool. I cannot stress enough how important it is that teachers adapt the interactive science notebook to their own teaching styles and elicit student feedback along the way. Regardless of the form it takes in the classroom, the interactive science notebook is an extremely effective constructivist innovation in enhancing general learning through the encouragement of writing across the curriculum, personalization, and metacognition strategies, while simultaneously serving to promote more specific inquiry-based science instruction by which students focus, experiment, reflect, and apply based on their personal connections to learning.

Robert Chesbro is an eighth-grade physical science teacher at Montgomery Upper Middle School in Skillman, New Jersey.

References

National Science Resources Center (NSRC). 2000. *Science and technology concepts for middle schools.* Burlington, NC: Smithsonian/The National Academies.

Young, J. 2003. Science interactive notebooks in the classroom. *Science Scope* 26 (4): 44–7.

Formative Assessment Probes

By Francis Eberle and Page Keeley

Students come into our classrooms with preconceived ideas. The formative assessment probes described here are questions informed by standards (AAAS 1993; NRC 1996) and research on student learning (Driver et al. 1994) that uncover students' ideas and ways of reasoning about common science topics. These probes can be effective tools to help teachers build a bridge between students' initial ideas and scientific ones. In this article, we describe how using two formative assessment probes can help teachers determine the extent to which students make similar connections between developing a concept of matter and a concept of rocks. Both probes require students to consider the properties of size, weight, shape, texture, or form in developing a concept of *matter* or *rock*.

The information uncovered through use of the probes informs instruction and can promote deeper conceptual understanding by helping students solidify an understanding of rocks and matter. These probes used together can help teachers learn whether their students connect the idea that matter comes in different sizes, shapes, textures, and forms and can have different properties while still being considered "matter" with the similar idea that rocks can come in different sizes, shapes, and forms and have different properties while still being considered a "rock." Neither "rocks" nor "matter" are defined by size, shape, texture, or form.

The following classroom snapshots show how these two probes helped a fifth-grade teacher uncover a similar conceptual rule students were using to form initial ideas about rocks as well as matter. Data from the students' ideas were used to design lessons from two different curricular units and help students make similar conceptual connections between physical properties in an Earth science context and physical properties in a physical science (matter) context.

Probing Students' Conceptions: Rock

Students worked through a lesson on rocks and minerals in which they examined rocks with magnifiers and performed various tests to observe their physical properties. The students recorded rock data, such as color, size, weight, hardness, texture, and form. The purpose of this lesson was to develop their measurement and observation skills as they apply to describing physical properties of rocks. The students shared their observations and compared different rock samples. Toward the end of the lesson, the teacher asked, "What is a rock?" Students provided their own definitions: "hard, rough things found on the ground," "heavy things that make up the Earth," and "large chunks made up of minerals." The teacher mentally noted the responses that mentioned weight, size, shape, and texture. She realized that for students to use their observations about the physical properties of rocks for further lessons, they needed to develop a common understanding of what determines whether "rocklike material" is considered to be a rock. Before ending the day's lesson, she decided to use the probe, "Is It a Rock?, Version 1" (Keeley et al. 2007; see Figure 1) to examine students' ideas further.

This particular probe is designed to elicit students' ideas about what determines whether something is called a rock. The probe does not seek a technical definition but rather is designed to reveal whether students believe rock material must be a certain size, shape, or texture to be considered a rock. Rocks come in many sizes, shapes, and textures, ranging from huge boulders to microscopic specks; from rough jagged rocks to smooth, round stones. Rocks can be described by their size and shape, and words like *boulder, cobble, gravel, sand, silt,* and *clay* have specific meanings related to the average size of rock fragments.

The teacher concluded the lesson and collected the students' responses to the probes, explaining that tomorrow they would further explore the idea of "what is a rock?" She was surprised to find that most students' conception of a rock depended on the size, shape,

Figure 1.

Is It a Rock? probe

Earth and Space Science Assessment **Probes** ⟨⟨20⟩⟩

Is It a Rock? (Version 1)

Which things on this list could be rocks? How do you decide if something is a rock? Put a X next to the things you think could be a rock.

___ jagged boulder   ___ smooth boulder

___ small stone   ___ large stone

___ pebble   ___ piece of gravel

___ piece of sand   ___ dust from two stones rubbed together

Explain your thinking. What "rule" or reasoning did you use to decide if something is a rock?

and texture of the rock. For example, many students responded that a piece of sand and the dust from rubbing two stones together were not rocks because they were too small. Some students said a rock had to be jagged. If it was smooth, then it was a stone.

In examining the teacher notes that accompanied the probe, the teacher found that the research summaries on student learning supported what she was finding in her students' ideas. For example, Driver et al. reports, "younger students often intuitively identify rocks through their weight, hardness, color, and jaggedness. Therefore, some students believe that rocks are larger, heavier, and jagged whereas smaller fragments are called stones instead of rocks (1994)." "Students have difficulty with the idea of rock types being a range of sizes such as boulder, gravel, sand, clay. They use these words in ways related to where they are found, rather than seeing them as rocks of different sizes" according to Keeley et al. (2007).

The next day, the teacher posted a list of the tallies of the items on the probe students considered to be "rocks." She asked the students to discuss in small groups their ideas about what determines whether the items on the list are rocks. Following the small-group discussion, the class now agreed that all of the items on the list, except for the piece of sand and dust from rubbing two stones together, could be considered rocks. They now decided that a rock could not be smaller than a piece of gravel and changed some of their ideas to agree that rocks could be different shapes and textures.

The teacher decided to further confront students' ideas with a demonstration involving actual rocks. She picked up a rock the size of a walnut and asked the students if it was a rock. All of the students agreed it was a rock. She asked them if it would still be a rock if she broke it into smaller pieces. The students replied that it would depend on how big the pieces were. The teacher then wrapped the rock in a towel and pounded it with a hammer. When she opened the towel, the rock was broken into smaller pieces. The students examined the pieces and agreed they were all still rocks. The teacher picked up a piece smaller than a pea and asked students if it would still be a rock if she broke this small piece into smaller pieces. The students began to reconsider their ideas and agreed it would be a rock, even if it got down to the size of a piece of sand. However, the students were still undecided about the dust from rubbing stones together. So, the teacher gave groups of students two stones and asked them to rub them together over a piece of white paper. The students observed the dust with magnifiers and discussed whether the dust was still "rock." Some students said it was no longer a rock because it was a powder. Other students argued that it was "rock powder," so it must still be a rock but in powder form. Many of the students changed their initial ideas after now realizing that rocks can be broken down into smaller and smaller pieces and still be rocks because they were made of the same material. They now agreed that size does not matter whether something is a rock. It's what a rock is made up of that matters.

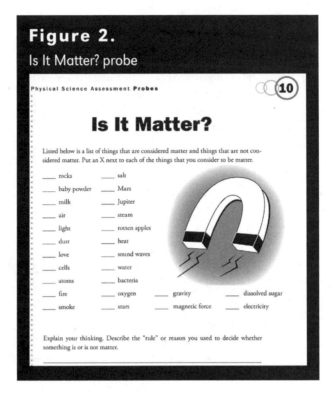

Figure 2.

Is It Matter? probe

Probing Students' Conceptions: Matter

These students lacked an understanding that the formation and composition of a rock is what makes a rock rather than the properties of size or texture of a rock. Several weeks later the teacher began a unit on physical changes in matter and decided to find out if students' ideas about what materials are considered to be matter were related to their initial ideas about what materials are considered to be rocks. Because both the rock unit and the matter unit involved related ideas about the physical properties of shape, size, weight, texture, and form, the teacher decided to probe the students' conception of matter and then try to link their ideas about matter to their prior ideas about rocks. Before beginning the unit on matter, the teacher asked students to complete the "Is It Matter?" probe (Keeley et al. 2005; see Figure 2). This probe is designed to elicit whether students can distinguish between things that are considered matter and things that are not.

The students shared their ideas in small groups and tallied their responses during a whole-class discussion. Again, the teacher noticed that materials on the list that were small, such as powders, or too small to even see, such as air or dissolved sugars, were not considered by many students to be matter. Students used reasons such as "It has to have weight" or "You have to be able to feel or see it." The teacher challenged students' ideas with an observation similar to breaking the rock and involved them in a demonstration and discussion about matter using sugar cubes, sugar granules, magnifiers, a small container of water, and stir sticks. Students observed the sugar cubes and agreed they were matter because you could see and feel them. The teacher asked them to crush the cubes and examine the pieces of sugar. Were the pieces still matter? Some students answered yes, and, when further probed to explain their thinking they said because "I can hold it," "I can see it," "It is hard," and "It takes up space." Others students said it wasn't matter because "It is in pieces" or "It doesn't hold together in one shape."

The teacher then asked if a single granule of sugar is matter. Some students said the granule is matter because they "can see it and it is part of the sugar cube, which is matter." Others said the granule wasn't matter because "It is too small." Then the teacher asked students to think back to the rock unit when they decided whether small pieces of a rock were still rock. Could the rules the students use for determining whether pieces of sugar are matter be similar to the rules used to determine whether pieces of rock were still rock? Now students were beginning to argue that it didn't matter how small something was, it was still matter, just like the small pieces of rock were still rock. It's just their size that changed, not what they were made of.

Next, the teacher showed the students all three forms of sugar again—the cube, sugar granules, and sugar dissolved in water. She asked again if the sugar cube is matter. The students resoundingly agreed it was because "It is solid," and they "can see it." The teacher asked if the sugar cube is the same thing as the sugar granules and the single granule of sugar. The students said the granules and the single granule are the same as the "clumped together" sugar cube so it's still "sugar matter." The teacher then asked them about the sugar dissolved in the water. Some answered it was no longer matter because you couldn't see the sugar. Others argued that the water gets sweeter when you put sugar in it so it must still be matter because it's there, even though you can't see it.

At this point, the teacher noted the different ideas students had about whether something like dissolved sugar could still be matter if you couldn't see it and her students' difficulty in accepting items on the probe like air as matter. She used this information to plan the next day's lesson on "invisible matter," leading students toward developing a particle conception of matter that is not defined by the senses of being able to see or feel matter.

After several more lessons observing and describing various forms of matter and their properties, noting how physical properties can change matter yet it still remains matter, the teacher brought the students back to the connection between the rock and matter unit.

She guided the students in concluding that although a rock's physical properties—such as size, shape, and texture—may change, it doesn't change the rock into something else; it is still a rock. A working definition was provided for them that rocks are one or more hard materials made of a mineral or combination of minerals. They then discussed their ideas about matter, making lists of what is matter and what is not. They discussed sizes of parts of matter, such as molecules in air, as being matter, emphasizing that the size is not a determining characteristic. They developed a working definition of matter as "the stuff things are made of."

Implications for Instruction

Understanding science requires a deeper knowledge than just knowing facts or the names of things. Instruction that focuses on just one learning goal in one context—such as rocks or matter, without connecting the two—can lead to isolated pieces of knowledge that extend similar misconceptions into other topic areas. Students need to be able to attach new ideas to a framework of science knowledge (NRC 2000). Teachers have opportunities to help students connect science topics when they are related to each other. When teachers do not provide opportunities to connect related ideas in science, it is not surprising students are unable to transfer ideas across topics.

As a result of examining students' ideas related to rocks and matter, the following instructional suggestions emerged:

- Provide students many opportunities to collect and examine a variety of rocks and matter and describe, rather than define, them according to their observable properties.
- Be clear with students about the terms and language you use and explain why particular words are being used, such as sand, boulder, gravel, and rock when teaching about rocks.
- Look at a whole cookie, and then break it into smaller parts. Have students decide if the pieces are still "cookie." Then try it with rocks.
- Help students develop operational definitions of rocks and matter, so when they are older they are able to bridge from their operational definition to a scientific one.

Looking at relationships between curricular topics and learning goals can be tricky, but doing so, as appropriate, can help students learn that science is not a set of isolated ideas. Looking for commonalities in students' ideas across contexts can help teachers make connections across curricular units like "Rocks" and "Matter" that are typically

Connecting to the Standards

This article relates to the following National Science Education Standards (NRC 1996).

Science Teaching Standards
Standard C: Teachers of science engage in ongoing assessment of their teaching and of student learning.

Content Standards
Grades 5–8
Standard B: Physical Science
- Properties and changes of properties in matter

Standard D: Earth and Space Science
- Structure of the Earth system

taught separately. Students' prior ideas may not change with just one instructional experience, so persistence, clarification, and repeated emphasis of these connections across topics will provide the opportunities necessary to help students better understand scientific ideas.

Francis Eberle is executive director, and Page Keeley is senior program director, both at the Maine Mathematics and Science Alliance in Augusta, Maine. They are coauthors of the books Uncovering Student Ideas in Science, *Volumes One and Two, available from NSTA Press.*

References

American Association of the Advancement of Science (AAAS). 1993. *Benchmarks for science literacy.* New York: Oxford University Press.

Driver, R., A. Squires, P. Rushworth, and W. Wood-Robinson. 1994. *Making sense of secondary science: Research into children's ideas.* New York: Routledge.

Keeley, P., F. Eberle, and L. Farrin. 2005. *Understanding student ideas in science. Vol 1.* Arlington, VA: NSTA Press.

Keeley, P., F. Eberle, and J. Tugel. 2007. *Understanding student ideas in science. Vol 2.* Arlington, VA: NSTA Press.

National Research Council (NRC). 2000. *How people learn: Brain, mind, experience, and school.* Washington, DC: National Academy Press.

National Research Council (NRC). 1996. *National Science Education Standards.* Washington, DC: National Academy Press.

Assessing Scientific Inquiry

By Erin Peters

Assessing student-led, open-ended scientific inquiry holds a unique problem for classroom teachers because of the diverse skills and content that emerge from student work. This article provides tangible strategies for teachers to assess divergent student-generated inquiry in a manner that is manageable for teachers, informative for students, and that demonstrates measurable academic growth. Using strategies illustrated in this article, teachers can improve inquiry assessment by developing a culture of assessment as information rather than judgment, developing relevant criteria for assessment of scientific thinking, and including vital elements in planning lessons in order to effectively inform instruction through assessment.

Information, Not Judgment

Establishing an environment in which students are not afraid of getting feedback is fundamental in assessing inquiry. In the current atmosphere of standards-based education and assessment, students are often left with the impression that the outcome of assessment is a final evaluation of their work in the form of an irrevocable grade. But assessment's main function is actually to determine the extent of student learning in order to inform future instruction, not to place a judgment on the value of work. Effective inquiry, because of its fluid nature, requires an environment in which students welcome assessment.

To accomplish the massive task of changing the culture of the classroom in terms of assessment, it is helpful for teachers to assign students ways to communicate informally. One way to provide informal assessment in inquiry is to have a two-way journaling activity from the beginning to the end of an inquiry project. This gives students a private way to discuss difficulties and to express their progress. Journals also give teachers a way to provide feedback to students to help guide their work

However, most middle school teachers face a time constraint when journaling with students. One suggestion that makes this assessment technique more manageable is to have students record their concerns and successes with their inquiry once a day from Monday through Thursday. On Friday, students should summarize their concerns and successes for the week, and the teacher can respond. This gives students the chance to reflect on their own work, synthesizes their progress, and condenses the workload for the teacher. Another method to make journaling more manageable is to have students jot down ideas as a group. If a teacher has 100 students and there are four members in each group, this process reduces the number of journals read by the teacher from 100 to 25. Having students jot down ideas as a group helps them to refine their ideas because the group has to collectively express their ideas. The main idea in the two-way journaling is to have students feel comfortable expressing their ideas without the fear of judgment. Establishing an environment in which students feel that they can freely describe their work without fear of failing opens the channels for communication that are necessary in the learning process.

Another way to create an environment in which assessment is not seen as a judgment is to develop methods of peer assessment and self-assessment. During the development of inquiry studies, students in different groups can sit beside each other and discuss their progress as well as their difficulties. This process gives students a chance to summarize their work and to identify any difficulties they may have. As an added bonus, students will often clarify complex issues when they talk out loud about their work. Figure 1 provides some sample questions that students can ask when conducting a peer review. Self-assessments are a way to help students clarify their work to date, and teachers can gather information about students' perceptions of their progress. Figure 2 shows a sample of a student self-assessment instrument. Since students are pursuing divergent topics and processes, it is imperative that they feel free to discuss their learning with others.

Criteria for Assessing Inquiry

Quality student inquiry often results in divergent directions of study within each class, which makes the creation of assessment tools difficult. Another complication of assessing inquiry includes the pursuit of topics for which teachers may not have content expertise. How

can you possibly assess each diverse project fairly? Three concepts that are essential to the construction of scientific knowledge can be used to help with this dilemma: ways of knowing in science, processes of science, and science content. All three concepts are necessary in scientific inquiry, so they should be an integral part of assessment.

Ways of Knowing in Science

Education researchers have identified some aspects of the nature of science that are appropriate for use in the K–12 arena (Abd-El-Khalick et al. 1998; Lederman 1992; McComas 2005). The nature of science includes the ideas that science is durable yet tentative, empirical evidence is required to back up ideas, historical and social factors influence the development of scientific ideas, science is a creative endeavor, science and technology influence each other but are not the same, laws and theories are two different ways of knowing, and habits of mind of science incorporate accurate record keeping and peer review. Aspects of the nature of science, such as the need for empirical evidence and the habits of mind of science, can be assessed in a practical way during student inquiry.

In assessing students' understandings of the need for evidence, teachers should look for student use of empirical evidence in gathering data during inquiry. That is, students should avoid using ambiguous or relative terms such as *colorful* or *big* in describing their observations. Instead students should use precise descriptions like *green, blue, and red* or standard units such as *27 centimeters* so that the descriptions can be understood by others. Another factor in assessing student orientation toward evidence is the ability to back up ideas using empirical evidence. Student work can be reviewed for the extent that each idea is justified by using empirical evidence gathered during the inquiry. A third factor that can be used to assess student inquiry work in terms of evidence is the willingness to change ideas in the face of evidence (Harlen 2007).

Figure 1.

Peer-review sample questions

	Meets expectations	Could use some improvement	Comments (must be filled out by reviewer)
Ways of knowing in science			
Are all ideas backed up with evidence from the inquiry?			
If the group changed its way of thinking about the inquiry, could it explain why? Was there a point in the inquiry where the group got stuck? How did it get over that barrier?			
Did the group go back to improve on their procedures and data? Could the group explain or document how its processes changed as it learned more about the topic?			
Did the group try to find out what scientists already know about the topic? Is there evidence that the group researched what is already known about this topic?			
Processes of science			
Did the group record observations that everyone, even those not involved in the inquiry, could understand?			
Did the group think about other ways to measure in its inquiry?			
Did the group try to predict what might happen in its inquiry?			
Did the group begin with a general question that was testable?			
As the group went through the inquiry, did more questions come out of the study?			
Did the group have a plan for its inquiry that made sense?			
Did the group follow the plan? If not, can it explain why it didn't follow the plan?			
Did the group make decisions about its conclusions that were based on the evidence?			
Are there better ways for the group to communicate ideas, procedures, or results?			
Science content			
Note to teachers: Use local standards to indicate student understanding of content.			

Figure 2.

Self-assessment sample questions

	Meets Expectations	Could use some improvement	Comments (must be filled out by reviewer)
Ways of knowing in science			
Can you connect all of your ideas with evidence found in the inquiry?			
Did you change your mind about the inquiry? Can you document how this happened?			
Would you make any changes in your procedure based on what you know now?			
How much research did you do to find out about your topic?			
Processes of science			
Are your observations as detailed as you can make them?			
Did you use the best tools to make measurements in the inquiry? Did you do research to find other tools that measure the same quantities? Could your data be more precise when you use these other tools?			
How did you know that your question that guided the inquiry was testable?			
Did you think of other questions as you progressed through the inquiry?			
Can you explain why your plan for inquiry was the best one for you?			
Could you communicate your processes, ideas, or results differently?			
Content			
Note to teachers: Use local standards to indicate student understanding of content.			

Often students cling to their preconceived notions even when the evidence gathered during the inquiry refutes their prior ideas.

Habits of mind in science have always been difficult to assess, but identifying important aspects of behavior in science may make this venture more tangible. Three important facets of habits of mind in science consist of the ability to construct meaningful questions, to choose tools that gather consequential data, and to infer from evidence. As students develop original questions for their initial inquiry, teachers can determine if students know the outcome of the inquiry by assessing prior knowledge. If students are aware of the outcome, they have not generated a meaningful question and the time spent on the inquiry could be used in more fruitful pursuits.

Student choice of tools can be assessed for their appropriateness in gathering the most precise and reliable data. For example, in an inquiry unit, students may choose to use a meterstick to measure the thickness of a dime although a Vernier caliper is available. Teachers can provide feedback to students to introduce the use of a Vernier caliper in order to measure small distances.

Habits of mind can also be assessed in terms of students' ability to infer from evidence. Students can demonstrate their ability to engage scientific habits of mind by explaining all possible inferences that can be made about their study and tightly linking their inferences to the evidence found in the inquiry. Assessing scientific habits of mind in three distinct forms—forming meaningful questions, choosing appropriate tools, and inferring from evidence—gives both teachers and students a solid framework.

Peer review plays a large part in the development of scientific ideas, so it is important that it has a role in the assessment of inquiry. Two factors that can be assessed in peer review are students' ability to communicate scientific ideas effectively to other groups, and the ability to look at other projects critically. Often students are afraid of hurting each other's feelings by making corrections on peer work, so teachers can provide students with assessment tools (such as the one described in Figure 1) to ensure suitable communication between peer groups.

Processes of Science

Some of the processes of science that can be assessed are observing, explaining, predicting, formulating questions, measuring, planning investigations, conducting investigations, and interpreting evidence. Not all processes are appropriate for all science inquiries, so teachers should choose which processes are useful for the particular inquiry unit students choose to follow. For example, if students are examining the food choices of mealworms, observation may be more useful than measurement in describing the results. Assessors of the inquiry unit could comment on the amount of detail that goes into the process of observing and make appropriate suggestions.

Science Content

Of course, content that is constructed during the inquiry unit is important to assess. Teachers can gauge their assessment of content in terms of the breadth and depth of content that is constructed during the unit. For example, if students are investigating the types of rocks that are found in the schoolyard, the breadth of the information can be measured in terms of completeness of the accounting of rocks. The depth of information can be assessed in terms of the research that goes into describing the rocks, identifying the rock formations, and describing the possible origin of the rocks. Helpful descriptions of core content information can be found in the *National Science Education Standards* (NRC 1996) or the *Benchmarks for Science Literacy* (AAAS 1993). Figure 3 presents a journaling tool that illustrates the use of the three major concepts—ways of knowing in science, processes of science, and science content—in assessing inquiry work.

Figure 3.

Assessment journal

	Date #1		Date #2		Date #3	
	Teacher comments	Student comments	Teacher comments	Student comments	Teacher comments	Student comments
Ways of knowing in science • Respect for evidence • Willingness to change ideas in the face of evidence • Willingness to critically review procedures, observations, and inferences • Willingness to use available knowledge						
Processes of science • Observing • Explaining • Predicting • Formulating questions • Planning and conducting investigations • Interpreting evidence • Communicating						
Science content (example) • Sediments of sand and smaller particles (sometimes containing the remains of organisms) are gradually buried and are cemented together by dissolved minerals to form solid rock again.						

Effectively Informing Instruction

Teachers can set the stage for effective assessment in inquiry by planning lessons that include three factors: (1) providing mechanisms to allow students to show what they know, (2) building multiple types of assessment into inquiry units, and (3) planning assessments for multiple audiences. Students should be given open-ended assignments so that teachers have complete and accurate information about students' conceptions and misconceptions. Since forced-choice assessments, such as multiple choice or fill in the blank, do not allow students to express their understandings, multiple types of assessments, such as oral reports, diagrams, or role playing, can be used to help students find a variety of ways to express their ideas effectively to a variety of audiences.

Let Students Show What They Know

Meaningful learning goals that can have more than one answer and open-ended questioning techniques are two characteristics that allow students to show what they know. It is difficult to aspire to deep student understanding of concepts if learning goals in inquiry units are superficial. Meaningful learning goals—for example, essential understandings (Wiggins and McTighe 1998)—provide students the opportunity to explore and connect new knowledge with prior knowledge. A mixture of open-ended communication processes such as written portfolios, oral presentations, flowcharts of ideas, and student-kept records help teachers to ascertain what knowledge students value and what they accurately comprehend.

Multiple Types of Assessment

Knowledge is difficult to assess accurately if it is not communicated well. Students can demonstrate their strengths and weaknesses in communication styles when offered multiple forms of assessment, such as written, oral, and diagrammatic. A variety of assessment types offers students a chance to write their understandings, speak about their understandings, and represent their understandings using symbols. Examples of student work products that can be assessed are as varied as student-kept records, portfolios, journals, rubrics, anecdotal notes, student-teacher conferences, and student-student conferences. Figure 4 shows some examples of how these products can be used to elicit student communication of their knowledge.

Frequent Feedback Loops

Students who receive frequent feedback about their ideas during the inquiry process tend to develop more complete understandings of science (Donovan and Bransford 2005). Time constraints make it difficult, however, for a teacher to provide frequent feedback to students. One solution to this problem is to assign students the task of presenting the information to a variety of audiences, using tools such as peer assessment and self-assessment. Peer feedback can give students multidimensional perspectives on work, which will lead to increased quality in student knowledge. Frequent peer assessment and self-assessment can result in the perception that assessment is not a judgment of students, but rather a method of providing important information to improve their work, resulting in increased understanding.

Assessment is important in guiding open-ended inquiry in productive directions. Frequent two-way communication of knowledge and skills, otherwise known as content and process, learned through inquiry is necessary in the construction of valid conceptions about phenomena. By developing a culture of assessment as information, planning lessons that allow open-ended communication, and establishing tangible criteria for scientific thinking, teachers can be well informed about student growth and can demonstrate measurable academic achievement.

Figure 4.

Student work products

Student products	Types of communication	How they could be used in assessment
Student-kept records	Written and diagrammatic	Teachers can establish benchmarks to be reached at certain points in the inquiry. When students reach a benchmark, teachers read the student-kept records of the inquiry and provide feedback on completeness of ideas, misunderstandings, scientific processes, and further study.
Portfolios	Written and diagrammatic	Instead of assessing the portfolio of work at the end of the project, teachers could assess the products as they are chosen for the portfolio. At the end of the project, teachers look at the totality of the work in the portfolio for an additional assessment of work.
Journals	Written	Students can write to teachers about the progression of learning goals, and teachers can comment on their progress and offer suggestions for additional study.
Rubrics	Written	Students can create their own rubrics to show what they consider to be quality work.
Anecdotal notes	Written	Teachers can observe learning in lab groups and write field notes on student progress, which are shared with students individually to enhance the learning experience in inquiry.
Student-teacher conferences	Oral	Teachers can interview students in a one-on-one setting using the three indicators for inquiry: ways of knowing in science, processes of science, and science content. The assessment journal in Figure 3 can be adapted for this type of assessment.
Student-student conferences	Oral	Students can interview students from other groups in a one-on-one setting using the three indicators for inquiry: ways of knowing in science, processes of science, and science content. The assessment journal in Figure 3 can be adapted for this type of assessment.

Erin Peters is an assistant professor of education at George Mason University in Fairfax, Virginia.

References

Abd-El-Khalick, F., R. L. Bell, and N. G. Lederman. 1998. The nature of science and instructional practice: Making the unnatural natural. *Science Education* 82 (4): 417–36.

American Association for the Advancement of Science (AAAS). 1993. *Benchmarks for science literacy.* New York: Oxford University Press.

Donovan, M. S., and J. D. Bransford, eds. 2005. *How students learn: Science in the classroom.* Washington, DC: National Academies Press.

Harlen, W. 2007. Assessment in the inquiry classroom. In *Foundations. Inquiry: Thoughts, views, and strategies for the K–5 classroom.* National Science Foundation. *www.nsf.gov/pubs/2000/nsf99148/ch_11.htm.*

Lederman, N. G. 1992. Students' and teachers' conceptions about the nature of science: A review of the research. *Journal of Research in Science Teaching* 29: 331–59.

McComas, W. F. 2005. Seeking NOS standards: What content consensus exists in popular books on the nature of science. Paper presented at the meeting of the National Association for Research in Science Teaching, Dallas, TX.

National Research Council (NRC). 1996. *National Science Education Standards.* Washington, DC: National Academy Press.

Wiggins, G., and J. McTighe. 1998. *Understanding by design.* Alexandria, VA: Association for Supervision and Curriculum Development.

Cartoons— An Alternative Learning Assessment

By Youngjin Song, Misook Heo, Larry Krumenaker, and Deborah Tippins

Wait! Before you grab that comic book out of some student's hands, maybe you should ask what the comic book does for the student that you haven't done. Perhaps you haven't tried to teach with some humorous cartoons? Nah, we all try that; many teachers are stand-up comedians in training. But have you thought about using cartoons and comics for assessing your students' science learning?

Science education reform documents in the United States, such as the *National Science Education Standards* (NRC 1996), envision that all students learn science with understanding. How do we, as science teachers, know that our students understand the science presented in the classroom? Our own teaching experience as well as research on science learning has provided evidence that assessment of student learning

is much more than just giving paper-and-pencil tests and grades. To fully understand student learning, we science teachers need to know the ideas that students bring into the classroom. Plus, good assessment calls for ongoing evaluation of students' progress and difficulties with learning on an everyday basis.

This approach to assessment emphasizes the inclusion of alternatives to traditional paper-and-pencil evaluations, that is, "alternative assessments." By using these, science teachers can obtain information about students' strengths and weaknesses in science while the learning is taking place. Alternative assessments can include portfolios, journals, concept maps, oral interviews, and so on. Cartoons are one tool that has been used successfully as a means of assessing student learning in science (Perales-Palacios and Vilchez-Gonzalez 2005). They

Figure 1.
Concept cartoon

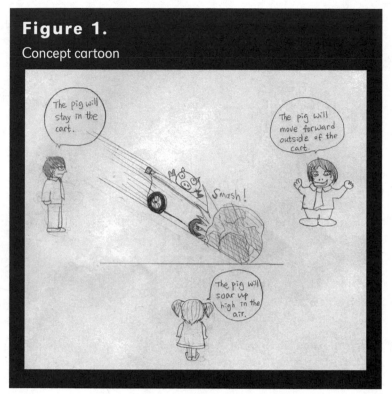

can be used at the beginning, middle, and end of a unit to assess students' prior knowledge and new learning. Recognizing the value of cartoons, we developed strategies for using them as an alternative assessment tool in middle school science.

We chose a unit on force and motion during which to use cartoons because research has shown that students come into a physical science class with preconceived notions about the topics, and have difficulties understanding these concepts (Wandersee et al. 1994). Alternative assessment strategies using cartoons can help science teachers to assess students' ideas, old and new, and difficulties they experience as they learn the force and motion concepts.

Assessing the Ideas Students Bring to the Classroom

In order to assess what students already know about a specific concept, we use a "concept cartoon," a term first coined by Naylor and Keogh (1999), to refer to a cartoon-style format that includes competing views or explanations of a specific phenomenon. To develop a concept cartoon, the teacher selects a science concept that will be explored in depth and for which he or she would like to see students' preexisting ideas. Then, the teacher draws or finds a cartoon that includes an everyday situation. To either of these, the teacher now adds several alternatives that depict students' common conceptual difficulties or confusions relevant to that concept. Teachers can decide what kinds of situations should be included in the cartoon based on their own experiences or the research literature. The cartoon should include three or more different ideas that students could have about the situation.

For example, Figure 1 is representative of a concept cartoon in our selected context. This cartoon illustrates the concept of inertia. When the cart hits the rock, the pig is supposed to keep moving in the same direction of the moving cart according to Newton's first law of motion, often referred to as the law of inertia. When a concept cartoon is used as a kind of pretest, students are given a copy of the artwork at the beginning of the lesson. Three or four students work together in a group and for a few minutes discuss each viewpoint represented in the cartoon until team members reach a consensus about a particular position. Once each group has arrived at a consensus, they take a minute to share the idea they have selected and explain their choice using a scientific rationale. After each group presentation, all students should be provided time to ask questions of the presenting team members.

Once this is completed, explain the scientific ideas contained in the cartoon to students. According to Newton's first law of motion, inertia is defined as the tendency of objects to resist changes in their state of motion; that is, an object in motion tends to stay in motion and an object at rest tends to stay at rest when no force is exerted on it. When students see this cartoon, however, different groups will express different viewpoints based on their prior knowledge and preconceptions. Through the above process, students should become aware of their own ideas, practice justifying their claims, consider alternative explanations, and finally adopt the scientific concept. In addition, while preparing the cartoon, we had the time to reflect on our own conceptions and became more familiar with common alternative conceptions our students would be likely to hold.

Assessing Students' Progress and Difficulties

Cartoons are especially effective in engaging students in scientific dialogue. Even the quietest students in class can be motivated to talk when a familiar cartoon character becomes the protagonist of their dialogue. Active dialogue facilitates student understanding of scientific concepts and also provides a context for teachers to recognize student progress and learning.

A second way of using cartoons is more open than the concept cartoon. In this approach, science teachers use a *cartoon cut,* that is, one image selected from a cartoon strip, comic book, TV animation, or other similar artwork. To have students articulate their thinking about a specific concept, teachers present a cartoon cut that contains a situation in which one or more scientific concepts are applied or misapplied. The difference between a concept cartoon and a cartoon cut is that a cartoon cut does not provide alternative viewpoints about a specific science concept within the cartoon. Rather, students have to find a "hidden" science concept. Furthermore, each group has to come up with its own scientific explanation about the situation instead of supporting one established viewpoint.

For example, many middle school students are likely to be familiar with the Warner Broth-ers' animations of Road Runner and Wile E. Coyote. In the animation, the coyote often falls faster than other objects so that he gets into trouble when hit by other falling objects. Students who understand free-fall motion in relation to Newton's second law can argue that the situation is nonscientific because all free-falling objects, which are falling under the sole influence of gravity, fall with the same acceleration regardless of their mass.

This example can be used to assess student learning while the concept of free fall is being taught. After having students watch a six-minute animation of Road Runner and Wile E. Coyote (see Internet for samples), the teacher can provide the cartoon cut or ask students to reflect on a situation that contradicts the scientific concepts illustrated in the film clip. Then, students can be asked to develop a scientific claim and list evidence to argue for and support their idea. In such contexts, the teacher has the opportunity to ascertain students' levels of understanding in relation to the concept, and students have the opportunity to reflect on their own understandings and practice communicating their scientific ideas.

One of the advantages of using a cartoon cut, especially a cut familiar to middle school students, is that it is effective in motivating ongoing discussion. The cartoon cut can provide teachers with information about where students are located in their learning and how the unit should progress. Furthermore, the cartoon cut can be used to assess how well students observe, gather facts, and then hypothesize which "laws of nature" are found in this cartoon universe and how they may or may not differ from ours.

Assessing Students' Application of Science to Everyday Life

Cartoons can also be used to assess students' learning outcomes and their ability to apply a science concept to everyday situations. We developed a cartoon project that provides students with an opportunity to draw cartoon strips and create stories. Figure 2 outlines a sample of a cartoon project guide. Teachers may adapt it to any science unit. The situation, which should contradict one of the science concepts they have learned, can come from students' lives or other cartoons, such as TV animations or favorite comic books. The situation must violate the principles underlying the concept. Students are asked to illustrate the situation in class by taking or copying a picture or drawing the scenario. In the classroom, students share their examples in small groups, discuss the situations, find plausible alternative situations, and finally make a cartoon strip and write an underlying story that corrects the flawed science of the original situation. All students' cartoon strips are exhibited, and their peers are asked to write an opinion about each cartoon strip in terms of the scientific plausibility and interest of the ideas. Each student's peer evaluation is useful as a supplemental means to further understand the writer's level of understanding. The entire process is assessed by a summative assessment rubric.

Figure 3 is a drawing done by a group of students as part of a cartoon project in a force-and-motion unit. Students found the situation in a TV animation in which two animals (the pursuer and the pursued) suddenly stopped on the edge of a cliff. Students thought that this situation contradicted the law of inertia since the animals could not stop immediately. Therefore, they drew a cartoon strip in which two animals fell down rather than halted, with a humorous ending.

In addition, the rubric in Figure 4 can be used to evaluate the entire process of a cartoon project in a force-and-motion unit, such as assessing students' ideas about force-and-motion concepts, the completeness of their work, and their creativity. Each student's written story can also be used as a supplemental assessment to further understand the student's conceptions.

Figure 2.
Cartoon-project guide

The cartoon project is designed to apply the scientific concepts to your everyday life. In this project you will create your own cartoon strip and story.

Procedure

1. Find a situation that contradicts the science concepts that you have learned. Your sources can be anything that you could observe, such as a real-life situation, TV animations, favorite comic books, and so forth. Make sure you cite the source.
2. Bring that situation into the classroom by taking a picture of it, copying it, or drawing the scenario.
3. In your group, share and discuss your situation and find alternative situations that match with scientific conceptions.
4. Based on your group's discussion, make a cartoon strip with an interesting story as a group. You can either choose one particular situation and add more cuts or use all the situations that your group members bring and mix them. When you make a story, use the scientific terms that you have learned.
5. After making your cartoon strip, tape it to the wall. Then, write your opinion about the other groups' work based on two criteria: scientific plausibility and interest of the ideas.

Teachers can modify this rubric for any science unit.

Assessment
Using cartoons as a summative assessment tool in the project is effective in many aspects. First,

Figure 3.
Students' sample work

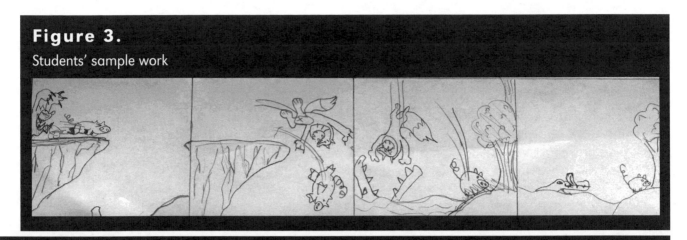

Figure 4.
Rubric for a cartoon project

	Outstanding	Good	Needs more work
Cartoon strip and story			
Use of scientific terms	Student often and correctly uses scientific vocabulary.	Student correctly uses a couple of scientific terms.	Student never uses or misuses scientific terms.
Understanding of Newton's laws of motion	Student shows evidence of clearly understanding Newton's laws of motion.	Student shows evidence of partially understanding Newton's laws of motion.	Student shows little evidence of understanding Newton's laws of motion.
Writing skill	Student organizes the story well and explains the situation clearly.	Student explains the situation clearly.	Student misses some parts necessary for the communication of the story.
Completeness	Student elaborates the drawing and finishes it.	Student creates a story but does not finish the drawing.	Student does not finish the drawing or the story.
Creativity	Student's ideas are sophisticated, humorous, and original.	Student's ideas are humorous and original.	Student's ideas are not original.
Peer evaluation			
Completeness	Student completes all the other groups' evaluations.	Student completes all but one or two groups' evaluations.	Student completes evaluations for less than half the groups.
Use of criteria	Student evaluates peers' products in terms of scientific plausibility and interest to others.	Student evaluates in terms of scientific plausibility.	Student evaluates in terms of interest to others or based only on the drawings.

it is relevant to students' interests. Second, it promotes students' skills of observation, establishment of hypotheses, and inductive thinking. Third, it enhances students' abilities to apply scientific knowledge to their real lives (who can deny that TV animations and comic books are a part of children's lives?). Fourth, it stimulates students' curiosity, creativity, and desire to express themselves by having their ideas represented in the form of interesting drawings and comic stories. Finally it offers an opportunity for teachers to assess student understanding in an authentic way.

Concluding Thoughts

We have introduced three ways of using cartoons as an alternative assessment tool in middle school science classrooms: assessing students' prior conceptions, assessing students' progress and difficulties with learning, and assessing students' learning outcomes. Using cartoons in a middle school is compatible with several characteristics of young adolescents (Forte and Schurr 1993). They are curious about the world around them, so they need varied situations for exploration. Young middle school students are more likely to be agents of their learning if they can use a familiar medium. Active rather than passive learning activities are preferred, so hands-on learning experiences are necessary. Students also need opportunities to express their creativity.

Cartoon strategies for assessment are useful for teachers as well. Students' abilities to discuss, draw, and write their own cartoons provide science teachers with a more complete picture of how their students understand scientific ideas. Besides assessment, these approaches can function as a powerful learning tool for students to interpret and synthesize scientific knowledge and to apply what they know. Using cartoons is much more exciting than simply providing facts. Though our examples involve a force-and-motion unit, we feel

sure other areas of science can be assessed in this same way.

Youngjin Song is a doctoral student in the science education program in the Department of Mathematics and Science Education, Misook Heo is a doctoral student in the gifted and creative education proam, Larry Krumenaker is a doctoral student in the science education program in the Department of Mathematics and Science Education, and Deborah Tippins is a professor in the department of Mathematics and Science at the University of Georgia in Athens.

References

Forte, I., and S. Schurr. 1993. *The definitive middle school guide: A handbook for success.* Nashville, TN: Incentive Publications.

National Research Council (NRC). 1996. *National Science Education Standards.* Washington, DC: National Academy Press.

Naylor, S., and B. Keogh. 1999. Constructivism in classroom: Theory and practice. *Journal of Science Teacher Education* 10 (2): 93–106.

Perales-Palacios, F. J., and J. M. Vilchez-Gonzalez. 2005. The teaching of physics and cartoons: Can they be interrelated in secondary education? *International Journal of Science Education* 27 (14): 1647–70.

Wandersee, J., J. Mintzes, and J. Novak. 1994. Research on alternative conceptions in science. In *Handbook of research on science teaching and learning,* ed. D.L. Gabel. New York: Macmillan.

Resources

Cary, S. 2004. *Going graphic: Comics at work in the multilingual classroom.* Portsmouth, NH: Heinemann.

Gonick, L. 1991. *The cartoon guide to physics.* New York: HarperCollins.

Internet

Concept Cartoons
www.conceptcartoons.com/index_flash.html
Paul Hewitt's Conceptual Physics media
www.conceptualphysics.com/books.shtml
Video clips featuring Wile E. Coyote
www.youtube.com (Search for Wile E. Coyote.)

Copyright Concerns

Even if it doesn't explicitly say so, every creative work, including cartoons, is copyrighted. This doesn't mean, though, that you can look but not touch. Guidelines for "fair use" in educational venues are found in the U.S. Copyright Office's *Circular 21,* "Reproduction of Copyrighted Works by Educators and Librarians" *(www.copyright.gov/circs/circ21.pdf).*

Briefly, teachers may make multiple copies for classroom use. No more than one copy per student. Usage must be at the "instance and inspiration of a single teacher" and when the time frame doesn't allow enough time for asking permission. Use it only for one course in the school and do this kind of copying no more than nine instances per class, per term (current news publications such as newspapers can be used more often). "Consumables" can't be copied. Don't use the cartoon every term; if you plan to, write for permission before your next usage. Higher authority cannot compel you to use it. Copying can't be substituted for buying the original resource, and you can make copies only from legally acquired originals.

As for video clips, teachers may use these materials in the classroom without restrictions of length, percentage, or multiple use. The material must be legitimately acquired (a legal copy). It must be used in a classroom or similar place "dedicated to face-to-face instruction" and is not for use as entertainment or reward. The use should be instructional. The place should be a nonprofit educational institution. You should check with your own local media committee for its policies as well.

Students have slightly more liberal guidelines than teachers; they may incorporate portions of copyrighted materials when producing projects for specific courses. The usage limits for them are no more than 5 images from one artist and no more than 10% or 15 images from a collection, whichever is less. So if a student photocopies a cartoon from one of his or her books to show you, it's apparently OK. Students must cite their sources.

Some of the above is derived from the Library Services copyright page at the University of Maryland University College *(www.umuc.edu/library/copy.shtml).*

Finally, there is no prohibition on displaying the original illustration in front of the class, on a document camera, Elmo, or opaque projector and adding your alternative choices for the cartoon cut on your own separate paper, blackboard, or PowerPoint slide. And nothing stops you from taking inspiration and doing your own cartoons with your own characters.

—*Larry Krumenaker*

Making Time for Science Talk

By Mark J. Gagnon and Sandra K. Abell

"A friend of mine who teaches fifth grade claims that discussion in science is key for her students' learning. I've tried discussion with my third graders, but it takes up a lot of time, and I don't think they get that much out of reporting what they found to each other. Am I missing something about the role of talking in science class?"

Do Elementary Students Benefit From Classroom Talk?

Cognitive scientists (Donovan and Bransford 2005) conclude that when teachers "simply give students the knowledge to incorporate, the practice and skill development of doing one's own mental search is shortchanged" (p. 579), but when students engage in classroom talk, they "become better at monitoring and questioning their own thinking" (p. 577). Science education researchers claim that elementary students have the ability to use science talk to explain, clarify, and justify what they have learned. In a study of British 10- and 11-year-olds, Sorsby (1999) found that students used the strategies of clarifying, reconciling, and persuading others during discussions. Furthermore, students use their everyday language to

help them reason and make sense of science. In a study of a sixth-grade urban, multiage, bilingual classroom, Warren et al. (2001) described how the "science circle" was structured to allow students to ask questions, challenge each other, ask for clarification, tell stories, and even joke. The students' everyday language was a deep intellectual resource that helped them to argue, categorize, organize, and theorize about science phenomena. However, not all classroom science talk leads to such results.

What Kind of "Talk" Are We Talking About?

Researchers who study science talk find that most classroom discussions limit students' opportunities for sense making. Carlsen (1992) found that the structure of classroom science

183

talk commonly followed "sequences of Initiation (usually a teacher question), Response (usually a student answer), and Evaluation (explicit feedback concerning the student's answer)" (p. 17). Lemke (1990) called this pattern *triadic dialogue* and asserted that this typical classroom structure is used to maintain control, not to help students generate science understanding. This "authoritative" approach (Mortimer 1998) encourages students to guess what the teacher is thinking, not to think on their own. Yet science discussions, if enacted differently, can help students learn science. Wertsch and Toma (1995) analyzed the kinds of talk in a Japanese fifth-grade classroom. They found that some talk served the authoritative function of conveying information, while "dialogic" talk helped students generate meaning.

How Can Dialogue Help Students Think About Science?

According to Lemke (1990), "True dialogue occurs when teachers ask questions to which they do not presume to already know the 'correct answer'" (p. 55). In dialogic science discussions, the students generate meaning from the classroom talk, rather than merely recite or report. Dialogic discussion is characterized by student spontaneity—comparing, expanding, and revising the ideas of others; and offering tentative explanations. Gallas (1995) found that her first and second graders could propose, support, expand, and revise their science theories, and, in doing so, generate new meanings. Gee (1997) described types of sense-making discussion found in a second-grade classroom where students designed and carried out investigations about plants. For example, in *design and discovery debate*, students discussed the success of the components of their investigations. In *anomaly talk*, students recognized unexpected outcomes. *Explaining talk,* the deepest kind of sense-making discussion, occurred when students interpreted their data through dialogue

with each other. Such dialogue can occur when teachers make time and space for it, in the form of "science talks" (Gallas 1995), "scientists meetings" (Reardon 1993), or "science circles" (Warren et al. 2001).

How Can Teachers Structure and Facilitate Scientific Discussions?

Elementary classroom teacher researchers Karen Gallas (1995) and Jean Reardon (1993) found that classroom science talk is a rich source of student thinking. Yet guiding dialogic discussions can be challenging for teachers. Here are some helpful strategies to get started on creating a classroom in which science talk is valued and practiced (see also Gibbons 2002):

- Hold discussions following a shared science exploration.
- Ask open-ended questions that require thoughtful discussion.
- Give students time to think about a topic by assigning a discussion topic for after recess or the next day.
- Provide discussion rules, including directions on how to listen.
- Ask students to discuss their ideas in teams before opening discussion to the entire class.
- Structure discussions so that all students have the opportunity to participate.
- Provide scaffolding for student talk by asking for clarification, probing for more information, and modeling science talk for the speaker.
- Instead of playing the role of evaluator after student responses, listen and wait for other students to respond.

Mark J. Gagnon has taught elementary and middle school science and worked with teachers in science professional development settings. He is a doctoral student in science education at the University of Missouri-Columbia. Sandra K. Abell is Curators' Professor of Science Education at the University of Missouri-Columbia (MU) where she directs the MU Science Education Center.

References

Carlsen, W. S. 1992. Closing down the conversation: Discouraging student talk on unfamiliar science content. *Journal of Classroom Interaction* 27 (2): 15–21.

Donovan, M. S., and J. D. Bransford. 2005. *How students learn: Science in the classroom.* Washington, DC: National Academy Press.

Gallas, K. 1995. *Talking their way into science.* New York: Teachers College Press.

Gee, J. P. 1997. Science talk: Language and knowledge in classroom discussion. Paper presented at the National Association for Research in Science Teaching, Chicago, IL.

Gibbons, P. 2002. *Scaffolding language, scaffolding learning: Teaching second language learners in the mainstream classroom.* Portsmouth, NH: Heinemann.

Lemke, J. 1990. *Talking science: Language, learning, and values.* Norwood, NJ: Ablex.

Mortimer, E. F. 1998. Multivoicedness and univocality in classroom discourse: An example from theory of matter. *International Journal of Science Education* 20 (1): 67–82.

Reardon, J. 1993. Developing a community of scientists. In *Science workshop: A whole language approach,* ed. W. Saul, 631–645. Portsmouth, NH: Heinemann.

Sorsby, B. 1999. The child's world and the scientist's world: Can argumentation help to bridge the culture gap? Paper presented at the Fifth International History, Philosophy, and Science Teaching Conference. Como, Italy.

Warren, B., C. Ballenger, M. Ogonowski, A. S. Rosebery, and J. Hudicourt-Barnes. 2001. Rethinking diversity in learning science: The logic of everyday sense-making. *Journal of Research in Science Teaching* 38 (5): 529–552.

Wertsch, J. V., and C. Toma. 1995. Discourse and learning in a classroom: A sociocultural approach. In *Constructivism in education,* eds. L. P. Steffe, and J. Gale, 159–174. Hillsdale, NJ: Lawrence Erlbaum.

Evidence Helps the KWL Get a KLEW

By Kimber Hershberger, Carla Zembal-Saul, and Mary L. Starr

Many teachers use Know-Want to know-Learn (KWL) charts and variations of them when teaching science to access students' knowledge on a particular topic and help students organize what they are learning during a science lesson or unit. We (a third-grade teacher, a university professor, and a professional development specialist) developed another variation—the Know-Learning-Evidence-Wonder (KLEW) chart—to add to the list. The idea for the modification arose from our observation that many teachers dismiss inquiry as impractical, interpreting science inquiry as free inquiry, a time in which children pursue questions of their choosing and conduct investigations over extended periods of time that is in short supply in elementary classrooms.

We wanted to change that perception and to encourage science inquiry of all kinds (long-term, short-term, open, and guided) in the classroom by highlighting the essential features of inquiry. And, because of the prevalence and popularity of KWL charts in elementary

instruction, it seemed like a reasonable and nonthreatening place to start.

Our adaptation differs from the traditional KWL chart because it emphasizes direct observation and using evidence to support what is observed, and it also encourages students to conduct further investigations based on what they observe. These inclusions help the KLEW chart align with the National Science Education Standards, which specifically emphasize the importance of engaging children in scientifically oriented questions, having students give priority to evidence and the development of evidence-based explanations, and justifying their proposed explanations (NRC 2000).

The following is a description of a KLEW chart developed during a unit on air and aviation for third grade students. Though this example addresses this topic, KLEW charts can be adapted for use with any science topic.

KLEW Into the Differences

A traditional KWL chart records what students

already Know about a topic, what students Want to learn about a topic, and, after explorations, what students have Learned about the topic. Similar to the KWL, the purpose of the *K* in our modification is to learn what students Know of a topic and to use that information to help guide instruction. However, the inclusion of the word *think* in these questions encourages students to share all their initial ideas, even those that might not be the best scientific explanation (Crowther and Cannon 2004). It also supports the idea that what students think they know can change as a result of the inquiry lessons.

L stands for "What are we Learning?" Learning occurs by conducting active investigations to find out about a topic. This differs from the traditional KWL because in a KWL, students' wonderings occur before investigation and then they conduct investigations and record what they found out in the L column. In KLEW, these activities are transposed. Learning precedes wonderings or what you want to learn about, which emerge through continued investigation and explanation building.

E stands for "What Evidence supports what we are learning?" Evidence is the data that results from the investigations. For students to record a statement under the L column, they must be able to provide specific data that supports the statement. This is a significant difference from the KWL—the KLEW chart makes evidence essential to the learning.

Finally, *W* stands for the wonderings—"What new Wonderings can we investigate?"—that occur as a result of students' investigative activities. Throughout the lesson or unit, students come up with questions and ideas that may further learning. These are recorded in the chart's final column. Emphasis is placed on asking testable questions.

Figure 1 shows how the KLEW categories played out in the air and aviation unit.

What They "K" About Air

Depending on what content is being explored and the time available, completing the K section of a KLEW chart can stretch from 10 minutes to a class period or more. Students are asked to share an explanation of the experiences that helped them Know the idea they are contributing to the chart. At this point in the unit, it is important to get ideas on paper. Because the KLEW chart is used throughout the unit as each new investigation takes place, students who don't contribute much at this initial time can be encouraged to contribute the next time.

In the aviation unit, the teacher began the unit by asking, "What do we think we Know … about air?" More than just hearing what students had to say, the KLEW chart provided a record of what students thought as the unit started, which was helpful in understanding what students did not know about air.

For example, students were not familiar with the properties of air necessary to understand flight principles, such as that air can apply force. Students were also confused about lift and how wing shape and airflow interact to provide lift. The teacher used the information students gave in the K column to tailor subsequent lessons to specifically address student confusion. In addition, she referred to the chart throughout the unit to help students reflect on their growing knowledge of the topic.

"L" with Bags of Air

After completing the K column, the students conducted an activity that explored some of the properties of compressed air. Each student was given a quart-size plastic bag securely taped to a straw so that the bag would fill with air when blown into. Students predicted which things in the classroom they thought they could lift with the air in the bag and what they would not be able to lift. Students believed that air could not lift heavy objects, such as a stack of books or a person, but that air would be able to lift a piece of paper.

Then, working in pairs, students went around the room and tested their predictions by putting the baggie under the object and blowing into the bag. Students soon discovered that the bag

Figure 1.

KLEW chart created as part of the air and aviation unit

What do we Think we **K**now?	What are we **L**earning?	What is our **E**vidence?	What are we **W**ondering?
Air is everywhere. Air has oxygen. We need air to live. Airplanes use engines to help them fly.	Air is strong → Air takes up space →	→ We lifted a computer, a bin of books, and a teacher with our air bags. → When we blew in the bags we could see the air made the bags get larger.	How do jets take off? How many math books can we lift with one bag of air? How many students can we lift using 10 air bags?

classroom that they were able to lift, including their teacher. The teacher then drew arrows to directly link the evidence to the related claim, reinforcing the importance of basing knowledge on evidence in science inquiry.

As the unit progressed, students conducted other investigations related to air and aviation to learn more about air, each time incorporating the use of a KLEW chart into the experience. However, no knowledge claims could be added to the KLEW unless evidence supported that knowledge claim.

After several weeks of air- or aviation-related investigations, class discussions began revealing a group of young scientists who gave priority to data, looked for patterns in those data, and generated explanations that were grounded in data. The children had begun to recognize that talking science involved providing support for the claims they wanted to make about phenomena. They were frequently observed launching into a justification of their claims without being prompted to do so.

of air could lift much heavier items than they initially predicted, including stacks of books, desks, and an empty aquarium. Students were intrigued and amazed with their findings.

Following the exploration with the bags of air, the teacher gathered students around the KLEW chart to discuss the investigation. The class spent some time talking about and demonstrating some of the things they were able to lift with their bags of air. Then, the teacher asked the students to make a claim about air as a result of their investigation. Students' knowledge claim was that air is strong, which was then included in the "What are we Learning?" column on the KLEW chart. In this case, students were using the word *strong* to describe the property of compressed air that enables it to hold things up.

"E" Is for Evidence

When students made the claim, the teacher asked them to provide Evidence (E) from their investigation that supported the claim. On the KLEW chart, students listed all the heavy things in the

What About Wonderings?

Wonderings—questions students asked while collecting data or discussing their results of their investigations—were recorded on the KLEW chart throughout the unit. In addition to recording what she heard students ask during the investigations, the teacher concluded each investigation by asking students if they had more wonderings about the concept under investigation. These Wonderings represented the W on the KLEW chart.

Wonderings were most often recorded on the chart as testable questions—if necessary, the teacher helped students frame their wonderings as testable questions. Whenever feasible, short lessons or extensions were planned to include the students' questions.

Positive Outcomes

One of the unexpected outcomes of adding evidence to the KWL format was that students began to suggest questions spontaneously as they worked together to construct evidence-based claims. Unlike the kinds of questions students tend to ask at the beginning of a unit, many of the questions generated within the context of investigations and explanation building were testable, such as "How many math books can we lift?" and "How many students can we lift using 10 air bags?"

Emphasizing evidence encouraged students to figure out new ways to collect more evidence through scientific investigations. The students were filled with ideas about modifications to existing investigations or designing new tests. Many of these suggestions were included seamlessly in the unit.

The KLEW chart aimed to increase opportunities for inquiry while providing teachers an instructional tool to organize students' ideas about their learning. The KLEW chart did that and more.

After using the KLEW chart throughout the aviation and a few subsequent units, the teacher observed that students wrote with greater depth about science topics. Students frequently referred to the KLEW chart to explain what they learned, and they used specific observations as evidence to support their claims.

We have used the KLEW chart in many settings and with different kinds of learners, including children and prospective and practicing teachers. The feedback is consistent. This new twist on an old favorite has the potential to go a long way toward supporting the vision of reform in elementary science teaching.

Kimber Hershberger is a third-grade teacher in the State College Area School District in State College, Pennsylvania. Carla Zembal-Saul is an associate professor of science education at Penn State University in State College, Pennsylvania. Mary L. Starr is a consultant who works with science teachers in their classrooms and provides professional development services in Plymouth, Michigan.

Connecting to the Standards

This article addresses the following National Science Education Standards (NRC 1996).

Content Standards
Standard A: Science as Inquiry
• Abilities necessary to do scientific inquiry

Science Teaching Standards
Standard C
Teachers of science plan an inquiry-based science program for their students.

Acknowledgment

This material is based upon work supported by the National Science Foundation (NSF REC 0237922). Any opinions, findings, and conclusions or recommendations expressed in this material are those of the authors and do not necessarily reflect the views of the National Science Foundation.

Resources

Crowther, D., and J. Cannon. 2004. From Know, Want, Learned to Think, How, Conclude, a popular reading strategy gets a science makeover. *Science and Children* 41 (1): 42–44.

National Research Council (NRC). 1996. *National Science Education Standards*. Washington, DC: National Academy Press.

Questioning Cycle

By Erin Marie Furtak and Maria Araceli Ruiz-Primo

Inquiry learning is an excellent way for students to get actively involved in science. It is essential that, while inquiry learning is in progress, teachers continuously elicit students' conceptions and take action to move students toward learning goals (Black and Wiliam 1998; Bell and Cowie 2001; Duschl 2003).

The Informative Questioning Cycle

During inquiry activities, teachers need to ensure their students are making progress toward learning goals. The informative questioning cycle can help teachers and students achieve these goals through simple techniques that can redirect and improve the quality of students' learning while it is in progress. The informative questioning cycle assists the teacher in making students' thinking explicit so the teacher can help students develop deeper understanding. The teacher begins by *eliciting* a response from students that reveals the state of the students' understanding. Next, the teacher *recognizes* the response by reflecting it back to the student or asking another follow-up question. The third step involves taking some form of *action* to help the student move toward the essence of the activity or concept. The process can be thought of as a cycle to reflect the ongoing nature of informative questioning throughout inquiry activities.

Setting and Aligning Learning Goals

Science inquiry units, like all other instruction, should have an ultimate goal to focus daily activities. Conversely, each daily activity should contribute in some way to reaching the ultimate goal. The goals for an activity can consist of learning about a concept, such as density, or developing a process skill, such as using a balance or constructing a graph properly.

A useful analogy for thinking about daily activity goals is the preparation of food. Different ingredients are combined together because of their individual flavors, and the flavors of these ingredients together create the taste of the dish. Similarly, each activity in an inquiry unit must have an essence that, when combined with those from other activities, contributes to the ultimate instructional goal.

To determine what the essence of an activity might be, a teacher may ask: "What will students need to know and be able to do at the end of the unit?" and "What are the concepts and skills students need to acquire during each of the activities to reach the goal?" If a certain activity does not contribute to the ultimate goal, the teacher should question why it is being included. Although competencies that satisfy the criteria for the ultimate goal are not developed in a single activity, the contribution of each activity toward the ultimate goal should be clearly understood for each classroom activity.

Eliciting Student Responses

Eliciting questions serves the purpose of drawing out what students know and are able to do and helping them learn how to share this information in an inquiry activity. Even for teachers who already use questions of this style, we suggest their purpose be changed to increase their informative potential. Asking students to provide evidence for an explanation, to share predictions based upon previous experiences, and to describe patterns in their data are all ways that the teacher can elicit students' thinking. Figure 1 includes a list of eliciting questions. Teachers should use the list as a source of suggestions, tailoring the questions to fit their own activities.

Eliciting questions may be used at any point in a lesson. For example, the teacher may use eliciting questions to determine students' prior knowledge when introducing a new activity, or to focus class discussion around an important concept at the conclusion of an investigation. In some cases the teacher may choose to develop eliciting questions in advance by writing them into a lesson plan. At other times, such as when the students are collecting data, the eliciting questions may be more spontaneous and responsive to what the students are doing at a given time.

Recognizing Student Responses

Once teachers have successfully elicited students' responses, they can acknowledge what the student has said in some way. Recognizing students' responses makes clear the students'

Figure 1.

Suggested questions for the eliciting stage of the informative questioning cycle

Types of eliciting questions Ask students to:	Examples
Provide evidence	What evidence do you have for your statement?
Formulate explanations	How do you explain the trend you see in the data?
Evaluate the quality of evidence	Based upon the methods you used, tell me what you think about the evidence you collected.
Interpret data or patterns	What does this pattern mean about the question you were asking?
Compare/contrast others' ideas	How is your idea different from Joe's idea?
Share observations	What did you observe as you were completing the activity?
Elaborate	What do you mean when you say that?
Take votes on ideas	How many of you agree with this idea?
Share everyday experiences	Have any of you encountered a similar phenomenon at home?
Use/apply known procedures	How do you draw a best-fit line?
Share predictions	What do you think will happen to the depth of sinking if I add more mass to this carton?
Define concept(s)	What do you think this word means?

Figure 2.

Suggested responses for the recognizing stage of the informative questioning cycle

Type of recognizing question or statement Teacher:	Examples
Incorporates student's comments into the on-going classroom conversation	Carlos is referring back to our discussion a few days ago, when we talked about how things sink when their density is greater than the medium.
Explores student's ideas	Alice, you suggested that the liquid looks very thick, so I'm going to pour it into this container so you can all see what she means.
Captures/displays student's responses	[Writes down student's responses on the board or easel for future discussion, comparing explanations, etc.]
Clarifies/elaborates based upon student's responses	You said things sink because they are heavy, but what are some heavy things that do not sink?
Takes vote to acknowledge student's ideas	How many of the rest of you agree with Blake?
Repeats or paraphrases student's words	You said the rock will sink because it has a greater density than the water?

contribution during whole class conversations or small group work and allows students to agree or disagree with what the teacher or other students have said. It should go beyond repeating students' words verbatim; rather, teachers should incorporate the student's comment into the ongoing classroom discussion (O'Connor and Michaels 1993), or rephrase the comment so that students can acknowledge or take credit for their responses (van Zee and Minstrell 1997). Note that this step in the cycle involves not only questions but also statements the teacher can make in response to a student comment. Figure 2 lists these and several other types of recognizing responses.

In some cases, the student's response will be unclear or incomplete. After recognizing the response, the teacher should return to the first step in the cycle and ask the student another question to elicit further information, such as asking the student to elaborate on a previous response, which will allow the teacher to continue the cycle in a more informed manner to help the student progress toward the ultimate learning goal of the activity.

Acting on Student Responses

Because one of the goals of informative questioning is to continually move students toward ultimate learning goals, the third part of the cycle, acting, involves using students' responses as an opportunity to advance student learning based upon information attained in the previous two steps. In our research, it is this final step that we found to be most powerful in terms of student performance on different types of

Figure 3.

Suggested strategies for the acting stage of the informative questioning cycle

Type of acting question or statement Teacher:	Examples
Promotes argumentation	[Providing counter-examples, encouraging students to address each other and to cite evidence for their claims.]
Helps relate evidence to explanations	The evidence in the graph shows us that as mass increases, depth of sinking increases. It looks like mass is at least one factor that contributes to why things sink or float.
Provides descriptive or helpful feedback	We're trying to develop a universal explanation for why things sink or float. Right now, you're just telling me why things sink. The next step for you is to learn about the variables that control why things float, to put that together as we develop our explanation.
Promotes making sense	This object is sinking because it has a density of 1.2, whereas this object floats because it has a density of 0.9. The difference is in the density of water, which is 1.0. Things with a density greater than 1.0 sink, and things with a density less than 1.0 float.

assessments because it leads students to learn the essence of the activity, which is necessary for them to reach the ultimate goal.

For example, if conflicting responses have been elicited from students, the teacher can encourage students to discuss their conceptions with each other by providing counter-examples or explanations, allowing students to argue their sides, always based on evidence. This process will help students evaluate for themselves what might be the best explanation and come to an agreement based upon the quality of the evidence provided to support the explanation.

The teacher can also act more directly in the form of providing meaningful feedback to the students. High-quality feedback consists of three steps: explaining the goal, explaining to the student where they are with respect to the goal, and suggesting steps the student might take to achieve that goal (Sadler 1989). There are a number of strategies teachers can employ in this final step (Figure 3).

Informative Questioning as Assessment for Learning

In the context of inquiry, telling students whether their responses are right or wrong focuses them on whether they have the correct answer, rather than allowing them to explore how they are coming to know what they know (Duschl 2003). Teachers should avoid the pattern of asking a question, receiving a response from a student, evaluating the answer, and moving quickly to the next question. The targeted actions possible in the informative questioning cycle can help students understand more clearly how they are thinking about concepts and processes and lead them to reach inquiry learning goals. A sample conversation incorporating the entire cycle is provided in Figure 4. The sample is based upon the investigation "Sinking and Floating Objects" from the *Foundational Approaches to Science Teaching* curriculum (Pottenger and Young 1992), in which students are provided with a collection of sinking and floating

Figure 4.

Sample learning conversation that demonstrates informative questioning during small group work

Ms. Yin's example		Role of question
Ms. Yin:	Can you predict the displaced volume of this floating object now that its mass is known?	Making a prediction (eliciting)
Rich:	I think that displaced volume will be about the same.	
Ms. Yin:	How do you know? Can you show me some evidence from your graph that supports your prediction?	Asking Rich to provide evidence (eliciting)
Rich:	I'm not sure. I don't see anything.	
Ms. Yin:	Can you give me an example from your data table?	Asking Rich to provide an example (eliciting)
Rich:	Well, I have this container of sand, and it floated. Its mass is 11.84 g, and it displaced 12 ml of water.	
Ms. Yin:	So Rich, you're telling me that the volume of displaced water is equal to the mass in this container of sand, based upon the data you collected in the activity?	Revoicing Rich's statement, noticing that Rich seems to understand the essence of the activity, but does not generalize from one object to the trend on the graph (recognizing)
Rich:	Yeah.	
Ms. Yin:	Okay Rich, you're telling me the relationship for this one object. Ayita over here is saying something else— I heard her say a few minutes ago that the graph shows that mass and displaced volume are equal for all objects. Rich, why don't you use your graph to see whether you agree or disagree?	Promoting argumentation (acting)

objects and are asked to determine if it is possible to predict the volume of water a floating object will displace if its mass is known.

Informative questioning helps the teacher become aware of the students' thinking and provides a basis for action. Practicing informative questioning is practicing high-quality informal formative assessment, which improves student learning. We have evidence that teachers using informative questioning had students who performed better on several types of formative embedded assessments, such as predict-observe-explain and open-ended questions, and summative assessments, such as performance assessments, predict-observe-explain, and open-ended questions, aligned with the learning goals of their curriculum (Ruiz-Primo and Furtak 2004).

Erin Marie Furtak is a research assistant in the School of Education at Stanford University in Stanford, California. Maria Araceli Ruiz-Primo is a senior research scholar in the School of Education at Stanford University in Stanford, California.

References

Bell, B., and B. Cowie. 2001. *Formative assessment and science education.* Dordrecht, Netherlands: Kluwer Academic Publishers.

Black, P., and D. Wiliam. 1998. Assessment and classroom learning. *Assessment in Education* 5 (1): 7–74.

Duschl, R. A. 2003. Assessment of inquiry. In *Everyday assessment in the science classroom*, eds. J. M. Atkin and J. E. Coffey, 41–59. Arlington, VA: NSTA Press.

O'Connor, M. C., and S. Michaels. 1993. Aligning academic task and participation status through revoicing: Analysis of a classroom discourse strategy. *Anthropology and Education Quarterly* 24 (4): 318–335.

Pottenger, F. M., and D. B. Young. 1992. *The local environment: FAST 1. Foundational approaches to science teaching.* 2nd ed. Honolulu: Curriculum Research and Development Group.

Ruiz-Primo, M. A., and E. M. Furtak. 2004. *Informal formative assessment of students' understanding of scientific inquiry.* In *Assessment for reform-based science teaching and learning,* ed. A. C. Alonzo (Chair).

Symposium conducted at the American Educational Research Association annual meeting, San Diego.

Sadler, D. R. 1989. Formative assessment and the design of instructional systems. *Instructional Science* 18 (2): 119–144.

van Zee, E., and J. Minstrell. 1997. Using questioning to guide student thinking. *The Journal of Learning Sciences* 6 (2): 227–269.

Thinking About Students' Questions

By Jaclyn Turner

Asking questions is a vital component in any classroom, but it is absolutely essential in a science classroom. As a science teacher, I know questioning plays a major role in the inquiry process and, in turn, students' learning. This article will discuss the importance of questioning skills and current research on questioning techniques. In addition, this article will present a series of lessons that improved the questioning abilities of my middle school students.

Significance of Questioning Skills

As a teacher, I understand the importance of building a trusting and positive relationship with each and every student. In order to accomplish this, I always make an effort to have individual conversations with students and give them opportunities to share their home lives, stories, and questions in class. However, sometimes these conversations and questions distract us from the many demands that are placed upon both teachers and students. During class, I never seem to have enough time to listen to all the interesting stories students would like to share or answer all the intriguing questions they would like to pose. Sometimes these questions and stories are on topic with the lesson or activity, and other times they are completely off topic. After class, I find myself wondering what caused the student to think about that particular story or question and more prominently, how I can include and follow through on more of these questions in the classroom.

Moreover, I recognize the significance of developing the curious and inquisitive minds of students. In addition to curriculum content, I hope to develop this trait of curiosity because I believe this to be not only an asset but also a necessity for becoming a successful student and possibly a scientist. I feel compelled to make students' questions a priority in the classroom because curiosity and questioning go hand in hand. How could I develop students' curious minds without recognizing and making their questions part of the classroom?

Research

Research shows that questioning is a vital component of scientific inquiry and the general learning process. According to Chin (2001), questioning is needed for students to be engaged and explore the topic and to make their own meaning of major concepts. Thier (2001) validates this point and goes even further to say that teachers need to redefine their teaching pedagogy by thinking in terms of questions and investigations rather than instruction and lessons. Harlen (1996) discusses the kinds of questions students ask, including the following: comments expressed as questions, philosophical questions, requests for simple facts, questions requiring complex answers, and questions that can lead to investigation by students. Harlen goes on to briefly describe strategies for teachers when responding to each of the five kinds of questions.

Lessons on Questioning Skills

My first step is to have students complete a questionnaire and self-assessment (see Figure 1) on issues related to questioning skills. I ask students to use as much time as they need. Most students finish within 15 minutes. During this time, I reassure students that there are no right or wrong answers and that I am only interested in their ideas.

Next, I present a series of five 40-minute lessons related to kinds of questions. In the first lesson, we discuss the types of questions, including factual, belief, opinion, interpretive, and good scientific questions. More specifically, we identify the different ways of finding the answers to these questions. For example, students point out how the answers to factual questions are found in books or on the internet, while the answers to belief, opinion, and interpretive questions depend on the individual being asked. More important, they state that the answers to good scientific questions can be found only by using science inquiry skills and completing an experiment.

As a whole class, students complete a chart (see Figure 2) on which they write down the meanings of the questions, examples of questions, and where to find the answers. In the second lesson, I place large pieces of paper around the room with the following headings: factual, belief, opinion, interpretive, and scientific. I then pass out an index card to each student with an example of each type of question. I ask students to read the question individually and go to the category in which they believe the question would belong. Next, I ask each student to read the question out loud and explain why he or she went to that category. I then ask the rest of the class if they agree or disagree with the way the question was categorized.

In the third lesson, I repeat the steps of the second lesson, but change the questions on the index cards to give students more practice describing and categorizing questions. At the end of this lesson, as a whole class, we make a master list of good scientific questions related to weather on a large piece of paper. Last, I reread each of the questions and ask students to pick their favorite question by a show of hands. "How does temperature change air?" is often a favorite and will be used as an example in the descriptions of the remaining two lessons. Due to lack of time, I end the lesson with the thought that this question needs to be changed and improved. As a result, the next lesson begins with the whole class going through the process of creating a question that will lead to an investigation.

During the fourth lesson, I first ask students to explain how we could actually determine the answer to the question, "How does temperature change air?" After sharing ideas, students realize that this question is not a good scientific question because it is unclear and unspecific, and that the first thing they need to do is refine it so we can devise an appropriate experiment to address it. With the help of a series of guiding questions, students are able to refine the question into, "How does temperature change the

Figure 1.

Questioning skills self-assessment

If someone asked the following questions, could you classify the questions according to how they could be answered?

F = factual question, it would be easy to look up the answer or just collect data without doing an experiment
B = belief or philosophical question, the answer would depend on someone's personal beliefs
O = opinion question, the answer would depend on someone's personal preferences
I = interpretive question, the answer would come from looking at lots of information and making an inference
S = scientific question, the answer would come from conducting an experiment during which we would change something and look for its effect

Read the questions carefully. Place an X in the column as to how you would classify each of the following:

	Factual	Belief	Opinion	Interpretive	Scientific
1. Why is the sky blue?					
2. What is the temperature of the inner core of the Earth?					
3. Is there a link between smoking and lung cancer?					
4. Where is the best vacation spot?					
5. Two students have built a robot, they ask: "How much electrical current does the robot's arm use to lift different weights?"					
6. What kind of a volcano is Mount St. Helens?					
7. Which is better, Coke or Pepsi?					
8. What is the function of chloroplasts?					
9. What is your favorite animal?					
10. Does fire in one part of a forest lead to more plant growth there than in other areas with no fire?					
11. What is the charge of a proton?					
12. What is the best biome to live in?					
13. Do plants need light in order to grow to a height of 2 feet?					
14. What material is the best conductor of heat?					
15. Did humans evolve from monkeys?					
16. How cold is the tundra?					
17. What is the best foundation to stand up against an earthquake?					

Figure 1. continues on next page

(Figure 1. cont.)

Choose one question from the previous list that is not an example of a good scientific question. Can you turn that question into a good scientific question?

Name three qualities of good scientific questions.

1.

2.

3.

Self-assessment (please circle answer)

1. I am confident when I ask questions in science class.	Strongly disagree	Somewhat disagree	Somewhat agree	Strongly agree
2. I know that there is more than one type of question.	Strongly disagree	Somewhat disagree	Somewhat agree	Strongly agree
3. I can name several qualities of good scientific questions.	Strongly disagree	Somewhat disagree	Somewhat agree	Strongly agree
4. I can explain the difference between a good scientific question and other types of questions.	Strongly disagree	Somewhat disagree	Somewhat agree	Strongly agree
5. When possible, I am able to turn other types of questions into good scientific questions.	Strongly disagree	Somewhat disagree	Somewhat agree	Strongly agree

way that air particles behave in a balloon placed on the mouth of a water bottle?"

We then identify possible materials, such as empty water bottles, balloons, bowls or containers, thermometers, and hot and cold water. Students form their own groups and are given time to plan their experiments. Students record the question, materials, and procedure in their science journals, which I then review. Prior to the fifth and last lesson, I assemble all materials and safety guidelines students will need. During the experiments, students record observations in their journals. I ask students to share the results of their experiments with the class and explain how the results could be used to answer the refined question.

My last step is for students to complete the original questionnaire and self-assessment (see Figure 1). I explain that the purpose of having them complete the questionnaire a second time is to determine what they gained from the lessons. I give students as much time as needed to complete the questionnaire.

Research

To determine how these lessons affected my students' ability to think about questions, I conducted an action research study with the 9 boys and 12 girls in my sixth-grade class. The five lessons were conducted over seven

40-minute class periods. Before the first class, students completed a questionnaire that tested their ability to identify qualities of good scientific questions and refine questions into inquiries. Students completed the questionnaire again after the final lesson. The percentage of students able to describe qualities of good scientific questions increased by 44%, and the percentage of students able to refine nonscientific questions into inquiry questions increased by 53%. These results show evidence of improvement in these questioning skills. The implications for my teaching are that I will implement a unit on questioning, specifically good scientific questions, at the beginning of the year before covering any content area in science.

Conclusion

Middle school students can be taught to differentiate between the various types of questions and, given explicit instruction, they can craft their own good scientific questions. Through this explicit instruction, students can discern the criteria of questions, specifically relating to good scientific questions that lead to inquiries that can be carried out in the classroom. More important, questioning can become a tool students will use throughout their educational careers. This type of questioning process allows students to create their own meaning and apply new concepts to their everyday lives.

Jaclyn Turner is a science teacher at Marshall Middle School in Billerica, Massachusetts.

Figure 2.
Experimenting with circuits

Type of question	Meaning	Example	Where do I find the answer?
Factual			
Belief			
Opinion			
Interpretive			
Scientific			

References

Chin, C. 2001. *Student-generated questions: What they tell us about students' thinking.* Singapore: National Institute of Education.

Harlen, W. 1996. *The teaching of science in primary schools.* London: David Fulton Publisher.

Thier, H. 2001. *Designing and assessing instructional materials based on guided inquiry.* Formerly available at *http://unr.edu/homepage/jcannon/thierAETS.htm*

The Eight-Step Method to Great Group Work

By Sally Steward and Jill Swango

Many science teachers already understand the importance of cooperative learning in the classroom and during lab exercises. From a theoretical perspective, students working in groups learn teamwork and discussion techniques as well as how to formulate and ask questions among themselves. From a practical standpoint, group work saves precious resources and reduces the cost of materials needed for invaluable inquiry-based, hands-on learning opportunities. For activities that require particularly pricey items, you can use larger group sizes, which enables you to offer your students the experience without being limited as much by expense. Many teachers, however, shy away from group work because they dread the headaches associated with getting adolescents into groups that actually work together rather than just group together.

Here are eight guidelines that will alleviate the stress of grouping your students and open up endless learning opportunities in a cooperative setting.

1. Make sure each student has a role to play in the group. Adolescents have not yet learned the fine art of delegation, so if you don't assign roles, one student often will end up doing all the work. A designated role or job description will help each student play a part in the success of the group. Some suggested roles: timekeeper, scribe, materials manager, and inquiry manager (the person who carries questions to the teacher from the group). You can develop your own roles for your students and use them each time your class does group work.

2. If the students are choosing and/or finding group partners, put a limit on the time they have. Thirty seconds is plenty. If they don't have a group by then, place them yourself. Limiting the time will help alleviate any panic your shy students may feel, because they won't have a long wait while they look around the room for a group. Adopt a cheerful, but assertive, voice and begin placing students with a resolute, "Here you go, Anne, you'll finish off this group nicely," or "Marcus, I want you to lend this group a hand today." Your guidance can also help ensure that the groups are as inclusive as possible.

3. Make sure each student has a copy of the directions to refer to, whether on a handout or written on the overhead or the chalkboard. If each student can refer to the directions, groups will be less likely to go astray and miss the point of the lesson. Written directions also eliminate the tendency of some students to commandeer the group and elect themselves in charge.

4. Place time limits on the tasks you want the groups to accomplish. This helps them stay on schedule and not get sidetracked with socializing. One of the most important life skills taught in middle and junior high school is time management. By assigning time limits to tasks, you are modeling for your students how they should prioritize the parts of an assignment to finish it properly. A clock counting down the time so students can keep track is helpful. You can be high tech by purchasing a timer you place on the overhead projector to display the time on a screen or low tech by using a simple egg timer that dings when the time is up. Be sure to check with your technology coordinator for ideas, because many schoolrooms have televisions and monitors that may include a countdown timer feature.

5. Float around the room during group work to provide guidance, answer questions, and keep groups focused on the assignment. Do not underestimate the value of proximity during group work. Although you may be tempted to sit at your desk and check e-mails or grade a few papers when the students are in groups, fight the temptation. Your presence will stave off misbehavior, and, through your observations, you will be able to redirect groups that may stray from the path you planned for the lesson.

6. If the assignment is for more than one day, write down the names of the members of the groups so your students don't forget where they belong the next day. Adolescents will prove time and again the old saying, "I would have remembered, but I've slept since then." Recording the names of group members will save you time and headaches during the second day of a group project.

7. Include the names of absent students in groups that will work for more than one day together. When accommodating students who were absent, don't worry about keeping group numbers equal. If one group grows larger than the others due to the addition of an absent student, so be it. It is preferable to have a slightly larger group than to save a place for an absent student only to find he or she has the chicken pox and won't return for two weeks.

8. Group work should never go home with a single student. It should remain in the classroom. Although students may plead with you to work on a project at home, the risk that they will be absent the next day or lose the work on the bus is too great. If groups want—or need—to spend extra time outside the classroom time on a project, make your classroom available before or after school, or during a study hall or flexible period.

If you follow these eight steps, you will be well on your way to nurturing collaboration among your students and opening your classroom to the benefits of cooperative learning. When it comes time to assess your students' group work, keep in mind that you should focus not only on the group's final product but also on the individual effort involved. If you are careful to make good observations of individual work during the group effort, you will have a basis for grading both the group's final product and each individual's efforts. This method of assessing will inspire all students to put forth their best efforts and eliminate any charges of one person having to shoulder the load for the entire group.

For more ideas about how to use group work and cooperative learning in your middle school science classroom, check out Chapter 5, "Cooperative Learning and Assessment" and Chapter 10, "Classroom Management" of *Help! I'm Teaching Middle School Science* from NSTA Press. The book can be bought at *www.nsta.org/store* in its entirety or in individual chapters.

Sally Steward is a science education consultant living in Danville, Indiana. Jill Swango is a science teacher at Brownsburg Junior High School in Brownsburg, Indiana. They are the authors of Help! I'm Teaching Middle School Science, *available from NSTA Press.*

Reference

Swango, C. J., and S. Steward. 2003. *Help! I'm Teaching Middle School Science*. Arlington, VA: NSTA Press.

Section 3
Science for All

Science for All

Recently I reviewed a textbook for my science methods course. After a glance at the table of contents, I quickly rejected it. I made the decision when I saw that one chapter was titled "Dealing With Diversity." How can you provide a positive learning environment for all students if you view diversity as something you have to "deal" with? Instead, we need to take the view exemplified in the title of an NSTA Press Journals Collection published in 2001, *Celebrating Cultural Diversity: Science Learning for All.* Diversity is what makes life interesting; it should be celebrated. In her introduction to the collection, Elizabeth Hayes outlines three elements that are required for a true multicultural science-learning environment: "First, the sense that all students can learn and do science; second, the view that each student has a worthwhile place in the science classroom; and third, an appreciation for the contributions of all cultures to our scientific knowledge" (p. vii).

Celebrating Diversity

Diversity strengthens a learning community. The single biggest factor in creating a learning community that celebrates diversity is the mindset of the teacher. All educators must reject the deficiency model. Diverse students do not have fewer experiences than students from the dominant culture. They have different experiences. Acknowledging, celebrating, and learning from these different experiences create rich learning opportunities for all students. Padron et al. (2002) describe this for Hispanic learners:

> Hispanic students need to be assured that they are important, and that they can make valuable contributions to society. When students are not given these opportunities to participate in the development of classroom activities and when their involvement is minimized, the implicit message is that teachers do not care about their experiences or what they have to say. For this reason, students may miss out on the type of classroom discourse that encourages them to make sense of new concepts and information. (p. 15)

Five or six years ago years ago, I attended a lecture about space shuttle safety by Dr. Jack

Bacon, a National Aeronautics and Space Administration engineer. He showed the power a diverse workforce creates by explaining that people with diverse backgrounds (such as ethnic, gender, and socioeconomic status) have different experiences throughout life and that the different perspectives they bring to the table illuminate problems. In his human differences textbook, Koppleman (2005) explains that diversity is regarded as positive when people engage in solving problems:

If we examine problems the same way, we would generate similar solutions. Williams (2003) described a problem-solving conference where a chemical company invited 50 employees that were women or people of color and 125 predominantly white male managers. When divided into problem-solving teams, half of the groups consisted of white males only and half included diverse members by both gender and race. Afterward, the company CEO said, "It was so obvious that the diverse teams had the broader solutions. They had ideas I hadn't even thought of… We realized that diversity is strength as it relates to problem solving, (pp. 442–443).

Culturally Responsive Teaching

Padron et al. (2002) describe culturally responsive teaching as incorporating students' everyday concerns, issues, and ways of knowing into the curriculum. According to Padron et al., culturally responsive teaching improves retention of new knowledge by working from students' existing knowledge base and improves self-confidence by emphasizing that existing knowledge. Culturally responsive teaching addresses the needs of students by improving motivation and engagement. Gay (2000) describes culturally responsive teaching as having these characteristics:

- It acknowledges the legitimacy of cultural heritages of different ethnic groups.

- It builds bridges of meaningfulness between home and school experiences as well as between academic abstractions and lived sociocultural realities.
- It uses a wide variety of instructional strategies that are connected to different learning styles.
- It teaches students to know and praise their own and each others' cultural heritages.
- It incorporates multicultural information, resources and materials in all the subjects and skills routinely taught in schools.

Lee and Fradd (1998) say that, traditionally, science has been taught with the expectation that students will understand and learn when teachers present the content in a scientifically appropriate way, with little consideration given to students' cultural understandings. This traditional practice may contribute to the underrepresentation of diverse students in science and their alienation from the subject. Nelson-Barber and Trumbull (1995) say, "When we pretend that domains of knowledge as taught in schools are neutral—not attached to particular ways of thinking, valuing and knowing—we excuse ourselves from acknowledging other equally valid perspectives and epistemologies and from creating ways for children to make connections and comparisons between different ways of knowing."

Lee and Fradd (1998) explain that there may be overlap between the culture of science and most cultures, because the scientific values of wondering, curiosity, interest, diligence, persistence, openness to new ideas, imagination, and respect toward nature are found in most cultures. Other values of science, however—such as thinking critically and independently, reasoning, using empirical criteria, making arguments based on logic, questioning, openly criticizing, tolerating ambiguity, and demonstrating evidence rather than deferring to authority—may not be as common in non-Western European cultures. For example, when students culturally value collectivism it becomes difficult to argue their perspective or critique others' ideas. Lee and Fradd (1998) identify three realms in which diverse students' cultural understandings are particularly important: knowing science, doing science, and talking science.

Knowing Science. Lee and Fradd (1998) say that the role of prior knowledge is especially important for diverse students. Because the knowledge students bring to the learning process may differ from the predominant culture, identifying relevant experiences can play a major role in linking what students already know with what they are expected to learn. By developing learning activities based on familiar concepts, teachers facilitate content learning by helping diverse students be more comfortable and confident with their work (Peregoy and Boyle 2000). According to Rivera and Zehler (1991) beginning by validating students' existing knowledge base can improve student knowledge acquisition and retention of new knowledge and develop a student's self-confidence and self-esteem. Nelson-Barber and Trumbull (1995) explain that teachers can use prior knowledge to introduce a topic by asking students to describe their own experiences, observations, and interactions with the topic itself. They argue that this type of teaching offers the potential for an active classroom role for each student because it requires student interpretation of ideas that they are familiar with.

Doing Science. Lee and Fradd (1998) say that diverse students may experience problems because they have not been encouraged to ask questions or devise plans for investigations on their own. Students from cultures that respect authority may be more receptive to teachers telling and directing them, rather than to inquiry. Rothstein-Fisch et al. (1999) contend that students from Hispanic and many non-Western backgrounds hold a collectivistic value system that emphasizes the importance of the group over the individual. Therefore, it is natural for Hispanic students to attempt to help each other,

even in situations where the predominant culture expects individual work. This may cause teachers to admonish them or accuse them of cheating. The authors describe a strategy used successfully by one teacher: When homework was passed out, students were allowed to discuss the questions but were not allowed to write down answers until they got home. This resulted in a 100% homework return rate!

Talking Science. Lee and Fradd (1998) explain that the correct use of vocabulary is an indicator of precision and sophistication of understanding. The correct use of vocabulary, however, becomes more difficult when comparable terms do not exist across languages. Therefore, meanings must be understood within cultural context. Rothstein-Fisch et al. (1999) argue that cultures that emphasize a collectivistic value system also emphasize the social context of learning: Students from these cultures often do not separate scientific information from the context in which they are embedded. This often conflicts with the culture of U.S. schools that emphasize information disengaged from social context. The authors describe a situation in which a park docent asked students what they knew about hummingbirds. The students proceeded to tell stories about their family experiences with hummingbirds. The docent was expecting scientific descriptions and grew frustrated. When he told the students to stop telling stories, they became silent. After the docent left, the teacher invited the students to tell their family stories. She wrote story highlights on the left side of the chalkboard and scientific aspects of the experiences on the right side. The teacher and class were able to value the stories and scientific information equally.

Authentic Activity

Culturally responsive instruction should include authentic activities. Authentic activities provide students with the opportunity to explore how the subject under study is socially relevant and connected to their everyday lives. Instruction should move away from using a collection of disconnected hands-on activities and toward interaction and manipulation of ideas that are valuable beyond the school walls.

The project conducted by Seiler (2001) provides an example of using authentic activities. Seiler developed a science study group specifically for African American male students. The Science Lunch Group consisted of eight African American males and the researcher, a white female. During the group meetings, topics emerged from student interests and included how drums make different sounds, how tall buildings are built, the physics of a wrecking ball, the chemistry of hair products, and the safety of cell phones. The emergence of these topics battles the perception that science is a collection of facts and leads to the idea of "reflexive science" that begins with what the students know, do, and want to do, instead of beginning with traditional school science. Students developed rich arguments that included the use of data, graphs, and multimedia. Most of the discussion involved student-student interaction and co-construction of knowledge. The researcher noted that the ability of the students to participate in scientific discourse (creation of scientific arguments) and their learning of specific science content knowledge increased during the Science Lunch Group meetings. Seiler concludes that teachers should create space in their instruction for their students' interests and cultural funds of knowledge. Lessons should connect science with students' ideas, interests, prior knowledge, and abilities. Seiler stated, "While grounding the content in topics connected with and sensitive to the lives and cultural histories of African-American students, I also believe that teaching of many critical skills (for science) can be based on abilities and cultural attributes already within the students' repertoires" (p. 1012).

The Articles

Article: Cultural Diversity in the Science Classroom

Key Ideas: The authors describe how cultural differences affect learning science, the ability of inquiry-based instruction to provide a bridge between cultural differences, and how teachers can support diverse students as they learn science.

Article: Capitalizing on Diversity
Key Ideas: The authors describe eight things a teacher can do to support science learning by students from diverse backgrounds.

Article: Supporting English Language Learners' Reading in the Science Classroom
Key Ideas: The authors provide a series of research-based strategies for helping English language learners in the science classroom.

Article: Science Success for Students With Special Needs
Key Ideas: Science for "all" students does not mean only students from diverse cultural backgrounds. In this article, the author describes multiple modifications that can be made to instruction to support learners with special needs.

Action Steps

1. Read the Principles for Culturally Responsive Teaching from Brown University's Teaching Diverse Learners web site: *www.alliance.brown.edu/tdl/tl-strategies/crt-principles.shtml*.

2. Develop a student assessment to evaluate the cultural responsiveness of your teaching. An example of a student assessment can be found at *http://crede.berkeley.edu/research/crede/standards/standards_7_worksheet.html*.

3. Search the internet to find programs focused on engaging girls in science. What features do these programs have in common? (This site is a good place to start: *www.girlsgotech.org/girls_go_tech.html*.)

4. Pick one topic from national or state science standards documents. How could

you connect this topic to the reality of your students' lives?

5. Select a science activity and describe specific things that you could do to support learners with special needs.

Reflection Questions

1. Read the following article from the National Science Foundation that describes five myths about girls and science: What can you do to engage girls in your future classroom? *www.nsf.gov/news/news_summ. jsp?cntn_id=109939*

2. Pretend that you are interviewing for a teaching position. How would you respond to this question: "What ideas do you have about diversity in the classroom?"

3. Review one resource from the "Lessons and Activities for Special Students" from this Education World article: *www. education-world.com/a_curr/curr139.shtml.* How does it help you support learning by students with special needs?

References

Lee, O. and S. H. Fradd, 1998 . Science for All, Including students from non-English-language backgrounds. *Educational Researcher* 27(4).

Koppleman, K. 2005. *Understanding human differences: Multicultural education for a diverse America.* Boston: Allyn & Bacon.

National Science Teachers Association Press. 2001. *Science learning for all: Celebrating cultural diversity.* Arlington, VA: NSTA Press

Nelson Barber, S., and E. Trumbul. 1995. *Culturally responsive mathematics and science education for native students.* San Francisco, CA: Far West Lab. for Educational Research and Development.

Padron, Y. N., H. C. Waxman, and H. H. Rivera. 2002. *Educating Hispanic students: Obstacles and avenues to improved academic achievement.* Santa Cruz, CA: Center for Research on Education, Diversity & Excellence, University of California—Santa Cruz.

Peregoy, S. F., and O. P. Boyle. 2000. English learners reading English: What we know, what we need to know. *Theory Into Practice* 39: 237–47.

Rivera, C., and A. M. Zehler. 1991. Assuring the academic success of language minority students: Collaboration in teaching and learning. *Journal of Education* 173: 52–77.

Rothstein-Fisch, C., P. M. Greenfield, and E. Trumbull. 1999. Bridging cultures with classroom strategies. *Educational Leadership.* April.

Seiler, G. 2001. Reversing the "standard" direction: Science emerging from the lives of African American students. *Journal of Research in Science Teaching* 38 (9): 1000–1014.

Williams, C. 2003. Managing Individuals and a diverse work force. In *Management,* 2nd ed., pp. 343–371. Versailles, KY: Thompson Southwestern.

Cultural Diversity in the Science Classroom

By Patrick L. Brown and Sandra K. Abell

"I teach in a growing area that becomes more culturally diverse each year. I am worried that I may not be reaching some of my fifth-grade class in science."

How Can Cultural Perspectives Affect Students' Views of Science and Science Learning?

When students come to science class, they bring a variety of perspectives formed in part from their cultural heritages, religious beliefs, and family backgrounds. This may create challenges for students whose experiences are different from typical "ways of knowing" promoted in school science. In Texas, Allen and Crawley (1998) studied fifth-grade Kickapoo (Native American) students' science learning. Students focused on their kinship with nature in interpreting their world, which often led to conflicts in science class. Studying Yupiaq children in southwestern Alaska, Kawagley, Norris-Tull,

and Norris-Tull (1998) found that students learned by listening to and mimicking stories that drew on integrated science knowledge. This conflicted with the textbook approach, which divided science into separate, seemingly unconnected, disciplines. Furthermore, the curriculum encouraged students to abandon their traditional worldview of science, which included themselves, nature, and the spiritual world. All students need experiences with school science that connect science with their everyday lives in familiar ways.

Second, students from different cultural backgrounds may have different styles of interaction that make it hard for them to perform in the ways their science teachers expect. In their study of Texas Kickapoo children, Allen and Crawley (1998) found that students viewed science learning as a cooperative venture and wanted to share answers and assignments. To the frustration of their teachers, they viewed their grades in science as a low priority. Anderson, Holland, and Palincsar (1997) found that learning science was difficult for sixth-grade students whose background was different from the language and interaction norms used in school science. For example, when creating a presentation to explain molecules and matter, the students focused on getting along with each other and creating an attractive and well-designed poster rather than giving priority to learning the science concepts. When student and teacher expectations differ, students may have a more difficult time learning science.

Can Inquiry-Based Instruction Help Bridge Cultural Backgrounds and Foster Science Learning Success?

The hands-on, minds-on nature of inquiry may help all students develop authentic science interactions and learn science in a context that is meaningful and relevant to their lives. Working with fourth-grade Haitian and Hispanic students, Fradd et al. (2001) investigated how students performed in an inquiry-based curriculum for teaching the water cycle and weather. Although many of the students came from homes where asking questions and debating was viewed as challenging authority, over time their teachers guided students to understand that questioning and debating are essential features of scientific inquiry. Fradd and Lee (1999) also examined how inquiry-based teaching influenced the fourth graders in developing science and English language skills. They found that by engaging in scientific inquiry, students benefited from working in groups, gained an understanding of the nature of science, and improved their English. In another study, third- and fourth-grade students from various linguistic and cultural groups developed enhanced understanding of science concepts and abilities to do scientific inquiry (asking

scientific questions, designing investigations, recording results, and drawing conclusions) by engaging in inquiry (Cuevas et al. 2005). As the above examples reflect, inquiry-based science instruction can indeed be effective in helping all students access the world of science.

How Can Teachers Best Support Diverse Cultural Backgrounds When Teaching Science?

Teachers can help all students learn science by allowing diverse approaches to scientific reasoning in their classrooms. For example, students might use both their first and second languages to engage in science. Jean-Charles, a student in a sixth-grade bilingual classroom, used English to clarify technical terms not present in his first language, Haitian Creole. By expressing his ideas in two languages, he used his full range of linguistic capabilities to develop more in-depth arguments and understanding of metamorphosis in mealworms (Warren et al. 2001). Students might also be encouraged to engage in creative thinking in science. Another student in the bilingual class, Emilio, designed an experiment to test whether ants prefer light or darkness. Unlike the typical science class in which students think about problems from an outsider's perspective, Emilio was encouraged to be creative and to think about being both inside and outside of the ants' habitat while designing his investigation. The interplay of Emilio's imaginative (insider) and evaluative (outsider) perspectives resulted in deeper reasoning about variables and experimental design. By opening up the science class to different languages and types of reasoning, teachers can encourage students to cross borders between their cultural backgrounds and the science classroom.

Patrick L. Brown is a former high school biology teacher and current doctoral student in science education at the University of Missouri–Columbia. Sandra K. Abell is Curators' Professor of Science Education at the University of Missouri–Columbia (MU) where she directs the MU Science Education Center.

References

Allen, N. J., and F. E. Crawley. 1998. Voices from the bridge: Worldview conflicts of Kickapoo students of science. *Journal of Research in Science Teaching* 35 (2): 111–132.

Anderson, C. W., D. J. Holland, and A. S. Palincsar. 1997. Canonical and sociocultural approaches to research and reform in science education: The story of Juan and his group. *The Elementary Science Journal* 97 (4): 359–383.

Cuevas, P., O. Lee, J. Hart, and R. Deaktor. 2005. Improving science inquiry with elementary students of diverse backgrounds. *Journal of Research in Science Teaching* 42 (3): 337–357.

Fradd, S. H., O. Lee, F. X. Sutman, and K. M. Saxton. 2001. Promoting science literacy with English language learners through instructional materials development: A case study. *Bilingual Research Journal* 25 (4): 417–439.

Fradd, S. H., and O. Lee. 1999. Teachers' roles in promoting science inquiry with students from diverse language backgrounds. *Educational Researcher* 28 (6): 14–20, 42.

Kawagley, A. O., D. Norris-Tull, and R. A. Norris-Tull. 1998. The indigenous worldview of Yupiaq culture: Its scientific nature and relevance to the practice and teaching of science. *Journal of Research in Science Teaching* 35 (2): 133–144.

Warren, B., C. Ballenger, M. Ogonowski, A. S. Rosebery, and J. Hudicourt-Barnes. 2001. Rethinking diversity in learning science: The logic of everyday sense making. *Journal of Research in Science Teaching* 38 (5): 529–552.

Capitalizing on Diversity

By Lenola Allen-Sommerville

Regardless of their cultural identity, students want to learn, produce more, and increase their level of achievement (O'Brien 1989). The challenge that science teachers face is to enable students of all ethnic and cultural backgrounds to accomplish these goals. Teachers must employ cultural knowledge, cultural sensitivity, and interpersonal skills when working with students; explore and develop expanded or new ways of teaching; and provide opportunities for students to maximize their learning potential.

As the population of the United States rapidly becomes more racially and ethnically diverse, students from various cultural backgrounds bring unique learning preferences and styles to the science learning environment. Cultural differences due to ethnicity, language variations, social class, and individual differences may influence these preferences and styles, which also will change as students age and gain experiences. There are also intraethnic and interethnic learning differences due to these cultural factors. Demographers predict that people of color will constitute one-third of the U.S. population by the turn of the century (CMPE 1988) and that American classrooms will begin to reflect a new majority—students of color, low-income students, and students of non-English-speaking backgrounds (Gomez and Smith 1991).

Teachers are continually challenged to meet the needs of all students, but understanding students' individual learning preferences is especially challenging because these preferences develop from early and continuing socialization patterns. Because learning preferences and styles have been identified as important variables in the scholastic success (or failure) of ethnic minorities in the United States, determining how these students process information in a science classroom can provide valuable information on which to base responsive instruction and educational experiences.

Recognizing that cultural differences influence students' learning experiences, the Learning-How-To-Learn coordinator and teachers in the program Science Bound were interested in knowing more about ethnic minority students and their learning preferences. Science Bound is an extension of (1) a two-year pilot project funded by the Iowa State University College Bound program and Ames Laboratory of the U.S. Department of Energy and (2) a three-year, $400,000 mentoring grant through the National Science Foundation.

It is a partnership between Iowa State University, the Des Moines Community School District, and technology-based businesses working together to increase the participation of ethnic minority students in science and technology and encourage them to prepare for careers as scientists, engineers, and technologists. University professors and district teachers plan and implement science- and mathematics-based curricula, including various programs and activities. Mentors help students see the applications of math and science as they relate to career opportunities, thus nurturing their science and technology potentials.

Learning-How-To-Learn, a component of Science Bound, includes, but is not limited to, goal-setting activities, becoming aware of preferences for studying and ways of most easily learning and remembering information, and finding out how to motivate oneself. Students who remain in the program for five years (grades 8–12), are accepted to Iowa State University in good standing, pursue a technology-based field of study, and receive a tuition scholarship from the university.

A priority of Science Bound is to work with students to assess how and when they process information and to determine their instructional preferences. One resource for diagnosing cognitive preferences and style is the cognitive domain of the National Association of Secondary School Principals' Learning Style Profile (Foriska 1992). The data supplied by the Learning Style Profile (LSP) allow teachers and others who work in teaching situations to diagnose students' strengths and weaknesses, ascertain students' learning preferences, and develop or modify instructional design and strategies to better match students' learning styles.

During the 1992 school year, 95 Science Bound students (American Indians, African Americans, Hispanic Americans, and Asian Americans) were administered the LSP. The LSP was hand scored in a three-stage process: scoring individual items, generating subscale raw scores, and determining subscale standardized scores. The score on a given subscale is the standard score for that subscale. The process of standardization was based on national data that were divided into categories of weak, low, or high; average or neutral; and strong. Reviewing these ranges provided the most useful basis for discussion of student and class results.

Analysis of the LSP showed that the majority of students were average to strong in willingness to work at a task until completion and in analytic, spatial, discrimination, and categorization skills. They had deficits in detecting and remembering subtle changes in information (memory skill) and grasping visuospatial relationships (simultaneous processing skill). Most students preferred hands-on or visual information to auditory. Fewer indicated below-average willingness to express opinions or speak out. Nearly half the students preferred working in small groups or pairs. As expected, members of the four ethnic groups also showed different learning preferences, with significant differences found between African Americans and Asian Americans. African Americans preferred categorization and verbal risk styles, whereas Asian Americans preferred spatial styles.

The Learning-How-To-Learn coordinator made the results of the LSP available to teachers, students, and parents and discussed how the information could be used to improve the student's learning outcome (at school and home). The student profiles showed that Science Bound students have the potential and capacity for science development and achievement. They can learn science. Students with strong cognitive skills (analytic, spatial, and categorization) are more ready for challenging instruction and are more capable of working at or beyond their grade level, whereas students with deficiencies in those areas benefit from focused problem-solving activities. Similarly, students with strong visual responses are likely to be less effective learners if instruction is strictly verbal (auditory). These students require assistance and practice to better appreciate and accept auditory information. Conducting these kinds of cooperative projects encourages cross-cultural communication and opportunities for academic peer influence.

Eight Successful Field-Tested Strategies

Identifying student learning preferences is one method for ensuring that students in multicultural settings learn science. Science teachers cannot expect to use the same traditional environments, instructional practices, and methods that were used in the past. We can no longer depend on old paradigms because they do not tap the academic potential of all students. We must become innovators in the quest to meet students' learning needs (Foriska 1992). A concerned and creative science teacher may replicate or modify the following strategies that have been successful for Science Bound teachers, mentors, and students:

1. Assume that students can learn. Avoid stereotypes that limit student success in selected subjects. Science Bound provides opportunities for students to visit a university campus and attend classes taught by professors, observe scientists in laboratories, work with mentors in the private and public sector, interact with college students, conduct research projects, and learn ways to reduce barriers to academic achievement.

2. Use exciting and challenging hands-on activities. Experienced teachers have indicated that instructional methodology can no longer be limited to using the science textbook supplemented with a few hands-on activities. Textbook science can turn off large numbers of ethnic minority students if it is the only way science is presented to them. Past Science Bound students interned with the state Department of Natural Resources in the areas of fisheries, wildlife, and law enforcement. They took samples of fish to determine a lake's

stocking needs, captured and banded geese and wood ducks to establish mortality and survival rates, talked with landowners about cropping for wildlife enhancement, and worked with the boating patrol to guarantee code compliance and check fishing licenses.

3. Talk to students about their learning styles. Encourage students to take more control of their learning and capitalize on opportunities for success. Through Science Bound staff, students have learned interesting things about themselves, such as the way they learn and study. After discussing their LSP profiles, students made comments such as, "I have strong spatial skills just like a scientist"; "This means I do better in the morning and should schedule hard classes in the morning, not my last two periods of the day"; "My analytical skills are weak"; and "I work best in small groups and hate to talk in class."

4. Develop a repertoire of content strategies and activities. Include a variety of cognitive/learning modes in your teaching style and assist students in moving from one preferred learning mode to a base of mixed preferences so they can benefit from information closely related to science. A 1992 summer algebra enhancement seminar introduced students to the basics of algebra through visual techniques and also provided a citywide support system to all Science Bound newcomers. A later seminar explored algebra concepts with manipulatives.

5. Learn about the history and culture of the various groups. To successfully integrate multicultural content into the curriculum, Science Bound teachers and mentors attended several sessions in which cultural information was disseminated. At one session, representatives of four ethnic minority groups in Iowa (Iowa Commission on the Status of African Americans, Iowa Commission on Latino Affairs, Iowa Governor's Advisory Board on American Indian Issues, and the Bureau of Refugee Programs) provided demographic and cultural information. This included, but was not limited to, characteristics of the population, family structure, customs, values, advocacy groups, organizations, and social-cultural concerns. The district's minority achievement program coordinator presented each participant with a report regarding the status of ethnic minority students in the district.

6. Help students see themselves as future scientists and appreciate the multicultural history of science. Students must realize that all cultures have made significant achievements in scientific fields and that a career in science is an exciting and realistic option for all people. Provide ethnic-minority role models. Do not underestimate the importance of seeing someone successful who "looks like you" doing and talking about science. Science Bound made concerted efforts to recruit ethnic-minority mentors, both male and female. The mentors work in hospitals, state government, research agencies, and the armed forces. Also, students have been provided lists of ethnic minorities who have made and are making important contributions to science and technology, such as Mae Carol Jemison, the first African American woman to fly in space.

7. Build opportunities for success into the curriculum and create climates conducive to learning. Avoid selling ethnic minority students short and underestimating their ability to succeed (Henson 1975). As a result of their efforts in a rocket-launching project at the annual picnic, several Science Bound students won scholarships to the U. S. Space Camp in Huntsville, Alabama, as participants in one of NASA's youth programs.

8. Provide diverse learning experiences. Engage students in both in-class and out-of-class learning opportunities. Field trips, such as visits to the Chicago Museum of Science and Industry, the Field Museum of Natural History, the Shedd Aquarium, and comparable institutions, are enjoyable and educational.

The Multicultural Classroom

Science teachers are encountering an increasingly broad range of students in their classrooms. These students bring individual and cultural differences that should be acknowledged as opportunities rather than deficits. As science teachers recognize this, they will realize that there is more than one way to learn science and that every student has a unique learning preference, style, and approach. The inclusion of the eight strategies in the curriculum has been quite beneficial for Science Bound students. Students' grades, motivation, cooperation, self-esteem, and attendance have all improved. Because these strategies met with such positive results with this multicultural group, they may also have success with students in other multicultural settings.

Lenola Allen-Sommerville is instruction parent family coordinator for Science Bound and an assistant professor of curriculum and instruction at Iowa State University.

References

Banks, J. A. 1988. Ethnicity, class, cognitive, and motivational styles: Research and teaching Implications. *Journal of Negro Education* 57 (4): 452–466.

Commission on Minority Participation in Education and American Life. 1988. *One-third of a nation*. Washington, DC: The American Council on Education.

Foriska, T. J. 1992. Breaking from tradition: Using learning styles to teach students how to learn. *Schools in the Middle* 2 (1): 14–16.

Gomez, M. L., and R. J. Smith. 1991. Building interactive reading and writing curricula with diverse learners. *The Clearing House* 64 (3): 147–151.

Henson, K. T. 1975. American schools vs. cultural pluralism. *Educational Leadership* 32: 405–408.

O'Brien, L. 1989. Learning styles: Make the students aware. *NASSP Bulletin* 73 (519): 86–89.

Supporting English Language Learners' Reading in the Science Classroom

By Greg Corder

S everal major organizations in the scientific community have communicated that there is a need for individuals to develop scientific literacy (AAAS 1993; NRC 1996; NSTA 2005). The skill to read and understand science-oriented information is an important means by which students can enhance their ability to acquire scientific literacy.

It might seem obvious that students with limited reading skills also have limited educational opportunities. Students acquiring English as their second, non-native language—referred to as English language learners—face this obstacle. Fortunately, a body of research has emerged that provides specific techniques for

supporting and developing their reading ability. These findings can be readily applied to the science classroom.

Students in the English language learner population are formally labeled as limited english proficient (LEP) by the federal government and most states. Although sharing a low proficiency skill of the English language, this rapidly growing segment of students is extremely diverse. They represent "every echelon of society from wealth, privilege, and education to poverty and illiteracy; they speak varying degrees of English" (Roseberry-McKibbin 2002, p. 13). Moreover, many immigrants, refugees, and migrants enter the United States with "limited, intermittent, or interrupted schooling" (Rivera and Vincent 1997, p. 347). Some English language learners are American born (Echevarria et al. 2004); others "enter the United States from many places. In the different countries of origin, curricular sequences, content objectives, and instructional methodologies may differ dramatically from American practices" (McKeon 1994, p. 46). An obvious language deficit challenges English language learners' academic success, while cultural and socioeconomic differences compound their education struggle.

The population of students classified as English language learners in American schools has and continues to experience major growth. Between the 1992/93 and 2002/03 school years, the total population of American students grew approximately 11%, while the population of identified LEP students grew approximately 85% (NCELA 2004). Moreover, Ruiz-de-Velasco and Fix reported that immigrant growth has been concentrated in urban areas, thus causing more extreme growth for those school systems (2000). Coupling their unique education needs with their population's growth makes the task of teaching English language learners seem daunting.

Setting a Language Objective

In general, stating an explicit objective for a lesson is considered a good teaching practice. An example of an objective in a science classroom might be "The student will determine the density of the sample." This example is a content objective and identifies "what a student should know and be able to do" (Echevarria et al. 2004, p. 21). English language learners' needs, however, extend beyond the science content alone. They need opportunities to listen, speak, write, and read English. Research suggests inclusion of language objectives along with content objectives (Echevarria, Vogt, and Short 2004, p. 22). Language objectives range from lower order, such as, "The student will underline unfamiliar words in the passage," to

higher order, such as "The student will read the four authors' descriptions and synthesize a model." The language objective's level should vary based on the language proficiency of your students.

All objectives must be comprehensible and explicitly communicated to students. The manner in which you direct students to an objective will determine its effectiveness: First, post the objective in a location that gives students easy access; second, orally state the objective; third, refer to the objective at the beginning and end of an exercise that demands reading. These steps will help your English language learners realize the importance of developing and practicing their reading skills.

Supplying Background Information

Many English language learners enter our classrooms with a different set of experiences than their fluent English-speaking counterparts (Echevarria, et al. 2004). This means that many of them lack the background knowledge required for reading that many texts may take for granted. Therefore, teachers must supply that necessary background knowledge.

It may be necessary for you to "model how to follow steps of directions needed to complete a task" (Echevarria et al. 2004, p. 25) such as a lab or project. As you model, you can think aloud by orally stating the objects you are manipulating and your thought process as you proceed. Modeling supplies English language learners with a visual image and accompanying terminology from which they can draw when encountering those terms and concepts in a reading passage.

When students encounter unfamiliar words, a reading passage becomes more difficult for them (Dale and Chall 1948; Klare 1974). To counter this, you can preteach key vocabulary. All difficult terms should be considered, even those that are not considered science vocabulary. For example, you can create and maintain a word wall by defining, discussing, and posting words that students identify as unfamiliar. This technique provides valuable prereading instruction, while creating a resource to which students can quickly refer and reinforce English language gains.

Linguistic Modification of Text

Reading is comprehensible only if a selection's linguistic complexity is within students' grasps. Finding and supplying resources that match a student's specific reading level and the desired curricular content is an ideal accommodation. However, availability and funding may limit your ability to do so. Therefore, linguistic modification of available texts may be necessary.

The level of text modification depends on an English language learner's level of need. Some strategies are less time consuming. Examples might include highlighting text, writing notes in the margin, or including illustrations to accompany each direction. However, more time-consuming methods, such as rewriting reading passages, textbooks, or directions, might be necessary to linguistically simplify the text.

Linguistic simplification does not mean that the text is "dumbed-down." When considering linguistic simplification, text adaptation must not "significantly diminish the content concept" (Echevarria et al. 2004). What is more, it is suggested that "the major concepts be retained and just the readability level of the text be reduced."

Researchers have identified several specific characteristics that affect a text's level of difficulty, and you can draw on their findings when simplifying your own texts:

- First, passages with longer words and longer sentences are more difficult to read (Bormuth 1966; Flesch 1948; Klare 1974).
- Second, passive voice is not always as clear as active voice (Forster and Olbrei

1973; Savin and Perchonock 1965; Slobin 1968). An example of passive voice is "The cause had been identified by scientists." An example of active voice is "Scientists identified the cause."
- Third, a long string of consecutive nouns elevates reading difficulty (King and Just 1991; MacDonald 1993).
- Fourth, a coordinate, or independent, clause is more difficult to read than a subordinate, or dependent, clause (Botel and Granowsky 1974; Wang 1970). A coordinate clause can stand by itself as a sentence, while a subordinate clause cannot.
- Fifth, an abstract statement is more challenging to comprehend than a concrete statement (Cummins et al. 1988). An example of an abstract statement is "Record your data." An example of a concrete statement is "Record the volume of the cylinders in Table 1."

Echevarria et al. suggested that the inclusion of idioms or slang may limit reading comprehension by English language learners (2004). Some examples of English idioms in a science classroom might include "hold on to your hats" to prepare students for surprising results or "don't beat around the bush" to encourage students to use their time wisely. Poorly collected data may be referred to using slang terms such as *garbage* or *trash*. Although rare in science texts and other resources, idiomatic phrases and slang terms should be avoided.

A fair degree of judgment is necessary when modifying text. For example, although converting an abstract sentence into one that is concrete may increase its length, that may be an acceptable compromise so as to clarify instructions. Linguistic modification may seem challenging at first, but with experience, the practice becomes easier and English language learners reap the benefits.

In a profession where teachers are burdened with more and more responsibilities and expectations, you may feel that linguistic modification takes away from preparing quality science instruction. If this technique seems overly time consuming, seek assistance. Many school divisions hire English as a second language (ESL) resource teachers. Depending on their designated role and training, they may be able to help. If you work with an interdisciplinary team of teachers, you may have access to a language arts teacher who is willing to lend a hand.

Conclusion

Reading ability can limit English language learners' success in the science classroom. However, these students need to develop their reading skills so that they can build scientific literacy, thus enhancing their contributions in society. Fortunately, educators can employ a number of specific techniques that aid English language learners as they strive to develop reading skills. Moreover, by gradually increasing student expectations and the degree of linguistic difficulty over time, students strengthen their language proficiency while lessening their reliance on their teachers.

Greg Corder is a teacher at Thomas Harrison Middle School and an instructor at James Madison University in Harrisonburg, Virginia.

References

American Association for the Advancement of Science (AAAS). 1993. *Benchmarks for science literacy.* New York: Oxford University Press. Available at *www.project2061.org/publications/bsl/default.htm.*

Bormuth, J. R. 1966. Readability: A new approach. *Reading Research Quarterly* 1 (3): 79–132.

Botel, M., and A. Granowsky. 1974. A formula for measuring syntactic complexity: A directional effort. *Elementary English* 49 (4): 513–16.

Cummins, D. D., W. Kintsch, K. Reusser, and R. Weimer. 1988. The role of understanding in solving word problems. *Cognitive Psychology* 20 (4): 405–38.

Dale, E., and J. S. Chall. 1948. A formula for predicting readability. *Educational Research Bulletin* 27 (1): 11–20, 28.

Echevarria, J., M. E. Vogt, and D. J. Short. 2004. *Making content comprehensible for English learners: The SIOP model.* 2nd ed. Boston: Pearson Education.

Flesch, R. 1948. A new readability yardstick. *Journal of Applied Psychology* 32 (3): 221–33.

Forster, K. I., and I. Olbrei. 1973. Semantic heuristics and syntactic trial. *Cognition* 2: 319–47.

King, J., and M. A. Just. 1991. Individual differences in syntactic processing: The role of working memory. *Journal of Memory and Language* 30: 580–602.

Klare, G. R. 1974. Assessing readability. *Reading Research Quarterly* 10 (1): 62–102.

MacDonald, M.C. 1993. The interaction of lexical and syntactic ambiguity. *Journal of Memory and Language* 32: 692–715.

McKeon, D. 1994. When meeting "common" standards is uncommonly difficult. *Educational Leadership* 51 (8): 45–49.

National Research Council (NRC). 1996. *National Science Education Standards.* Washington, DC: National Academy Press.

National Science Teachers Association (NSTA). 2005. *Strategy 2005 goals.* Arlington, VA: NSTA. Available at *www.nsta.org/main/pdfs/Strategy2005.pdf.*

Porter, R. P. 2000. Accountability is overdue: Testing the academic achievement of limited English proficient students. *Applied Measurement in Education,* 13 (4): 403–10.

Rivera, C., and C. Vincent. 1997. High school graduation testing: Policies and practices in the assessment of English language learners. *Educational Assessment* 4 (4): 335–55.

Roseberry-McKibbin, C. 2002. *Multicultural students with special language needs: Practical strategies for assessment and intervention.* 2nd ed. Oceanside, CA: Academic Communications Associates.

Ruiz-de-Velasco, J., and M. Fix. 2000. *Overlooked and underserved: Immigrant students in U.S. secondary schools.* Washington, DC: Urban Institute.

Savin, H. B., and E. Perchonock. 1965. Grammatical structure and the immediate recall of English sentences. *Journal of Verbal Learning and Verbal Behavior* 4: 348–53.

Slobin, D. I. 1968. Recall of full and truncated passive sentences in connected discourse. *Journal of Verbal Learning and Verbal Behavior* 7: 876–81.

Stewner-Manzanares, G. 1988. *The bilingual education act: Twenty years later.* Washington, DC: National Clearinghouse for Bilingual Education.

Teachers of English to Speakers of Other Languages (TESOL). 1997. *ESL standards for pre–K–12 students.* Alexandria, VA: TESOL.

U.S. Department of Education. 2001. Public Law Print of PL 107-110, the No Child Left Behind Act of 2001.

Wang, M. D. 1970. The role of syntactic complexity as a determiner of comprehensibility. *Journal of Verbal Learning and Verbal Behavior* 9: 398–404.

Science Success for Students With Special Needs

By Marcee M. Steele

No Child Left Behind required a science component to state tests beginning in 2007. Special education legislation (Individuals With Disabilities Act amendments) emphasizes the placement of students with mild disabilities in the general education classroom. Therefore, students with learning, behavior, and communication disorders typically learn science from classroom teachers rather than in separate special-education classes. They will be required to pass the same standardized science tests as the children without disabilities, but many of their characteristics interfere with success in science. Deficits in memory, low-level reading and writing skills, language difficulties, organizational problems, and social-emotional issues are just a few of the characteristics that can impede science achievement and standardized test performance. This article highlights instructional, study, and test-taking strategies useful in preparing *all* students, but particularly students with mild learning challenges, for success in science class and hopefully on high-stakes tests as well.

Teaching Strategies

Below are suggestions for instructional modifications that teachers can do to help students with learning problems understand science concepts.

Collaborate with special education and general education teachers. Collaboration is essential for planning instructional strategies that will be effective for students with learning and behavior disorders. When special education and science teachers plan and teach together, the combined expertise in individualization and science content will foster development of appropriate lessons for all students.

Create lessons based on themes or big ideas. Many science standards and programs emphasize broad concepts for organizing science instruction, and this approach can benefit students with memory problems. They will have fewer ideas to learn at one time and more practice with the concepts as they are covered across many science lessons. Lessons based on themes help students with mild disabilities focus on a few important ideas rather than getting lost in numerous details. For example, the theme of energy could be the foundation for subsequent units on sound, light, electricity, heat, food, and machines rather than planning separate units on each of these topics without showing connections.

In addition, the major science themes integrate and relate ideas across the curriculum, thus giving even more review in another context for students who have problems with memory and generalization. For example, in a unit on weather, students can use mathematical skills when they measure with a barometer, relate to social studies when they compare weather patterns across a country or state, and incorporate literature by reading and writing stories focused on weather conditions.

Incorporate explicit instruction on the lesson topics. Although most science standards emphasize a constructivist classroom and inquiry science lessons, giving some explicit instruction to students with mild disabilities is beneficial. Directly summarizing the key points learned from a lesson provides students with notes on the new information for later study. For example, before a lesson on sound, teachers could preview key concepts and terms such as *vibration, sound waves,* and *echo* by providing explanations and definitions using PowerPoint slides, handouts, or dictation. At the conclusion of the lesson, the key concepts can be discussed again so that students have the opportunity to put the ideas in their own words and relate them to real-life examples.

Use graphic organizers and visual representations. Teachers can prepare notes as organizers for presentation before, during, and after the lesson. The notes can be outlines, key ideas, critical questions, or sentences with blanks for students to complete.

At the start of a lesson, graphic organizers can relate new material to previous information, introduce new concepts, explain related assignments, discuss the purpose of the lesson, and clarify difficult terms. After the lesson, teachers can present summaries, key questions, and lists of important concepts for emphasis. A set of questions, for example, for a lesson on the atmosphere might ask students to explain ways that air protects people, reasons that smog is harmful, and uses of oxygen.

Visual representations can be useful for students with difficulties in processing and reading comprehension. Graphic organizers, tables, and charts are helpful visual displays that can represent key ideas and their relationship to each other. Pictures that represent ideas can be beneficial for comprehending and conceptualizing. Charts of solids, liquids, and gases; acceleration graphs; and diagrams of moon phases, for example, clarify the concepts and their relationships.

Model behaviors and strategies you want students to follow. When teachers assign small-group tasks in the elementary science class, it is helpful to prepare students so that everyone has a chance to participate. Teachers can model appropriate strategies such as measuring small objects with a ruler prior to a group task involving classification of plants by size. It is also important to assist students with language and learning problems as they prepare reports and projects so they will have success in that format. Group and partner activities can be valuable but need to be explained clearly, with specific rules and tasks for each student involved. Each student might have a different task, such as placement of objects to be used in an experiment on magnetism, slowly pushing a bar magnet toward the object, slowing pushing a horseshoe magnet, measuring the length, recording results, and reporting to the class.

Students with reading disabilities may benefit from modifications regarding science textbook use if a textbook is used. Highlighting key passages for students; eliminating sections that are not as critical; using visual representations of material such as charts and outlines; reviewing vocabulary before the lesson; and clarifying the parts of the textbook such as glossary, index, and appendix are useful strategies. In addition, teachers can model outlining using textbook features such as titles, headings, and subheadings and taking notes from the textbook in forms such as lists and summaries.

Study Strategies

In addition to instructional modifications for teachers, there are numerous study strategies for students that can help students get the most out of the science instruction.

Study guide use. Before a science lesson, teachers can create and distribute study guides with key questions, lists of main ideas, and definitions. Teachers can then instruct the students to use them after the lessons to help them focus by reciting the answers, definitions, and main ideas aloud or with a partner. The guides can be particularly useful for students with attention, memory, and organizational deficits.

Material review tips. Study strategies that emphasize organizational skills can lead to better performance on high-stakes science tests. Teachers can set aside time at the end of each unit to ensure that all students have related materials or assign partners to ensure that all books, guides, charts, and resources are available to complete homework assignments. Teachers can also set (or even require) a study goal of a certain number of minutes each night after completing written science assignments. Contracts, grades, and other incentives can ensure this extra time is used effectively. Even 5 or 10 minutes will establish a pattern of reviewing each night rather than waiting to study all material the day before the test. Teachers could even set aside class time each day or week for students to review new material and encourage this practice.

Many students with learning disabilities and attention deficits are not active learners and do not use strategies to help them comprehend and remember new material; however, they can learn to employ specific study strategies when they are trying to understand and memorize. Strategies in which students preview, read, and then check their comprehension can be rewarded and modeled. These strategies may include using or making flash cards with questions on one side and responses on the other for independent review of key material; mnemonic strategies to memorize information, such as names of bones and energy forms, by associating with pictures, first letters, and keywords; and various self-instruction study strategies, such as revising notes, writing summaries, and making visual representations such as charts and diagrams. These facts and terms then provide a foundation for activities and projects involving the creation of meaning such as important uses of energy and purposes of various bones in the body.

Note-taking practices. Elementary teachers can incorporate instruction on note taking into science lessons so students with learning, memory, and attention problems will be able to generalize and use the strategies immediately with science content. To help students improve their note-taking skills, teachers can model how to identify main ideas and concepts for notes or provide framed outlines with some information completed and blanks for students to fill in as they listen or read. Highlighting is another note-taking strategy that teachers can explain, model, and reinforce.

Strategies for Tests

In addition to instructional modifications and an emphasis on study skills, it is also useful for teachers to provide students with test-taking strategies. These tips are useful in all testing situations, including high-stakes science tests.

Practice appropriate strategies before the test. All students should be taught general test-taking behaviors, such as healthy eating, appropriate sleep habits, wearing comfortable clothing, and staying calm during the test. Also helpful for all students is practicing analyzing directions and questions to be sure students are responding to all parts and interpreting accurately before writing answers.

Some test-taking strategies are more effective at addressing some learning challenges than others. For example, students with attention problems likely will benefit from practice staying on task for longer periods of time, while students with memory problems might better benefit from practice using concepts they have rehearsed and memorized in response to test questions. For some students, test-taking strategies should be taught, practiced, and then reviewed just before the test. This is helpful for students with processing and memory problems to remember to use the strategies during the test.

Taking the test. Whether teachers use traditional tests or more inquiry-focused tests, teaching students to preview an entire test and then start on the questions that they know best will help them. They may want to mark questions that are more difficult so that they remember to complete them later. Practicing activities with test directions related to science questions is particularly beneficial for students with learning and communication disorders who may not be familiar with terminology frequently used to describe science tasks, questions, and experiments. Teachers can discuss key vocabulary such as *explain, describe, compare,* and *analyze* to show students how to determine the type of response needed based on these words.

Students can also learn to write down a few key words to help with memory as they read the questions and make lists or outlines before writing responses to essay questions. Then they can refer to these words as they are answering the questions.

Finally, teach students to underline or highlight key words when taking tests to be sure they follow directions accurately. Students should be encouraged to check that they have answered all questions and that their responses include all needed information before they complete their exams.

The strategies summarized in this article are appropriate for use in other subjects as well, including mathematics and social studies. Although the recommendations are critical for the success of students with mild learning disabilities, the ideas are beneficial for all students. With deliberate attention to these topics, you can provide students with the tools they need to succeed in class and on tests.

Marcee M. Steele is a professor of special education at the University of North Carolina-Wilmington in Wilmington, North Carolina.

Resources

Breidel, D. C., S. M. Turner, and J. C. Taylor-Ferreira. 1999. Teaching study skills and test-taking strategies to elementary school students. *Behavior Modification* 23 (4): 630–646.

Brighton, C. M. 2002. Straddling the fence: Implementing best practices in an age of accountability. *Gifted Child Today* 25 (3): 30–33.

Cawley, J. F., and T. E. Foley. 2002. Connecting math and science for all students. *Teaching Exceptional Children* 34 (4): 14–19.

Cawley, J. F., T. E. Foley, and J. Miller. 2003. Science and students with mild disabilities. *Intervention in School and Clinic* 38 (3): 160–171.

Freund, L., and R. Rich. 2005. *Teaching students with learning problems in the inclusive classroom.* Upper Saddle River, NJ: Pearson Merrill Prentice Hall.

Hammel, D. D., and N. R. Bartel. 2004. *Teaching students with learning and behavior problems.* Austin: Pro-Ed.

Mastropieri, M. A., and T. E. Scruggs. 2007. *The inclusive classroom: Strategies for effective instruction.* Upper Saddle River, NJ: Pearson Merrill Prentice Hall.

Mercer, C. D., and A. R. Mercer. 2005. *Teaching students with learning problems.* Upper Saddle River, NJ: Pearson Merrill Prentice Hall.

Olson, J. L., and J. C. Platt. 2004. *Teaching children and adolescents with special needs.* Upper Saddle River, NJ: Pearson Merrill Prentice Hall.

National Research Council (NRC). 1996. *National Science Education Standards.* Washington, DC: National Academy Press.

Palincsar, A. S., S. J. Magnusson, K. M. Collins, and J. Cutter. 2001. Making science accessible to all: Results of a design experiment in inclusive classrooms. *Learning Disability Quarterly* 24 (1): 15–32.

Polloway, E. A., J. R. Patton, and L. Serna. 2005. *Strategies for teaching learners with special needs.* Upper Saddle River, NJ: Pearson Merrill Prentice Hall.

Section 4

Science Teaching Toolbox

Science Teaching Toolbox

The articles in this section (and those in the last section, Section 5) describe strategies that support the foundation laid in the first three sections. Because it is not possible to provide a comprehensive overview of all teaching strategies, this section will focus on introducing a few important issues: reading and writing in science, integrating other disciplines, integrating technology, and teaching science to young children.

This section takes a different format. Instead of reading an introductory essay, you will plunge directly into the articles. A few reflective questions included at the beginning will guide your thinking about these articles.

Reflection Questions

Think about these questions as you read the articles:

1. Explain how ideas presented in these articles support a learner-centered, assessment-centered, and community-centered classroom.

2. How do these articles promote science inquiry or other aspects of a "knowledge-centered" classroom?

3. How do the ideas in these articles support science learning by students from diverse backgrounds?

The Articles
Reading and Writing Strategies

Article: Erupting With Great Force
Key Ideas: The authors provide examples of how to help students understand expository text through poetry, rap, drama, and other types of performances.

Article: Developing Strategic Readers
Key Ideas: The authors describe four strategies that can improve student learning as students interact with science texts.

Article: 14 Writing Strategies
Key Ideas: The authors explain why writing is important to scientists and characteristics of

good writing assignments. Then, they present 14 examples of types of writing responses.

Article: Science the "Write" Way
Key Ideas: The authors describe ways to help students use writing to learn science through journaling, charting, and writing student-authored books.

Integrating Other Disciplines

Article: Connecting With Other Disciplines
Key Ideas: The authors provide a rationale, caution, and action steps for integrating science with other disciplines.

Article: Art and Science Grow Together
Key Ideas: The authors describe a project that involved integrating art and science during a long-term investigation into growing plants from bulbs.

Article: En"Light"ening Geometry for Middle School Students
Key Ideas: The authors describe an activity in which students learn about reflection, refraction, and symmetry as they increase their understanding of light and geometry.

Article: A Blended Neighborhood
Key Ideas: The authors describe an activity that integrates science, math and social studies as students research, explore, and model their neighborhood.

Integrating Technology

Article: Cell City WebQuest
Key Ideas: Webquests are internet-based activities that foster authentic learning. The authors describe a webquest that helps students understand the names and functions of organelles in cells.

Article: Using Web-Based Simulations to Promote Inquiry
Key Ideas: The authors describe how they used

a virtual fruit fly experiment to help students understand phenotypes and inheritance.

Article: Making "Photo" Graphs
Key Ideas: This article describes how to use a digital camera to help students build graphs of plant growth.

Article: Learning With Loggerheads
Key Ideas: This article describes one example of using real data from the internet in the science classroom. The authors explain how they used sea-turtle tracking data with third grade students.

Article: Up-to-the-Minute Meteorology
Key Ideas: The authors describe how to access and use real-time weather data.

Teaching Science to Young Children

Article: What's the Matter?
Key Ideas: This article describes a series of explorations that young children can do with ooblek and gloop. Students describe and compare characteristics of the two materials.

Article: Discovery Central
Key Ideas: This is another article that describes using learning centers to help students learn science while using multiple inquiry skills.

Article: It's a Frog's Life
Key Ideas: The author describes a long-term natural investigation that her preschool students did with tadpoles. Students asked and tried to answer questions about the life cycle of frogs. Although this investigation occurred spontaneously, it is possible to purchase safe frog habitats and tadpoles to replicate this activity. By using a safe frog habitat, issues of frog mortality should also be reduced.

Article: The Science and Mathematics of Building Structures
Key Ideas: In this article, preschool students

conduct inquiry and learn about science and
math as they build structures.

Erupting With Great Force

By Ann Bullion-Mears, Joyce K. McCauley, and J. YeVette McWhorter

"Miss, do we have to read the textbook today?"

"I don't get it, teacher. What does this word mean?"

"This book is bo-o-oring! Can't we watch a video?"

Middle school science teachers frequently hear these comments when they use a textbook as a vehicle for instruction. Many teachers resort to giving notes or lectures to simplify the information and thus avoid the moans and groans of their students. The dilemma is real—how do teachers help students understand expository text?

Expository text is challenging (Young and Vardell 1993). Many middle school students lack the experiential background necessary to understand the content. Textbooks frequently develop multiple concepts using unfamiliar vocabulary in a brief passage. Middle school students also experience difficulty with the expository organizational patterns of description, sequence, cause and effect, and compare and contrast. Science textbooks often switch from cause and effect to comparison/contrast to illustrate a single concept. Expository text also displays information in a variety of graphic formats such as graphs, charts, pictures, and diagrams. Students must navigate the various organizational patterns, the development of multiple concepts, and the graphic formats to determine textual meaning.

Not only is the text challenging, but adolescent readers also vary greatly in physical, emotional, social, and cognitive development. Students move alternately and rapidly between concrete and abstract forms of thinking (Irvin 1998). They are gaining the ability to be reflective, analytical, and introspective about thoughts and feelings. As adolescents experience internal cognitive changes, external expectations for academic behavior also change. The language structures used by teachers and text are longer, more formal, more complex, and involve students in acquiring the language of instruction (Combs 2003). In addition, adolescents face inconsistent expectations regarding the reading of textual materials. The use of text appears to vary greatly during middle school and some doubt exists about the amount of text middle school students actually read (Irvin 1998). Matching content learning expectations with adolescent developmental abilities poses a special challenge to the middle school teacher. The question is "How can teachers direct the energies and interests of teenagers into a productive learning outcome?" One answer to this question is performing text.

Performing text in the form of choral reading, rap, reader's theater, and/or simulations offers students a powerful vehicle for understanding and recalling key concepts and significant details culled from textual material. The rhythmic beats, clear images, and social interactions inherent in performing text help students develop mnemonic devices to retain content (Bullion-Mears et al. 1997). Creating a script, poem, or lyrics to perform requires repeated readings of a text, a practice that increases participants' comprehension, reading rate, and enjoyment (McCauley and McCauley 1992; Young and Vardell 1993). As an added benefit, performing text also provides an exciting change from oral recitations of textbook materials.

Creating Performance Materials

Alhough poems, scripts, raps, and simulations can be located in print and online, the process can be time consuming and the material may be inappropriate. That's the bad news. The good news is that expository text from a newspaper, book, encyclopedia, magazine, or textbook can be rewritten for performance. For example, the excerpt below is taken from *101 Things Every Kid Should Know About Science* (Beres 1998).

> A volcano is a hole or a crack in the crust of the Earth that lava and ash come out of. Volcanoes are often pictured as large cone-shaped mountains that spit out tons of flowing lava from the top. Some volcanoes do look like this, but there are other volcanoes that are nothing more than long cracks in the ground that ooze lava. Some volcanoes are dead, meaning they don't erupt anymore and are not expected to erupt in the future. If a volcano is fuming—letting out smoke, oozing, or erupting—it is "active." A volcano is considered "alive" if it's expected to erupt sometime in the future.

> Volcanoes erupt because of heat and pressure underground. Magma (liquid rock) is as far as 90 miles below the Earth's surface. Blobs of hot liquid magma and gas are less dense than the surrounding rock so that they start to move upward. As gas moves toward the surface, it expands and looks for a place to escape. The gas finds its way to the surface of Earth through a vent and brings hot molten rock with it. When magma reaches the air, it is called lava. Sometimes volcanoes just ooze slowly, but other times an explosion shoots the hot red rock high into the air! The "smoke" that fills the sky during and after a volcanic eruption is a thick cloud of ash. (Beres 1998, p. 35–36)

This text can be rewritten for performance. The following procedures (Bullion-Mears et al. 1997), though developed for found poetry, are easily adapted to create rap lyrics, reader's theater scripts, and simulations.

When introducing the procedure, select a passage containing a difficult or key concept, procedure, or process of 150 to 300 words. Next, copy the passage onto a sheet of paper, double-spacing the text to make it easier to examine and edit. Teachers may also want to create a transparency with enlarged text for demonstration purposes with the whole class. At this point, the students need an introduction to found poetry (or raps, reader's theater, or simulations). Found poetry involves the rewriting of an existing narrative or expository passage into a poetic format. Because the textual content is set, the student writer is able to focus on distilling and emphasizing meaning.

Next, demonstrate the poem-writing process to the whole class. With the students, carefully read the passage, highlighting key words and concepts. Delete dull, uninteresting, or unnecessary words. Dunning and Stafford (1992) suggest cutting the original passage in half. Punctuation may be deleted and capitalization may be changed. Adding words to the passage should be avoided, if at all possible. However, up to two words may be added to ease transitions or to help the poem make sense. Other small changes, such as changing possessives, plurals, and tenses, may be made to the text. Then arrange the material into poetic lines. Emphasize meaning by placing words in various and unique ways on the page. Through questions and prompts, lead students to share in the examination, condensation, and design of this first poem. Reading aloud as students arrange the text will help them to hear differences in meaning and emphasis. Space the words out or runthemalltogether to indicate timing. Keywords can be highlighted by placing them on a line by themselves, by writing them in a larger size, or by using boldface or a different color or type of print. Try more than one format. Finally, title the poem and include the proper citations.

After this initial demonstration, the class can be broken into small groups of students (three to six) to experiment with the process using a related text. Interesting comparisons can arise when groups develop distinctive poems based on a common text. As students grow more adept with the process, they can perform the examination and writing in pairs or individually, using either a uniform text or different texts related to the same topic. Text passages can also be lengthened. Figure 1 includes an example and student instructions for creating a found poem.

When poems are complete, they can be displayed around the classroom or they can be performed using choral reading techniques. Poems can be assessed on the inclusion and correctness of major conceptual principles. Ultimately, the comprehension of the concepts can be evaluated by oral and/or written questions.

Performing Expository Materials

Performing text uses voice combinations and contrasts to create meaning and highlight particular vocabulary and concepts. Choral

Figure 1.

Writing a "found poem"

1. Select an interesting or important passage of 150 to 300 words from a newspaper, book, encyclopedia, magazine, or textbook.

2. Copy the passage onto a sheet of paper, double-spacing the text to make it easier to examine and edit. Carefully read the passage, highlighting key words and concepts. Delete dull, uninteresting, or unnecessary words, and punctuation.

3. Arrange the material into poetic lines. Try more than one format.

4. Title the new text "Found Poem." Under the title write "words from" and the article or passage title, publication source, date, and page number(s). At the end of the poem write "arranged by" and your name or the class designation.

Found Poem

Words from Beres, S. 1998. *101 things every kid should know about science*, pp. 35–36. Los Angeles, CA: Lowell House Juvenile Books.

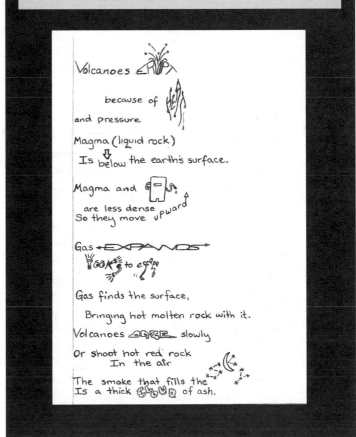

reading, the most familiar of the performance techniques, can use solo, duet, or choral voices in unison or antiphonally. Antiphonal arrangements can be accomplished through the physical division of a class into two parts or according to gender and having each section recite alternate lines or stanzas. Separating the class by gender encourages the development of interesting contrasts between male and female voices.

Rapping is a favorite among middle school students (Morrell and Duncan-Andrade 2002). This performance style adds strong beats, forming a hip-hop style of rhythmic talking. These beats can act as a mnemonic device to help students retain information. Reader's theater is more formalized. Readers use little, if any, movement. They stand or sit in assigned places (different levels add interest) and hold scripts in their hands throughout the performance. The power of reader's theater lies in the ability of the reader to bring the character to life through voice and facial expression (Young and Vardell 1993; Prince and Jackson 1997; El-Hindi 2003).

Choral reading, rap, and reader's theater use the same general performance procedures. Before beginning, introduce the rap or reader's theater script. As a class, closely examine the rap or script. Help students discover the key elements, the purpose of a repeating chorus between verses, and how the beat was developed. Talk about whether or not rap needs to rhyme. Discuss the role of the narrator in the script. If using a student- or teacher-created rap or script, give credit to the source of information and have students compare the two texts. Discuss the voice tones (volume, emotional quality, pacing), rhythms (speed, syncopation, emphasized beats), or movements (bodily and facial) demanded by the rap or script. Model the reading. Read with expression, using drama, sound effects, and/or movements. For raps, establish a strong beat by clapping hands or snapping fingers. Students love it when teachers get into it by moving with the rhythm Assign students to perform words, lines, stanzas, or roles. Initially, group students together; as they become more experienced, encourage solo performances. Perform the rap or script for each other and for other classes.

Once students have been introduced to the performance styles and techniques, they can create their own adaptations of content area materials using the instructions in Figure 2. Rap lyrics and reader's theater scripts can be assessed on the inclusion, accuracy, and sequencing of content and vocabulary. Performances can be assessed on delivery (volume, pacing, enunciation, intonation), poise, and expressiveness.

Performing Simulations

Simulations show a simplified model of a situation, problem, activity, procedure, or process. Creating a simulation involves students in translating abstract textual concepts into a concrete model. Motion, noise, and simple props help students demonstrate concepts (Freiberg and Driscoll 1992; Orlich et al. 1994). For example, to simulate a volcanic eruption using the Beres's (1998) text, quickly diagram the steps of an eruption: quiescence, internal rumblings, full eruption (see Figure 2). Translate the drawing into body motions and sounds that demonstrate the disturbance a volcano causes to Earth's surface. Focus on the commotion that accompanies the magma and gases as they gain momentum. To illustrate the hot magma, students can squat or sit on the floor moving back and forth. As the magma mixes with gases, students can move to crouching positions and intensify their sounds and movements. For the final stage, students leap upward, placing arms wide open and making swooshing sounds to show the power and dynamic effect of a volcanic eruption. Everyone in the class participates in the actions. Use debriefing to check for student understanding of basic concepts and processes.

Simulations are active and require student engagement to enhance concept development;

Figure 2.
Creating and performing a rap or reader's theater script

1. Select a text from a newspaper, book, encyclopedia, magazine, or textbook that explains a science concept.
2. Copy the passage onto a sheet of paper, double-spacing the text to make it easier to examine and edit. Carefully read the passage, highlighting key words and concepts. Delete unnecessary, repetitive, or uninteresting information.
3. Personify inanimate objects and abstract concepts. For raps, use verses and a chorus as found in song writing. Emphasize the beat by adding hand claps or finger snaps. Use scriptwriting techniques for reader's theater; a narrator can provide a frame for the performance and bridge gaps in the action.
4. Practice the poem, rap, or script in a group or with the whole class. Encourage everyone to join in. When performing, read with expression, using drama, sound effects, and/or movements.

Volcano: A Reader's Theater
Narrator: The scene opens 90 miles below the Earth's surface. It's a tense time. Heat and pressure are building. We are about to witness a volcanic eruption. Try to stay calm.

Magma: I am Magma. I am hot liquid rock waiting—waiting to escape upward.

Gas: I am Gas. I form in the bowels of the Earth. I know that Magma wants to escape, so I help.

Magma/Gas: Together we are less dense than the surrounding rock, so we look for places to work our way toward the surface.

Vent: Come this way, Magma and Gas. I am Vent. Follow me to the top. I'll even throw in a few rocks to make the journey exciting.

Rocks: Good choice. We love to become hot and molten.

Narrator: And so Magma, Gas, and Rocks choose to either ooze forth quietly or burst forth unabashedly.

Today they feel more like a burst. Listen now. I hear them coming.

(Explosion sounds)

Magma/Gas/Rocks/Vent: Look at us! Hear us! Tremble. We are awesome!

Narrator: (As the explosion sounds slowly die away) And so, a volcano. Active. Pulsing. Fuming. (No more sounds) And afterward there lingers a thick cloud of ash. The tension is gone. All is quiet. Earth, once again, rests.

Volcanoes: A Rap (Clap or snap your fingers for each x in the chorus.)

Chorus
Hot **x** hot **xx** it's hot
Say hot **x** hot **xx** it's hot

Verse 1
Ya better never go near the volcano
It might look nice, but it's not. Down below
It's bubblin' and boilin', it's waitin' for a ride.
It'll sure find a groove to get outside.

Chorus
Verse 2
It finds a nice vent; now the journey is fast.
Here it comes, movin' up—ya hear a blast.
Lava's pourin' and hissin' and shootin' high.
There's tons of ash fillin' up the sky.

Chorus
Verse 3
Later things change, that volcano is through.
The noise stops, ash leaves, sky is blue.
But don't let the quiet fool your father and your mother
Cause way down there, there is always another.
Pssssssssssssssssss! Hot! Hot! Yeah!

therefore, students should create their own simulation. The instructional procedures in Figure 3 optimize the opportunities for creating successful simulations.

Begin by selecting a text; one that shows a clear process or procedure works best. Read the selection aloud several times; ask students to highlight key words and concepts and to brainstorm ways to illustrate the process, procedure, or action to an audience. You may use a quick drawing or rough diagram to clarify key concepts. On an overhead or chalkboard, delineate clearly the steps the students will use to demonstrate the process. Assist students in translating the steps into body movements and sounds. Simple props can help to clarify ambiguous actions. Students then prepare for the performance and present to the class. Because of the speed with which a simulation is enacted, students need to perform it more than once. Once completed, students need an opportunity to talk about their simulation. Videotape of the performance is helpful with debriefing and can be used in future discussions and reviews of the concepts. Student reflections on the accuracy and portrayal of the content determine mastery of the concepts.

Final Thoughts

Performing text is a technique that builds on the social and energetic nature of middle school students and helps them create detailed and vibrant mental pictures that enhance comprehension. Performing expository text engages students with the material they are studying as they communicate and collaborate with their peers in preparing and practicing text. Even reluctant readers and shy introverts find it almost impossible to be uninvolved in a classroom that is working with performing text.

Lifting concepts from expository text off the page and into the minds of middle school students is certainly a challenge. Performing text is a vehicle to give those informational words the wings needed to be understood, seen, and felt.

Figure 3.
Creating and performing simulations

1. Select a text that shows a clear process or procedure. Read through the text several times, highlighting key words and concepts.

2. Brainstorm ways to illustrate the process, procedure, or action to an audience. A drawing, diagram, or chart helps to clarify and delineate key concepts.

3. Translate key concepts into body motions and sounds. Use simple props to clarify meaning.

4. Practice the simulation several times prior to performance.

5. Deliver an overview of the topic and key concepts to prepare the audience for the simulation. Perform it!

6. Be prepared to talk about your simulation once you have finished.

Choral reading, rap, reader's theater, and simulations can help replace the moans and groans of the middle school reader and the "Miss, do we have to read our textbook today?" with excitement and interest.

Ann Bullion-Mears is an assistant professor at Angelo State University in San Angelo, Texas. Joyce K. McCauley is a professor at Sam Houston State University in Huntsville, Texas. J. YeVette McWhorter is an associate professor at Georgia Southwestern State University in Americus, Georgia.

References

Beres, S. 1998. *101 things every kid should know about science.* Los Angeles, CA: Lowell House Juvenile Books.

Bullion-Mears, A., J. Y. McWhorter, C. Haag, M. Cox, and S. Hickey. 1997. *Extending literacy across the disciplines: Reading and writing poetry in middle school classrooms.* Washington, DC: ERIC Document Reproduction Service. ED410587

Combs, M. 2003. *Readers and writers in the middle grades*. 2nd ed. Upper Saddle River, NJ: Merrill Prentice Hall.

Dunning, S., and W. Stafford. 1992. *Getting the knack: 20 poetry writing exercises*. Urbana, IL: National Council of Teachers of English.

El-Hindi, A. E. 2003. Integrating literacy and science in the classroom: From ecomysteries to readers theatre. *The Reading Teacher* 56 (6): 536–38.

Freiberg, H. J., and A. Driscoll. 1992. *Universal teaching strategies*. Boston: Allyn & Bacon.

Irvin, J. L. 1998. *Reading and the middle school student: Strategies to enhance literacy*. Boston: Allyn and Bacon.

McCauley, J. K., and D. S. McCauley. 1992. Using choral reading to promote language learning for ESL students. *The Reading Teacher* 45 (7): 526–33.

Morrell, E., and J. M. Duncan-Andrade. 2002. Promoting academic literacy with urban youth through engaging hip-hop culture. *English Journal* 91 (6): 88–92.

Orlich, D. C., R. J. Harder, R. C. Callahan, and H. W. Gibson. 1994. *Teaching strategies: A guide to better instruction,* 4th ed. Lexington, MA: Heath.

Prince, N., and J. Jackson. 1997. *Exploring theatre.* Minneapolis/St. Paul, MN: West Publishing.

Young, T. A., and S. Vardell. 1993. Weaving readers theatre and nonfiction into the curriculum. *The Reading Teacher* 46 (5): 396–406.

Developing Strategic Readers

By Jennifer Jones and Susie Leahy

As elementary students progress from *learning to read* toward *reading to learn*, it is vital that they become strategic readers. A strategic reader is one who understands when and how to use a strategy to comprehend text. Although some students use strategies naturally during the reading process, most students must be taught how to think during reading. The strategies presented here—Question-Answer-Relationships (QARs), Wonder Notebooks, and Reciprocal Questioning (ReQuest)—aim to do just that and are appropriate for use with science texts.

Questions Are Key

One of the key factors in reading success—and also success in science inquiry—is an ability to ask good questions. Questioning techniques are prevalent in many schools; however, in many instances, questioning is used to evaluate comprehension, rather than to develop comprehension skills (Blachowicz and Ogle 2001). In most classrooms, the teacher does most of the questioning, often using the I-R-E approach (Mehan 1979; Blachowicz and Ogle 2001). The I-R-E approach involves an *I*, or *initiation*, by the teacher, such as asking questions about a reading selection. Initiation is followed by an

R, or *a response*, from the student(s), which is in turn followed by an *E*, or an *evaluation*, by the teacher regarding the students' responses. This method is actually more appropriate for assessing student comprehension than for facilitating it. Questions allow students to interact with the text, evaluate the text, and make connections to it.

Research suggests that questioning is most effective when students are involved in the process (Beck et al. 1996; Raphael and Wonnacott 1985), such as in the strategies described in this article. Most important, these strategies can help students learn for themselves how and where to find the information to answer questions.

Question-Answer-Relationships

Question-answer-relationships (QARs) are a well-researched method for teaching questioning as a reading strategy (Raphael 1984; Raphael and Au 2005). The Question-Answer-Relationship technique engages students in the questioning process and teaches students that questions often require different sources of information to answer them. QAR is basically a structure by which students categorize questions according to four types. Each type of question requires different skills to answer it, thus allowing students to become aware of the thought processes and resources necessary to thoughtfully ask and answer questions.

To implement QARs in the classroom, teachers must first introduce the four types of questions to students and also provide students with practice in categorizing questions. To begin, students and the teacher can categorize teacher-generated questions together. As the class practices categorizing the questions, the teacher asks students to explain why they categorized each question as they did. Later, students can practice categorizing their own questions in small groups and with partners as the teacher moves among the groups asking students to explain their reasons behind their categorizations. Eventually, students will be able to independently apply the QAR questioning strategy without support.

The four question types are as follows:

- *Right There* questions are questions in which there is one answer that can be found directly in the text. Students should be able to answer such questions with ease, even underlining the answers in the text.
- *Think and Search* questions are also found in the text but encompass more than one answer. Students must put different parts of the text together in order to answer this type of question.
- *Author and Me* questions are not found directly in the text. This type of question requires the reader to "read between the lines," using information from the text coupled with personal background knowledge and prior experiences. In essence, Author and Me questions require the reader to make inferences as they negotiate information from the text with their own knowledge base.
- *On My Own* questions appeal to students' experiences and feelings on a topic and can sometimes be answered without reading the text.

Figure 1 lists an example of each type of question based on the Matter and Energy section in *Harcourt Science Fourth Grade Text* (Jones et al. 2002).

Color-coded sticky notes can help students reinforce the message of each question type (Lawrence 2002). For example, *Right There* questions might be written on green sticky notes, because students can go straight to them without stopping. Yellow sticky notes can be used for *Think and Search* questions, because they require the reader to slow down a bit. Red (or dark pink) sticky notes can be used for *Author and Me* questions, because they require the reader to stop and think in more depth.

Generating questions facilitates deeper thought than merely answering questions. To generate questions, students must revisit the text, process the important elements of the text, and determine the sources needed to generate and answer questions in a thorough manner. In other words, students must know the content before they can ask a good question about it.

Research has shown that training and practice with QARs improves text comprehension, particularly for implicit or Author and Me questions (Schoenbach et al. 1999). The technique has also proved motivating for some students. Many teachers use student-generated questions on quizzes (giving the question writer credit for his or her work) or have students peruse peer-generated questions during free time in the classroom. Seeing their own questions being used as part of the classroom activities is inspiring to students and encourages them to employ deeper thought with their questions.

Wonder Notebooks

The Wonder Notebook strategy is useful for sparking students' curiosity and questioning skills. To use this strategy, a teacher first models and shares her own questions, "those things she wonders about and longs to explore further" (Harvey and Goudvis 2000, p. 86). Following the modeling, students are encouraged to write

Figure 1.
QAR Question examples and explanation

Question Type	Question	Explanation of Use
Right There	*What is kinetic energy?* (Answer: energy in motion) *What does the word* thermal *mean?* (Answer: heat)	These Right There questions address important terms in the reading selection but only require surface-level thought processes. Right There questions are excellent for highlighting important terms and concepts, teaching note-taking, and locating important information (Raphael and Au 2005).
Think and Search	*Using the text, name two examples of kinetic energy.* (Possible answers: ball flying through the air, cart moving through the grocery store, etc.)	This Think and Search question requires the reader to read across the text, searching for more than one simple answer. Students may still use the text explicitly to answer the question; however, it requires more reading across the text. Think and Search questions often involve listing examples or naming steps in a process. This question type often facilitates students in locating facts, summarizing information, and using text structure to identify important information (Raphael and Au 2005).
Author and Me	*If I have a pint of boiling water, and I have a gallon of boiling water, which container has more thermal energy and why?* (Answer: The gallon of water has more energy because the text says more matter equals more particles, which equals more energy.)	In order to answer this Author and Me question, the reader must go beyond the text. He or she must take information the author has provided and apply it to a situation outside of the text. Author and Me questions require higher-level thinking and generally require students to go beyond the text, applying knowledge in real-world scenarios, making simple and complex inferences, and/or distinguishing between fact and opinion (Raphael and Au 2005).
On My Own	*Have you ever used a thermometer? In what ways did you use it?*	This On My Own question asks students to share their experiences in connection with a portion of the text. There is no right or wrong answer; however, the question facilitates text-to-self connections. On My Own questions are excellent for prereading science selections or after-reading discussions.

down three things related to the topic they wonder about in their own personal "Wonder Notebooks."

For example, after reading about electricity, one fourth-grade student was curious about how electricity enables lamps to give light or how it powers our computers. This student jotted down the following questions in her Wonder Notebook:

- How does something that I can't see (electricity) make my desk light work?
- How does the electricity actually get to my computer?
- How is lightning created?

From the Wonder Notebooks, students then organize their questions into categories for further investigation. Typically, students need guidance from the teacher to determine appropriate categories.

This guidance occurs when the class gathers to share their questions after students have jotted down their questions independently. Together, the class can group their questions into broader categories, such as electrical conductors or electricity in the natural world. By working as a group, the teacher has an opportunity to "think-aloud" and model her thinking processes for the students. This helps strengthen the students' own ability to generate thoughtful, on-target wonderings.

After the questions have been categorized, the teacher and students reread the questions in each category to determine if there are overarching questions about the concept addressed in the categories (do students have overall wonderings about what types of materials serve as electrical conductors under the Electrical Conductors category?). The teacher would then use the I Wonder questions under this category and apply them to hands-on science experiments that students can conduct to answer their questions.

Reciprocal Questioning

Reciprocal questioning (ReQuest) engages students in questioning with the teacher during classroom discussion (Manzo 1969). The object of ReQuest is not to evaluate students' comprehension of science material but to stimulate students' critical-thinking and reasoning skills via this questioning technique (Vaughn and Estes 1986).

In a ReQuest reading, students read a science text with the mindset that they will be the ones asking the questions; therefore, they must know the content reasonably well to be able to ask intelligent questions of the teacher (McKenna 2002).

To begin, both students and teacher read a small predetermined portion of the science text. The teacher closes his or her book, and the students ask the teacher any question related to the selected portion of the reading. The teacher must answer the question as completely and accurately as possible. The teacher follows his or her answer by providing students with feedback regarding the quality of their questions. Next, the process is repeated but the teacher asks students the question. The teacher's questions provide a model for the quality of the questions.

For example, after a group of fourth-grade students and their teacher read a section called "What are living things?" from a textbook, the teacher closed her text and students asked her, "What is an organism?" The teacher responded with an accurate and complete response: "I am an organism. I know this because the book says organisms need food, water, and oxygen; are made of parts; and each part has a job for keeping the thing alive."

Next, it was the teacher's turn to ask students a question based on the reading. She said, "Plants are organisms, too. Explain why a tomato is also an organism."

By following students' question with this statement, the teacher was modeling higher-level questioning because her question asked students to provide reasoning for their responses. In addition, her question helped students make meaningful real-world connections with information provided from the text because to answer this question, students must take what the text told them about plants and the characteristics of organisms and apply this outside of the context of the text selection.

Summing Up
Using these three questioning techniques can help your students learn to think more deeply about the topics presented. For the strategies to be truly effective, however, teachers have to model each strategy and provide significant guided practice before students can independently engage in such strategic endeavors while reading. Once students are comfortable with the techniques, they will be armed with three powerful tools to use continuously as they learn about the world around them.

Jennifer Jones is a reading specialist and an assistant professor of education at Radford University in Radford, Virginia. Susie Leahy is the director of reading in the education department at the University of Richmond in Richmond, Virginia.

Resources
Blachowicz, C., and D. Ogle. 2001. *Reading comprehension: Strategies for independent learners.* New York: The Guilford Press.

Beck, I. L., M. G. McKeown, J. Worthy, C. A. Sandora, and L. Kucan. 1996. Questioning the author: A year-long classroom implementation to engage students with text. *The Elementary School Journal* 96 (4): 387–416.

Harvey, S., and A. Goudvis. 2000. *Strategies that work: Teaching comprehension to enhance understanding.* York, ME: Stenhouse.

Jones, F., M. Frank, G. H. Krockover, M. P. Lang, J. C. McLeod, C. J. Valenta, and B. A. V. Deman. 2002. *Harcourt science, fourth grade text.* Orlando, FL: Harcourt.

Lawrence, K. M. 2002. Red light, green light, 1-2-3: Tasks to prepare for standardized

tests. *The Reading Teacher* 55 (6): 525–528.

Manzo, A.V. 1969. ReQuest procedure. *Journal of Reading* 13 (2): 123–126.

McKenna, M. C. 2002. *Helping struggling readers, grades 3–8.* New York: The Guilford Press.

Mehan, J. 1979. *Learning lessons.* Cambridge, MA: Harvard University Press.

Raphael, T. E. 1984. Teaching learners about sources of information for answering comprehension questions. *Journal of Reading* 4: 303–311.

Raphael, T. E., and K. H. Au. 2005. QAR: Enhancing comprehension and test taking across grades and content areas. *The Reading Teacher* 59 (3): 206–221.

Raphael, T. E., and C. A Wonnacott. 1985. Heightening fourth-grade students' sensitivity to sources of information for answering comprehension questions. *Reading Research Quarterly* 20 (3): 282–296.

Schoenbach, R., C. Greenleaf, C. Cziko, and L. Hurwitz. 1999. *Reading for understanding: A guide to improving reading in middle and high school classrooms.* San Francisco: Jossey-Bass.

Vaughn, J. L., and T. H. Estes. 1986. *Reading and reasoning beyond the primary grades.* Boston, MA: Allyn & Bacon.

Connecting to the Standards
This article relates to the following National Science Education Standards (NRC 1996):

Teaching Standards
Standard B:
Teachers of science guide and facilitate learning.

Content Standards
Standard A: Science as Inquiry
• Abilities necessary to do scientific inquiry
• Understanding about scientific inquiry

14 Writing Strategies

By Thomas Turner and Amy Broemmel

I n 1905, a young scientist named Albert Einstein published a three-page paper presenting his theory of relativity. That brief paper was a major step in revolutionizing how physicists throughout the world thought, and it would change the way that the world in general thought about science (Penrose 2005). That a relatively small piece of writing could be so important certainly illustrates the significance of writing to science. Good scientists record what they do—their results, procedures and operations, observations, and hypotheses, as well as their problems and questions.

Scientists need to develop their writing skills for a number of reasons:

- Writing down their ideas and describing what they do and find give scientists and those that read and depend on their work a more accurate record from which to attempt to replicate results.
- Written accounts of what scientists observe, which are recorded at the time of their observations, help scientists remember more accurately and completely.
- Written summaries of scientific work allow scientists to synthesize bodies of work and look at them holistically so that they

or other scientists can extend and develop ideas further.
- Written notes about their work allow scientists to reflect on and process what they have observed.
- Written presentations of their work allow scientists to share and publicize their findings, get credit for their work, and, as a result, claim the benefits of their successes.
- Written descriptions of planned work enable scientists to obtain funding to continue their often-expensive work.
- Written summaries of their ideas allow scientists to share the importance of their work with nonscientists.

Why We Need to Teach Writing

Any science teacher who wants his or her students to be engaged in real science is going to engage them in real science writing. Students do not intuitively know how to do such writing, nor is instruction in scientific writing necessarily or even likely going to occur in other school subjects. This writing instruction can serve two purposes. It can increase science understanding and engage students in activities that are useful in the assessment process in science itself. Montgomery (2005, p. 28) points out that student writing provides the teacher with "a tangible demonstration of learning and gives students the opportunity to connect their personal experiences to the content." Montgomery goes on to say that well-crafted, thoughtfully planned writing assignments require the student to do a "deep analysis of subject material."

Well-designed science writing assignments essentially have three critical attributes:

1. They provide authentic purposes for writing.
2. They motivate students to want to write and to do science.
3. They help students plan and structure both their writing and their science activities.

These attributes are inextricably and symbiotically related. They combine to make the writing assignment comprehensible, authentically important, and feasible. Matsumura and his colleagues (2002) found that the cognitive challenge of the writing assignment had a significant effect on the quality of students' final drafts. That is, when students felt that assignments were cognitively challenging and satisfying to complete, they worked more effectively in producing a finished writing product. Writing experiences should help students feel good about their own writing.

Writing in science should begin with clear, imaginative writing purposes and stimuli that are then scaffolded in such a way that students are able to find an organizational structure for their writing. Writing fluency is often enhanced and supported by experiences like brainstorming or free writing.

Writing Assignments That Work

Writing in *The American Scientist*, Gopen and Swan (1990) said, "The fundamental purpose of scientific discourse is not the mere presentation of information and thought, but rather its actual communication" (p. 550). Of course, much of the public and many scientists would question this idea because they often think that scientific concepts, data, and analysis are extremely complex, difficult, and abstract. Like Gopen and Swan, however, we would argue that what matters most in scientific writing is that a majority of the reading audience accurately perceives what the science writer has in mind, and, that when science writing improves, it is a sign that the thinking is better. In the interest of promoting such thinking, we would like to offer 14 examples of different kinds of writing assignments that can provide legitimate, purposeful writing practice while promoting solid science learning and review.

1 *Writing hypothetical letters*—Often scientists share their observations and questions as well as their differences of opinion by letter or, in today's world, by blogs and e-mail messages. A very simple yet effective example of a scientific exchange can be seen in the children's book, *Dear Mr. Blueberry,* by Simon James (1996). In this book, James has created a story line through an exchange of letters between a little girl named Emily and her teacher, Mr. Blueberry. Read the book aloud and talk about how Emily seeks help, information, and even opinion but is strongly true to her own observations. Students can work collaboratively to create their own hypothetical exchange of letters between themselves and a scientist or teacher. An important lesson of this poignantly sweet book is that a person should believe in the power of evidence even when it contradicts authority. A second lesson is that it is possible to do this without being disrespectful to authority. In adapting the activity for class, students, in their letters, can share observations about some theme or topic. If possible, the return letters by the authorities or scientists can come from older children or parents with science backgrounds. This could also be accomplished electronically in collaboration with university students studying to be science teachers.

2 *Process steps analysis*—After observing or taking part in a demonstration of a scientific process, the class could discuss what they saw. After talking the observations through, they can analyze and document the sequential steps that they would need to completely replicate the demonstration. In some cases, in which it is safe and feasible, students might even have the opportunity to recreate the demonstration following their own steps.

3 *Identifying critical attributes*—Small groups of students are asked to look at something. This can be an object of any kind or even a plant or an animal. Each group has a different object. They are given the opportunity to make a thorough examination and to identify its critical attributes. Critical attributes are those observable qualities that make the object, plant, or animal unique, allowing it to be distinguished from all others. The groups can then compile a list of what they believe to be the critical attributes of what they have seen. The lists are shared with the whole class, and students attempt to match the correct item with the critical attribute list. If accurate matching is not possible, students are encouraged to revisit and revise their lists.

4 *Collaborative writing of scientific stories*—The teacher begins by reading (or having the students read) a science-related trade book. Fiction books, such as *How Groundhog's Garden Grew* (Cherry 2003), and nonfiction books, such as *One Tiny Turtle* (Davies 2001), can be used effectively for this activity. After students have become familiar with the story, the teacher needs to start a discussion focusing on the scientific content or process described in the book. Once the teacher is satisfied that students understand the science of the book, he or she has the class sit in a circle on the floor. Three clipboards with paper are given to students positioned at equal intervals around the circle. Each student

holding a clipboard is asked to think about the science described in the book and then writes one sentence that describes the first event in the book. They then pass the clipboard to the right. Students are instructed that when they receive a clipboard, they need to read what has been written up to that point on the paper and then write an additional sentence describing the next event in the scientific process described in the story. Each paper will, in the end, contain a complete retelling of the story in the sequence it occurred. (Three papers are used to provide a means of keeping students engaged and to document student understanding of various parts of the content and process.)

5 *Chain of evidence*—Because most students have watched many television shows dealing with forensic evidence in criminal investigations, their observation experiences can be used as the basis for writing activities. First, the teacher identifies a crime that the team will investigate. Appropriate possibilities could include robberies, kidnappings, acts of vandalism, or simple crimes that happen around the school every day. (Avoid scenarios involving violent or graphic crimes.) Begin with a brainstorming session. Have the class create a detailed summary of the chain of evidence leading to the arrest and trial of a suspect in their invented crime. Encourage them to use rich details with leading questions, such as: What kind of evidence are we going to look for? Where are we likely to find evidence? How do we distinguish evidence related to the crime from what we would normally expect within the crime scene? What are some different ways of reconstructing the crime based on the evidence? What possibilities does the evidence suggest?

As an alternative to providing students with only the hypothetical crime, the teacher could also provide a list of "suspects" with a brief introduction to each. Students might then choose a "guilty" suspect and create a well-reasoned written explanation of fictional clues and evidence that could lead to the suspect's arrest. Students then have to learn the difference between being reasonably sure that someone is guilty and having sufficient evidence to bring them to trial and then having enough evidence to convict. Students can assume the roles of judge and jury in response to one another's assembly of evidence, ultimately deciding if the written chain of evidence is sufficient to lead to a trial and subsequent conviction.

6 *Accident report*—In this activity, a teacher creates an accident scene by either using photos or actually staging an accident. Examples of cases might include lunchroom mishaps such as spilled trays; a playground incident such as a fall from a piece of equipment, someone being hit by a ball, or a collision between two running students; or a classroom situation such as stacks of papers falling on the floor and getting mixed together. After examining the accident scene and gathering evidence, the accident-scene investigators are asked to write reports based on their observations. In very small groups, students then read each other's reports, noting inconsistencies or missing details.

7 *Label analysis*—The teacher first organizes students into groups and then provides each group with an empty package or label for some product. The products can be foods, medicines, household cleansers, or anything else with a label that lists its ingredients. Each group then writes a description of what they know about the product based on the list of ingredients—in other words, what the contents list tells you, and what it doesn't tell you. For example, if something advertised as a juice product has little or no actual fruit juice in it, what does that mean? What does the label tell you about nutrition? What are the risks and benefits of using the product?

8 *Technical directions*—The teacher begins by giving students toys or models that

require some assembly. Students are then asked to take the role of the marketing staff at the product's manufacturing company. Students must first practice assembling the toy or model, carefully noting the quickest, most efficient steps for assembly. Then, they are responsible for writing the directions that will be included on the package. Finally, students attempt to assemble other groups' toys or models using the new directions.

9 *Scientific directions*—The teacher organizes the class into small groups and assigns each group a familiar location within a short distance from the school. Each group then discusses the best route to the assigned place and writes directions for getting there using landmarks based on scientific observations taken along the route. For example, the directions could include descriptions of plants, geological formations, or environmental cues. As a follow-up, have students see if they can navigate to a spot using others' directions.

10 *Scientific reporting*—After a discussion of the essentials of accurately reporting scientific observations, students are organized into groups. Each group is given a video recording of a scientific experiment and asked to create a detailed list of observations that someone could use to recreate the experiment. The group is allowed to view the video as many times as they like to ensure that their observation list is accurate and complete. (See Resources for recommended video collections.)

11 *Proposal writing*—The basic function of a proposal is to describe and pitch to others ideas for projects, papers, and research studies. Proposal writing is an essential activity for many scientists, and the skills needed to write proposals should be developed as early as possible. Instead of simply assigning projects and research reports, teachers can provide general parameters for the intended assignment—for instance, research related to rock formation or a project depicting a food chain. Proposal-writing activities can begin with a simple brainstorming for project ideas. The fundamental question is, What do we want to do? After generating a list of ideas, the teacher can then lead students through the process of selecting and refining a single idea from the list. The next step is to create a proposal outline. To help students with this the teacher may have a set of specifications or even provide a simple outline such as the following:

- Title (a proposal…)
- Abstract or summary
- An introduction giving background and explaining the situation
- A statement of the project problem to be solved
- Some suggestion or suggestions about solutions to the problem
- Some explanation of how you will solve the problem
- An outline describing the proposed project outcome
- A step-by-step description of your research methods
- Conclusions

After the outline has been created, assign a different group to write a draft for each part. Finally, piece together the proposal, editing each part so that it is consistent with the rest. The combined class effort can then serve as a model for small groups or individual students to develop their own proposals.

12 *Pourquoi story writing*—Pourquoi (*pourquoi* is French for *why*) stories are fictional explanations of natural phenomena. They are usually based upon definitive descriptions of the phenomena themselves. One example is "How the Elephant Got His Long Trunk." A series of logical plot actions are described, connecting the

main characters in the story to the creation of the phenomena. Provide students with a list of natural phenomena, and have them create their own pourquoi stories for one of these. Stress the importance of including scientific facts in explanations. Examples of appropriate subjects include why magnets attract, why we have tornadoes, why snakes shed their skin, why hens cackle and roosters crow, why owls hoot, how squirrels got their bushy tails, and why volcanoes erupt.

13 *Preparing descriptive research through web quests.* Web quests are designed to be structured inquiry activities in which information is drawn from the internet. Web quests focus the learners' time on using information rather than looking for it, and emphasize thinking at the levels of analysis, synthesis, and evaluation. Essentially, students are directed to a sequenced series of specific websites to solve a structured inquiry problem. A number of websites provide examples of web quests (see Resources). An example of a teacher-created web quest might ask students to determine which simple machines would be most effective in performing a particular multistep task. The web quest would be designed to lead students to a series of websites that present verbal and/or pictorial information about simple machines. Students would use the information to develop a written solution to the problem. Teachers can also train students to develop their own web quests as an alternative means of demonstrating understanding of particular scientific content and/or processes.

14 *News clip observations*—The teacher shows short news film clips without sound. These clips may show natural disasters, the effects of weather, destruction brought about by human effort, or other science-related concepts. Students then write descriptions of the event based on their observations. After students have completed their descriptions, replay the film clip with sound and ask students to compare the accompanying news commentary to what they wrote.

Final Note

A science class is not complete unless it helps students learn to think like scientists, and writing is an essential part of such thinking. The 14 writing experiences described here for integrating meaningful, interesting writing into science are not intended to be followed to the letter. Rather, they are all adaptable ideas. Neither are they intended to replace traditional science instruction. If we want our students to think like scientists, however, then it is only logical that we should ask them to observe, document, and write like scientists, as well. We believe that these and other thoughtfully structured writing activities can be integrated into science classrooms in a way that addresses curriculum; provides alternative, authentic means of assessing student understanding; and motivates students to become actively involved in the learning process.

Thomas Turner is a professor and Amy Broemmel is an assistant professor in the Department of Theory and Practice in Teacher Education at the University of Tennessee in Knoxville, Tennessee.

References

Cherry, L. 2003. *How groundhog's garden grew*. New York: Blue Sky Press.

Davies, N. 2001. *One tiny turtle*. Cambridge, MA: Candlewick Press.

Gopen, G. D., and J. A. Swan. 1990. The science of scientific writing. *The American Scientist* 78 (November-December): 550–58.

James, S. 1996. *Dear Mr. Blueberry*. New York: Scholastic.

Matsumura, L. C., G. G. Patthey-Chavez, R. Valdes, and H. Garnier. 2002. Teacher feedback, writing assignment quality, and third-grade students' revision in lower- and higher-achieving urban schools. *Elementary School Journal* 103 (1): 3–25.

Montgomery, M. 2005. Authentic science writing. *Principal Leadership: High School Education* 5 (6): 28–31.

Penrose, R. 2005. *Einstein's miraculous year: Five papers that changed the face of physics*. Princeton, NJ: Princeton University Press.

Resources

Web Quests
The WebQuest Page
   http://webquest.sdsu.edu
Teachnology
   www.teach-nology.com/teachers/lesson_plans/ computing/web_quests/science/
Science web quests
   www.can-do.com/uci/k12-lessons.html

Science the "Write" Way

By Valarie L. Akerson and Terrell A. Young

Learning to write well is a long process that comes through teacher modeling, instruction, practice, and feedback. Luckily, the writing process can be used to improve science learning, too. Here are a few good writing suggestions that integrate science while helping students develop their informational writing skills.

Science Journals

There is perhaps no better place than a science journal for students to develop informational writing skills. Daily journal prompts are one way to encourage students to write expansively about developing knowledge (see Figure 1 for sample journal prompts).

In journals, students make records of what they are doing in investigations—they organize data by creating tables and write observations based on their investigations. They record, via drawing and writing, characteristics of what they are observing, such as what a pill bug looks like and how it reacts in different settings. In using the journal in this way, students learn that making records of actual observations is something scientists often do and is a useful kind of nonfiction writing.

Beyond recording observations, students can use journals to write inferences based on

their observations. For example, if students observe that pill bugs prefer walking on dirt, they could infer that the dirt is more like their natural environment—thus making meaning of their observations. Students will find that inferences made from early observations may change as they make more observations. This tentativeness in inferences is an intrinsic part of the nature of science, but by making the recordings in their journal students can track their ideas over time and note any observations that lead to a change in inference.

Observations Versus Inference Charts

Another tool that supports science learning while developing informational writing skills is the observation versus inference chart—we've used this chart successfully to introduce primary students to the distinction between *observation* and *inference*. On the chart, one column is labeled "Observations" and the second is labeled "Inferences." During a class discussion following an exploration, the teacher records student observations under the Observations column and then asks students to make inferences about what those observations mean on

Figure 1.

Sample journal prompts, followed by examples of typical student responses

TREES
What do you think is a tree? How is it different from other plants?
I think a tree is wood and leaves. Trees are bigger than plants.

What do you think a tree is made of?
Trees are made of wood and leaves.

What are the parts of the tree? Draw a tree.
Leaves and the wood trunk (later in the unit they add other parts, such as roots)

(After we find a tree to "adopt") What is our tree like? What is special about our tree? How do you think our tree might change over time?
Our tree is big. It is special because it is ours! It has big leaves.

Why do you think trees are different shapes? Why do you think their leaves are different?
Because the leaves catch the sun in different ways.

(After several weeks) How does our tree look different? How does it look the same?
The trunk still looks the same. It is getting leaves!

What different shapes of leaves did you find? How can we sort our leaves?
I am putting the big ones together, then putting the spikey ones, and then the skinny ones.

What things can you tell me about a tree now? How do you think it is different from other plants now?
Trees are a kind of plant.

the Inferences column.

For example, after students have had time to observe snails up close, the teacher would collectively record students' observations—"The eyestalks move when I touch them," for instance—on the chart, then ask students to infer the meaning behind the observation—in this case, perhaps, "Because they are trying to move them out of my way—to keep them safe." The teacher can record the response on the inferences side.

After a few examples, students will begin making good distinctions between observations and inferences, and they can be given similar smaller charts for individuals or small groups of students to record their observations and inferences about other investigations on their own.

Student-Authored Books

To gain simultaneous insights into a content area, research, and literacy, students can research and write their very own book on a theme, such as "A Book About Scientists." Individual students or small groups can research subtopics—"What do scientists do?" "How do I become a scientist?" "What do scientists do in their spare time?"— and write chapters for the books (Figure 2). The chapters usually begin as notes from research or interviews of scientists.

Once the chapters are compiled, students then create a table of contents and a reference list to demonstrate that nonfiction writing must be based on accurate information. Next, students can illustrate the chapters with their own drawings.

Afterward the book can be published for their classroom enjoyment. Publishing a book is another good place to reinforce accuracy in writing in terms of spelling and conventions and the process of writing. Notes that students have taken previously can be written in draft form to be edited by the students later as they work on the computer to type their chapters.

We keep copies of our student-authored books in free reading–time tubs, so students can

Figure 2.

Sample chapter from a student-authored book, "What Is a Scientist?"

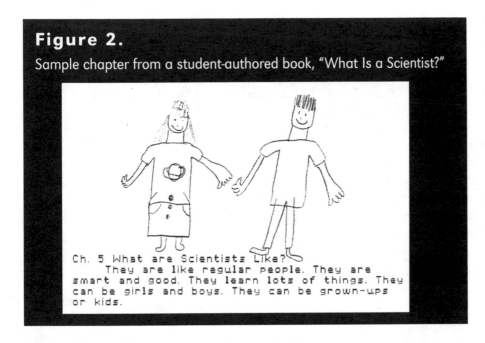

Ch. 5 What are Scientists Like?
   They are like regular people. They are
smart and good. They learn lots of things. They
can be girls and boys. They can be grown-ups
or kids.

The student who gets "L" might study lemurs. That student would then write an informational page about the lemur, illustrate it, and, when all pages are complete, the teacher would compile the book as a class alphabet book. Teachers can involve their students with similar projects related to nonfiction counting books (see Resources). April Pulley Sayre and Jeff Sayre's *One Is a Snail, Ten Is a Crab: A Counting by Feet Book* (2003) is ideal for intermediate students, because readers are required to count, add, and multiply the feet of various creatures. Using *Counting Wildflowers* (McMillan 1986) as a model, a first-grade teacher can take digital pictures of animals on a class field trip to a farm. Students can then record information about what they experienced on their field trip.

revisit their work, encouraging both recall of information about scientists and the importance of writing informational text.

Custom ABC Books

For younger primary grades, have students collectively create informational text in the form of an alphabetical or counting book. Students will not only be practicing writing and research content; they'll be learning how to gain information from nonfiction text and group it into categories.

Start out by reading examples, such as George Ella Lyon's (1989) *A B Cedar: An Alphabet of Trees,* George Shannon's *Tomorrow's Alphabet* (1996), or Kathy Darling's *Amazon ABC* (1996), then assign a content area to students or have them pick their own content area. Next, assign individual students a letter or a number. Each will research information related to that content and write an informational page that relates to their assigned letter or number.

For example, primary students might study organisms, and each child in the class could be assigned a letter of the alphabet and select an organism to study that begins with that letter.

E-mails to Scientists

Finally, students can pursue science learning by writing to real scientists. Most appropriate for older elementary students, having students e-mail a scientist provides an opportunity for students to compose their own questions about science content. Or, students could interview scientists about how they became scientists and the kinds of work they do. Students could use these e-mail conversations as a basis for a nonfiction report on that scientific specialty. They could even be required to ask the scientists how they use writing in their work.

Teachers can find contact information for scientist e-mail pals by contacting local universities and science labs. For instance, Indiana University houses a science outreach office in their college of arts and sciences with staff whose purpose is to make contacts between university science faculty and K–12 education. A similar office is located in Washington State at the Pacific Northwest National Laboratory's Office of Science Education, which not only provides scientists to visit classrooms and interact with students but also provides professional development opportunities for teachers. Teachers can find similar opportunities for contacts with scientists in their own local areas.

Reports and Other Uses

Nonfiction writing can also be used to help students develop understandings of science as inquiry, as students record observations, inferences, and results of investigations, and write formal reports to share with peers. Students can also use writing to design their own investigations, leading to a further understanding of investigations as recommended by the *National Science Education Standards* (NRC 1996).

Writings Are Assessments

Incorporating various nonfiction writing activities such as those suggested above not only facilitates students' thinking about science content, but it also results in material and work that can help teachers assess student understanding.

For example, observation versus inference charts can be used to capture a picture of what the whole class understands about a given topic. If a student records an observation of an investigation exploring whether pillbugs prefer light or dark environments as "Pillbugs love the dark," the teacher will know that the student is confusing the observation with an inference. The teacher can then ask the student to describe how he or she knows that pillbugs "love the dark." When the students states that it is because pillbugs tend to stay in the dark side

of their environment, the teacher can point out to the student that moving to the dark side is the observation and the inference is that they "love the dark."

Similarly, individual journal writings can be used to assess what individual students understand about a science content area. In a unit exploring electrical circuits, students could be asked to respond to a journal prompt of "How do you think electricity works?" several times throughout the unit. Initially the student may respond with something like "Electricity is lightning," whereas later in the unit the student may respond with something like "Electricity makes things work," and finally the student may respond with something like "Electricity works through a complete circle—a circuit." Thus, the teacher can track the development of the student's idea over time, from less informed to more informed views.

Whether supporting content learning, guiding teacher instruction, or furthering the development of students' literacy or science process skills—or all of the above—nonfiction writing opportunities are an essential aspect of science learning from which teachers and students benefit in many ways.

Valarie L. Akerson is associate professor of science education at Indiana University in Bloomington, Indiana. Terrell A. Young is professor of literacy education at Washington State University in Richland, Washington.

Resources

Atwell, N. 1990. *Coming to know: Writing to learn in the intermediate grades.* Portsmouth, NH: Heinemann.

Brown, J. E., L. B. Phillips, and E. C. Stephens. 1993. *Toward literacy: Theory and applications for teaching writing in the content areas.* Belmont, CA: Wadsworth.

Calkins, L. M. 1994. *The art of teaching writing.* Portsmouth, NH: Heinemann.

Chapman, M. L. 1995. The sociocognitive construction of written genres in first grade. *Re-*

search in the Teaching of English 29 (2): 164–192.

Darling, K. 1996. *Amazon ABC.* New York: Lothrop, Lee, and Shepard.

Ehlert, L. 1990. *Fish eyes: A book you can count on.* San Diego: Harcourt.

Hadaway, N. L., S. M. Vardell, and T. A. Young. 2002. *Literature-based instruction with English language learners.* Boston: Allyn & Bacon Longman.

Hughey, J. B., and C. Slack. 2001. *Teaching children to write: Theory into practice.* Upper Saddle River, NJ: Merrill/Prentice Hall.

Lyon, G. E. 1989. *A B Cedar: An Alphabet of Trees.* New York: Orchard Books.

McMillan, B. 1986. *Counting wildflowers.* New York: Lothrop, Lee, and Shepard.

National Research Council (NRC). 1996. *National Science Education Standards.* Washington, DC: National Academy Press.

Noyce, R. M. and J. F. Christie. 1989. *Integrating reading and writing instruction in grades K–8.* Boston: Allyn and Bacon.

Pomeroy, D. 1996. *One potato: A counting book of potato prints.* San Diego: Harcourt.

Sayre, A. P., and J. Sayre. 2003. *One is a snail, ten is a crab.* Cambridge: Candlewick Press.

Shannon, G. 1996. *Tomorrow's alphabet.* New York: Greenwillow.

Connecting With Other Disciplines

By Meredith A. Park Rogers and Sandra K. Abell

Question: I never seem to be able to cover everything in my curriculum. With the recent focus on assessing student achievement in literacy and math, I find little opportunity to teach anything else. How can I possibly prepare students for those tests and still help them make meaningful curricular connections to science?

How Can Interdisciplinary Instruction Help Students Learn All Subjects Better?

Interdisciplinary instruction is a way of approaching curriculum by organizing content and processes from more than one discipline around a central theme, issue, problem, topic, or experience (Jacobs 1989). The *National Science Education Standards* (NRC 1996) calls for interdisciplinary instruction to strengthen student science learning. Researchers have found that reading and writing instruction can connect to science through the reciprocal use of process skills, such as observing, comparing/contrasting, inferring, explaining with evidence, and communicating (Baker and Saul 1994; Casteel and Isom 1994; Glynn and Muth 1994). Other researchers describe connections between science and mathematics that include using mathematical representations and developing problem-solving skills within the context of science (Frykholm and Glasson 2005; Lehman 1994). By weaving big ideas and important skills from different disciplines, teachers can maximize classroom time and reinforce concepts and skills across subjects.

How Do Students Learn in Interdisciplinary Settings?

Instructional approaches that integrate curriculum have gained support from the field of cognitive science, in which researchers suggest that learning big ideas and frameworks is more powerful than learning individual or fragmented ideas (Caine and Caine 1993; Donovan and Bransford 2005). Interdisciplinary instruction encourages connections among disciplines to help learners construct stronger knowledge schema. Nuthall (1999) studied British elementary students' learning in an integrated science and social studies unit on Antarctica. He found compelling evidence to support an interdisciplinary approach. Because students could approach the content from different angles based on their interests, involvement, and background knowledge, there were greater opportunities to learn. The knowledge that the 12-year-olds built while learning about Antarctica across several disciplines affected the ways they organized new experiences and transformed them into new knowledge. For example, giving students opportunities to learn about Antarctica in both science and social studies contexts allowed for students' individual differences to be addressed and increased the chance that the students would make some connection to their background knowledge. When students had multiple ways to encounter and represent knowledge, their networks of associations were more complex. Evidence from this study suggests that linking science and reading, writing, social studies, and mathematics through common themes or topics creates the potential for more effective learning.

What Are Cautions About Using an Interdisciplinary Approach?

For all the potential benefits, an interdisciplinary approach also generates concerns. The first concern is that blurring disciplinary boundaries devalues the content of each discipline and student learning becomes superficial (Beane 1995; Dickinson and Young 1998). Roth (1994) expressed the concern that, in elementary classrooms in which thematic interdisciplinary approaches are used, the science instruction that occurs may do more harm than good. In particular, "the content of theme units often [does] not focus on the powerful ideas or organizing concepts from the disciplines" (p. 44). When teachers create interdisciplinary units around themes such as "teddy bears" or "apples," the curricular connections may be forced and important science concepts underemphasized.

The second concern is that an interdisciplinary approach may benefit one discipline more than another. Nixon and Akerson (2004) studied fifth graders who learned science integrated with reading and writing. Science and reading

were successfully integrated in this classroom. However, the focus on science content hindered students' development of various writing skills. Nixon and Akerson suggested using science as a bridge for reading and writing when "the writing structure is familiar to the students and is being used to explore new science content, [or] the writing structure is open-ended so the students are not confined to a specific pattern, [and] when reading for information is connected to students' own questions" (p. 214).

How Can Teachers Use Science to Develop Meaningful Interdisciplinary Connections?

Park Rogers (2006) studied a team of four second-grade teachers who used science as the basis of their interdisciplinary curriculum. She found that they meaningfully integrated science, literacy, and mathematics in three ways: (1) by emphasizing process skills across subject areas, (2) by valuing inquiry as a common tool for learning, and (3) by employing a learning cycle model of instruction in all disciplines.

Teachers can start the process of designing interdisciplinary units by examining the standards in different curricular areas and finding commonalities. One place to start is with the *National Science Education Standards* (NRC 1996) unifying themes. The unifying themes (e.g., systems, change, models), as well as connected tools (e.g., measurement, representations), and shared processes (e.g., observing, predicting) are places for making meaningful curricular connections across disciplines.

Next, teachers can design interdisciplinary contexts in which students can achieve the standards. For example, investigations of local issues can engage students in thinking about science and social science concepts and help develop their understanding of probability and data analysis, which are parts of the mathematics standards. Asking students to examine representations of the Moon in various picture books can help them develop a critical stance toward reading and hone their concept of phases of the Moon (Abell et al. 2002). Using learning cycles to teach other subjects can promote inquiry throughout the curriculum. In these ways, teachers can find more time for science and maximize the connections that students make in their learning.

Meredith A. Park Rogers is an assistant professor of science education at Indiana University. Sandra K. Abell is Curators' Professor of Science Education at the University of Missouri-Columbia (MU) where she directs the MU Science Education Center.

References

Abell, S. K., M. D. George, and M. Martini. 2002. The Moon investigation: Instructional strategies for elementary science methods. *Journal of Science Teacher Education* 13 (2): 85–100.

Baker, L., and W. Saul. 1994. Considering science and language arts connections: A study of teacher cognition. *Journal of Research in Science Teaching* 31 (9): 1023–1037.

Beane, J. A. 1995. *Toward a coherent curriculum.* Alexandria, VA: Association for Supervision and Curriculum Development.

Caine, R. N., and G. Caine. 1993. Understanding a brain-based approach to learning and teaching. In *Integrating the curricula: A collection,* ed. R. Fogarty, 9–20. Arlington Heights, IL: IRI/Skylight Training and Publishing.

Casteel, C. P., and B. A. Isom. 1994. Reciprocal processes in science and literacy learning. *The Reading Teacher* 47 (7): 538–545.

Dickinson, V. L., and T. A. Young. 1998. Elementary science and language arts: Should we blur the boundaries? *School Science and Mathematics* 98 (6): 334–339.

Donovan, M. S., and J. D. Bransford. 2005. *How students learn: History, mathematics, and science in the classroom.* Washington, DC: National Academies Press.

Frykholm, J., and G. Glasson. 2005. Connecting science and mathematics instruction: Pedagogical context knowledge for teachers. *School Science and Mathematics* 105 (3): 127–141.

Glynn, S. M., and K. D. Muth. 1994. Reading and writing to learn science: Achieving scientific literacy. *Journal of Research in Science Teaching* 31 (9): 1057–1073.

Jacobs, H. 1989. *Interdisciplinary curriculum: Design and implementation.* Alexandria, VA: Association for Supervision and Curriculum Development.

Lehman, J. R. 1994. Integrating science and mathematics: Perceptions of preservice and practicing elementary teachers. *School Science and Mathematics* 94 (2): 58–64.

National Research Council (NRC). 1996. *National Science Education Standards.* Washington, DC: National Academy Press.

Nixon, D., and V. L. Akerson. 2004. Building bridges: Using science as a tool to teach reading and writing. *Educational Action Research* 12 (2): 197–217.

Nuthall, G. 1999. The way students learn: Acquiring knowledge from an integrated science and social studies unit. *The Elementary School Journal* 99 (4): 303–341.

Park Rogers, M. 2006. *Achieving a coherent curriculum in second grade: Science as the organizer.* Unpublished PhD diss., University of Missouri–Columbia.

Roth, K. 1994. Second thoughts about interdisciplinary studies. *American Educator* 18 (1): 44–48.

Art and Science Grow Together

By Pat Stellflue, Marie Allen, and D. Timothy Gerber

When a science teacher, an art teacher, and a botany professor team up to talk about—plants, of course—things really get growing! As part of a longstanding partnership with the biology department at the University of Wisconsin–La Crosse, our school has been involved in numerous successful plant projects over the years. But, by far, the most exciting and creative project we've collaborated on was our recent integrated science/art study, "Plants, Pots, and Paints." This interdisciplinary project was successful in connecting content across disciplines (science to art) and for motivating fourth- and fifth-grade students to create something beautiful both they and our entire community can enjoy.

Planting Bulbs

It all began with an August meeting in which we brainstormed core science and art concepts. In science, we emphasized the idea that plants have structures that serve different functions in growth, survival, and reproduction. In art, we focused on understanding and applying media techniques and processes, and using knowledge of structures and functions. We then identified different hands-on experiences students could participate in based on these core concepts, such as growing, drawing, painting, and dissecting plants. We also created a time line to coordinate our overlapping project activities (Figure 1).

Figure 1.

Project timeline

Month	Activity	Grade
Oct – Nov	Bulb planting in schoolyard and science experiment setup	Fourth
Dec	Clay pot construction in art class	Fourth
Dec – Feb	Bulb cold treatment	Fourth
Feb	Planting cold-treated bulbs in pots	Fourth
Mar – Apr	Plant growing, observing, and dissecting in science class	Fourth
Apr – May	Drawing, painting, and other media in art class	Fourth and Fifth
May	Plein-Air artists visit	Fifth

Our focus was on upper elementary students because they would have the requisite skills for creating the artwork. Our fourth-grade science curriculum includes detailed instruction in flower and plant parts. What the students learn in fourth grade would be applied in work with visiting artists in fifth grade.

We chose bulbs for this project because they are perennial, they bloom during the school year, and they can be "forced" to bloom in containers with proper cold treatment (see Lawniczak et al. 2004 for more information on cold-treated bulbs).

Following instructions supplied with the bulbs, during October and November fourth-grade students planted an outdoor garden (an area of the schoolyard tilled by the district's building and grounds department) with crocus, iris, and daffodil bulbs purchased from a local garden center. We funded the first year of the project through two grants and a bulb sale.

The outdoor gardens would be an "outdoor art" installation and also supply cut flowers in the spring for the science and art classrooms. The outdoor gardens were also the site of a science experiment.

To provide plants before spring blooming, we planned to force daffodil and tulip bulbs for indoor blooms. In December, we placed bulbs in egg cartons and covered them with damp (not wet) newspaper strips. Students took the cartons home and refrigerated the bulbs for a 12-week cold treatment.

Utilitarian Art

The art portion of the project focused on clay pot construction and plant illustration techniques. In addition to being artwork themselves, the pots would also conveniently serve as containers for the forced bulbs.

While the refrigerated bulbs were being "cold treated," students made clay coil pots using clay rolled into long tubes that were then coiled to make the body of the pot. After the pots were constructed, they were fired, glazed, and fired again in the art room's kiln. Another option, for teachers without access to a kiln, would be to purchase terra-cotta pots, paint them with acrylic paints, and seal them with lacquer or polyurethane. If you choose to do this, make sure your students follow all safety precautions when working with glazes, paints, or any other chemical.

When the cold-treated bulbs were returned to school and removed from the egg cartons, students planted one or more bulbs (depending on pot size) in their clay pots, covered them with potting soil, and watered them. Each pot had drainage holes, so students also made matching trays to catch the water. The planted pots were placed in the science classroom.

Scientific Subjects

In March, before spring bloom, we used purchased cut flowers to practice plant-illustration techniques with a variety of media, such as pencil, ink, scratchboard, and watercolor, in art class (see Resources). Students drew a large, single-stem flower and outlined it in pen and ink or brush and ink. Students then added color and identified flower parts. The idea was for the illustrative drawings to be informative, not just decorative.

In the spring, flowers from both the containers and the schoolyard were used as subjects for drawing and painting using various illustration techniques.

Fourth-grade students also spent time creating a value scale showing the lightness and darkness of a color and working with color classification using a Munsell color chart made with standardized color chips. Fifth-grade art students spent part of one day outdoors working on canvas boards with a local plein-air art group. Plein-Air Painters of America is an organization devoted to outdoor, open-air, painting from life.

Students critiqued completed works of art individually and in groups. Students' understanding of technique was also assessed.

All Hands on Plants

The science portion of the project focused on using crocuses, daffodils, and tulips as model organisms to teach life science concepts in an extensive unit on the structure and function of plants' leaves, stems, and roots.

Students used Geoscopes (30× portable indoor/outdoor lighted microscopes, see Resources) to examine the growing plants and their structures in the garden. Because other grades had planted gardens next to the school as well, students were able to examine several types of plants and various vein patterns in the leaves.

After planted pots of bulbs were transferred from the art classroom, students observed their growth in the classroom. Students were able to observe different stages of plant development.

After reaching maturity, blooming plants were used for illustrations. Drawings were labeled to include grade-appropriate science vocabulary (e.g., *stem, leaves, roots, stamens, pistil, petals*).

After the tulips bloomed, they were removed from their containers and dissected. Observations of the entire plant were necessary to understand the function of all plant parts. Finally, a discussion of plant form and function was conducted with a local university botanist to address misconceptions about plants.

Each student's level of understanding of plant biology was formally assessed. Fourth-grade science tests included questions on plant structure and function. Students' illustrative drawings were also assessed for accuracy.

Bulb Growth Experiment

Some of the outdoor bulbs planted in the schoolyard in the fall were used in a science inquiry. A dozen tulip bulbs were planted at each of three different depths: at the surface, at a normal planting depth of 15 cm, and at 30 cm deep. The goal of the experiment was to determine optimal planting depth. Because instructions that came with the bulbs suggested planting at 15 cm, this depth was used as the control in the experiment.

Students were to measure survival and height of the plants grown at different depths and compare growth of the bulbs planted at the surface and at 30 cm depth against survival and growth of the control plants. Unfortunately, the bulbs were planted too far away from the school, and the local deer population ate all of the tulips. This led to a fruitful discussion about other environmental factors that could kill or damage plants.

After spring bloom, the students discovered that deer don't eat daffodils. Next year's fourth-grade class will repeat the experiment with daffodils.

Integration Grows

Students were very motivated by their plant and art studies—and learning was enhanced in both subjects because of the integration. For example, in art class, students developed observations skills as they learned new plant-illustration techniques. Having learned more about plants' form and function in science class, students applied that knowledge to their drawings. Also, after dissecting plants in science class, their drawings were more informed and detailed.

On the flip side, in science class, students took better care of their plants because they had made the pots and drainage trays in which the bulbs were planted. They were also able to use drawing and painting techniques learned in art. Overall, the best outcome of the project was seeing how the separate disciplines of art and science could be brought together effectively to create a bigger, better whole. Now, with the success of our school's plant projects, we've begun to pass the information along to other elementary teachers in our district. We want to encourage them—and you—to conduct similar studies at other schools. Integrating art and science will likely grow on you, too.

Pat Stellflue is an art teacher, and Marie Allen is a fourth-grade teacher, both at Eagle Bluff Elementary in Onalaska, Wisconsin. D. Timothy Gerber is an associate professor of biology at the University of Wisconsin–La Crosse in La Crosse, Wisconsin.

Acknowledgments

The authors thank plein-air artists from La Crosse, Wisconsin (B.H. Decker, D. Cuta, D. Marusarz, L. Steine, M. Thompson) and Eagle Bluff Elementary Library Media Center Director S. Coorough for their help with this project. Funding was provided through grants from Wisconsin Society of Science Teachers (WSST), Onalaska Foundation for Excellence in Education (OFFEE), and Eagle Bluff Elementary PTSO.

Resources

Lawniczak, S., D. Gerber, and J. Beck. 2004. Plants on display. *Science and Children* 41 (9): 24–29.

National Art Education Association (NAEA). 1994. *The national visual arts standards.* Reston, VA: NAEA.

National Research Council (NRC). 1996. *National Science Education Standards.* Washington DC: National Academy Press.

Sherlock, S. 2004. *Botanical illustration: Painting with watercolors.* London: B. T. Batsford.

Sherwood, S. 2001. *A passion for plants: Contemporary botanical masterworks.* London: Cassell.

Wood, P. 1994. *Scientific illustration.* New York: John Wiley.

Internet Resources

ASPB (American Society of Plant Biologists). Principles of Plant Biology
www.aspb.org/education/foundation/principles.cfm

Plein-Air Painters of America
www.p-a-p-a.com

Connecting to the Standards

This article addresses the following National Science Education Standards (NRC 1996):

Content Standards
Standard C: Life Science
Grades K–4
- The characteristics of organisms
- Life cycles of organisms
- Organisms and their environments

Grades 5–8
- Structure and function in living systems
- Diversity and adaptations of organisms

En "Light"ening Geometry for Middle School Students

By Julie LaConte

Many science topics can naturally be integrated with a variety of mathematical concepts, including the study of light and optics. Working collaboratively with the math teacher on my team, I integrated the concepts of light, optics, and geometry to create a set of hands-on activities in which students can explore the properties of light energy while building their understanding of geometric concepts.

One of the main concepts included in the National Science Education Standards, Content Standard B, focuses on the transmission of light, involving both reflection and refraction (NRC 1996). The activities that follow were designed to help students understand the concepts of refraction and reflection and can be conducted over a one- to two-week period. These activities were completed while the math

teacher on our team was simultaneously teaching a variety of geometry concepts.

Reflection

We begin with a study of reflection, a topic with which students should already have practical experience. We introduce an activity that has been modified from an AIMS *Pieces and Patterns* activity titled "Mirrors That Multiply" (Hillen 1986). I provide two small, square mirrors of the same size to pairs of students. I use unbreakable plastic mirrors that are approximately 10 cm × 10 cm. These are available through a wide variety of science supply catalogues and teacher supply stores. Any small, square mirror will work for this activity. After donning safety goggles and listening to reminders about sharp edges, students begin their exploration of reflection by carefully touching one edge of each mirror together, creating a hinged effect. Students then place a small object—such as a coin or game piece—between the two mirrors. Students move the mirrors closer together and then spread them further apart on the "hinge," examining the resulting effect on the image in the mirror. Specifically, students are looking for the relationship between the angle of the mirrors and the number of images created.

I have students experiment with this technique for a few minutes and then place a piece of paper underneath their mirrors. They use their pencil to draw and label the angles created as they shift the mirrors and then measure these angles with a protractor or angle ruler. Students create a chart with the measurement of the angle in relation to the number of images produced in the mirrors. Over time, students see that as the angle measurement decreases, the number of images produced in the mirrors increases. This activity coincides with their study of types of angles in math class, so they are able to name the angles created by the mirrors as obtuse, right, or acute. Students also have experience naming, measuring, and estimating angle degrees from math class.

After experimenting with the relationship between the angles and resulting images, students use a flat, or plane, mirror to explore the law of reflection. For this experiment, pairs of students get a plane mirror (I use the same mirrors from the last activity), a small block of clay (one small block of clay per pair, stiff enough to support the mirror), a piece of graph paper, and two small toothpicks. Students position the mirror on the graph paper so it runs along the x-axis. They place the block of clay behind the mirror to prop it in an upright position along the x-axis, trying to get the mirror to stand as straight as possible. If the mirror leans, it will distort the image slightly. The mirror should be centered on the graph paper so the y-axis runs through the center point of the mirror. Students then place the end of one toothpick on the origin

and position it so it runs diagonally across the lower right-hand quadrant of the graph paper. They make a mark with a pencil at the end of the toothpick and label it point A. They observe the virtual image created in the mirror and position the second toothpick so it is in a straight line with the virtual image of the first toothpick in the mirror. Thus, the second toothpick has one end at the origin and it runs diagonally across the lower left-hand quadrant of the graph paper. Students make a mark at the end of this toothpick and label it point B (see Figure 1).

Moving the toothpicks off the paper, students connect points A and B to the origin with straight lines. They use an angle ruler or protractor to measure the angles created by point A and the x-axis, as well as those created by point B and the x-axis. Students should notice that the angles are the same, or very close to the same. From this quick experiment, students are able to see the principle behind the law of reflection, that the angle of light approaching the mirror (angle of incidence) is equal to the angle of light reflecting off the mirror (angle of reflection). Students can continue to experiment with this law by slightly shifting the position of the toothpicks, drawing new points, and measuring again. The law should hold true with the toothpicks in any position in front of the mirror.

After the hands-on portion of this experiment, I assess by showing students a diagram of a plane mirror with a beam of light coming toward it. Students have to label this as the incident beam and then measure the angle of incidence. Then, they have to draw in the reflected beam at the appropriate angle and label the angle of reflection and the reflected beam. I give them two or three of these as an assessment.

Symmetry

After building on students' math skills of naming, estimating, and measuring angles, we continue to use mirrors to reinforce the geometric

Figure 1.

Mirror images

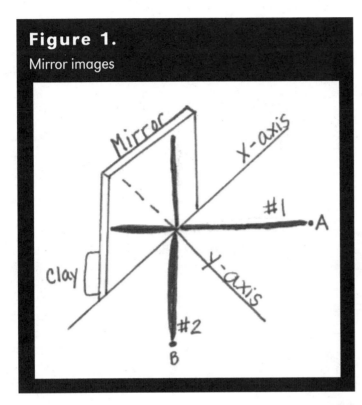

their own patterns and challenge their classmates to complete the flip of their image (see student samples in Figure 2). We compare the reflections created to other geometric transformations they are learning about in math class, including translations and rotations, looking for similarities and differences. In the past, I have assessed their understanding of the concept of reflection by observing their grid patterns to ensure that they are shading correctly to show the reflection and accurately flipping the image across the axis.

Refraction

The final, and most extensive, light and geometry activity is adapted from an AIMS activity called "Bent on It" (Mitchell 1998). This activity focuses on the concept of *refraction*, or the

transformations they are learning about in math class. I give students a paper with a variety of large letters and simple shapes on it (a heart, smiley face, polygon, etc.) modified from an AIMS *Pieces and Patterns* activity titled "Halves and Halve-nots" (Hillen 1986). Students use small square mirrors to find the lines of symmetry in the shapes and letters, and then mark them using dotted lines. Students are challenged to find all lines of symmetry and draw an object of their own that they can trade with a friend to find the lines of symmetry. Upon completion of the symmetry activity, students use their mirrors to demonstrate the geometric transformation of a reflection, or flip. I provide students with small grids that have been divided in half, with one side showing a shaded pattern. Students then hold their mirrors on the dividing line and observe the reflection of the pattern in the mirror. They shade the reflection, or flip, of the pattern on the opposite side of the dividing line. Again, students are encouraged to create

Figure 2.

Student samples

Light Refraction Activities

In these experiments, you will be examining how light refracts through different media. But first, you will need to prepare the path that light will travel. Answer all questions on another sheet of paper.

Part A: Light Refraction Lab
Procedure

1. Plot the following points on your graph paper. Label each point with the designated letter.

(0, 0) = O	(-9, 9) = A	(-9, 3) = B
(-9, 0) = C	(9, -8) = D	(9, -3) = E
(0, 9) = F	(0, -9) = G	(9, 0) = H

2. Connect the points
   - Connect points A, O, and D with a blue line.
   - Connect points B, O, and E with a red line.
   - Connect points F, O, and G with a green line.
3. Name the angles. Remember, acute angles measure _____, right angles measure _____, and obtuse angles measure _____.
4. What type of angle is
   - angle AOC
   - angle BOC
   - angle AOH
   - angle BOH
   - angle COF
5. Estimate the angle measurement of the given angle.
   - angle AOC
   - angle BOC
   - angle AOH
   - angle BOH
   - angle COF
6. Measure the angles. Use your angle ruler to find the actual measure of each angle.
   - angle AOC
   - angle BOC
   - angle AOH
   - angle BOH
   - angle COF
7. Test the path of light. (Make your observations looking down onto the paper, as your teacher shines the light for you.)
   - Place the laser pointer on point D and shine it along DA.
   - Place the laser pointer on point E and shine it along EB.
   - Place the laser pointer on point G and shine it along GF.

   What medium is the light traveling through? How does light travel?
8. Take the clear container and place the long side of it along the x-axis of your graph. (Make your observations looking down onto the paper, as your teacher shines the light for you.)
   - Place the laser pointer on point D and shine it along DA.
   - Place the laser pointer on point E and shine it along EB.
   - Place the laser pointer on point G and shine it along GF.

   What medium is the light traveling through? How does light travel?
9. Add water to the container so it is half full. Starting at point G, have your teacher shine the light along GF. Look down into the water. Can you see the beam of light?
10. Add a few drops of milk to the water and swirl it around. Again, start at point G and have your teacher shine the light along GF. Look down into the water. Can you see the beam of light now? Why?
    - Place the laser pointer on point D and shine it along DA.
    - Place the laser pointer on point E and shine it along EB.

    What do you observe about the path of light when the water is added to the container? Why does that happen to the light?
11. Observe as the teacher places the laser pointer on point G and shines it along GF through the water. Does the light bend? Why or why not?

Part B: Light Refraction Challenge
Procedure

1. Have your teacher place the laser pointer on point D and shine it along DA through the water.
2. Make a new point on the graph paper where the light is refracted to and label it point X. What kind of angle is XOC? What is the measure of angle XOC?
3. Compare angle AOC to XOC. What is the difference between the two angles? (This is called the angle of refraction.)
4. Have your teacher place the laser pointer on point E and shine it along EB through the water. Make a new point on the graph paper where the light is refracted to and label it point Y. What kind of angle is YOC? What is the measure of angle YOC?
5. Compare angle YOC to BOC. What is the angle of refraction?

bending of light as it passes through different media (see Light Refraction Activities Sheet, Part A). For this activity, students work in groups of four. Each group will need a large, clear container with flat, rather than sloped or curved, sides. Plastic shoebox containers work well, are available at a wide variety of stores, and are not expensive. The group also needs water (enough to fill the container halfway), a few drops of milk, a large piece of graph paper (11 × 17 or larger), an angle ruler or protractor, and red, blue, and green colored pencils. A laser pointer will also be used by the teacher for the group.

This activity begins with students plotting nine different points on their graph paper. Students then connect three points with a blue line, three points with a red line, and three points with a green line (see Light Refraction Activities Sheet). Students then name the angles as acute, right, or obtuse, estimate their measure, and then find their actual measurement. Then, the teacher operates the laser pointer and students observe the path of light as it travels along different lines they have created. They place the clear container over the graph paper along the x-axis and shine the laser along different lines, observing the path of light by looking down into the empty container. Students add water and a few drops of milk and repeat their observations. When the water and milk are added, students can see the beam bend as it passes through the water/milk mixture in the container, resulting in a new line created by the laser. As an extension, students can plot this new line and measure the resulting angle of refraction (see Light Refraction Activities Sheet, Part B).

Conclusion

After completing these light activities, students have grasped not only the scientific concepts of reflection and refraction, but strengthened their understanding of often abstract geometric topics with frequent practice and hands-on experimentation. Although the materials and setup of some of the experiments can be unwieldy, the resulting authentic experience they provide students is worth the effort. By taking a little extra time to coordinate our light and geometry units, the math teacher and I have been able to provide students with a practical application of geometry and the visual representation of the transmission of light in an engaging context.

These activities are just a few selected ones that I do during an entire light/optics unit. Throughout the unit, students receive hands-on experience with geometric concepts. As they are learning about angles and angle measurements, they are able to see the application of these geometric concepts in the real world in how they relate to reflected images. Students notice that, as angles change, the appearance of the reflected image changes as well. They see how the light is refracted at an angle as it passes through different media, and we again discuss this in terms of the real world and relate it to our previous study of the atmosphere. We discuss how the refraction, reflection, and scattering of light as it passes through the atmosphere affects the colors and visual effects we see in our sky. We extend these activities with simulations modeling mirrors in the real world where students have to set a mirror at a certain angle so a driver in a car has optimal vision from the side mirrors. Understanding the law of reflection allows them to set the mirrors at the best position based on the angle created between the driver and the mirror. Students are also challenged to use mirrors to "see" around barriers and find a pathway using the appropriate angles to position the mirrors for a clear view around the model objects.

Julie LaConte is a classroom teacher at Hoech Middle School in St. Ann, Missouri.

References

Hillen, J. 1986. *Pieces and patterns: A patchwork in math and science.* Fresno, CA: AIMS Education Foundation.

Mitchell, D. 1998. Bent on it. *AIMS Education Foundation Magazine* 13 (5): 7–10.

National Research Council (NRC). 1996. *National Science Education Standards*. Washington, DC: National Academy Press.

A Blended Neighborhood

By Chris Ohana and Kent Ryan

When eight-year-old Chris walked into the room one morning, he saw a peculiar sight in the class's three-dimensional neighborhood model: A 7.5 cm homemade garbage can had been placed near his personal prism and rectangular home. He looked at it and said to no one in particular, "Hey, who put this cylinder in my yard?" With those words, we knew that our integrated curriculum that blended science, mathematics, and social studies was on the road to success.

Who would have imagined that building a neighborhood model with a lively group of six-, seven-, and eight-year-olds would be the perfect vehicle to make connections between content areas and their standards? Luckily, we tried it, and the resulting multidisciplinary project became a favorite classroom investigation that motivated both students and teachers all year long.

This is the story of our project.

A Burst of Inspiration

Having taught science, mathematics, and social studies as discrete subjects in previous years, we—a team of two classroom teachers and a science specialist—were searching for a way to integrate instruction and to erase grade distinctions in our multiage classroom. We had done well in blending other curriculum areas, but science and mathematics were more difficult. We saw several opportunities to make connections to the district's curriculum in geometry.

As we contemplated ways to integrate mathematics, we were also planning a social studies unit on neighborhoods in which students would study our local area's history, architecture, and businesses. In this unit, we wanted students to create their own buildings and businesses and construct a three-dimensional model neighborhood in the classroom, incorporating into these experiences lessons from both social studies and mathematics.

As we brainstormed, we realized that building the model would give us an opportunity to blend science learning into the unit as well. The first- and second-grade science curriculum included forces and simple machines. The science teacher pointed out that exploring these topics would help students' understanding of the requirements for building neighborhood structures—from playground equipment to engineering plans—which would strengthen the neighborhoods unit both literally and figuratively.

Figure 1.

National standards from science, mathematics, and social studies covered in aligned unit

Science Content Standards (NRC 1996)	Mathematics (NCTM 2000)	Social Studies (NCSS 1994)
A: Science as Inquiry	Standard: Problem-Solving	Principle: Social studies teaching and learning are powerful when they are meaningful, integrative, value-based, and challenging.
B: Physical Science Properties of objects and materials Position and motion of objects	Standard: Geometry Spatial sense Investigate and predict combining, subdividing, and changing shapes	Thematic Strand: People, Places, Environment Maps Data Scale
D: Earth and Space Science Properties of materials	Standard: Geometry Describe, model, and classify shapes	Thematic Strand: People, Places, Environment Geographic features
E: Science and Technology Abilities of technological design	Standard: Connections	Thematic Strand: Science, Technology, Society Social Studies programs should include experiences that provide for the study of relationships among science, technology, and society.
G: History and Nature of Science Science as a human endeavor	Standard: Connections	Thematic Strand: Power, Authority, Governance Technology and transportation Needs and wants

Aligning Subject Standards

Excited by the prospect of the integrated units, we—with significant contributions from a student teacher—began planning and coordinating our teaching. At first, we saw major obstacles. There were objectives in each subject that lacked clear or consistent connections to the others. We solved this problem by aligning the content areas (see Figure 1). To do that, we looked at the scope of each separate unit and identified points where the three units overlapped. Then, we decided to teach the units in such a way that the overlapping points were taught roughly at the same time.

For example, when aspects of the science unit supported something in geometry and/or social studies, we taught them on the same day and made explicit references from one to the other. However, not all of our lessons would align. There were lessons in mathematics, social studies, and science that needed to be taught for the integrity of that subject but that lacked a clear connection to the other content areas; this was okay, the important factor was not to force any connections.

With these thoughts in mind, we sketched out a "tentative" project time line to present the unit. We anticipated that teaching the integrated units would last about three months. We began the study with the science unit and introduced the social studies and mathematics units about two weeks later. We found, however, that the nature of our collaboration allowed us to continuously make connections between content areas all year long, right from the project's start.

Forces and Arrows

In all three content areas the units began with explorations—of balance (science), shapes (mathematics), and neighborhoods (social studies). The science portion began with an expansion of a unit on balance and motion. Students used balances and mobiles to develop the concept that things move when forces are not balanced. The students manipulated weights on a balance to see that the mass had to be equal on both sides. If one side had more mass, it moved. The same was true with mobiles. If the mass was unequal, then the one with more mass fell down.

After exploring motion, students balanced objects (cardboard frogs on wires and potatoes on forks) to try to keep them still. These activities helped to develop the concept that when forces are balanced, there is stability. If the cardboard frog listed to one side, more force—for example, a gentle push—had to be placed on the opposite side to counterbalance it.

During these explorations, students were introduced to an elementary version of a force diagram (a diagram using arrows to represent all the forces acting on an object, their direction, and their magnitude). We introduced this idea using a bowling ball placed on the floor.

We asked, "What is the force pulling the ball down?" and then drew an arrow pointing down to represent gravity. "What keeps the ball from falling into the Earth?" Then we drew an equal-sized arrow pointing up to represent the floor. *Equal arrows + Opposite directions = No movement.* Next, we asked, "What if I kicked the ball?" "What direction is the force?" "Is there an opposite force?" If not, the ball will move.

Students drew arrows to designate direction and magnitude of forces. We explained that when the arrows didn't "cancel" each other out, movement would occur.

We talked about the idea of opposing forces with the example of a stalemate in a tug-of-war: Students pull from one direction. Other students pull from the other side. If no one is stronger or bigger, the rope stays where it started. If there is a strong kid on one side, their arrow gets bigger and the rope moves.

Students also applied the concept of opposing forces to the strength of structures. A building stands when the forces are balanced. Certain structures, such as a triangle or arch, are strong because they help to balance the forces. We looked for evidence of triangles in buildings. Roofs were one place where triangles were easily found. Walls were a source of confusion—shouldn't they be triangles, too? We showed students that although walls look like rectangles, they are built or reinforced with triangles. Photographs of a building site showed students the innards of a wall and the triangular bracing inside.

Getting in Shape

The mathematics work during the first week was also important. Students began to visualize how different shapes could be manipulated to make other shapes, added to their problem-solving strategies, and learned the vocabulary necessary to communicate about shapes with the teachers and each other.

Over the course of the week, students worked in groups of four at five learning centers that explored geometric and spatial relation concepts, spending a total of 30 to 40 minutes at each center. The centers were as follows:

- Tangrams—Students solved tangrams (puzzles) or created their own.
- Pattern Blocks—Students created patterns and designs that used lines of symmetry or worked on pattern-block puzzles.
- Geoboards—Students made different geometric shapes on the geoboard (a plastic board with 25 evenly spaced pegs on which rubber bands can be placed to create various shapes and patterns), working either individually to recreate patterns or with partners to present challenges to each other.
- Pentominoes—Students completed puzzles or created their own.
- Clay and Sticks—Students created two- and three-dimensional structures from chunks of clay and two sizes of bamboo skewers.

Neighborhood Research

During the week that students started the geometry unit, they also began the social studies unit by observing the neighborhood around them. One afternoon, we sat in front of an easel and recorded everything we might see on a neighborhood walk. The next day, clipboards in hand, we took that walk. The children took note of buildings, street signs, and the people we saw. Cameras helped us document our walk. As part of our neighborhood study, we dropped the film off at a nearby photo store. The following day, armed with neighborhood pictures, students sorted the photographs and plotted them on a large, mural-sized map of the neighborhood that we had created in advance by enlarging a city map.

This led us to introduce the project: Create a model neighborhood. Naturally, students were intrigued by the opportunity to create a make-believe neighborhood. The next few days passed quickly as we began questioning the students about the different places where people live and work. Our social-studies lessons continued as we again sorted copies of the pictures, this time to create a graph of business and family dwellings. We also sorted businesses according to whether they provided goods or services.

"Structure" Science

Now that we had completed our initial explorations, it was time to begin preparing for the construction of the neighborhood. Applying their recently learned "shape" vocabulary from their mathematics unit, students made craft-stick models of triangles and rectangles by joining the drilled ends of the craft sticks with brass fasteners.

Then, we led students to a discussion of what happens when the structures are placed under a pushing force or a pulling force: The triangle holds its shape while the rectangle can be manipulated into all sorts of configurations. We asked, "How can the quadrilateral be made into a strong shape?" Make it into two triangles by connecting the diagonals.

Next, students constructed a rectangular box using clay and bamboo skewers. They hung loads (steel washers) on the structure until it failed. Then they repeated the process on a triangular prism made of the same materials. It held dramatically more weight. The students were starting to understand the advantage of triangles.

The students then explored an "edible" challenge: Construct the tallest building possible using toothpicks and marshmallows. The students attempted all different types of configurations. Many students reverted to the rectangular house idea. They quickly discovered that only those structures bolstered by triangles had a chance to get very tall.

Businesses and Blueprints

During social studies time, each student was asked to identify a business that he or she would like to own. Each child then named the business and wrote a business plan. These plans, after rounds of peer editing and conferencing, were "published" and displayed in the classroom.

The next step was to create the exterior of the business in a drawing we called "blueprints." The students were encouraged to be detailed in their work. How could they make their building strong and attractive to potential customers? Students' businesses ranged from private goods business, such as restaurants, clothing stores, and convenience stores, to public service providers, such as fire stations, libraries, and even a zoo.

We Are Builders

To prepare for the impending construction phase, students again returned to our learning centers for mathematics exploration. This time, the focus was on developing a sense of three-dimensional shapes. Small groups of students met with teachers during center time so the students could better develop their understandings of the attributes and names of two- and three-dimensional shapes. They were also shown examples of three-dimensional shapes when laid flat. They cut out shapes and attempted to configure them into common shapes. The students were given homework assignments to identify spheres, cylinders, cubes, and pyramids in their home. We did the same in the classroom.

Once the students were comfortable with the names and strengths of the various shapes and had each completed a business plan and blueprint, they chose the shapes needed to build their business. There was serious discussion as students decided which shapes to use. One student suggested to another that, in the interest of seating capacity, she might think about using a rectangular prism instead of a cube.

Buildings were constructed of poster board and cardstock paper. Cylinders were made from paper towel tubes. In the end, most students chose a rectangular prism for the building and triangular prism for the roof, although some chose cube and pyramid designs. They then used their skills at visualizing flat patterns for three-dimensional designs to create their own pattern for their building. Students, using some trial and error, often folded their construction-paper designs as they were cutting to make sure the pattern would work to make their desired shape. When some rectangular walls displayed structural weaknesses, students remembered a solution from science: triangular bracing.

Making Room

After folding and taping, the next step was to find a spot for each business in our neighborhood. In the interest of space, we created two neighborhoods. For platforms we used 1.2 m × 1.2 m pieces of plywood that were covered by green paper for grass and black construction paper for streets. As the businesses went up, students noticed there was something missing: houses.

After a minilesson in social studies on houses, students added duplexes, apartments, and houses. The skyscraper apartment building gave the science teacher an excuse for an impromptu discussion about the center of mass, recalling previous lessons on balance. Recess found many students electing to stay inside to work on their neighborhood.

A Place With Flavor

Soon the two models were filled with names like the "Rainforest Cafe," "McDonnell's Boys Stuff," and "Peden's Library." The neighborhood developed its own flavor. The integration up to this point had been relatively easy, but there were standards in which we wanted students to deepen their understanding. For example, in social studies, students were expected to understand and use the cardinal directions.

In math, students were expected to know the difference between open and closed shapes.

To dig deeper into the geography objectives, we created a simple cardinal direction game. Students "drove" a car along the roads of the neighborhood while describing their route to the class. The rest of the class was then asked which direction the car was facing. A correct answer won control of the car. Another game involved following directions and pinpointing the location of a car.

To deepen students' understanding in some geometry standards, we again used a car and the neighborhood—this time to create open and closed shapes. In this game, the teachers "drove" the car through the neighborhood, describing the route to the class. Students followed along, determining whether the route represented a closed shape (one that separates one space from another) or an open shape (such as a square with only three sides), and recorded the shape on their geoboards.

Assessment: Clipboard Cruising

How did we know the project worked? We used a variety of methods to assess student understanding. Formal methods included a geometry test from the publisher of the adopted mathematics curriculum. In science, student understanding was gauged through their oral presentations about the choice of shapes for the model neighborhood and the consequences for strength. Students answered, "What forces would the shape need to sustain?" and "How would their shapes meet the challenge?"

Informal assessment methods involved the teacher art form, "clipboard cruising." On our clipboards were the objectives for the units and the students' names. When we noticed a certain behavior or understanding, we noted it on the clipboard. This gave students another way, beyond paper-and-pencil tests, to demonstrate their understanding in the subjects.

Going and Growing

Although nearly every student mastered the district objectives for science, mathematics, and social studies, the unit never really ended. The students kept adding to the neighborhood long after the formal instruction had ended. Trees showed up, a zoo was added. Street signs and lights appeared to control the growing traffic. Playgrounds featured monkey bars bolstered with triangles, and students frequently gave directions to neighborhood sites using north, south, east, or west.

Not every lesson was connected to other content areas. Still, this unit gave us the opportunity to align three different content standards in a creative way. The connections that punctuated the different units helped us bridge the curricular areas and reinforce the concepts. But beyond content, we were also able to integrate higher-order thinking skills. Each of the content standards contains a strand on inquiry or problem solving. The inquiry and problem solving required for the neighborhood project wove together the three disciplines.

Another major benefit was the chance to work together with our colleagues. We learned more about each other's curriculum strengths and, in the process, became better teachers. We have worked on this unit for three years, and we still have plans to expand and amend it. Next year, we hope to bring in the art teacher. She wants to include a unit on Alexander Calder's mobiles—another natural fit with geometry and forces.

And the neighborhood could use a little art.

Chris Ohana is an assistant professor of elementary education at Western Washington University in Bellingham, Washington. Kent Ryan is a reading consultant with the Iowa State Department of Education in Des Moines, Iowa. They previously taught together at Martin Luther King Elementary in Des Moines and would like to thank Toni Hayes, the third teacher involved with this project and a tremendous source of knowledge, inspiration, and friendship.

Resources

Gonsalves, P., and J. Kopp. 1995. *Build It! Festival.* Berkeley, CA: Great Explorations in Math and Science.

Kluger-Bell, B. 1995. *The Exploratorium guide to scale and structure.* Portsmouth, NH: Heinemann.

Lawrence Hall of Science. *Balance and Motion.* Berkeley, CA: Author.

National Council for the Social Studies (NCSS). 1994. *Expectations of excellence: Curriculum standards for the social studies.* Washington, DC: Author.

National Council of Teachers of Mathematics (NCTM). 2000. *Principles and standards for school mathematics.* Reston, VA: Author.

National Research Council (NRC). 1996. *National Science Education Standards.* Washington, DC: National Academy Press.

Westley, J. 1988. *Constructions.* Sunnyvale, CA: Creative Publications.

Cell City Web Quest

By Clay Rasmussen, Amy Resler, and Audra Rasmussen

When faced with a dwindling budget and supplies, I began using more online resources to provide students with engaging, affordable activities. Web quests, online activities that require students to read, analyze, and synthesize information found on the web, are one of my favorite ways of facilitating instruction and student inquiry. In this article, I will describe how I use a web quest called Cell City to teach students the names and functions of all the major cell organelles.

City in a Cell

Prior to the activity, I save the URL of the web quest in the Favorites folder on each of the computers students will be using. Each group of four or five students will need access to at least one computer. As part of the web quest, students are asked to construct their own cell city, so I make sure that storage space is available for their creations.

To begin, I divide students into groups and ask them to review the web quest online (see summary of activity in Figure 1). The web quest takes students through a series of worksheets that help them learn the names and functions of cell organelles. The worksheets contain internal and external links for stu-dents to follow—no time is wasted aimlessly surfing the web. Each link (vetted for accuracy and appropriateness), provides definitions, images of organelles, and explanations of how the organelles function. Other links take students to the worksheets and grading rubrics (Figure 2). After they have completed the worksheets, students begin designing and building their cell cities.

Why Use It?

There are several levels of assessment for this web quest. The first level of assessment is a rubric that can be used as is or amended to fit personal styles to assess student learning. It is easy to see if the worksheets are being completed correctly, but what is more important is being able to determine if students can make the correlations between the function of a cell organelle within a cell and the function of a cell organelle in their city. This project is a memorable activity that promotes long-term retention of the concepts involved. When I bump into former students and strike up a conversation, without fail they recall the function of the organelles they used to build their cities.

Figure 1.

Cell City web quest

Purpose(s) or learning goals

Both plant and animal cells are very complex. For some students, trying to remember which organelles can be found where and what their specific functions are can be a difficult task. This web quest will help students understand how a cell is similar to a city and then apply these concepts to an actual cell. Although this project is very simple as compared to the actual cell and how it functions, hopefully it will be a starting point from which students can build.

Introduction

How does a cell function like a city? Think about the sights and sounds of a city. You see people and cars moving about, buildings, restaurants, and lights everywhere. What a flurry of activity!

Cells, the basic units of life, can be compared to a city. Cells are building and breaking down material. Cells release energy from foods, and then use that energy to make needed cell parts. Cells function to make your body operate like a well-run city.

Task

1. Use this web quest site to research the functions of cell organelles and to complete both the cell questionnaire and cell diagram.
2. With your group, complete the city structure sheet.
3. In your group, work together to plan and create a rough-draft blueprint of your cell city.
4. With your group, create a model of your cell city.
5. Each group member will choose a different career and complete the job associated with that role.
   a. Travel agent: You will create a brochure for your cell city.
   b. Newspaper journalist/newscaster: You will write news articles regarding "Cell City" news.
   c. Musician/poet: You will compose and perform a song or compose and recite a poem.

Procedure

1. Research each cell organelle to determine its function. Also, label the parts of the cell on the diagram. Below you will find a list of the cell organelles. Click on each organelle, and you will be taken to a link that will help you find answers for your cell questionnaire and to label your diagram. Click on the back arrow on the toolbar to return to this page after completing your research.

- Nucleus
- Lysosome
- Mitochondria
- Endoplasmic reticulum
- Vacuole
- Cell wall
- Chloroplast
- Cell membrane
- Cytoplasm
- Golgi apparatus

2. In your group, discuss how each organelle corresponds to an actual city structure. Each group member needs to fill in his or her own city-structure sheet.
3. As a group, make a rough-draft blueprint of your cell city. It should include labels for all cell organelles and their corresponding city structure. Together, give your cell city a name.
4. As a group, make a 3-D model of your cell city with materials from home. Be sure to label all cell organelles and corresponding city structures. Your model should look like your blueprint!
5. Each member will choose one of the following careers and complete the job associated with that role. Click on any job below for detailed instructions.

- Travel agent
- Newspaper journalist/newscaster
- Musician/poet

Conclusion

Although this activity seems simple, cells are very complex. You will be able to better understand the interrelationship of the cell's organelles through this comparison to a city. This introduction to cells will prepare you for more detailed instruction in the future.

Figure 2.
Grading rubrics

Cell City evaluation

	0 points	**3 points**	**5 points**
Organelles represented	none	most	all
Construction of city	falling apart	one-month warranty	lifetime guarantee
No. organelles labeled	none	most	all
City structures identified	none	most	all
Accuracy of organelle structure	none	most	all
Creativity	boring	meets basic requirement	one of a kind
Neatness	sloppy	meets basic requirements	outstanding
City named	none	general	unique
Rough draft (drawing)	none	most structures identified	exact blueprint
Presentation of cell city	none	adequate	outstanding
Total points earned:			

Job evaluation

	0 points	**5 points**	**10 points**
Organelles represented	none	1–2	3
Accuracy of organelle information	wrong	mostly correct	completely accurate
Creativity	boring	meets basic requirements	one of a kind
Presentation	none	adequate	outstanding
Followed directions	not at all	mostly	exactly
Total points earned:			

Conclusion

The activity addresses several of the National Science Education Standards

- Content Standard A: Science as Inquiry
- Content Standard C: Life Science (structure and function in living systems; reproduction and heredity; regulation and behavior; populations and ecosystems; diversity and adaptations of organisms)
- Content Standard E: Science and Technology (abilities of technological design; understandings about science and technology).

It is also a great interdisciplinary approach to teaching that combines creative writing, art, spelling, language arts, and mathematics. Cell City is also easy to implement, and students are quick to adapt to this new learning style. I spend time working with students the first couple of days to help them get on track, but after that I mainly float from group to group providing encouragement and redirecting their work when needed.

This project generates a lot of enthusiasm, and students often ask to come to my classroom before school, at lunch, and after school to work on their cities. Students enjoy having the opportunity to be creative and work with their hands. Students also enjoy having their work displayed in the library so that it can be shared with the rest of the school.

Clay Rasmussen is a doctoral student in the Department of Secondary Education at Utah State University in Logan, Utah. Amy Resler is a science teacher at Westlane Middle School in Indianapolis. Audra Rasmussen is a science teacher at Northview Middle School in Indianapolis.

Resources

Cell City web quest
  www.msdwt.k12.in.us/web quests/RasQuest/ Cell_City.html
San Diego State University web quest page
  http://web quest.sdsu.edu

Using Web-Based Simulations to Promote Inquiry

By Mel Limson, Crystal Witzlib, and Robert A. Desharnais

That inquiry-based curriculum programs have positive effects on cognitive achievement, process skills, and attitudes toward science is widely accepted (NRC 2000). Science teachers seek engaging, effective, and inquiry-based activities that are standards-aligned and convenient to implement in their classrooms. For many years, the web has provided teachers and students with a vast resource of factual information (some of it multimedia). More recently, websites have been developed where teachers can obtain effective inquiry-based tools for teaching science. We report on how one of these sites, the Virtual Courseware Project (*www.sciencecourseware.org*), was used to engage students in an inquiry-based study of the principles of genetic inheritance.

About the Project

The Virtual Courseware website has a free suite of activities for both the life science laboratory and Earth science field studies that can be used by students ranging from middle school to high school, or in the college classroom. Virtual Courseware activities are innovative, experimental simulations that emphasize the inquiry process. Students learn by doing: making observations, proposing hypotheses, designing experiments, collecting and analyzing data generated by the software, and synthesizing and communicating results through an online notebook and report. The activities also include an online assessment quiz that consists of randomized, interactive questions. Students' answers are graded automatically and stored in a database server hosted by the Virtual Courseware Project, and a printable certificate of completion is issued for each student. The certificate of completion is generated automatically after a student has taken the quiz and is presented to the student together with the quiz results.

Teachers can access student and class results, allowing them to quickly gauge how well the key concepts were understood. Additionally, teachers have the option of modifying the grading rubric and guiding questions for the laboratory report, a feature that makes Virtual Courseware adaptable for different populations of learners. Examples of Virtual Courseware appropriate for middle school science students include *Drosophila,* for studying the principles of genetic inheritance; Natural Selection, for studying evolution; Relative Dating, for studying geological time; and Faults, for studying geological patterns.

We used the *Drosophila* simulation for two main purposes. First, we wanted students to grasp how phenotype alone can be used to determine what traits are passed from parents to offspring. By observing patterns of inheritance, recessiveness or dominance can be hypothesized. Secondly, we wanted to expose students to the inquiry process. *Drosophila* was used in both Gifted and Talented Education (GATE) and nonGATE seventh-grade classes at the culmination of the genetics unit. Before using the activity, students knew only how to determine offspring by using genotypes and Punnett squares.

Virtual Experiments

The *Drosophila* activity transforms the traditional fruit-fly laboratory experience into a virtual experiment. Students first register and create an account with a class code that is generated when the teacher sets up the class. The class account stores students' notebooks, reports, and quizzes, which remain accessible for student review during subsequent sessions. The use of a class code also permits the teacher to view the notebook, grade and comment on the report, and analyze the quiz results. After logging on, students see a lab bench with the equipment necessary to perform the fruit-fly experiments (Figure 1). Throughout the activity, students can add images, data, and additional notes to the online notebook accessible through the Notebook tab. Once the report is activated by the teacher, the Report tab guides students in writing their online lab reports. After the teacher has activated the quiz, students can use the Quiz tab to answer a series of interactive and randomized questions related to the tasks they perform with the activity. Using the Options tab, students can turn on or off the sounds, transitions, and on-screen directions.

In a typical experiment, students (1) select a male and female fly with specific traits, (2) mate these two parent flies, (3) observe and record the characteristics that are passed on to their offspring, and (4) analyze the results and provide a hypothesis ratio based on the outcome of the experiments. Offspring from one cross can also be mated to produce a second generation. The computer in the Lab Bench tab allows students to order flies with different

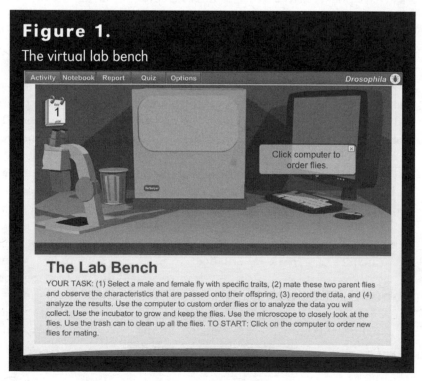

Figure 1.

The virtual lab bench

The Lab Bench

YOUR TASK: (1) Select a male and female fly with specific traits, (2) mate these two parent flies and observe the characteristics that are passed onto their offspring, (3) record the data, and (4) analyze the results. Use the computer to custom order flies or to analyze the data you will collect. Use the incubator to grow and keep the flies. Use the microscope to closely look at the flies. Use the trash can to clean up all the flies. TO START: Click on the computer to order new flies for mating.

combinations of mutations or to analyze the data that are collected.

Designing an experiment begins with the Fly's Supplies screen (Figure 2). The fly being customized is in the view on the left half of the screen, along with a list of its characteristics. Visible mutations are chosen from a tabbed catalog on the right. Up to three traits may be selected for any single experiment. Possible choices include gender and 30 traits in nine different categories: bristles, body color, antennae, eye color, eye shape, wing size, wing shape, wing vein, and wing angle. Thousands of experimental combinations are possible. In the simplest case, students choose one mutation and cross it with a normal wild-type fly. For example, a female with vestigial wings and a wild-type male can be ordered and added to the shopping cart. At checkout, images of these flies can be recorded directly into the online notebook.

The next steps occur at the Lab Bench. The customized flies are shipped, unpacked, added to a mating jar, and placed in the incubator to initiate mating. A 10-second animation shows the development of flies through a normal life cycle. Another animation shows the offspring flies being anesthetized with ether in preparation for viewing under the microscope.

Data collection occurs in the Microscope View (Figure 3), where students can automatically sort flies based on their phenotype. A table in the upper right of the screen lists the gender, count, and phenotype of each group of flies. By clicking on a button, students can send their data to the Lab Bench computer for later analysis. Clicking on a fly pile zooms the view to a single fly. Students can save the fly image in their online notebooks and add them later to their reports.

Drosophila allows multiple generations. Students can choose two flies in the microscope view for a new mating. Multiple generations allow students to see examples of classic Mendelian genetic ratios. For example, the second generation of offspring from a mating between

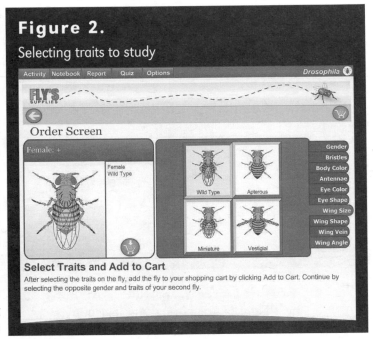

Figure 2.

Selecting traits to study

Figure 3.

Viewing flies in the microscope

a vestigial-winged female and wild-type male is shown in the Microscope View in Figure 3. The second generation is now sorted into four piles and the data (gender, count, and phenotype) are listed in the upper-right section. Because vestigial

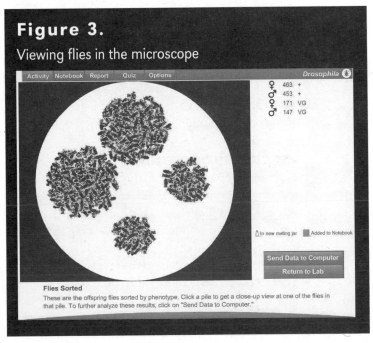

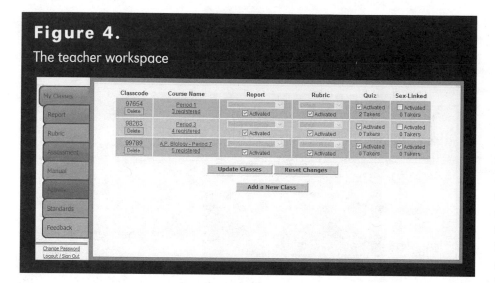

Figure 4.

The teacher workspace

The teacher can modify the online default report guide and grading rubric to make it appropriate for middle school students (Figure 5a). Each section, header, and line of text can be customized using the Report and Rubric Editor tabs in the Teacher Workspace. Furthermore, the teacher can save versions under different names and associate each version with a particular class in the My Classes tab. Once students submit a final report, the teacher can easily grade and comment on it through the report link on the Assessment tab (Figure 5b).

In our classroom implementation, we compiled a student-preparation worksheet that included four predetermined fruit-fly crosses as guiding examples (Figure 6) and other websites (see Resources) on fruit flies and their use in genetics. The *Drosophila* activity was introduced to students by guiding them through an animated tour and other components of the website.

wings are a recessive trait, these data show a 3:1 ratio between the normal and mutant flies.

Drosophila also allows test crosses. In this case, an offspring fly in the microscope view is added to the mating jar and then a new fly from the store can be used for a mating with the offspring fly. Test crosses with a recessive fly allow students to distinguish between flies with the same phenotype but different genotypes.

Data analysis occurs in the Computer View. Data transferred from the microscope appear in tabular form. Students can propose a numerical hypothesis for the expected ratio of the different fly phenotypes and see how well their hypothesis matches the data. A chi-square statistical analysis is also an option. All data tables and analyses can be saved in the online notebook.

Teacher Preparation

Teacher preparation for the activity is fairly simple. A *Teacher Registration and Workspace Guide* and a *Teacher Manual* are both available on the website. In the online Teacher Workspace, the teacher can register multiple classes, and class codes are automatically generated (Figure 4). These codes are given to students to use when they register so that their notebooks, reports, and quiz results are accessible by the teacher.

Using *Drosophila* in the Classroom

Drosophila was used as a weeklong activity at the culmination of a monthlong unit on genetics. A summary of how we used the *Drosophila* simulation with students in five middle school classes is shown in Figure 7. Although the activities were designed to accommodate one student per computer in a classroom or computer lab, working in pairs or in small groups was also effective. If there is limited access to computers in the classroom, the teacher can demonstrate the activity using the self-animated tour or by setting up and using an example student account. Students can then complete the activities on their own time as a homework assignment if they have access to computers connected to the internet. We provided students

Figure 5.

(a) Report Template and Rubric Editors (b) Grading Rubric for assessment of student

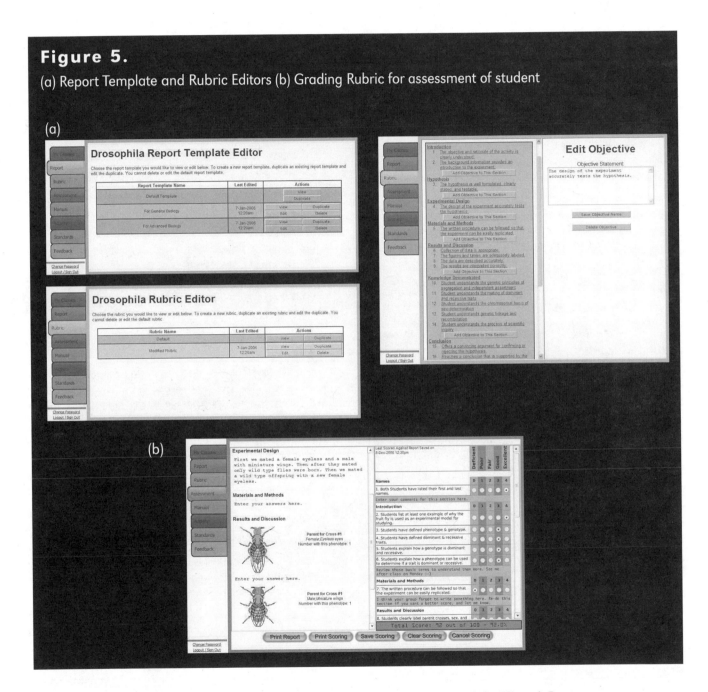

a list of local, public libraries with computers and internet access they could use during after-school hours. The website is database-driven and has dynamic features (student and teacher accounts), and thus can be used on any computer connected to the internet. No student or class information is stored on the local machine.

On the day we started the Virtual Courseware lab, students were required to do two of the four crosses that we assigned. Advanced students in the GATE classes were to pick one of four crosses to complete and were required to do one cross of their own. Again, the flexibility for customization of Virtual Courseware permits differentiated in-

Figure 6.
Supplemental student-preparation worksheets

Drosophila melanogaster (fruit fly) preparation

A quick and simple introduction to *Drosophila melanogaster*
   www.ceolas.org/fly/intro.html

Directions: You will need the internet for this assignment. Use the websites listed to answer the questions.

Mutant fruit flies
www.exploratorium.edu/exhibits/mutant_flies/mutant_flies.html

Read this entire site and answer the questions below. This site gives examples of fruit-fly mutations.

1. A mutation is any change in the genetic message carried by that gene that makes some trait of an organism different from normal, for example, having six fingers rather than five. Are all mutations bad?

2. What does it mean for a fruit fly to be "wild type"?

3. What color will an ebony fruit fly be?

4. Can a fly be "eyeless"?

5. What will fruit flies accumulate around?

6. How long is the life cycle of a fruit fly?

7. How many pairs of chromosomes do fruit flies have?

8. Besides the fruit fly, name two other insects that have had their entire genome sequenced.

Drosophila
www.sciencecourseware.org/vcise/drosophila

This is the website we will be using in class for our lab next week. Please spend some time investigating the site and answering the questions below.

Click on the blue tab on the left that reads Tour. Use the red arrows on the upper right to go from page to page. This will take you through the entire experiment we will be doing. Wait until the timer gets to the end before you move on to the next page, or you will miss information.

9. Who will give you your class code?

10. For what is the incubator used?

11. To start an experiment, what must you click on?

12. What must you click on to have the flies delivered to the Lab Bench?

13. Can your report be printed?

14. Are the questions the same each time you take the quiz?

After you finish the tour, click on the red tab on the left labeled User Homepage. On the lower right you can click on a button labeled Enter as a Guest. Click this button and enter. Important: DO NOT CLICK on the BACK button of your web browser or it will bring you back to the homepage!

15. Click on the computer.

16. Click on Order Flies.

17. Order a female with purple eyes (found under Eye Color) and a male with curly wings (found under Wing Shape). After ordering the flies you will have to check out.

18. Click on the box to unpack your flies and follow the directions given to you in the yellow boxes.

19. Sort your flies when you get to this step.

   a. How many piles will be formed?

   b. Will any of the flies have purple eyes? If yes, how many? If no, what does this tell us about the trait for purple eyes?

20. Go to Analyze Results.

   a. What was the total number of flies that were the offspring of this mating?

21. Go back to order more flies. Try mating at least two more fly types. Experiment and have fun trying to learn the program.

Drosophila

Directions: Use any two of the following matings to write a detailed lab report for the *Drosophila* activity. Make sure to save your experimental findings in the online notebook so that you can use that information for your report. You will find the online report on the *sciencecourseware.org* website.

1. Female Eyeless (Eye Shape) and Male Miniature (Wing Size)

   Observe the results and save to notebook.
   Mate the male offspring with a new order of Female Eyeless.
   Observe the results and save to notebook.

2. Female Wild Type and Male Dichaete (Wing Angle)

   Observe the results and save to notebook.
   Mate the Male Dichaete offspring with a new order of Female Dichaete (Wing Angle).
   Observe the results and save to notebook.

3. Female Purple Eyes (Eye Color) and Male Yellow Body (Body Color)

   Observe the results and save to notebook.
   Mate the Female Wild-Type offspring with Male Purple Eyes.
   Observe the results and save to notebook.

4. Female Lobe (Eye Shape) and Male Shaven (Bristles)

   Observe the results and save to notebook.
   Mate the Lobe Male with a Wild-Type Female.
   Observe the results and save to notebook.

Figure 7.

Summary of implementation in the middle school classroom

Day	Activity focus	Comments
Day 1	Students introduced to website and animated tour. Students picked partners. Partners registered for student accounts.	Partnering allowed students to exchange ideas and decreased the amount of grading. Students' first initials and last names were combined to register a single account.
Days 2–3	Report activated for partners. Partners followed worksheet with predetermined fruit-fly crosses. Gifted and Talented Education (GATE) students picked one of four crosses to complete and performed a cross on their own; non-GATE students picked two of the four crosses to complete. Partners began composing report using data saved into notebook.	Software allows teacher to • modify the Report Guide, • modify the Scoring Rubric, • decide when to activate the report, and • decide when to activate the quiz. Students can access the web-based program, notebooks, and reports at home or at the public library. Student results and teacher assessment saved to server, not on local machine.
Day 4	Quiz activated for extra credit. Students worked in pairs, some took quiz multiple times. Certificates of completion printed. Partners continued composing reports.	Quiz is advanced for seventh graders. Quiz cannot be edited by the teacher because of its interactive nature. Several students repeated the quiz until they got correct answers. This contributed to their learning. Students excited by the printable and personalized certificate of completion.
Day 5	Reports due by time-stamp deadline.	Reports, notebooks, quiz answers, and scores can be viewed through the Teacher Workspace. Reports were graded online using the previously customized rubric. Students were able to view their grades and teacher comments on their reports by logging in to their accounts.

struction among all learners. Although the GATE students finished the activity much faster, the non-GATE students performed and understood just as much as the advanced students.

Students were quickly engaged and amused at the entertaining, yet accurate simulation, while instinctively using the activity. Partners worked together, and surprisingly, some groups began checking on the various outcomes that other groups were obtaining and providing hypotheses for one another. At the end of the class period, we followed up with a short group discussion on using the activity. As instructors, we enjoyed observing the camaraderie of students that led to a true learning environment while we circulated through the computer lab room and only occasionally guided some partner groups in an inquiry-directed manner.

The assessment components of the activity are the report and quiz. All student groups were required to compose their reports by following the teacher-designed report guide and by importing images and tables saved into their notebook. Virtual Courseware provides teachers the flexibility to modify and customize the default report guide template and the grading rubric for the student reports. Furthermore, teachers have the discretion to assign the work as group or individual work. In our case, we assigned students to work in pairs or groups of three. The report guided students to state their hypotheses, explain their results, and defend their conclusions. All students successfully completed reports and were given full credit for the assignment. Because it was designed for high school students and its interactive nature could not be edited by the teacher, the quiz was an extra-credit, optional assignment. The quiz addresses the learning objectives of the activity, but the details of the questions are randomized each time it is rendered. Students were challenged by the quiz in the *Drosophila* activity, but many of them retook the quiz several times, improving their performance and, in the process, their learning. Students had an incentive to complete the quiz—a printable, personalized certificate of completion that has been programmed into the activity. Both assessment components, the report and quiz, have a date and time stamp associated with every save and can be monitored from the Teacher Workspace. Thus, the teacher can set a deadline for students to complete the experiments and submit their report or take the quiz.

Observations of Inquiry

We were pleased by the amount of inquiry learning resulting from this activity. Students were able to justify the explanations of their scientific experiments, and independently formulated and tested alternative hypotheses to see how genetic patterns would be inherited. For example, a pair of students was surprised to find that after two generations their flies turned out to have yellow-colored bodies, despite having red-colored parents. They tracked the gene by writing down the chain of events and discovered that the recessive trait in the yellow flies came from the grandfather.

Both low- and high-achieving students were constantly engaged. It was unusual for students to be disciplined or asked to stay on task because they wanted to use the program. Though it was

rarely necessary during the activity in our computer lab, we enforced a policy that grading points would be deducted if we found students going to other websites not directly related to *Drosophila*. One of the most rewarding moments occurred when a student said, "I went home and almost finished the report last night on my computer." At the time this student had 13 missing assignments, but was now putting in time outside of class!

The response to the *Drosophila* activity was better than we expected. Students were excited and motivated to think and discover, and several told us that they hadn't understood genotype and phenotype before mating the flies. Students grasped the basic concepts more fully by applying and discovering the principles they had learned earlier in our genetics unit.

Mel Limson is the K–12 education programs coordinator at the American Physiological Society in Bethesda, Maryland. Crystal Witzlib is a former seventh-grade science teacher at the John Muir Middle School in Burbank, California. Robert A. Desharnais is a professor of biology at California State University, Los Angeles.

Acknowledgments

The Virtual Courseware Project is funded by the National Science Foundation and the California State University.

Reference

National Research Council (NRC). 2000. *Inquiry and the National Science Education Standards*. Washington, DC: National Academy Press.

Resources

Mutant fruit flies
   www.exploratorium.edu/exhibits/mutant_flies/ mutant_flies.html
The Virtual Courseware Activity: *Drosophila*
   www.sciencecourseware.org/vcise/drosophila
The Virtual Courseware Project
   www.sciencecourseware.org
The WWW Virtual Library: A Quick and Simple Introduction to *Drosophila melanogaster*
   www.ceolas.org/fly/intro.html

Making "Photo" Graphs

By Julianne Doto and Susan Golbeck

Collecting data and analyzing the results of experiments is difficult for children. We found a surprising way to help our third graders make graphs and draw conclusions from their data: digital photographs. The pictures bridged the gap between an abstract graph and the plants it represented. With the support of the photos, students analyzed the results of their experiment and represented them graphically. In addition, children learned about plants according to state science standards while integrating the data analysis components of state math standards.

Planting Seeds

Unbeknownst to the class, Wisconsin Fast Plants actually grow shorter and produce larger canopies when given excess fertilizer. Students would soon discover this through collecting data and analyzing their own graphs.

Taking Pictures

By Monday of the week following planting, most of the plants were between 1 and 2 cm tall. With some teacher assistance, partners photographed their plants. To ensure the photos were taken from the same distance, a diamond drawn on top of a white plastic shelf specified where children should place the planter. We arranged boxes and books so that the camera would be at the correct height. An "X" marked on the floor with tape controlled the students' distance from the plant. They wrote their student numbers and the color code for their plants (plants were labeled with colored toothpicks) on a white board behind the plant. Finally, yellow paper was placed behind the control group plants and white paper was placed behind the treatment plants (Figure 1).

Pairs repeated the procedure for each of their four plants. We took photographs every Monday for four weeks, documenting the plants' entire life cycles.

Taking Measurements

After taking the photographs, students measured their plants using centimeter rulers and recorded the measurement in a data table. It was important to take the pictures before measuring, because sometimes plants were damaged in the act of measuring. I later entered the heights into an Excel spreadsheet.

Figure 1.

As students photographed their plants, they distinguished the control and treatment groups with colored paper.

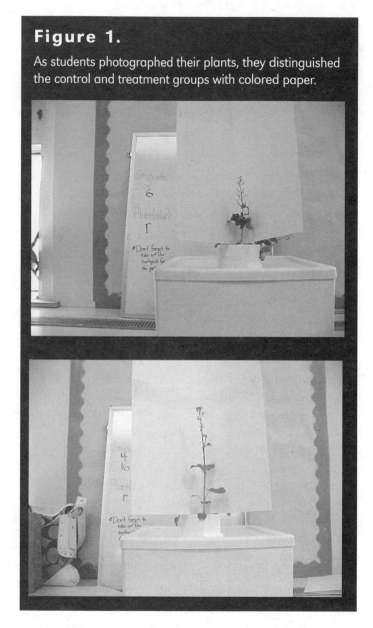

Printing Photographs

Printing the photographs that would illustrate the graph was surprisingly easy. After transferring the photos to a computer, I inserted the images one at a time into individual cells in the Excel file. Once the picture was inserted, its corresponding cell on the next page (if printed back to back) was filled with that plant's height.

We cropped the photos to fit inside their designated cells as follows:

1. Insert photos with → Picture → From File.
2. Click on the picture, and use the picture toolbar (View → Toolbars → Picture) to crop the images to the width of the planter.
3. Shrink photo so the planter is the width of a cell, making all of the plants to scale. Click on the photo, and then drag the corner until it is small enough to fit in the cell.
4. Add heights to cells to the right of the photos by looking at the student data tables (Figure 2).
5. Using a laser or photo printer, print the photos and heights back-to-back.
6. Print out student data tables with all the heights for the week.

Creating Graphs

The graphs were introduced as a way to organize our data so that others could look at a graph and see how tall the plants grew. We discussed how the graphs would help us see which group was growing taller. We showed students a list of data without tables, and then they compared that to the same data presented in a table. The students recognized the table made the data much easier to read and understand.

Each week, students were given the assignment of creating a graph with the following supplies: chart paper, scissors, pencils, markers, glue sticks, a table of plant heights, and the photo printouts. Students were given time to discuss the layout and create their own graphs during the first and second weeks. Because the heights were on the back of the photos, they had to figure out how to convey that data once the photo was glued down and that data obscured.

We discussed the photos and what they added to the graph. The photos helped students understand what the values on the graph represented. Instead of being naked numbers, the numbers had a visible reference in the picture.

The photos reminded children that their graph consisted of the whole sample of plants.

Comparing Treatments

At first, it was confusing for children to compare two different treatments in one graph. Some completely ignored the treatment group during the first week and graphed solely based on plant height. Instead of separating "fertilizer" from "no (extra) fertilizer," they lumped both treatment groups together, making it difficult to see which group grew taller. We returned to the earlier discussion about the need to compare the fertilized group to the plain group. If we mixed up all of the numbers, how could we compare them? Eventually students understood they were trying to figure out which group grew better (fertilizer or no fertilizer) and that they had to graph by treatment.

At first, the majority of students included only values that were found in the data, which is typical of this age group (Nemirovsky and Tierney 2001). For example, if there were no 4 cm plants, then their scale read 3 cm, 5 cm, 6 cm, etc. We discussed why it was important for people to see what data was missing and therefore to include all of the values in the range of the scale (terms they had learned in a previous graphing unit).

Some students separated plants by treatment group but made no effort to sort plants sequentially by height. When heights were not arranged sequentially with an axis on the graph, it was difficult for students to compare the two treatment groups of fertilizer and no fertilizer. Students were prompted to line up the data—to make the axes for the fertilizer and no-fertilizer groups the same scale so that they could easily compare them. We compared graphs that lined up and those that didn't. Students agreed that the lined-up ones were easier to read.

Analyzing Results

Once the graphs were finished, children agreed that the no additional fertilizer plants had grown

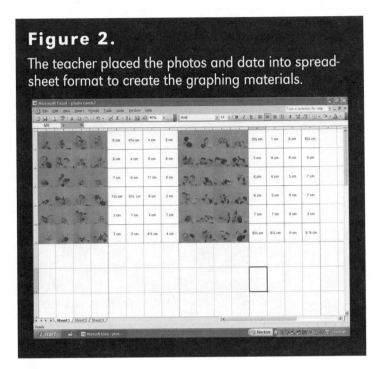

Figure 2.

The teacher placed the photos and data into spreadsheet format to create the graphing materials.

better. They were taller and some were flowering, compared to the extra-fertilizer group, which were stunted and brown in some cases. During a whole-class discussion of our results, some mentioned how too much medicine was bad for you, so too much fertilizer might also be bad for plants.

Learning Outcomes

At the end of the unit, students were assessed with a graphing conference in which they were shown graphs and asked to interpret them. Then, children were given a data table and asked to construct a graph. All except three students made frequency graphs, and about half were able to read a bar graph representing frequencies.

When a passing teacher asked two children whether extra fertilizer helped their plants grow, they promptly and adamantly said it had not. "It's easy to look at the pictures," said one student about her "photo graph." "Look how much better no fertilizer did," replied her partner.

Upon taking the last set of pictures, students pollinated the flowers and then a week later harvested the seedpods. We were already wondering what to graph next.

Julianne Doto is a teacher at Washington School in West Caldwell, New Jersey. Susan Golbeck is an associate professor of educational psychology at Rutgers University in New Brunswick, New Jersey. Special thanks to Sally Joseph, Sandy D'Orio, Gilda Sibelia, and Susan Smith for their assistance with the project.

References

National Research Council (NRC). 1996. *National Science Education Standards*. Washington, DC: National Academy Press.

Nemirovsky, R., and C. Tierney. 2001. Children creating ways to represent changing situations: On the development of homogenous spaces. *Educational Studies in Mathematics* 45 (1): 67–102.

Connecting to the Standards
This article relates to the following National Science Education Standards (NRC 1996):

Content Standards
Grades K–4

Standard A: Science as Inquiry
- Abilities necessary to do scientific inquiry
- Understanding about scientific inquiry

Standard C: Physical Science
- Life cycles of organisms
- Organisms and environments

Science Education Program Standards
Standard C
The science program should be coordinated with the mathematics program to enhance student use and understanding of mathematics in the study of science and to improve student understanding of mathematics.

Learning With Loggerheads

By Christine Lener and Theodora Pinou

Kids tracking sea turtles? No, it's not a description for a new nature show on TV, it's a lesson, and it could be happening in your classroom. Sea turtle biologists worldwide are currently working together to track turtles to learn about sea turtle behavior and migration in an effort to conserve these endangered animals. We developed a unit using a modified version of published tracking activities (Sera and Eckert 2005) for third-grade students in which students develop and share computer-generated maps that are based on authentic data. With this information, students can evaluate sea turtle life history, behavior, and environmental hazards, just as scientists are doing today. Now, with only an internet connection, your students can engage in the global mission of sea turtle conservation while at the same time learn about the importance of technology in conservation and understanding of biodiversity.

Satellite Telemetry

Humans are able to track sea turtles across the world's oceans and follow their extensive migrations in real time through satellite transmission technology or telemetry. How does telemetry work? A biologist attaches a transmitter to the carapace (shell) of a sea turtle, usually at a nesting beach. When the turtle surfaces to breathe, the transmitter's antenna sends signals to satellite receivers that pinpoint the turtle's location and migratory pattern. A sea turtle can surface as often as every 10 minutes, sending multiple data points to satellite processing centers. Scientists translate these signals into points of latitude and longitude, which help them monitor and map sea turtle movements. Scientists then post these data onto a collaborative sea turtle monitoring site, *www.seaturtle.org*, so they can communicate with colleagues globally about sea turtle movements throughout the world's oceans.

This sea turtle site is also accessible to educators on any basic internet server to teach students about sea turtle migration and mapping. In preparation for the activity, it's best if teachers reserve a computer lab ahead of time. In cases where computers are limited, teachers can group as many as three children to work cooperatively or rotate children between computer stations and manual mapping of the tracking points. Teachers are strongly encouraged to prepare for this exercise by accessing the tracking data beforehand and modifying the points of latitude and longitude by rounding off to the nearest whole number. Our experience is that, if the data are not rounded, finding the specific decimal places to plot becomes confusing for the children.

Preparing to Track

On the first day of the unit, we begin by asking the class about migration: What animals do you know that migrate? Why? Responses are written on the board and typically include whales, birds, and butterflies. Children often explain that migration occurs because animals are following their food or are migrating in response to the changing of the seasons. It is during this first day that students are introduced to sea turtles (*Caretta caretta*) and the idea that sea turtles also migrate due to seasonal changes that affect water temperatures and food supply. In addition, sea turtles migrate to find a mate and to find appropriate beaches to build nests and lay eggs.

Background information on sea turtle life history, migration, and threats to sea turtle survival can be read together in class and discussed as a whole-group activity. Alternatively, the teacher may choose to send home reading materials for students to read as homework before the lesson. Such information can be found in the Sea Turtle Migration Tracking and Coastal Habitat Education Program educator's guides (see Resources). These readings introduce students to sea turtle tracking patterns. For example, tracking points recorded from land indicate nesting (laying eggs); tracking points recorded offshore of the nesting beach indicate internesting (a female can return to nest multiple times in one season, revealing a zigzag pattern); and the foraging grounds where turtles feed are clustered record tracking points at the end of the migration pattern. The migration pattern is the line drawn between the internesting and foraging grounds.

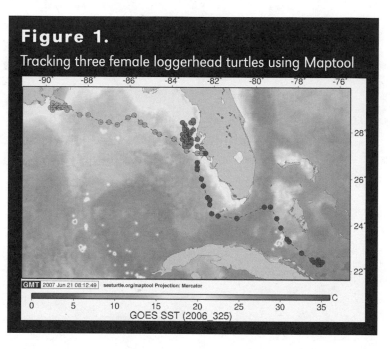

Figure 1.

Tracking three female loggerhead turtles using Maptool

The next day, we establish a baseline understanding of mapping skills by giving students a graphing assignment called "A Pointy Turtle" (Prime 1997). This activity helps students learn how to find points on a table and then connect the points to draw a graph. This activity reinforces the importance of connecting points in a defined order by revealing the outline of a turtle only when points are connected sequentially. This graphing activity prepares students for connecting the sea turtle tracking points according to the date the signal was reported.

Next, students are introduced to a *tracking map* (Figure 1), which is a record of a turtle's travels. Teachers can obtain samples of tracking maps in advance of the lesson through *www.seaturtle. org*. These maps can also be used to integrate geography, such as names of oceans, continents, compass rose, longitude, and latitude.

The Tracking Begins

On the third day, choose an ocean you want to concentrate your tracking activities on with students. Our class chose to study the Gulf of Mexico because they sponsored turtles through

Figure 2.

Tracking map of the Gulf of Mexico with lines of latitude and longitude

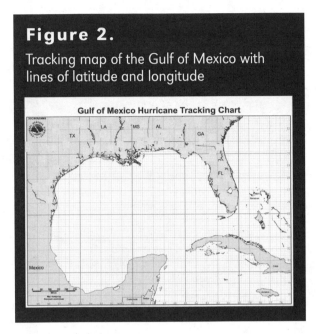

a pattern. If this is not done, students can get frustrated when plotting points in close proximity that when connected don't show a trajectory of travel.

Recommended strategies for teachers include partitioning the data by seasons, so different groups can map the location of a turtle during different seasons and then come together to discuss the annual pattern. Alternatively, groups can compare different turtles that all start at the same nesting beach and examine if their migration is different, as shown in Figure 1 for Ariel, Talulah,

the Mote Marine Lab Sea Turtle Tracking Program in Sarasota, Florida. The teacher traveled to Mote Marine Lab and attached the transmitters on several nesting female loggerhead turtles herself. When she returned to school, her students named and tracked these same turtles. Students were given a hurricane tracking map of the Gulf of Mexico (Figure 2) with pronounced lines of latitude and longitude to use for manual mapping. Maps can be customized for a desired area from the National Weather Service or from the *seaturtle. org* tracking homepage (see Resources).

Teachers access tracking data by going to *seaturtle.org* and clicking the "Tracking" icon. Next, they find the "For Teachers" heading in the menu on the left. Then, under the "Tracking Data" heading, they click "Access Data" and access the data by geographic project or sea turtle species. In this case, the teacher selected Casey Key Loggerheads (the sea turtle group the class was tracking in the Gulf), and then selected a specific animal (Talulah), hit "Submit," and all 48 tracking points were listed. To reduce confusion generated by the large number of data points, the teacher summarized the travel to 14 points (Figure 3) that when connected will reveal

Figure 3.

Modified telemetry points for mapping by students

TALULAH'S SATELLITE TRACKING DATA

DATE	LONGITUDE	LATITUDE
7/19/2006	82.5 W	27.0 N
7/20/2006	83.0 W	27.0 N
7/22/2006	83.0 W	26.0 N
7/25/2006	82.0 W	25.0 N
7/30/2006	82.0 W	24.0 N
7/31/2006	81.0 W	24.0 N
8/01/2006	80.0 W	25.0 N
8/02/2006	79.5 W	25.0 N
8/03/2006	79.0 W	24.0 N
8/06/2006	78.5 W	23.0 N
8/07/2006	78.0 W	23.0 N
8/12/2006	77.0 W	22.5 N
9/13/2006	77.0 W	22.0 N
10/15/2006	77.0 W	22.0 N

and Genie. Completion of this manual mapping can take as much as three lessons. (Students are given approximately three seasons of data to plot over three class periods.)

Inquiring About Behavior

Once students have generated migration maps, we review terms like *nesting beaches, internesting behavior, foraging behavior,* and *migration.* Teachers can assess learning by recording student ability to label these behaviors and locations on their maps. Teachers can also assess student ability to add to their migration analysis project the location of where the sea turtle was tagged, number of days spent internesting, the direction of the migration, where the foraging ground is, and how they know this. Using a rubric, the teacher assesses student ability to plot latitude and longitude on a map and connect these points by date and to describe movements of the turtle's life history (Figure 4).

Once students have had a chance to map by hand, they can spend another class period entering points of migration into *seaturtle.org*'s Maptool (see Resources). Maptool also permits students to add layers of information, such as coastlines, country names, currents, and sea surface temperatures (SST). Here students can label land masses, oceans, and direction of migration. Then they can predict what factors may have influenced the migration; for example weather may account for Virginia's unorganized pattern. These maps can then be discussed as a class. Ariel stopped transmitting signals after 94 days of being tagged. She was last tracked into an area with a high concentration of red tide (which was likely fatal), and Genie and Talulah migrated to different foraging grounds (Figure 1). Virginia's transmitting signal continued after the storm, demonstrating that turtles can endure many natural disasters like hurricanes.

Finally, we integrate literacy and writing by requiring each student to write a one-page journal entry explaining what the sea turtle may be

Figure 4.

Learning with loggerheads rubric

Objective #1: Upon completing this assignment, you will be able to record and graph sea turtle travels using research data (1 point each).

1. Shows a beginning level of performance.
2. Shows development and movement toward mastery of performance.
3. Shows mastery of performance.

Objective #2: Upon completing this assignment, you will be able to describe movements of sea turtle life history (nesting, internesting, migration, foraging) by examining tracking data (1 point each).

1. Shows a beginning level of performance.
2. Shows development and movement toward mastery of performance.
3. Shows mastery of performance.

Objective #3: Upon completing this assignment, you will be able to discuss environmental factors that may influence sea turtle migration (1 point each).

1. Shows a beginning level of performance.
2. Shows development and movement toward mastery of performance.
3. Shows mastery of performance.

experiencing while traveling. Students develop public-speaking skills by sharing their journal entries with their peers. Students are assessed by the correct usage of the behavioral terminology in their writing and speaking and in their ability to predict what environmental factors are influencing the migration, such as season and food, water temperature, disease, and storms. Each of these factors can be examined empirically by visiting the National Oceanic and Atmospheric Administration (NOAA) website, which tracks, documents, and reports such data at *noaa.gov*. In addition, Maptool permits migration maps to be constructed with overlaid sea surface temperature (SST), vegetation index, and other factors that can help explain turtle migrations.

Student Success

We found that when children are given an opportunity to map animal travels in real time—just like scientists—they independently inquire why the animals exhibit certain migratory patterns. Students began wondering if turtle movements observed were due to environmental dangers, such as commercial fishing, recreational boating, and pollution. They also considered changes in the turtle's food supply due to seasonal changes in sea surface temperatures and ocean currents. We believe that when satellite telemetry technology is brought into the classroom to investigate the phenomenon of migration, elementary students improve their conceptual understanding of science and technology, their personal and social perspectives of science, and their understanding of organisms and life history.

The students at our school look forward to this unit every fall with great anticipation and enthusiasm because they understand the real-time setting and are excited about where the turtles are moving. This active interest initiates much discussion about conservation in the classroom. Parents have reported that their children are excited to share maps, journal entries, and questions at home, engaging their family and friends in their science class experience.

Christine Lener is the lower school science and technology specialist at Wooster School in Danbury, Connecticut. Theodora Pinou is an assistant professor at Western Connecticut State University, also in Danbury, Connecticut.

Resources

National Research Council (NRC). 1996. *National Science Education Standards*. Washington, DC: National Academy Press.

Prime, C.S. 1997. A pointy turtle. In *Zoobooks: Turtles*, eds. T. Biel and J. Bonnett Wexo, p. B. Poway, CA: Wildlife Education.

Sera, H., and K. L. Eckert. 2005. *Endangered Caribbean sea turtles: An educator's handbook*. Beaufort, NC: Wider Caribbean Sea Turtle Conservation Network.

Internet

AccuWeather.com Hurricane Center
http://hurricane.accuweather.com/hurricane/tracking.asp?partner=accuweather
Caribbean Conservation Corporation and Sea Turtle Survivor League Educator's Guide
www.cccturtle.org/satellitetracking.php?page=educatorsguide
Seaturtle.org Maptool
www.seaturtle.org/maptool
Seaturtle.org Satellite Tracking
www.seaturtle.org/tracking/index.shtml?project_id=67
Seaturtle.org Educator's Guide
www.seaturtle.org/documents/Educators_Guide.pdf
Seaturtle.org Tracking Teaching Resources
www.seaturtle.org/tracking/teachers

Connecting to the Standards

This article relates to the following National Science Education Standards (NRC 1996):

Content Standards
Grades K–4

Standard C: Life Science
- The characteristics of organisms
- Organisms and environments

Standard E: Science and Technology
- Understanding about science and technology

Up-to-the-Minute Meteorology

By Mervyn J. Wighting, Robert A. Lucking, and Edwin P. Christmann

If you are looking for up-to-the-minute weather information, chances are you'll turn to The Weather Channel or visit a website such as *www.weather.com* or *www.accuweather.com*. You should also turn to these resources to help teach your students meteorology. Of course, students should still be taught how to gather their own data using hands-on instruments such as thermometers, barometers, weather vanes, wind gauges, and rain gauges. Once they have mastered traditional data collection techniques, however, introduce them to the wealth of data, lesson plans, and simulations offered online and on television. Here are a few of our favorite weather-related resources.

Weather on the Web

The Weather Classroom (*www.weather.com/ education*), which is available from The Weather Channel, is a comprehensive collection of weather-related internet links for teachers. Once you set up a free teacher account, you can access lesson plans, interactive multimedia, newsletters, and caches of other teaching resources.

For example, a thematic lesson titled RAYS Awareness gives you a video clip from Weather Channel meteorologist Jennifer Lopez and four *Standards*-based lesson plans (Hot Colors, Light Reading, A [Time] Piece of Pizza, and Seed vs. Seed) that can be used with your middle school students. The unit and activities are designed to focus on the dangers of ultraviolet radiation to skin. The lessons include scientific experiments, creative writing exercises, mathematical calculations involving Sun protection factors (SPF), and explorations of how various cultures and economies are affected by the Sun.

In addition to the variety of weather units and lessons available for classroom use, teachers can tape episodes of The Weather Classroom, which airs Monday and Thursday from 4–4:30 A.M. EST. Topics of episodes have incluedd winter weather, careers in meteorology, weather and geography, and tornadoes. A teachers guide for each episode created by veteran teachers can be found on the website. Each guide contains background information, activities, and study questions. Additionally, some of these guides contain sophisticated data-gathering forms and matrices.

Another offering on The Weather Channel site is Project SafeSide, which was developed in partnership with the American Red Cross. SafeSide explores the effects of extreme weather such as hurricanes, tornadoes, floods, lightning, extreme heat, and winter storms.

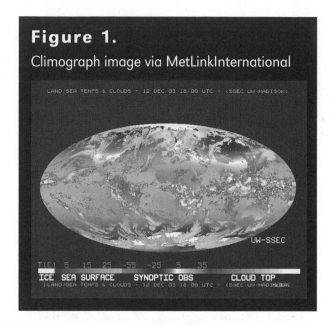

Figure 1.

Climograph image via MetLinkInternational

One part is designed for grades K–4 and the other for grades 5–12. Both include hands-on activities, cross-curricular extensions, and instructions for conducting a severe weather simulation. Students are encouraged to develop a family disaster plan to protect and prepare themselves and their families for a weather emergency.

Finally, encourage your students to visit *www. weather.com/learn/dave*, where they will find a wide range of weather-related information for incorporation into their assignments.

Global Perspective

If you are interested in global meteorology, check out the MetLinkInternational Project at *www.metlink.org*. This project is the result of a partnership of The Royal Meteorological Society, Project Atmosphere Australia, and MetLinkInternational. Students around the world use the site to exchange weather observations using an online database. For example, students in the United States can exchange weather information with classes in Oman, India, and Australia. Teachers can find additional project suggestions from participating schools from around the world.

Daily images of the entire globe are provided that show cloud movement and other atmospheric events using still photos, movies, and weathercams. With the click of a mouse, students can see fog surrounding the Eiffel Tower or a sunrise in Hong Kong. Figure 1 is an example of a Climograph image, which shows worldwide temperatures.

For another fascinating set of images, check out the many photos of lightning at *thunder.msfc. nasa.gov* (see Figure 2). At this link, your students can observe data on the global frequency and distribution of lightning as observed from space by NASA's Optical Transient Detector.

Grab Bag

Another useful site is *www. education.noaa.gov*, home of the National Oceanic and Atmospheric Administration's education resources. Here you will find lists of free and inexpensive

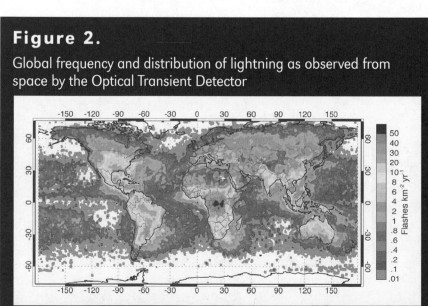

Figure 2.

Global frequency and distribution of lightning as observed from space by the Optical Transient Detector

classroom materials, such as booklets, videos, software, and posters. You'll also find a collection of K–12 weather and climate activities and study guides on weather topics. Another site that caught our attention was the Global Weather Services vision of weather in the distant future, which can be viewed at *www.ucar.edu/pres/2025/web*. There researchers project weather patterns for the year 2025 using video images of real and model data.

Flight Into the Fury

From the safety of your classroom, students can join the crew of the 53rd Weather Reconnaissance Squadron and take an interactive flight into the eye of a hurricane by visiting *www.hurricanehunters.com*. This site has excellent videos, an interesting narrative, and plenty of pictures of storm systems. Another site that your students can use for investigating severe weather is *www.tornadoproject.com*, which gives students scientific information about tornadoes and explains some of the hazards associated with them.

Conclusion

Teachers need to take full advantage of the ubiquitous up-to-the-minute information that is available at our fingertips. Otherwise, students might not make the connections between school and our increasingly technological world.

Mervyn J. Wighting is an assistant professor of education at Regent University in Virginia Beach, Virginia. Robert A. Lucking is a professor and chairman of the curriculum and instruction department at Old Dominion University in Norfolk, Virginia. Edwin P. Christmann is a professor and graduate coordinator of the mathematics and science teaching program at Slippery Rock University in Slippery Rock, Pennsylvania.

What's the Matter?

By Susie Barcus and Mary M. Patton

I f you want to create an intriguing, hands-on environment in which young children can explore an unknown substance and examine its properties, then oobleck (or gloop) may be just what you need.

Making Sense of Properties

If your students have had little or no experience investigating materials and describing the properties of a substance, begin by holding up a piece of chalk, or other item, and asking the children to tell about what they already know from using it (Sneider 1985). Next, ask the children to describe what they can observe about its properties, including color, size, shape, texture, weight, hardness, and odor.

By listing these properties, the children will be able to see that a property of a substance is something that can be seen, heard, smelled, or felt by the senses or detected by various instruments such as microscopes, thermometers, and scales (extensions of the senses). Remind the students not to use their sense of taste.

Exploring Oobleck

To segue into an exploration of oobleck, read to the children *Bartholomew and the Oobleck* (Geisel 1949), in which a king's wizards make green oobleck fall from the sky.

Another popular story describes oobleck as a strange substance brought back from a planet in a different star system by a space probe (Sneider 1985).

By the time you have finished reading these stories, the children will be eager to get their hands on this unusual substance, which seems to be both a liquid and a solid at the same time.

A Sticky Situation

First prepare a batch of oobleck (see Figure 1 for the recipe) and store it in an airtight container until you are ready to begin.

Set up workstations by covering tabletops or laying paper on the floor to accommodate groups of three to four children. Provide each workstation with a sheet of paper and pencils for students to record observations and questions.

Set up a master supply table with a variety of nonstandard tools of investigation, such as potato mashers, eggbeaters, sections of wire mesh, plastic knives and spoons, straws, string, toothpicks, and metal washers. Also, although oobleck dries quickly and brushes off easily, you may want to supply children—especially younger ones—with plastic capes. Then give each child a sample of the oobleck.

When the children begin their explorations, encourage them to investigate the oobleck using only their senses. Ask them, "How does the substance look? What does it feel like? Does it have a distinctive odor?"

As the children scoop up handfuls of oobleck and watch it run through their fingers and down their arms, they will make many observations, such as, "It jiggles!" or "It crusts!" Children may also describe the oobleck by comparing it to a more familiar substance like gelatin, toothpaste, or candle wax. Explore alongside the children and you, too, will find your hands dripping with oobleck.

Further Exploration

Next, invite each group to extend its exploration by choosing one or two tools from the master supply table. Children may wonder, "Can it be whipped with an eggbeater or forced through a piece of wire mesh?" or "What happens when you place a piece of ice in the oobleck or add more water or cornstarch?" The children's own questions will determine the direction of their investigations and the tools they choose to carry them out.

As the children's observations become more refined and focused, their comments will indicate that they are no longer simply exploring the oobleck itself but are using the oobleck as a tool for thinking about the transformations they are witnessing. Some of our students wondered aloud, "When I squeeze the oobleck in my hand, it melts. Why does it do that? Is it because of the heat from my hand?" and "When I blow on the oobleck with a straw, it separates. Then it goes back together again. Why does that happen?"

At the end of the period, return the oobleck to its airtight container to be used for further explorations on the following day. Or, better yet, send it home in plastic bags for the children to

explore with their families. Also include a copy of *Bartholomew and the Oobleck* and a journal for recording the family's observations.

Since dried oobleck is easy to brush off and sweep up, make sure that the children allow the oobleck to air-dry on hands and utensils, then rub off as much of the powder as possible before washing up. Allow leftover oobleck to dry, then dispose of it in the trash (do not dispose of oobleck in drains, since it will clog pipes).

Gloop and Oobleck

Gloop (see recipe in Figure 1) is as fascinating a substance as oobleck, yet it has distinctly different properties. It can be stretched, pulled, mashed, bounced, or cut and is often compared to products such as Silly Putty or Gak.

Allow the children to explore gloop in the same way as they explored oobleck. Then ask students to compare the two substances during a class discussion that allows the children to articulate their discoveries and clarify their findings. Encourage the children to discuss what these substances are made of, describe how they are alike and different, analyze what makes them change, and suggest other areas for further exploration.

Raising the Standard

As part of the content standards for physical science in grades K–4, the National Research Council recommends that children develop an understanding of the properties of objects and materials (1996).

The council further states that "when carefully observed, described, and measured, the properties of objects, changes in properties over time, and the changes that occur when materials interact provide the necessary precursors to the later introduction of more abstract ideas in the upper grade levels" (1996, p. 126).

By introducing children to the use of their senses to make observations about the physical properties of materials, these activities

Figure 1.

Recipes

Oobleck

This recipe comes from *Oobleck: What Do Scientists Do?* (Sneider 1985). To make oobleck, you will need

- four 454 g boxes cornstarch,
- 1600 mL water,
- green food coloring,
- and additional cornstarch or water for experimentation.

Add desired amount of food coloring to 1 L of water. Pour the green water into a mixing bowl and add the cornstarch and another 600 mL of water. Swirl and tip the bowl to level the contents, then set the bowl aside for a few minutes. To mix the oobleck, slip your fingers under it and lift it from the bottom of the bowl to the top. Continue mixing until the oobleck has achieved an even consistency. The oobleck should flow when you tip the bowl but feel like a solid when you hit it or rub your finger across the surface. Store in an airtight container.

Gloop

This recipe for gloop is adapted from *The Sandbox Scientist* (Ross 1995). To make gloop, you will need

- 475 mL white school glue,
- 355 mL water at normal room temperature,
- 240 mL warm water, divided evenly between three cups,
- and 15 mL borax powder.

Add the room temperature water to the glue in a mixing bowl. In another bowl, dissolve the borax powder in the warm water. Slowly pour the dissolved borax into the glue and water mixture, stirring constantly. Remove the gloop from the bowl and knead it for about one minute until it is smooth and has lost its stickiness. Store in an airtight container.

help provide a foundation for future scientific inquiry.

In addition, when you see how engaged your students are by these science activities, you will fully agree that the minimal amount of money and effort needed to provide the activities is a worthwhile investment.

So, raid the pantry, loot the laundry room, and pillage the school supply closet. Some irresistible adventures with science await!

Susie Barcus is a graduate student of education and Mary M. Patton is an assistant professor of early childhood education, both at Texas Christian University in Fort Worth.

Resources

Geisel, T. S. 1949. *Bartholomew and the oobleck*. New York: Random House.

National Research Council. (1996). *National Science Education Standards*. Washington, DC: National Academy Press.

Ross, M. E. 1995. *The sandbox scientist: Real science activities for little kids*. Chicago: Chicago Review Press.

Sneider, C. I. 1985. *Great explorations in math and science (GEMS). Oobleck: What do scientists do?* Berkeley, CA: University of California.

Discovery Central

By Jaimee Wood

Spring is an exciting time in my—or any—kindergarten classroom. The children are communicating better, and they have begun working more independently. Their critical-thinking skills are growing each day.

Last year, as the warm days of spring teased our senses, a plant unit seemed especially enticing, so I created four interactive, plant-themed learning centers that developed science-process skills, including observing, comparing, recording data, collecting data, sorting, and classifying.

The centers addressed four curriculum areas—mathematics, fine arts, communication arts, and science, and they incorporated the use of a journal in which students wrote or drew every day, further developing students' improving communication skills. Though the tasks at each center embraced different parts of the curriculum, they all related to plants and gave children a chance to get their hands dirty and experience the joy of discovery and exploration—an important goal of our kindergarten science curriculum.

Although my choice was plant-themed learning centers, the approach can be used effectively with nearly any topic, and I encourage you to try learning centers with your students. The lessons at our centers came from my local curriculum, the AIMS book *Primarily Plants* (Hoover and Mercier 1990), and Successlink—a Missouri Department of Education website where educators share teaching ideas (see Internet Resources).

Where Do We Start?

Before preparing the centers, I did a preassessment to find out what students knew about plants. I asked students to write down the four most important things that plants need. Some ideas students listed were "family," "homes," "dirt," "water," "bugs," and "food." Their answers told me I had a lot of work to accomplish in this unit.

My objective with the learning centers was to help students build background knowledge about plants and practice their science-process skills. First, I wanted to find out what my students knew about plants and what they wanted to learn about plants. Together the class created a K-W-L chart ("What I Know," "What I Want to Know," and "What I Learned"). Students knew "plants grow everywhere," "plants are green," "plants don't eat food," and "plants are in dirt." They wanted to know the following:

- Why are plants green?
- How do plants grow?
- Do plants need water?
- Are flowers plants?
- Do all plants have leaves?

This chart became a great learning tool throughout the unit: As students discovered new information about plants, we referred back to our K-W-L chart and recorded their findings on the What I Learned part of the chart.

Sorting Seeds

At the first center, I provided chart paper, small paper cups, a hand lens, and assorted seeds: lima beans, kidney beans, popcorn, sunflower seeds, garbanzo beans, and black-eyed peas. Students counted the seeds and then grouped the seeds by recognizable traits, such as color, size, shape, and texture.

Students also weighed the seeds. The students estimated how many seeds it would take to balance one teddy bear. They then weighed the seeds and recorded their results.

Finally, students made drawings of the seeds in their journals and recorded their observations and questions, such as "Will all of these seeds grow?" and "Why are the seeds different colors?"

An extension of this activity is to plant the seeds so students can answer such questions as "Which seed will sprout first?"

Painting With Nature

The art center followed a brief lesson on the plant parts in which students learned that the stem supports the upper parts of the plant; the roots anchor the plants in the soil; the flowers are the reproductive parts of the plants; and the leaves are the part of the plant where food is made.

At this center, the objective was to reinforce students' knowledge of plant parts by painting a plant using items from nature. I provided various items from nature—flowers with stems, pinecones, leaves, corncobs, and celery stalks as well as paint, paper, and easels.

"How do we paint without paintbrushes?" was the response I heard from my kindergartens at the art center. I encouraged the students to use their imagination and be creative and showed them one example using a celery stalk.

The children were asked to include the correct plant parts in their "plant" painting and to identify the parts of the plants with which they painted (such as the leaf). Afterward, we displayed plant posters around the room and at the center to help students remember the new names they had learned.

Listening and Writing

At this center, students started out by listening to stories about plants (see Resources). Next, they illustrated their favorite parts of the books and explained their illustrations on paper and orally.

Students also completed a booklet from AIMS called "What Do Plants Need to Grow?" (see Internet Resources). Students colored and decorated the booklet as they wished. The book started with "plants need soil," and then continued to add a plant need on each page.

Planting Seeds

Now it was time for the students to predict and experiment with their own plant. The objective of the final center was for students to watch a bean seed grow. I gave each student a small clay pot or Styrofoam cup, potting soil, and a bean seed.

Students planted their seeds and chose a spot in the room to place their plant. They were instructed not to move their pots during the growth period. I wanted them to see that seeds grow when the conditions are right.

Students also wrote in their science journal many times during this process. The students illustrated the growth process of their plants every day in their journals. I asked them to include anything they did to their plant, such as water it or measure it.

Sprouting Knowledge

After completing all of the learning centers, we talked about all we had learned about what plants need to grow. Students had observed that plants need sunlight and water through their growing experiment.

The kindergarten classroom is a safe and familiar environment in which students can develop the scientific skills of observing, sorting and organizing, comparing, predicting, experimenting, evaluating, and applying. Science centers help build students' self-esteem by giving them hands-on experiences. Students were given time to familiarize themselves with the materials at each center, encouraged to make their own observations, and allowed to proceed at their own learning pace, giving them a sense of control and ownership while exploring science.

Through the learning centers, my students had experienced science in a personal way that provided a sense of accomplishment and gave them wonderful memories of their kindergarten class, too.

Jaimee Wood is a kindergarten teacher at La Plata R-II School District in La Plata, Missouri.

Resources

Carle, E. 1991. *The tiny seed*. New York: Simon and Schuster.

Ehlert, L. 1987. *Growing vegetable soup*. New York: Harcourt.

Hoover, E., and S. Mercier. 1990. *Primarily plants*. Fresno, CA: AIMS Education Foundation.

National Research Council (NRC). 1996. *National Science Education Standards*. Washington, DC: National Academy Press.

Internet Resources

AIMS

www.aimsedu.org

Successlink

www.successlink.org

Connecting to the Standards

This article relates to the following National Science Education Standards (NRC 1996):

Content Standards
Grades K–4

Standard C: Life Science
- The characteristics of organisms
- Life cycles of organisms
- Organisms and environments

It's a Frog's Life

By Audrey L. Coffey and Donna R. Sterling

A Note from the *Science Scope* Editor

I was captivated by this article the first time I read it. It captures the essence of inquiry. The children and the teachers had a serendipitous encounter with an unknown. The teacher and students worked together to unravel the mystery and discover that the coolest possible thing happened: They had frogs! They then went about researching, studying, and observing the eggs as they changed to tadpoles and then frogs.

As we re-read the article and consulted with the NSTA Safety Committee, some concerns emerged. What are the safety issues with keeping a wading pool in a preschool? What pathogens might lurk in the murky water? What about mosquitoes? What might be the consequences of handling for the frogs? For the children? The most simple and elegant of lessons—"kids and frogs"—is riddled with potential risks for amphibians and humans alike.

Granted, this experience isn't likely to be replicated, but because of the safety and health concerns associated with it, we are offering the following guidelines and suggestions when studying live animals or plants:

- Know all the possible risks. Make sure that children wash their hands thoroughly after handling any animal. There are obvious dangers with wading pools and small children. In addition to creating the danger of drowning, water kept more than a few days can harbor increasing colonies of bacteria. These bacteria can be passed to children as they dip their hands into the water and proceed to put a finger or two into their mouths. They need not drink it to ingest it.

- One solution would be to remove the eggs from the pool and bring them to an indoor aquarium, allowing you to change the pool water every few days without disturbing the frogs. If you remove the eggs (see next bullet), be sure you know what the organisms require.

- Leave the animal or plant as undisturbed as possible. If an animal (or plant) must be brought indoors, be sure to know its requirements first. Consult someone from a department of natural resources or a comparable expert to learn about the needs of the animal and if keeping it is advisable. If you cannot identify the animal by species, resist the temptation to bring it indoors.

- Minimize or eliminate physical contact with the animal. Frogs have very sensitive skin. Soap residues or lotions can kill frogs or make them ill. Amphibian skin must also stay moist, so any time they are handled, hands should be wet. Unfortunately, this leads to slippery frogs that may become airborne and potentially flattened.

- Please consult the NSTA guidelines and your district policy on safety before keeping any classroom pet or animal.

We chose to share this story because it is an exemplary article about *real* inquiry. It is also a cautionary tale about supervising this type of naturalistic investigation and serves as a study in how to protect all of the creatures involved. With these considerations in mind, we encourage teachers to investigate the natural world with children.

The NSTA guidelines for working with animals in the classroom are available in *Safety in the Elementary Science Classroom,* published in 2003 from NSTA Press. The NSTA position statement "Animals: Responsible Use of Live Animals and Dissection in the Science Classroom" can be read at *www.nsta.org/about/positions.aspx.*

Now, enjoy the wonder of these preschool students as they embark on this surprising inquiry experience.

Chris Ohana

As the owner, director, and head teacher of a small preschool that serves three- to five-year-old children, my main interest is discovering the wonders of the world with my students. Many early childhood educators extol the virtues of water play at this age, and I am no exception. To teach observation skills, cause and effect, volume, properties of water, and more, there's no substitute for that magical substance we call H_2O.

In my school our water table is a sturdy blue baby pool with a drain that sits outside on a gravel circle on the playground. With buckets, sieves, cups, funnels, large plastic aprons, and seasonal changes, water can provide endless learning experiences and—as I discovered quite unexpectedly one summer day—can be the source of a teachable moment too good to pass up.

What's That?

Teachable moments are just that—moments a teacher can use spontaneously to add to students' life experiences and enrich their learning. I experienced one last August as my students and I clustered around our pool on water center day. To my dismay, the pool cover had been left off the previous night. "What's that?" children asked as they pointed at something in the pool.

"Oh, just some bugs that landed in the water overnight," I quickly answered, my mind preoccupied with the task of draining and cleaning the pool. "What's *that?*" they asked again, still pointing. This time, I really stopped to look. There, floating in several jellylike masses were little, black, round ... eggs! What a teaching moment. I immediately called the class together and explained they were *frogspawn,* or eggs. The children loved the word *spawn.* They loved the eggs. Immediately, they wanted to know what would hatch from the eggs.

When I answered "tadpoles" and saw their expressions, I knew I would not be draining the pool any time soon. It had turned into a frog pond overnight. As we went back indoors, my brain was humming with the implications: fitting real-life learning experiences into our curriculum, safety, and logistics.

Standing by my new pond that afternoon, I realized I knew very little about frogs. I knew I'd have to do my homework (research) to create and plan age-appropriate learning experiences for my students, and I knew I'd have to identify the skills I wanted them to master. Right away, I thought of observation skills. Starting our frog adventure with observation activities would heighten children's interest in frogs and give me time to put together cohesive learning experiences for further study.

Safety First!

The children were more excited than I'd ever seen them. Immediately, they wanted to put their hands into the pond and grab the eggs. My first job was to teach them how to study animals safely. Back in the classroom, we reviewed germs and how they are transmitted. I showed children pictures of what germs look like under a microscope and introduced the term *bacteria*. After explaining that germs are invisible, we pretended tiny pieces of paper were bacteria. To help the children understand how bacteria travel, we scattered the pieces of paper all over the classroom. Our strategy to prevent bacteria from spreading to us or from us to the frogs was to wash our hands before and after our observation studies.

Second, I did not want the children to harm the eggs/tadpoles/frogs in any way during our study. We discussed how to treat animals carefully and how to be gentle with animals, so they would not be squished or dropped. I told students that the classroom aide and I would be the only people to scoop up eggs and tadpoles, so the eggs would not get hurt.

Third, I had to ensure the children's safety working around standing water. Normally the pond is covered unless the class is working there, and now I couldn't cover it. Because West Nile virus is a concern in our area, I decided to check the pond every morning for mosquito larvae and to scoop it out in advance before any student visited the pond—however, during the study no mosquito larvae materialized.

The children and I created pond rules to keep ourselves safe. This is what the children came up with:

- Work at the pond only when an adult is with you.
- Wear protective clothing, such as aprons, to stay dry.
- Kneel down when looking in the pond.
- No drinking pond water.
- No running around the pond.
- Do not splash in the pond water.
- Do not touch eggs or other creatures in the pond.

Many of these rules had already been established in the context of the water center. However, with the new name *pond* I wanted to make sure students would follow water safety rules no matter what the context.

Frogspawn Hatch Quickly

To study our frogs, I decided to start each day with an observation period of about 30 minutes. During this time, we would focus on making observations and discuss what we saw. Our first observation day was wonderful. The children wore aprons and crowded around the pool on their knees. Their eyes were drawn to the blobs of jelly floating around in the water. We taped a large piece of chart paper to the wall of the preschool on which to record our observations. Using markers, the children took turns helping to draw a large picture of the pond.

The children gathered in a circle on our vinyl outside floor, and I scooped up a clump of eggs using a small bucket. The bucket was passed around the circle, and we discussed the eggs' color, size, number, and what we thought might hatch. Students estimated there were about 100 eggs. One child noticed that not all of the eggs looked the same. Sure enough, some blobs were more clear and seemed to be squiggly. After each child looked at the eggs in the bucket, they went to the chart paper and drew frogspawn on our pond picture.

The next day, the children were even more excited about the pond. What seemed like hundreds of tiny tadpoles were now squiggling around in the water, including some still in jelly blobs. We repeated the procedure of the day before, writing our observations, passing around a small sample in the bucket, and drawing tadpoles on the chart paper. When all the children began asking, "What will they eat?," I knew we'd have to begin our frog research right away.

Asking and Answering Questions

Back in the classroom, we discussed what we knew about ponds, tadpoles, and frogs. Basically, students knew that ponds were outside, had fish and frogs in them, and were muddy. Tadpoles were "cute," and frogs were green, ate bugs, and could jump and say "ribbit" or "croak." During this discussion, I had each child think of a question about frogs that they wanted to answer. The range of their questions ensured that we would cover a variety of topics. Here are a few examples.

- "What kind of frogs are they?"
- "How do they jump? How will we find them if they jump away?"
- "Are tadpoles fish?"
- "Why do they change?"
- "What do they eat?"

I decided to focus on "Are tadpoles fish?" and "Why do they change?" first. After all, the tadpoles were changing rapidly and the life cycle is a fascinating topic. After our observation time each day, I read books about fish and amphibians to the children.

We looked for anything in the books that matched what we were seeing in the pond. We made a chart listing the differences so the children could see why the frogs were amphibians and understand what an amphibian is.

Typically, story time was followed by a hands-on activity. For example, students made clay models of each stage of the frog's life cycle, and we learned or created songs about frogs and their changes. Students' favorite activity was to pantomine the life cycle of a frog.

From Tadpole to Frog

As the tadpoles grew larger, I supplied each child with a clear plastic cup (8 oz) in which stu-

dents could observe a tadpole up close. Because the children had been extremely careful and respectful of the rules thus far—and it was taking too much time for me to catch a tadpole for each child with our aquarium net—I decided to let the children try to carefully scoop up a tadpole using their plastic cups. They scooped in groups of three students at three different points of the pond. Students who became careless—standing up, throwing water, or trying to grab with their hands—were not allowed to continue. I soon discovered that children were more adept than I was at collecting tadpoles.

The plastic cups had a magnifying effect, so students could really see the details on the tadpoles. As the tadpoles swam around in the water in the cup, the children were amazed at how quickly the tadpoles were changing. Within a week, some tadpoles had back legs.

After the observation period, students returned the frogs to the pond. During each observation period the children were wondering if they were scooping up the same tadpole as the day before. As the adult frogs appeared, we added some fireplace-sized logs for them to sit on. The frogs were tiny, ranging from marble to superball size.

To get a frog in their cups, students would hold the cup close and lightly tap the frog from behind. The frog almost always jumped right into the cup. It was very difficult to keep the adult frogs in the cup. Many times they would jump out and away into the grass. I did not allow the children to chase them for fear that the frogs would be stepped on and killed.

I asked the children to document the changing tadpoles every day by drawing what was in their cup. They dictated a sentence to be written with each change. Within a month, each child had created a book about the change from tadpole to frog.

What Kind of Frog?

Meanwhile, I filled our classroom with many posters and books about the life cycle of a frog, and I incorporated frogs into our curriculum in any way I could. For mathematics explorations, we graphed how long it took for the frogs to change in our pond. (It took a total of three months for all of the tadpoles to change. We wondered why some tadpoles took a week and others months. The children thought the faster changing tadpoles were stronger or were eating all the food in the pond.) We estimated how many frogs we had in each stage of development. The first week we felt we had about 50 tadpoles in the pond. The second week we had about 10 with front or back legs. By the third week we estimated 30 of them had front or back legs and maybe 10 that were still just a tail. By the fourth week we estimated we had 10 frogs. We never had more than 10 frogs at any one time, because they would leave the pond soon after becoming adults.

The frogs were small (approximately 2 cm compared with 4 to 5 cm as tadpoles), smooth, and light green in color. The children observed that the frogs had three sticky toes on each foot, which were tickly. Because there were algae growing in the pond and various tiny water bugs swimming around, we guessed that was what the tadpoles and little frogs ate. Based on information from our resource books, we decided that we had a type of tree frog.

Learning Opportunities

During our frog days of summer, we took field trips to local ponds to see if what was happening in our pond was also occurring in real ponds. I introduced students to the concept of the pond as a habitat, and students and I started looking for other aspects of pond life. Our pond now had a great algae community, several types of aquatic insects, and a lily pad I purchased at a garden center. I also prepared slides with our pond water to look for microscopic animals in the water using our video-screen microscope. The learning experiences seemed as if they would never end.

To check my students' progress, I developed several activities to see if they understood the life cycle and characteristics of amphibians. First, I made cards showing the different stages of a frog's life cycle. The children were tested individually by having them arrange the cards in the correct order. All of the four- and five-year-olds could do this easily. Of my five three-year-olds, only two could put the cards in the right order consistently.

Second, I presented the students with picture cards of different body parts of many amphibians, fish, mammals, and insects. The children were asked to build a frog and to put their frog into one of four habitat backgrounds (sky, ocean, pond scene, and forest). All of the children could do this consistently.

I also evaluated the pictures and models the students made for accuracy and details. During our many discussions I could tell which students were retaining information and which were forgetting information previously presented.

Leaving the Pond

As the frogs matured and left the pond, the children's distress at losing them grew. By the third month, it was increasingly obvious that soon there would be no frogs left in the pond. The children begged to keep some of the frogs. I decided that to continue exploring the idea of habitat, we would construct an indoor terrarium for a few of our frogs.

I found an old 20 gal aquarium and set it up next to an aquarium already in the classroom. We filled the terrarium using dirt, rocks, and moss from our school-yard. A layer of dirt was put in and rocks, moss, and a small branch were arranged on top. A shallow pool was created in the center by putting a small bowl in the dirt layer. We filled the bowl with water from the pond.

Finally, it was time to put in our frogs. I decided five frogs would be appropriate for the space we had, and the students and I transferred them indoors. The children were ecstatic. The frogs did very well for two weeks. However, for some reason, one by one, the frogs would go into the water and drown. Within a month, we lost all five of our frogs.

We tried to prevent the frogs from drowning, but decreasing the water did not help, and local pet stores that carried frogs did not offer us any advice, nor could I find information about our problem on the internet or in the books I had. The students were sad but did not seem too upset.

We added a discussion of death to our life cycle. We shared stories of any pets anyone had lost before. They told me how they felt sad and missed their old pets. We talked about accidents and old age deaths. We decided the frogs had accidental deaths, because they kept going in the water in their terrarium and drowning. As a group, we decided the frogs were better off left outside so they could live a normal frog life. The children were happy at the thought that, if they looked carefully enough, they could still get to see frogs outside.

In retrospect, I would not attempt the indoor terrarium again. We are planning, however, to create a permanent pond on our school property, so we can study frogs and their habitat all year long and, with much scrubbing, regain our water center on the playground.

Audrey L. Coffey is the director of Discovery Preschool Learning Center in Manassas, Virginia. Donna R. Sterling is associate professor of science education and director of the Center for Restructuring Education in Science and Technology at George Mason University in Fairfax, Virginia.

Resources

National Research Council (NRC). 1996. *National Science Education Standards*. Washington DC: National Academy Press.

Connecting to the Standards
This article relates to the following National Science Education Standards (NRC 1996):

Content Standards
Grades K–4

Standard A: Science as Inquiry
• Abilities necessary to do scientific inquiry

Standard C: Life Science
• Characteristics of organisms
• Life cycles of organisms
• Organisms and environments

The Science and Mathematics of Building Structures

By Ingrid Chalufour, Cindy Hoisington, Robin Moriarty, Jeff Winokur, and Karen Worth

Imagine preschool children playing with blocks—nothing unusual about that, right? Well, now imagine these children using blocks to conduct a rich science inquiry that integrates mathematics and science skills—from exploring shape, pattern, measurement, and spatial relationships to developing understandings of stability, balance, and properties of materials. Sound impossible? It's not.

Students in a Head Start program in Boston, Massachusetts, did just that, and the success of their learning experience was inspiring. Their teacher and a group of curriculum developers who worked with her as she conducted this integrated unit wrote this article to share their story and thoughts. Through this classroom's experience, you will see that you can use everyday activities—like building blocks—as a basis for meaningful learning that meets national educational standards in science and mathematics.

Identifying the Standards

The idea for the integrated unit came about as we reflected on the science that normally took place in the teacher's classroom and realized that neither the science table, with its collection of shells, bird nests, and magnets, nor the planned activities, such as mixing cornstarch and water, were engaging students in rich science inquiries—inquiries that would give students reasons to measure, count, or look for patterns. The children loved to build, and, as we talked together, the potential for integrating science and mathematics in block play became clear. We started by identifying some developmentally appropriate concepts that could be the focus of the children's block play.

In science, we identified stability, balance, and properties of materials as concepts to explore. In mathematics, we identified numbers and operations as concepts students would use as they collected data about their structures.

In addition to these discipline-specific concepts, we identified several concepts and processes that were part of both the science and mathematics standards. For example, standards in both science and mathematics identify shape, pattern, measurement, and spatial relationships as important concepts for study. Similarly, both disciplines identify questioning, problem solving, analyzing, reasoning, communicating, connecting, investigating, and creating and using representations as processes central to engagement with each subject.

Together we created a Venn diagram (Figure 1) to clarify our thinking and to show the relationships between the content and processes presented in the *National Science Education Standards* (NRC 1996) and the *National Association of Teachers of Mathematics Principles and Standards for School Mathematics* (NCTM 2000). The figure's center area points out the unit's areas of overlap, while the areas on the right- and left-hand sides point out the targeted concepts specific to each discipline.

Readying the Classroom

Having identified the standards that would guide the teaching and learning in the block unit over the next several months, the teacher set about transforming the classroom to best meet the unit's learning goals and the needs and interests of her students.

To begin, she created an environment for inquiry by enlarging the block area, creating additional building centers and adding foam and cardboard blocks to the collection of unit, hollow, and tabletop blocks. She also temporarily removed Legos from the block collection. Though the children loved Legos, they tended to use them to build solid, squat structures, and she wanted them to experiment with materials

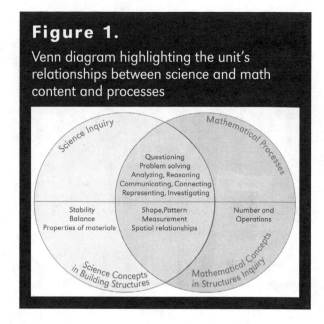

Figure 1.

Venn diagram highlighting the unit's relationships between science and math content and processes

that did not stick together. She hoped the various other kinds of blocks would entice students to explore the relationship between the kind of materials they used for building and the balance and stability of their structures. The Legos would be reintroduced later in the exploration so students could compare them to the other building materials.

In addition to changes in the block areas, the teacher displayed books and posters of structures around the classroom, such as the Eiffel tower, the Empire State Building, and various other buildings and bridges. For easier access to the blocks and to facilitate cleanup, she labeled shelves with pictures of each kind of block, which provided students the added benefit of practicing their problem-solving skills as they compared shapes and their attributes.

Before the unit began, we all worked with the blocks to explore how they balanced and how different designs and kinds of materials affected a structure's stability. This experimentation was a big help when the classroom teacher later observed students' block play to consider the mathematics and science concepts they were exploring.

Open Exploration

Twenty-four children, speaking eight different languages, arrived in the classroom in mid-September. For the first month of school, the teacher's goal was to engage students in building and provide opportunities for students to wonder, question, and develop initial understandings of properties of materials, stability, and balance.

Every day students explored, via trial and error, what the materials could and could not do. They discovered quite a bit about their triangle-shaped blocks. For example, they determined it's possible but not easy to balance a rectangular-shaped block on the point of a triangular one; they noticed that two triangular blocks together can be used instead of one square block, but only if the triangular blocks are laid on their flat sides. They agreed that triangular blocks are not strong when you try to stand them up as a square: The two triangles slip away from each other.

Every day at the class's morning meeting, the teacher got students excited about using the building materials. She talked about the children's buildings or drawings from the previous day's block play and then shared a picture of an interesting building (the Taj Mahal, for example) or introduced a new kind of building material.

During the daily choice time or activity time (about an hour each day), the children worked in three block centers. During this time, the teacher walked around the classroom, observing the different ways children built and expressing interest in students' block play. She asked children to tell her about their buildings, described interesting features of their structures aloud, and sketched and photographed children's buildings.

Toward the end of each week, she engaged children in talking about the patterns and designs they were using. These weekly science talks helped children articulate, examine, and defend their developing ideas about how to build strong buildings: what materials were best and which blocks were good at the bottom.

To stimulate these conversations, the teacher referred to the drawings and photographs and to excerpts from conversations she'd had with children about their structures' stability (for example, "You need to use big blocks on the bottom and smaller ones on top if you want to have a strong building" or "If it starts to wiggle, you need to hold it with your hands").

As students became more comfortable with their building experiences, the teacher began to highlight the science and mathematics in her children's open exploration of building structures.

She used comments like "The block under your house makes for a strong foundation" and "The block between these walls is balancing on its end!" to focus attention on their structures' designs and stability and relative position in space. In so doing, she addressed a section of the NCTM geometry standard as she modeled vocabulary, such as *under* and *between,* that children need to learn as they talk about location and space.

As she communicated her interest in the various ways children had designed and balanced their structures, the teacher supported each child's development of new science and mathematics language and modeled its use. This enabled the children to communicate better with one another, an element of both the NSES's and the NCTM's communication standards.

Questioning and Investigating

A few weeks into the open exploration of building structures, the teacher noticed students' preoccupation with building straight up. She decided to help students focus their inquiry on the question they all seemed to be asking through their building behavior: How tall can we build?

She brought the children together and showed them photographs of the various towers they'd been building out of different kinds of blocks. She articulated their question, "How tall can we build?," and asked for predictions.

Some children used movement, some used numbers, and others described height in terms of other objects ("as tall as the door," for example) to answer how tall they could build. The teacher recorded students' ideas in words, numerals, and sketches, and she helped interested groups and individuals plan their investigation by working with them to figure out who was going to build where during the upcoming choice time. Children could select in which of the three different building centers they were going to work. Some children partnered up; others worked solo.

Now that the children's science investigation focused on a single question, the teacher facilitated this part of the inquiry differently. She used morning meetings for the next few weeks to refer children to the previous day's data, plan their day's work, or make predictions about what they might discover.

During choice times, she encouraged children to represent their towers' heights in two dimensions and three dimensions, and she helped children measure their towers, count the blocks, and compare heights. And she used their weekly science talks to help students analyze their data and support their developing theories about building tall towers with evidence from their own experiences.

For example, in one science talk, the teacher shared photos and representations of the children's towers and, together, they compared the numbers of blocks on towers of different sizes. Students were able to easily observe that the taller towers had more blocks.

In another talk, students discussed which kinds of blocks—unit blocks or cardboard blocks—made the tallest towers. The teacher asked students probing questions, such as "Why do you think the cardboard blocks fell down more than these cylinders?" to encourage students to elaborate on their ideas. In this way, the teacher was able to shift the children's focus from the effects of design on their towers' height and stability to the effects of the properties of the building materials themselves on the stability of a tall structure.

As she worked with her class, the teacher deepened students' science and mathematics learning in several ways. For example, she

- identified questions to focus the inquiry;
- helped children collect data using photographs, drawings, models, counting, and measuring;
- used informal conversations and whole-group science talks to help children communicate and analyze their data; and
- encouraged students to use representations and other data to articulate theories they developed about how design and properties of materials affect a tower's stability.

Of course, by encouraging students to articulate theories and use evidence from their work to support their ideas she also addressed NCTM's process standards: reasoning and proof; data analysis and probability; and communication. Children also measured and counted with a purpose: to collect data that would help them answer their questions, "How tall can we build?" and "Which blocks make the tallest towers?"

Tying It Together

As the children's interest in building tall towers began to wane, the teacher suggested they hold an open house so they could share their investigation of the ways materials and designs affect tall structures' stability.

When the visitors came, students challenged their guests to build tall, stable structures. They passed out clipboards and markers and invited the guests to draw their structures and write about the strategies they'd used to make their structures stable. Photographs, charts, and documentation panels were hung around the classroom, and the teacher encouraged the visitors to ask the children about them.

The teacher also referred to the experience and shared examples of students' work in parent-teacher conferences to discuss how their children's social/emotional, language, and mathematical skills and understandings had developed in concert with their developing understanding of inquiry, stability, balance, and properties of materials.

Beyond Blocks

Building with blocks clearly offered this teacher and her students rich opportunities to integrate mathematics and science. Other science topics can also offer similar opportunities.

For example, try adapting the Venn diagram in this article to facilitate a life science inquiry, such as a study of organisms in the environment. Replace the physical science concepts related to building structures, currently listed in the bottom left-hand section of the diagram, with age-appropriate concepts related to life science, such as life cycle, characteristics of living things, and habitat.

Think about a rich classroom environment including many plants representing a good variety, as well as several terrariums representing different local habitats. Think about taking children outdoors each day to observe their natural surroundings. Try to fill out the rest of the Venn diagram.

You might include opportunities for three-, four-, and five-year-olds to use patterning, counting, measuring, and spatial relationships to describe what children notice and think about the growth and development of living things. With a little consideration, it is possible to create integrated science and mathematics units that keep the integrity of each subject and also highlight the overlapping processes and concepts central to both subjects.

Ingrid Chalufour is a project director with the Center for Children and Families at Education Development Center (EDC) in Newton, Massachusetts; Cindy Hoisington was a classroom teacher at Action Boston Community Development South Side Head Start in Roslindale, Massachusetts, when she helped develop the activities discussed in this article; Robin Moriarty is a curriculum developer in the Center for Science Education (CSE) at EDC; Jeff Winokur is a senior research associate at CSE and an instructor at Wheelock College in Boston, Massachusetts; and Karen Worth is a senior scientist in CSE and a graduate level instructor, also at Wheelock College.

Resources

National Association of Teachers of Mathematics (NCTM). 2000. *Principles and standards for school mathematics.* Reston, VA: Author.

National Research Council (NRC). 1996. *National Science Education Standards.* Washington, DC: National Academy Press.

Connecting to the Standards

This article relates to the following National Science Education Standards (NRC 1996):

Content Standards
Grades K–4
Standard A: Science as Inquiry
- Abilities necessary to do scientific inquiry

Standard B: Physical Science
- Properties of objects and materials
- Position and motion of objects

This article relates to the following Principles and Standards for School Mathematics (NCTM 2000):

Grades PreK–12
Algebra
- Understand patterns, relations, and functions

Geometry
- Analyze characteristics and properties of two- and three-dimensional geometric shapes and develop mathematical arguments about geometric relationships
- Use visualization, spatial reasoning, and geometric modeling to solve problems

Data Analysis and Probability
- Formulate questions that can be addressed with data and collect, organize, and display relevant data to answer them

Communication
- Organize and consolidate mathematical thinking through communication

Connections
- Recognize and apply mathematics in contexts outside of mathematics

Representation
- Create and use representations to organize, record, and communicate mathematical ideas

Section 5
Teaching Science Content

Teaching Science Content

Traditionally, when someone thinks about science, he or she thinks about the major school science disciplines: physical science (physics and chemistry), life science, Earth science, and space science. There is more to understanding science, however, than just the content of these disciplines. The National Science Education Standards (NSES) (NRC 1996) outline eight content categories of Standards that identify the science content and processes that students should master during their K–12 education. Every state has adopted science standards that are at least loosely based on the NSES. Many districts have also created standards or benchmark documents based on state and national standards documents. The articles in this section complement those in sections 1 through 4 by showcasing a variety of activities that can be effectively used as part of an instructional sequence to help students meet your instructional goals related to the content Standards.

See the Standards matrix on pp. 341–343 for information on how the articles connect to the Content Standards.

The eight content categories in the NSES include:

Unifying concepts and processes in science. This category of Standards is unique from the others. It describes concepts, processes, and underlying principles that unify science disciplines throughout K–12. There are four unifying concepts and processes described in this category for students K–8:

- *Systems, order, and organization:* Students should think and analyze in terms of system and understand the order and organization of concepts, processes and events.
- *Evidence, models, and explanation:* Students should use natural evidence (from investigations, experimentation, or research) to support explanations and create models to assist in understanding how things work. Models can take the form of physical objects, illustrations, mental constructs,

mathematical equations, and computer simulations.

- *Change, constancy, and measurement:* Students should understand how concepts and processes change or remain constant. They should be able to use multiple systems to measure change.
- *Evolution and equilibrium:* Evolution in this standards category does not only refer to biological evolution. Students should understand concepts and phenomena and how they have changed over time. The general idea of evolution is that the present arises from forms of the past. Equilibrium describes a steady state where changes occur in offsetting directions.
- *Form and function:* Every object has a form and a function that are often interrelated. The form of an object describes its physical structure. Function describes the purpose or capability of an object.

Science as inquiry. This category of Standards describes the skills and understandings that students need in order to use the processes of science to engage in scientific reasoning and critical thinking as they develop their understanding of science.

The concepts for students K–8 are
- abilities to do scientific inquiry, and
- understanding about scientific inquiry.

Physical science. This category of Standards describes the subject matter of physics and chemistry. The major ideas presented in these standards include matter and energy, forces, position and motion, and interactions of matter and energy.

The concepts for K–4 students are
- properties of objects and material,
- position and motion of objects, and
- light, heat, electricity, and magnetism.

The concepts for 5–8 students are
- properties and changes of properties in matter,

- motion and forces, and
- transfer of energy.

Life science. This category of Standards describes the subject matter of biology and the interaction between living things and their environment. The major ideas presented in these standards include continuity and change in living things, characteristics of organisms, and organisms and their environments.

The concepts for K–4 students are
- characteristics of organisms,
- life cycles of organisms, and
- organisms and environments.

The concepts for 5–8 students are
- structure and function in living systems,
- reproduction and heredity,
- regulation and behavior,
- populations and ecosystems, and
- diversity and adaptations of organisms.

Earth and space science. This category of Standards describes subject matter of Earth systems, planetary science, and astronomy. The major ideas presented in these standards included characteristics of Earth materials and resources, history and evolution of the solar system and universe, geology, meteorology/climatology, and oceanography.

The concepts for K–4 students are
- properties of Earth materials,
- objects in the sky, and
- changes in Earth and sky.

The concepts for 5–8 students are
- structure of the Earth system,
- Earth's history, and
- Earth in the solar system.

Science and technology. This category of Standards describes the relationship between science and technology and the application of science and technology. This category also provides standards for technological design and decision-making.

The concepts for K–4 students are

- abilities of technological design,
- understanding about science and technology, and
- abilities to distinguish between natural objects and objects made by humans.

The concepts for 5–8 students are

- abilities of technological design and
- understandings about science and technology.

Science in personal and social perspectives. The Standards in this category help students understand and act on personal and societal issues related to scientific understanding.

The concepts for K–4 students are

- personal health,
- characteristics and changes in populations,
- types of resources,
- changes in environments, and
- science and technology in local challenges.

The concepts for 5–8 students are

- personal health,
- populations, resources, and environments,
- natural hazards,
- risks and benefits, and
- science and technology in society.

History and nature of science. This category includes Standards that use the history of science to help students understand different aspects of scientific inquiry, the human aspects of science, the role of science in culture, and contributions to science made by people from diverse cultural backgrounds.

The concept for K–4 students is

- science as a human endeavor.

The concepts for 5–8 students are

- science as a human endeavor,
- nature of science, and
- history of science.

Action Steps

1. Read through the NSES content standards. Select one of the standards categories and describe what students should be able to know and do by fourth grade and eighth grade at *www.nap.edu/readingroom/books/nses/overview.html*.

2. Read Chapters 4, 5, and 10 of AAAS's *Science for All Americans* at *www.project2061.org/publications/sfaa/online/sfaatoc.htm*. (Rutherford, F. J., and A. Ahlgren. 1998. New York: Oxford University Press.)

Reflection Questions

Think about these questions as you read the articles:

1. How do these articles help students understand the nature of science through science inquiry?
2. Pick one of these articles and describe how it fits within the four lenses of learner-centered, knowledge-centered, assessment-centered and community-centered teaching. How would you change the activity to improve its alignment with these lenses?
3. Pick any article from this book and describe how it helps students gain an understanding of standards E, F, and G of the National Science Education Standards, which can be found at *www.nap.edu/readingroom.books/nses*.
Standard E: Science and Technology
Standard F: Science in Personal and Social Perspectives
Standard G: History and Nature of Science

The Articles

Content Standard B: Physical Science
   Article: Film Canister Science
   Key Ideas: The authors describe a series of activities, using simple materials, to help students learn about properties of materials.

Article: Breaking the Sound Barrier
Key Ideas: This article describes a series of stations that can be used to help students understand the science of sound.

Article: What's Hot? What's Not?
Key Ideas: The authors describe how they use the tale of "Goldilocks and the Three Bears" to launch an exploration of the factors that affect the cooling of oatmeal.

Article: Circus of Light
Key Ideas: This article describes stations that give students the opportunity to explore characteristics of light. In addition to the stations, the authors describe "The Forum," a class discussion about what students learned and questions they have about their light explorations.

Article: Building Student Mental Constructs of Particle Theory
Key Ideas: The author describes demonstrations that he uses to help students identify their understanding of the particle nature of matter.

Article: You Can Always Tell a Dancer by Her Feet
Key Ideas: This article uses examples from the students' lives (such as shoes, ballet, and snowshoes) to engage students in exploring the concept of pressure.

Content Standard C: Life Science
Article: Trash or Treasure?
Key Ideas: In this activity, students determine how their trash affects animals and their habitats.

Article: Inquiring Into the Digestive System
Key Ideas: This article describes an inquiry project that allows students to apply their knowledge of the digestive system.

Article: Beak Adaptations
Key Ideas: In this article, the author uses a variety of objects—such as a spoon, tongs, and turkey baster—to help students understand the process of natural selection.

Article: Choice, Control, and Change
Key Ideas: Students apply their knowledge of science to the real-world issue of childhood obesity and healthy eating.

Article: Are There Really Tree Frogs Living in the Schoolyard?
Key Ideas: In this article, the authors describe how to conduct field research in the schoolyard. Students learn about tree frog habitats, conduct field sampling of the schoolyard, and analyze data to determine if the schoolyard is an appropriate habitat for tree frogs.

Article: The Alien Lab: A Study in Genetics
Key Ideas: The author describes a fun activity that introduces students to genetics.

Content Standard D: Earth/Space Science
Article: Light Foundations
Key Ideas: In this activity, young students learn that light travels in straight lines and use that information to help understand the path of the Sun across the sky.

Article: They're M-e-e-elting!
Key Ideas: This article describes activities that allow students to explore the melting and retreat of glaciers in Antarctica.

Article: The Dimensions of the Solar System
Key Ideas: In this article, students use Google Earth to create a model of the solar system that is accurate for planet size and distance.

Reference

National Research Council (NRC). 1996. *National Science Education Standards.* Washington, DC: National Academy Press.

American Association for the Advancement of Science (AAAS). 1998. *Science for all Americans.* New York: Oxford University Press.

Quick-Reference Chart of Articles and Content Standards

Film Canister Science

By Andrew Ferstl and Jamie L. Schneider

Opaque film canisters are readily available, cheap (usually free from a local film processing store), and useful for scientific inquiry in the classroom. Recently, we pilot tested an integrated science class for elementary education majors. The first goal of our integrated science class was to overcome the common elementary education major's aversion to science. A goal of this course was to use teaching methods and activities that preservice teachers could readily transport to future classrooms. We modeled how to teach science by having the preservice teachers do the activities that they will use in their class. We also modeled how a strand within the Physical Science Standards could be explored at numerous levels of development from lower elementary levels to middle and high school levels (NRC 1996).

Because supplies are limited in many classrooms, we used film canisters in a number of inquiry activities, including a "black box" activity and several activities on sinking and floating properties related to density and to Archimedes' principle. As described, the activities in this article were written for preservice teachers. However, our intent for this article was to describe activities that could be used at elementary, middle, and high school levels. For instance, the black box and the initial floating and sinking activity could be used at the elementary level with modifications to the instructions and expectations, and the more mathematically based activities on density could be used at the middle and high school levels. Overall, these activities address Standards related to the nature of science, specifically to scientific inquiry; physical properties including mass, volume, density, and floating and sinking; and mathematic patterns and relationships (see Connecting to the Standards).

Learning About Science Process

Film canisters were first used in our class to help students discover ideas about the process of science. We took a well-known black box activity (Dickey 1995) and substituted film canisters as the black box (Figure 1). Students completed this activity on the second day of class. Students enjoyed the activity because they felt as though they were solving a mystery. Through discussion, students realized that each group solved this mystery using relatively similar scientific approaches, including making observations

Figure 1.
Black box activity

Objective
Introduce the process of science.

Materials and setup
Each group has two opaque film canisters with something inside of each; an empty canister; and a clear plastic bag of items that could potentially be in the canister, such as a button, a piece of string, some cloth, and a needle. One of the canisters has an object that is in the plastic bag. This is a different object for each group. The other canister has an object that is not in the plastic bag. This item is the same for each group. Also in the room are mass balances.

Student instructions
The instructions are very basic and intentionally vague. We ask students to figure out what is in the canister without opening it. We also inform them that the plastic bag contains potential candidates for the item in their canisters. Students can use the empty canister to help them evaluate and guide their inquiry. Students are asked to record their testing strategies, predictions, observations, and conclusions in a journal.

Instructor note
Instructors can tailor this experiment to fit the ability of their students. Students usually overlook the adjective in the phrase *potential candidates* and instead tend to focus solely on the items in the bag. This outcome is significant because not all of the experiments that we do in science give the results that we expect, which is a good thing. During the activity, many students will ask for guidance. Knowing that students are fully capable of accomplishing the task, instructors should encourage them to do the best that they can, but intentionally avoid giving an answer.

Results
Most students will shake the mystery container, and as a result, get tactile information as well as auditory information. Students will typically weigh the canister and its contents. They will usually fill the empty canister with the plastic bag items to try to reproduce what they have observed—in terms of weight, tactile information, and sound. Sometimes, students will recognize that the sound they hear in the mystery canister is not similar to a sound that they can reproduce with any single object. Students usually resolve this discrepancy by saying that there are multiple objects in the canister. For example, a pin in a canister would sound muffled if a piece of cloth was also in the canister. Students with a very light object that made very little sound (like a piece of string) were often convinced that their canister was empty.

Discussion/conclusion
Groups publish the results of their inquiry (what they predicted and what was actually in each canister) on the blackboard and we discuss, as a class, the procedures they used to decipher the contents of the canisters. This leads to a discussion about the nature of science. In the context of the canister, whose contents were not in the plastic bag, we also discuss that science is constantly discovering new, unexpected ideas and facts and then fitting these into an existing framework.

Figure 2.
Floating and sinking activity 1

Objective
Sorting objects based on sinking and floating properties.

Material and setup
Each group was given a tub of water and a variety of items including a wooden pencil, a toothpick, a craft stick, several buttons (some plastic and some metal), a piece of Styrofoam, a paper clip, and a plastic spoon.

Student instructions
We ask students to predict which items will float and which items will sink. Students then test their predictions by placing the items into the tub of water. Students are asked to record their testing strategies, predictions, observations, and conclusions in a journal.

Instructor note
Some students might get one object to float whereas another group will get the object to sink. For example, some plastic spoons will float if they are lowered gently onto the water with the "open side" up. But if you place the plastic spoon completely under the water and get rid of any air bubbles,

it might sink. This is an opportunity to discuss a good testing strategy. Namely, how do we know if it really floats or sinks? The best way is to place it under the water and get rid of air bubbles. If it floats it will pop back up; if it is going to sink, then it will fall to the bottom of the tub.

Note that this method also eliminates any effects from surface tension. For example, a paper clip that is carefully placed on the top of the water could float because of surface tension even though its density is greater than one. But if you put the paper clip under the water and avoid the surface tension, it will always sink.

Results
Most types of wood will float. Some plastics will float but some will sink; it's nice to have a variety here.

Discussion/conclusion
Ask for things in common among the objects that floated or sank.

Follow-up activity
Brainstorm with the class what factors influence floating and sinking.

and predictions/hypotheses, developing and using experiments to test their predictions, and drawing conclusions. Students also learned an important lesson: Scientific explorations do not always have yes-or-no answers. Careful and unbiased data analysis is essential because the unexpected is always possible.

Sinking and Floating Concepts
A little later in the school year, we used film canisters to explore the concept of floating and

sinking, from which we developed the concept of density. The concept of density is difficult for students to master (Stepans 2003; Kessler and Galvan 2003). We recognize that density and floating and sinking are different concepts—density is an object property whereas floating and sinking is the result of the relationship between two materials (Libarkin et al. 2003). We believe, however, that mingling these concepts helps students understand density. To help students master these concepts, we used

Figure 3.
Floating and sinking activity 2

Objective
To explore how mass and volume affect floating and sinking.

Material and setup
Each group was given five film canisters, a tub of water, and 50 pennies.

Student instructions
We ask students to determine, with the given equipment, how volume and mass affect floating and sinking. They are also reminded that a good experiment only changes one variable at a time. They are asked to record their testing strategies, predictions, observations, and conclusions in a journal.

Instructor note
After the Floating and Sinking Activity 1 (Figure 2), students suggested that mass and volume play a role in determining floating and sinking. This activity further explores this relationship.

During the activity, we monitor student progress and offer advice on how to perform the experiment. Students can change the mass and keep the volume constant by using one film canister and adding more pennies. Conversely, they can hold the mass constant and change the volume by adding film canisters. In this case, they will need to start with one canister and add around 30 pennies to it—this way it will sink and they will see that by increasing the volume enough, the object will float. The way to change the volume is by using the fact that most film canisters are slightly tapered and thus they can be stuck inside each other. Further instructions are given during the activity: A film canister, without a lid, weighs about the same as one penny; thus, to keep the mass constant in this process, they will need to remove a penny to compensate for the increase in mass due to the second film canister.

If a shallow tub is used, it is possible for one part of the canister to touch the bottom of the tub while another part floats on the surface. From this observation, students might conclude that the canisters are sinking or floating—depending on their perspective. This situation should be discussed with the students. To avoid this problem, use a deeper tub or evenly distribute the 30 pennies among the canisters so that they float or sink evenly.

Beware of potential student pitfalls here. Students may naively predict that if it takes 14 pennies to sink one canister then, for five canisters, it would take 5 x 14 = 70 pennies. This is not true because when two film canisters are put together, the volume has not exactly doubled since part of one canister is inside the other. Also, the additional film canisters do not have caps (as is the case with only one canister) and thus the mass of the object does not increase proportionally.

Results
It takes about 14 pennies to sink one film canister and, thus, about three canisters to float the 30 pennies used.

Discussion/conclusion
In the ensuing class discussion of the results, we highlight the fact that increasing mass tends to sink the object; yet increasing volume tends to float the object. Thus, in the language of mathematics, the "sinking property" of an object (which is associated with density) is directly related to the mass but must be inversely related to the volume.

Follow-up activity
To check student understanding, we ask students to apply their findings and predict how many pennies it will take to sink five film canisters. Then they test their prediction with the available equipment.

several activities that built upon one another, eventually leading to density.

In the first activity on floating and sinking (Figure 2), we gave each group of students a tub of water and a variety of items, including a wooden pencil, a toothpick, a craft stick, several buttons (some plastic and some metal), a piece of Styrofoam, a paper clip, and a plastic spoon. Students predicted whether each item would float or sink and then tested their predictions. Not surprisingly, many students predicted, for example, that the wooden pencil would sink but that the toothpick would float. For the expert, this is an obvious contradiction; both objects are made of wood and thus have the same density, which is less than water, so both should float. After the activity, we had a classroom discussion about students' predictions and results to try and tease out their misconceptions ("the physical size of the object matters").

For this activity to produce valid results, it was imperative for students to avoid surface-tension effects by first placing the object under the surface of the water, then releasing it to determine whether it floats or sinks. (For example, a paper clip can sometimes "float" because of surface tension, but it should sink because paper clips are more dense than water.)

To conclude this activity, the class developed a list of possible factors that determine floating and sinking. Students offered the following ideas: density, weight, size, material that the object is made of, the force that is put on it, force of water, solutes in water, water tension, and volume. Even though some of these ideas were incorrect, we did not immediately correct students because we wanted them to confront their misconceptions through further experimentation and inquiry.

Mass and Volume

In the second floating and sinking activity, we explicitly asked students to explore mass and volume (Figure 3). We used the film canisters for an inquiry-based activity in which students adjusted the mass of the canister by adding pennies or adjusted the volume by combining canisters. The general result of this activity was that the *sinking property* (as we termed it) of an object increases with added mass (adding more pennies eventually got the object to sink) and that the sinking property decreases with added volume (adding more canisters eventually gets the object to float).

In the language of mathematics, the sinking property is proportional to mass but inversely proportional to volume. In other words, we are led to the mathematical formula for density (density = mass/volume). When doing this activity, it is important to distinguish object density versus material density. For example, pennies have a material density that is greater than the density of water (1 g/mL); therefore, pennies sink in water. However, the penny/film canister system can float because the object density is less than the density of water. The material density of a penny is m_{penny}/V_{penny} but the object density of the canister system equals $[m_{canister} + m_{pennies}]/V_{canister}$. For the case of sinking and floating it is the object density that matters. An application of this concept would be to ask students: If steel is denser than water, then why does a steel ship float?

Alternatively, students could explore this concept via the classic clay boat experiment. In a clay boat experiment, students are given a ball of clay and asked to make it float by changing the shape of the clay. Although the volume of the clay is constant, the volume of the clay boat object (air + clay) can be greater than the original clay, making the density less than water. Students at this point will, we hope, see that it is object density, not surface tension, that is usually important for floating and sinking.

Because the second floating and sinking activity led to the idea of object density, we then introduced the concept that the material density is an intrinsic property of the material. Three objects of the same material but different size were given to students who were then asked to predict whether each object would float or sink. Students tested the idea and were asked to measure the density of these objects and compare it to the density of water.

From this discussion, the class concluded that objects with a density greater than water will sink. So, we developed another activity based on saturated saltwater (density = 1.2 g/mL) that also used the film canisters. Students were asked to determine how many pennies it would take to sink a film canister in this water. For a final activity with the film canisters, we asked students to come up with a way to quantify the observation that more-dense objects, which still float, sink further into the water. This is Archimedes' principle (Loverude, Kautz, and Heron 2003). This exercise was unique because we required the students to graph their data (i.e., object mass versus volume displaced). Graphing data is something that the novice usually does not think about doing, but it is an important scientific tool used to detect trends. In this manner, we were able to tie this activity back to the question of how we do science.

Overall, we found film canisters to be surprisingly versatile and useful as a tool for stimulating scientific inquiry. Our hope is that these preservice teachers will consider using more hands-on science activities with their students because they now more clearly and confidently understand complex scientific principles and they know that expensive equipment is not always needed to study science. Preservice teachers will also see how a strand in the Physical Science Standards can be continued and connected as their students advance through the grades.

Andrew Ferstl is an associate professor of physics at Winona State University in Winona, Minnesota, and Jamie L. Schneider is an assistant professor of chemistry at the University of Wisconsin–La Crosse in La Crosse, Wisconsin.

Acknowledgments
The authors thank colleagues Kimberly Bates, Melanie Reap, and Cathy Summa, who also participated in the development and facilitation of this class. This work was funded in part through several grants including a NASA Opportunities for Visionary Academics grant (#NAG5-9388), a Winona State University Longterm Improvement Award, and a Minnesota State Colleges and Universities Learning by Doing Award.

References
Dickey, J. 1995. *Laboratory investigations for biology.* San Francisco, CA: Benjamin/Cummings.

Kessler, J. H., and P. M. Galvan. 2003. *Inquiry in action; Investigating matter through inquiry.* 2nd ed. Washington, DC: American Chemical Society.

Libarkin, J. C., C. D. Crockett, and P. M. Sadler. 2003. Density on dry land. *The Science Teacher* 70 (6): 46–50.

Loverude, M. E., C. H. Kautz, and P. R. L. Heron. 2003. Helping students develop an understanding of Archimedes' principle. I. Research on student understanding. *American Journal of Physics* 71 (11): 1178–1187.

National Research Council (NRC). 1996. *National Science Education Standards.* Washington, DC: National Academy Press.

Stepans, J. 2003. *Targeting students' science misconceptions: Physical science concepts using the conceptual change model.* Tampa, FL: Showboard.

Connecting to the Standards
The National Science Education Standards (NRC 1996) addressed in these lessons include

Science as Inquiry
- Understandings about scientific inquiry (K–12)

History and Nature of Science
- Science as a human endeavor (K–4)
- Science as a human endeavor and nature of science (5–8)
- Science as a human endeavor and nature of scientific knowledge (9–12)

Physical Science
- Properties of objects and materials (K–4)
- Properties and changes of properties in matter (5–8)
- Structure and properties of matter (9–12)

Breaking the Sound Barrier

By Tom Brown and Kim Boehringer

Student interest in science has been amplified at our elementary school. During a recent unit on sound, students in a fourth-grade class participated in a series of dynamic sound learning centers followed by a dramatic capstone event—an exploration of the amazing Trash Can Whoosh Waves. It's a notoriously difficult subject to teach, but, for our fourth-grade students, this hands-on, exploratory approach ignited student interest in sound, promoted language acquisition, and built comprehension of key science concepts.

A Sound Background

The lessons began with an introductory discussion about sound. First, the teacher asked students to brainstorm what they knew about sound and what they wondered about it. Most students had heard of sound waves, but they couldn't explain exactly how they worked. Other students connected the idea of vibrating objects to sounds but couldn't expand on that information.

The teacher explained that, when our vocal chords vibrate, they produce waves that travel through the air. When these waves enter the ear

of a listener, they can be interpreted as *sounds*. Our vocal chords can vibrate at different rates, and, the faster they vibrate, the more waves per second they produce and the higher the pitch (frequency) of the sound. A soprano singer produces more waves per second than someone who sings bass. Some students placed a hand on their vocal chords and quietly hummed high and low notes to see if they could tell any difference.

Next, the class discussed that sound waves carry energy that affects humans in various ways. For instance, prolonged exposure to high-intensity (energy) sound waves causes inner ear damage that, in turn, will cause hearing loss. They talked about ways to prevent hearing loss, such as by keeping their headphones down to a reasonable level and by using earplugs when they are working in loud environments.

To conclude the introduction and to help guide students in their hands-on explorations to come, the teacher asked students to brainstorm some questions about sound in their science journals. Students' most common questions were "What is sound made of?" and

"How do we hear sound?" While enthusiastically acknowledging their inquiries, the teacher suggested that today's explorations would help them to find answers to these questions.

She encouraged them to make careful observations, record their data, and write about their thinking in their sound journals.

Center Time

Each center included a mini-exploration that addressed a sound-related concept along with one or two guiding questions. The center activities originate from teacher-centered sound demonstrations that have been modified into student-centered explorations as part of a professional development project we have participated in called SMATHematics (see Internet). Students spent 10 minutes at each of the centers with time being split equally between performing the activity and writing their observations and ideas in their sound journals.

Tuning Fork Vibrations

Science Concept Introduced:
Students will understand that sound is produced by vibrating objects and that some objects vibrate faster (with a higher pitch) than others.

Materials:
Tuning forks of various sizes (see Internet Resources), plastic glass of water, paper towels, sound journals.

Procedure:
Students struck a tuning fork against the heel of their shoes and then closely observed the vibrations, being careful not to place it too close to their ears. Then, students exchanged tuning forks with each other and observed the differences in sound with shorter and longer forks. Finally, students struck the tuning fork and placed the tines of the fork into a plastic cup of water and observed. Students used paper towels to clean up before rotating to the next station.

Guiding Questions:
Explain how you think the tuning fork caused the water to splash. This demonstration helps students see that sound waves carry energy that can affect the things around them. In this case, the vibrations from the tuning fork transfer much of their energy to the water causing it to splash, much to the delight of the students.

Why does one tuning fork sound different from another? By carefully listening to each of the different tuning forks, students recognize that shorter tuning forks vibrate faster (with a higher pitch) than the longer tuning forks. They can begin to understand that certain characteristics of vibrating objects can affect the quality of the sounds that are produced.

Recording Data:
At this center, students were asked to record their observations and draw a sketch of what they observed when placing a tuning fork in water. They were then asked to predict and explain the differences in sound between a longer and shorter tuning fork.

Rubber Band Guitars

Science Concept Introduced:
The pitch (speed) at which an object vibrates depends on characteristics of the object, such as length, thickness, and tension.

Materials:
One shoe box for each group so that each group can construct their own guitar, scissors, variety of rubber bands, sound journals.

Procedure:
Students cut a 3 in-wide hole toward one end of the shoe box. They then stretch three or four rubber bands of varying thickness around the shoe box and across the hole. Students then pluck each of the strings and listen carefully for differences in the sounds.

Guiding Questions:
Explain how the rubber band produced sound when you plucked it. The pitch of the vibration depends on both the mass (thickness) of the rubber band and the tension on the rubber band. The heavier the band, the lower the pitch, and the tighter the tension on the band, the higher the pitch of the vibration.

Why do you think the rubber band vibrates louder on the guitar than it does all by itself? The air by the hole of the guitar moves back and forth as the string vibrates. This causes the air to resonate with the string, and together they produce a louder sound. This question was probably too difficult as kids had a hard time answering it.

Recording Data:
At this center, students were asked to record their observations and explain why they thought that each of the rubber bands sounded different.

Drum It Up
Science Concept Introduced:
Vibrations can move through different objects and materials.

Materials:
Play drum, drum sticks, uncooked rice, sound journals.

Procedure:
Students placed a small handful of rice on top of the drum and tapped gently with the sticks. Students observed and listened closely as the rice bounced up and down.

Guiding Questions:
What do you think caused the rice to move? The vibrations from the drum were transferred to the rice causing it to vibrate (move) up and down.

How could you tell the drum is vibrating even if we didn't have any rice? You can tell the drum is vibrating because you can hear the sound produced by the drum. Sounds are produced by vibrating objects—in this case, the drum.

Recording Data:
In their sound journals, students drew a picture of what they thought was occurring at this center.

The First Phone
Science Concept Introduced:
Vibrations can move through different objects and materials, including strings and cups and air.

Materials:
Four plastic cups with small slit cut in the bottom, two 40 in pieces of cotton string, four paper clips, transparent tape, sound journals.

Procedure:
Students tied a paper clip onto each end of the string and then threaded the paper clips through the slit on the bottom of the cup and secured the paper clip with tape. Then they repeated the process for the other cup. Students held the cup to their ear and gently pulled the string tight. They then took turns plucking the string and listening closely to what they heard. Some even tried to talk to each other through the cups. The students were surprised by how well the vibrations could travel through the string and to their ears. Although the words themselves were not understandable, they could also transmit the vibrations from their voices back and forth to each other.

Guiding Questions:
How do you think the sound is getting from one cup to the other? Sound can travel through many materials including solids, liquids, and gases. In this case, the sound travels through the string, cup, and air before reaching your ear. Although most students seemed to recognize that the vibrations moved through the string and cup, they were most interested in writing about how they could feel the vibrations that were produced.

Do you think that real phones work in the same way? Explain. No, real phones don't act in the same way. Traditional phones convert sound waves into electrical waves, which are sent to the receiver and then converted back into sound waves. Cell phones are actually miniradios that use radio waves to communicate. Most of the students thought that real phones did not act in the same way. One wrote, "No, because it is a cup and the phone is electricity."

Recording Data:

At this center, students were asked to record their observations and describe what they heard when they listened with the cup.

Assessment and Reflection

During these investigations, the teacher observed that her students were "totally immersed in the content and were not apprehensive about any language barriers that they would normally have encountered." According to Maatta et al. (2006), inquiry science provides an arena in which English language learners can try out their ideas about science using their expanding second-language skills. Hands-on activities involving opportunities to read, listen, talk, and write are key to improving students understanding of both science content and the English language.

Upon completion of the exploration, the class discussed each center and the teacher highlighted key concepts. Using simple sentence structures and speaking slowly, she wanted to make sure that her students understood that sound was produced by vibrating objects, that objects vibrate with different pitches, and that sound waves carry energy in ways that affect humans. She then had her students repeat and rephrase the main ideas to each other in their own words, making sure to enunciate the words clearly. In doing so, she provided the scaffolding and language support that was needed for her English language learners (Rice et al. 2004).

By having students write about what they explored in class, she also helped develop their understanding of how language is related to meaning within a particular subject area. In simulating the actions of scientists, students were asked to make

and record careful observations as they completed each of the sound centers. After diligently constructing and testing his rubber band guitar, one student wrote that "by stretching the string [rubber band] and by sliding your finger on the string you can change the pitch of sound." By participating in purposeful, guided experiences related to key ideas about sound, students were able to build their academic understanding of sound.

As a wrap-up for this lesson, most of the students were asked to write a paragraph in their journal explaining what they learned about sound. Recognizing that academic writing poses a challenge to most English language learners, the teacher allowed students to complete their journal in various ways (Bravo and Garcia 2004). The students with limited English proficiency were allowed to draw and label their ideas relating to the tuning forks, drums, or phones. Others were encouraged to use diagrams and concept maps to help organize their ideas. These modifications, and the supportive comments on sticky notes that the teacher included when returning their journals, enabled students to demonstrate their growing understanding and feel successful in their pursuit of scientific understanding.

A Blast of a Finale

As a culminating event, the teacher used a trash-can wave generator (See Figure 1 for building instructions) to "blast" each student with a "silent" sound wave (because of their low frequency). To produce the wave, the teacher pulled the handle back on the trash can and then pushed it quickly into the can. The teacher moved around and aimed a wave at each student. Students had a rare and delightful opportunity to feel the waves because of the strong pressure (amplitude) that was readily detectable as the passing waves pushed against their faces.

After each group had their chance to shoot their own sound waves by moving the handle quickly or slowly, the teacher explained that, as with the tuning forks, the pitch of a sound depends on how fast the waves are produced by the vibrating object (or trash can). She then spoke with a female voice as she shot several waves quickly and then switched to a malelike voice as she shot a few slowly.

The trash-can wave generator demonstration was a fitting end to a memorable hands-on experience about sound. Having worked through the sound learning centers previously, students were comfortable discussing their ideas and observations about the trash-can wave generator and they were eager to apply their new understand-

Figure 1.

Instructions for building the trash-can wave generator

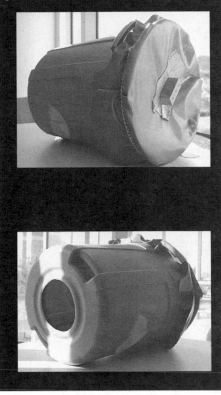

1. Use a utility knife to cut a 4–5 in round hole in the middle of the bottom of a round plastic trash can (20–30 gallons).

2. Cut a piece of shower liner (available at home supply stores) or some thick plastic about 12 inches wider than the can opening on each side.

3. Attach a handle to the middle of the liner: a small piece of wood attached with a screw and a washer (see photograph).

4. Place the liner across the trash can and center the wood handle. Push in the liner so that it bows slightly into the can and allow the liner to overlap the edges of the can. Secure the liner to the can with tape or a bungee cord.

Your amazing wave generator is now ready for use.

ings to the demonstration at hand. The ease of discussion and the quality of students' comments let the teacher know that the concrete hands-on experiences had truly helped her students begin to develop a foundation of understanding about sound—a difficult topic for many students to understand.

Tom Brown is assistant professor of elementary science education at Kennesaw State University in Kennesaw, Georgia. Kim Boehringer is a fifth-grade teacher at Fair Oaks Elementary School in Marietta, Georgia.

Resources

Bravo, M., and E. Garcia. 2004. *Learning to write like scientists: English language learners' science inquiry and writing understandings in responsive learning contexts.* Paper presented at AERA Annual Meeting, San Diego, CA.

Maatta, D., F. Dobb, and K. Ostlund. 2006. Strategies for teaching science to English learners. In *Science for English language learners*, eds. K. Fathman and D. Crowther. Arlington, VA: NSTA Press.

National Research Council (NRC). 1996. *National Science Education Standards.* Washington, DC: National Academy Press.

Rice, D. C., N. E. Pappamihiel, and V. E. Lake. 2004. Lesson adaptations and accommodations: Working with native speakers and English language learners in the same science classroom. *Childhood Education* (80): 121–127.

Internet

Educational Innovations
   www.teachersource.com
Flinn Scientific
   www.flinnsci.com

SMAThematics

http://webtech.kennesaw.edu/tbrown/curiosity/sound.htm

Connecting to the Standards
This article relates to the following *National Science Education Standards* (NRC 1996):

Content Standards
Grades K–4
Standard C: Physical Science
• Position and motion of objects

What's Hot? What's Not?

By Sandy Buczynski

When Goldilocks finds three bowls of porridge at different temperatures in the three bears' house, she accurately assesses the situation and comes up with one of the most recognizable lines in children's literature, "This porridge is too hot; this porridge is too cold; and this porridge is just right!"

Goldilocks's famous line is a perfect lead-in for an inquiry with upper-elementary students that explores the concept of heat energy as measured by temperature. In the investigation, students consider the variables that might account for temperature differences between each bear's porridge. For example, if Papa Bear has the hottest bowl of porridge, does he also have the largest bowl size? I've conducted this inquiry with groups of fifth and sixth graders and also with preservice students with good results. It's fun to observe students as they make surprising discoveries—for example, that a quantity of porridge in a smaller bowl will retain heat energy longer than a large bowl with the same quantity of porridge—and start considering that Papa Bear's bowl could have been the smallest bowl on the table.

I Heard, I Wonder

On the first day, I read "Goldilocks and the Three Bears" with emphasis on the porridge section of the story:

> Once upon a time, a little girl named Goldilocks went for a walk in the forest. After a while, she came upon a house. Goldilocks was hungry. So she knocked on the door and, when no one answered, she walked right in.
>
> At the table in the kitchen, there were three bowls of porridge.
>
> She tasted the porridge from Papa Bear's bowl.
>
> "This porridge is too hot!" she exclaimed.
>
> So, she tasted the porridge from Mama Bear's bowl.
>
> "This porridge is too cold," she said
>
> Then, she tasted Baby Bear's bowl of porridge.
>
> "Ahhh, this porridge is just right," she said happily and she ate it all up.

Students wrote observations in their science notebook about what they heard concerning the

Figure 1.
Student observations and questions

I heard	I wonder
1. There were three bowls of porridge.	1. Were the bowls different sizes? Did the bowls have lids? Were the bowls different shapes?
2. The porridges were different temperatures.	2. What could cause the porridges to be different temperatures?
3. Goldilocks tasted each bowl to determine its temperature.	3. Could the temperature of the porridge be taken with a thermometer?
4. All the porridge in the last bowl was eaten.	4. Was Goldilocks hungry? (this is NOT a measurable question)

bowls of porridge in a column with the heading "I Heard" (Figure 1).

Next, we discussed students' observations to see if what they heard in the story led them to wonder anything. Maybe Mama Bear fixed her bowl of porridge first, so it has been on the table the longest, allowing heat energy to dissipate and causing the porridge to grow cold. Or, maybe Papa Bear had a greater quantity of porridge, which retained heat energy longer, explaining why his porridge was too hot. Or, maybe a bit of cool milk was added to Baby Bear's bowl, lowering the initial heat energy immediately to ensure his porridge was just right.

Students' reasons for the varying porridge temperatures included

- size of the three bowls;
- composition of bowls (glass, ceramic, wood, plastic, metal);
- covering of bowl (with lid, without lid);
- amount of porridge in each bowl;
- whether a cooler or hotter substance was added to porridge after preparation;
- length of time each bowl of porridge had been sitting on table; and
- shape of bowls (square, round).

Then, we discussed some heat energy concepts and reviewed the idea of a *measurable question*. A measurable question is a question about which numeric data can be collected. For example, a measurable question based on the Goldilocks story might be be, "How fast do different amounts of oatmeal lose heat?" Students would measure both the temperature of the oatmeal and periods of time, such as five minutes, 10 minutes, and so on.

Research Design
Although students had come up with numerous potential reasons for differences in the oatmeal's temperature in our discussion, for practical purposes we decided to focus on four factors: bowl size, amount of oatmeal in the bowl, whether the bowl was covered or uncovered, and whether an additional substance (milk) added to the oatmeal cooled it faster. Students divided into lab groups based on their interest in the investigation topic.

In this guided inquiry, each group changed only one variable—this is the *manipulated* variable (the condition that is purposely changed or altered). All other conditions of the experiment

Hot Stuff

Heat is energy. Temperature is not energy but rather the measure of it. The amount of heat energy in a substance depends on the characteristics of the particles (molecules) that make up the substance. These characteristics include speed of particles, mass (the size or number) of particles, and the type of particles. If heat energy is added to a substance, the result is that the temperature will go higher. Higher temperatures mean that the particles that make up a substance are moving (vibrating) with more energy. The converse is also true; if heat energy is removed, the temperature will go lower.

To ensure accurate collection of data during this activity, I have students practice reading a thermometer (see Internet). Taking the time to discuss thermometer readings helps students conceptualize what temperature readings might be considered in the "hot" range (e.g., 40°C–100°C) and where a "cool" temperature reading (e.g., 0°C–20°C) might fall on a thermometer. Soon students begin to associate a number (in degrees Celsius) on the thermometer with a range of what might be considered hot to Goldilocks!

remained the same. For example, the group investigating whether the "amount of porridge" influences temperature kept constant the size, composition, shape, and depth of bowl; lid use; amount of stirring; amount of hot water added; temperature of initial water; type of porridge used; even the particular thermometer used to measure heat gain or loss. The only variable changed was the porridge portion. Because only one variable was changed, any temperature differences observed could be attributed to that one variable.

Next, we discussed the *responding* variable—the measurement that results from changing the manipulated variable (in these investigations, measuring heat by taking the porridge's temperature).

After identifying the variables, each group established a prediction. Although formal hypotheses (testable explanations) are beyond the targeted grade levels, students can begin to learn the logic by completing "If/Then" statements with an explanation. IF this is done (manipulated variable), THEN this will happen (direction of responding variable). Aligning the prediction with the variables establishes

what will be measured in the experiment. For example, "IF the same amount of porridge is put into different size bowls, THEN porridge in the largest bowl will stay hot longest."

Finally, each group wrote a procedure for its experiment, providing enough detail in the instructions so that another group could follow its directions. Once the groups were comfortable with the variables and had recorded their predictions and plans in their science notebooks, they were ready to proceed with the experiments, which were conducted the next day.

Investigation Day

I assembled the materials for the four experiments, which included various shapes of plastic food-storage bowls with lids, instant oatmeal packets for the porridge, measuring cups, and an electric hot pot to provide the heated water. For safer science, keep heated water within a warm temperature range (40 to 60°C) that is measurable with a student thermometer. I boil water in the hot pot, then pour out half and replace it with room temperature water. Only the teacher handles the hot pot. Also, be sure students use alcohol—not mercury—thermometers, and

Figure 2.

Student investigation plan

Prediction:

IF the amount of porridge is increased, THEN the temperature of the porridge will stay hot longer.

Variables:

Manipulated:
Amount of porridge

Responding:
Temperature of the porridge

Constant(s):
Size of bowls
Shape of bowls
Number of times stirred
Temperature of water
Room temperature

Materials:
Three packets of instant oatmeal
Three same size, round plastic bowls
Thermometers
Timer
Heated water
Plastic spoon
Measuring cup

Procedure:

1. Line up three identical bowls. In the first bowl pour in one-half packet of instant oatmeal. In the second bowl pour in one whole packet of instant oatmeal, and in the third bowl pour in 1½ packets of instant oatmeal.
2. Add one-half cup of water from the kettle to each bowl.
3. Stir the water and oatmeal together in each bowl 10 times.
4. Put a thermometer in each bowl and take an initial reading.
5. Record the temperature in science notebook.
6. After 5 minutes take another temperature reading and record.
7. Continue until 4 readings are complete (15 minutes).

Data Chart:

Manipulated Variable	Temperature in Degrees Celsius (Responding Variable)			
Time in minutes	0	5	10	15
½ packet of oatmeal	50	41	33	25
1 packet of oatmeal	50	46	39	35
1½ packets of oatmeal	50	48	45	40

do not permit students to eat the porridge.

Students investigated the following four predictions:

- IF porridge is put into different size bowls, THEN porridge in the largest bowl will stay hot longest.
- IF a bowl of porridge is covered, THEN porridge will stay warm longer than if uncovered.
- IF the amount of porridge in a bowl is increased, THEN the greater the amount of porridge, the longer it will stay hot.
- IF a cold substance (like refrigerated milk) is added to the porridge, THEN the porridge will cool faster than porridge without something added.

Each group picked up its needed materials and followed the procedures it had established for their experiment. Figure 2 describes the student investigation plan for the group comparing amounts of porridge, and it includes their data table. Other groups had similar worksheet plans for their predictions.

From Data to Graphs

Each group was required to record its data on a chart. Some scaffolding is usually necessary to guide the conversion of these data tables into graphs that can be analyzed. To begin, we first considered whether a line graph or bar graph would best represent the data. Generally, continuous data, such as temperature, is represented with a line graph and discrete data (data that falls into categories), such as number of people, colors, or favorite food, is represented with a bar or pie graph.

For this experiment, students were looking at change in temperature over time, so we put time on the X-axis and the responding variable of temperature on the Y-axis. This graph represented the rate of heat loss or gain. If your students are comfortable with graphs, point out that the lines between data points are *interpolations*—explain that we don't have the data for those points, but if we did, we could predict it would be near that line.

A separate graph can be constructed for each manipulated variable or different colored markers used to put all data on one graph. The graph can be called the relationship of manipulated variable to responding variable and the axes of the graph are always labeled with units of measure. Students can use the information illustrated in the graph to analyze trends and patterns in data.

What Happened?

In describing what happened in the experiments, I ask students to consider their results from all angles:

- What is the summary or big picture of the results?
- What was the highest and lowest temperature (range)?
- Did the responding variable show an overall increase or decrease (temperature trend)?

Examining the big picture is a good place to reconnect the experiment with the story. Ask

- If the temperature of all experimental bowls of porridge went down over the 15 minutes, does that mean that the porridge was getting cooler or warmer? When students answer "getting cooler," they are making connections between decreasing temperature readings and loss of heat energy making the oatmeal cooler.

- Would Goldilocks consider the porridge at 50°C hot? If 100°C is the boiling point of water and 0°C is the freezing point of water, students can recognize temperature readings within a relative hot and cold range. The range in this experiment usually runs between 21°C and 50°C, so students will agree that 50°C would be at the hot end.

Conclusions and Beyond

As we concluded the lessons, students examined their predictions to determine if they were supported or not supported, and we talked about some additional questions that arose from the experiments, including the following:

- Would the results be similar if a different type of porridge were used?
- Would the temperature readings be different if the porridges were heated in the microwave oven?
- Would the results be different if they used Styrofoam bowls instead—does insulation play a role in heat retention?
- What would happen if we placed the bowls of oatmeal in the sun and in an air-conditioned room to see if outside temperature is a factor?

Finally, we discussed if procedures were compromised in any way (spills, constants not held, thermometer misreading), which may have introduced factors that could have affected the accuracy of the data or affected their conclusions. For example, one group held the bowls in their hands during the experiment. In hindsight, the students realized body heat could have influenced their results.

Assessing Students

To assess students' learning, I used a rubric (Figure 3) designed to provide constructive comments and questions on students' progress.

Figure 3.
Assessment rubric

Criteria	Beginning Scientist	Developing Scientist	Accomplished Scientist
Investigation Skills	Try to make your "I wonder" question measurable. What information needs to be collected to answer the question?	Accurate data supported your measurable question. How could your results change the story of "Goldilocks and the Three Bears"?	All components of your investigation are accurate. Each bear is matched with his/her bowl of porridge. Three cheers!
Understanding Temperature	Practice reading a thermometer. If the reading is high, does this mean something is HOT or COLD?	Think about what might cause the porridge to get cooler/warmer. How would changing ONE variable affect the temperature readings?	You connected your manipulated variable to heat retention/loss as measured by temperature. Congratulations!
Collaboration	Most scientists work together—won't you?	You had some great ideas—also consider your lab partners' ideas!	You worked productively with lab partners! Thank you.

If a student's performance is in the "beginning scientist" range, the rubric will provide direction for the student to take in order to move up to the "developing scientist" range by offering ideas on how to improve understanding of scientific investigation.

Learning to design a measurable question, accurately read a thermometer, and making a connection between the temperature reading and amount of heat energy present in the bowl of porridge were the intended learning outcomes from these investigations. In addition, I hoped students would be able to incorporate their investigation into a wider framework and begin to analyze relationships among data. By thinking critically, students learn to reason from evidence.

At the completion of this activity, students were doing just that. Some students were already thinking about how to apply this investigation strategy to other pieces of children's literature. Students were discussing that, for *The Three Little Pigs,* manipulated variables might be how much fan power would be needed (or at what distance a fan would need to be placed) to knock down houses constructed of sugar cubes (bricks), toothpicks (wood), or broom straw.

Sandy Buczynski is an assistant professor at the University of San Diego in San Diego, California.

Acknowledgments
Many mahalos to the lively Liberty Elementary sixth-grade class of Annie Humphrey for field-testing this activity. Thanks also to Donna Barnes for her close reading of the first draft of this activity, and to Bobbi Hansen's multiple subject preservice teachers for valuable input in developing this lesson.

Resources

National Research Council (NRC). 1996. *National Science Education Standards*. Washington, DC: National Academy Press.

Internet

The Story of Goldilocks and the Three Bears
www.dltk-teach.com/rhymes/goldilocks.htm

Connecting to the Standards
This article relates to the following National Science Education Standards (NRC 1996):

Content Standards
Grades 5–8

Standard A: Science as Inquiry
• Abilities necessary to do scientific inquiry

Standard B: Physical Science
• Transfer of energy

Circus of Light

By Juanita Jo Matkins and Jacqueline McDonnough

Imagine a classroom containing several small groups of students engaged in various science activities at stations around the room. At regular intervals, the groups move to another station. After about 45 minutes the children have worked at all the stations and return to their desks, discussing the questions posed at the different stations. The teacher then leads the class in a discussion about the science topic, using the experiences at the stations to guide the students to understandings about the topic. This class just performed a "science circus."

A science circus is a set of activities done in any order that together illustrate complementary properties of a science topic. As in a traditional circus, several "performances" occur at the same time, and students focus their attention on one activity while others are going on. Similar to the ringmaster of a circus, the teacher guides and directs students as they circulate through the stations.

In this article, we describe the light-based science circus we developed and tested with a fifth-grade class at Blackwell Elementary School in Richmond, Virginia.

Why Do a Science Circus?

Many science topics are complex, and two or three activities are often insufficient to support student concept development. How can teachers fit more activities on a topic into the classroom schedule? Our answer was to alter the pattern of doing science activities in sequence and instead do several at the same time. With the time saved, we had more time to lead discussions with the entire class, helping construct understandings about the topic.

There are three steps to a science circus on any topic: (1) the *hook,* a question that generates student interest in the topic; (2) the *activities* that explore that question and other aspects of the topic; and (3) the *forum,* the teacher-led class discussion of the topic.

For our study of light, our hook was a thought-provoking question related to a misconception many children and adults have about being able to see an object even though there is no light shining on the object: "If you were in a completely dark room, would you be able to see anything?" The students were divided over the answer. Several insisted you could see in complete darkness, while others argued you had to have some light. We led them to the second step of the circus by explaining we were going to do some activities that might show them the answer to that question. The science circus activities are described in Figure 1.

We planned our five circus activities—Bouncing Light, Bending Light, Light in the Darkness, Me and My Shadow, and Making a Rainbow—by first identifying the basic understandings about light we wanted to introduce to students. These understandings are consistent with the National Science Education Standards

Figure 1.

Five-ring science

Bouncing Light. We set up the materials for this station—a flashlight, a tennis ball, a large mirror, and a powder puff with some talcum powder on it—in a dark corner of the classroom with enough space for students to bounce a ball back and forth.

Do and Discuss

1. Bounce the ball at different angles. Compare the angle of the ball's path as it approaches the floor with the angle of its path as it leaves the floor.
2. Place the mirror face up on the floor and "bounce" the light beam from the flashlight off the mirror, then at different angles. Shake the powder puff over the light beam to help you see the path of the light.
3. Compare the angles of the light beam approaching and leaving the mirror.

Science Log Questions

1. Draw pictures of the path the ball takes to and from the floor.
2. Draw pictures of the paths the light beam takes to and from the mirror.
3. How do the angles of the light beam approaching and leaving the mirror compare with the angles of the bouncing ball approaching and leaving the floor?

Bending Light. At this station, students observed a pencil in an empty glass and in a glass of water.

Do and Discuss

1. Place the pencil in the empty glass. Look at the pencil from the top and the side. Predict what the pencil will look like in the glass of water.
2. Put the pencil in the glass of water. Look at the pencil from the top and the side.

Science Log Questions

1. Draw what the pencil looks like in the empty glass and in the glass of water. What appears to happen to the pencil?
2. What ideas do you have about this effect? (Hint: Think about how water is different than air.)

Light in the Darkness. For this station, we placed a large cardboard box on its side on a table and draped a sheet over it (to make it completely dark inside). Inside, we placed a flashlight, a mirror, a piece of white paper, and a small object (a toy cow).

Do and Discuss

1. Put your head in the box and cover up with the sheet. Can you see the object?
2. Shine the flashlight on the object. What do you see now?
3. Predict whether you can see the object without shining the flashlight straight at it.

4. Aim the flashlight behind you. Can you see the object?
5. Hold the mirror out beside you and aim the flashlight at the mirror. What do you see now?
6. Hold the piece of paper out beside you and aim the flashlight at it. What do you see now?

Science Log Questions

1. What were the sources of light in this activity?
2. Were you able to see the object when you shined the flashlight behind you? How about when you used the mirror and the piece of paper?
3. Which way was it easiest to see the object? Why?
4. Draw the direction the light energy travels when you can see the object. Include the light source, the object, your eye, and anything else you think helped you see the object.

Me and My Shadow. This activity requires a fairly dark area, a light source (such as an overhead projector or a lamp), a screen or blank wall, and a set of pictures of shadow creatures (shapes) students can form with their hands, such as a bird, a dog, and an elephant.

Do and Discuss

1. Hold your hand in front of the light and observe what happens.
2. Remove a shadow creature card from the bag. (Don't tell what it is.) Take turns with your teammates making the shadows. Guess what the others are making.
3. Can you make your shadow creature grow bigger? Smaller?

Science Log Questions

1. Sketch your idea of the path the light traveled.
2. Why do you think the size of the shadow changed when you moved your hands?

Making a Rainbow. At this station, we set two prisms next to the teacher's overhead projector.

Do and Discuss

1. Hold one prism in the path of the light coming from the projector and find the rainbow. Determine where the light emerges from the prism.
2. Hold the second prism in the path of light coming out of the first prism. See if you can position the second prism so the rainbow becomes white light again.

Science Log Questions

1. Draw the path of light going into and out of the prism. What happens in the first prism that makes the rainbow appear?
2. Draw your idea of what happens when you use the second prism to make the light white again.

on light (NRC 1996). We wanted the students to explore the following ideas:

- Light travels in a straight line.
- The *angle of incidence* of light striking a reflecting surface is equal to the *angle of reflection*.
- Light is necessary for us to see.
- Light *refracts* or bends when it passes through substances of different densities as it travels to our eyes.
- Visible light has all the colors of the rainbow in it.

Directions were posted at each station, as were questions to be answered in the students' science logs. The student teams had seven minutes at each station, and we gave students extra time to finish their written responses once all activities were done. Students were encouraged to discuss their observations with the teacher and their classmates throughout the circus.

The Forum

When students completed the circus activities, it was time to discuss what they discovered in the forum. During the circus we paid close attention to what students were saying to each other, and we noted what students were saying about each activity. We used this information to guide our questions during the forum.

We wanted students to construct the scientific ideas for themselves with only a little guidance from us. We had already planned to use certain questions to guide the forum discussion, and we added questions inspired by student interactions.

The questions were all intended to guide the students into realizing how each activity related to the specific characteristic of light it was helping to demonstrate. Because all of the students had completed each activity, they were able to draw upon their own observations and experiences as a foundation for discussion and for the development of concept understanding

about the topic. What follows is how the light discussion progressed.

Light Travels in a Straight Line.
We began by discussing the Bouncing Light activity, asking "Did the light from the flashlight travel 'every which way'?" Students commented that they had observed the light traveling in a straight line from the flashlight and talked about using the powder puff and mirror to see the path the light took when it left the flashlight.

Next, we discussed Me and My Shadow by asking, "What did you do to make the shadow larger?" Students commented that the shadows got bigger when they held the creatures (their hands) closer to the light source. "Why do you think that happens? Could it have anything to do with the path light travels?" One child suggested, "The closer to the light that you hold the shadow creature, the more light you block. That's why the shadow gets bigger. The light is traveling in a straight line and it's blocked by the shadow creature—it can't go around." The class agreed with the comment, and we then asked, "Do you all feel okay about making a rule about the way light travels through the air?" The entire class agreed, "Light travels in a straight line" was a good rule.

The Angle of Incidence Is Equal to the Angle of Reflection.
We asked, "In the Bouncing Light activity, what happened to the light when it left the mirror?" In previous classes, students had learned about *acute* (less than 90 degrees) and *obtuse* (greater than 90 degrees) angles. In this activity, students observed that when light traveled to the mirror at an obtuse angle, it came out at an obtuse angle, and that when light traveled to the mirror at an acute angle, it came out at an acute angle.

When asked, the class was unanimous in agreeing that the angle going in was the same as the angle of light coming out. We explained that the angle going in was called the *angle of*

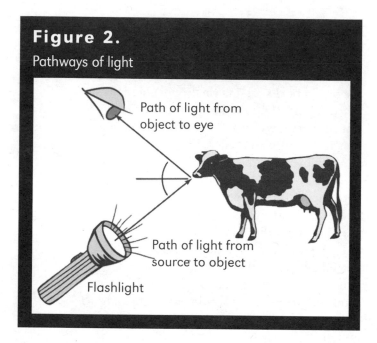

Figure 2.
Pathways of light

Path of light from object to eye

Path of light from source to object

Flashlight

incidence and the angle going out was called the *angle of reflection.* We put the new vocabulary into their previously agreed-upon observation about the angles being equal. They agreed that "The angle of incidence is equal to the angle of reflection" was a good rule for light reflecting off a mirror.

Light Is Necessary for Us to See.

Did the students remember our hook question, "If you were in a completely dark room would you be able to see anything?" What did they think now? They agreed that they had to have the flashlight on to see the toy cow in the box. We asked, "Where did the light start, and how did the image get to our eyes?" We drew an eye, a flashlight, and a cow on the board, and asked the class how we might draw arrows to show how light helped us see (Figure 2). The students said the light started with the flashlight. Some thought light went to the eyes next, and some thought light went to the object.

We explained we see things because light strikes those things and that light, or part of it, is reflected into our eyes. It is the light entering our eyes that sends the signal to our brain about the appearance of the object. With our human senses, we cannot tell when light leaves a source and hits an object and is then reflected to our eyes. It's just too fast.

Light Bends, or Refracts, When It Passes Through More Than One Substance as It Travels to Our Eyes.

"What about the pencil in the glass of water [Bending Light]?" we asked, "Does the pencil look different in the water?" Everyone agreed the pencil in the glass of water looked like two pencils under the water. Why did they think it looked like this? One student suggested, "It might be something about the surface of the water because when you look on the side it looks different."

We explained something happened when light traveled into and out of water that was different from light traveling in air, and it made the pencil look bent or crooked. The light slowed down in the water, causing the path of the light to shift slightly as it traveled through the water. All the light waves reflecting off the part of the pencil under the water hit our eyes at a different place than they would if the pencil were not in the water.

We said that light is *refracted* when it shifts or moves in its path from the object to our eyes, leading us to see the object as bent or crooked—or making it appear like two pencils under the water.

Visible Light Has All the Colors of the Rainbow in It.

Refraction also was evident in our last activity, Making a Rainbow. Sometimes refracted light waves spread out so we can see the different colors that make up visible light. White light is a combination of the colors that we see when we see a rainbow. When white light is absorbed incompletely (part of it is reflected to our eyes), then we see the color that is the part of white light that was not absorbed. That is why we see colors. Shining a strong light (like an overhead projector light) through a prism can spread out the waves so we see the different colors.

Some students wondered if the colors in the rainbow were always in the same order, like the colors in the prism. We wrote ROYGBIV on the board and told them those letters stood for the colors in the rainbow—red, orange, yellow, blue, green, indigo, and violet, also called the *visible spectrum*. We explained that there are other "colors" in the rainbow that our eyes cannot respond to, such as infrared and ultraviolet.

Turning on the Light

Providing hands-on science experiences for elementary children can be a challenge because of the difficulties of allotting the time and finding the necessary materials. A science circus format makes the task of designing good science lessons easier, because less time and fewer materials are needed than when doing activities sequentially or individually.

Perhaps the greatest benefit to teachers of using the science circus format is not the ease of use but the outcomes produced when students generate their own understandings through interaction with real phenomena. In one day of science activities these elementary students observed phenomena, compared ideas with others, and tested new ideas against their old ideas to see if they needed to change their old ideas. The students had joined Isaac Newton in the quest for understanding the mysterious substance known as light.

Juanita Jo Matkins is an assistant professor in the Graduate School of Education at George Mason University in Fairfax, Virginia, and Assistant Director of the Center for Restructuring Education in Science and Technology. Jacqueline McDonnough is an assistant professor of science education at Virginia Commonwealth University in Richmond, Virginia.

Resources

National Research Council (NRC). 1996. *National Science Education Standards*. Washington, DC: National Academy Press.

Koch, J. 1996. *Science stories: Teachers and children as science learners*. Boston: Houghton-Mifflin.

Internet

Properties of Light
sol.sci.uop.edu/~jfalward/physics17/chapter12/chapter 12.html

---

Connecting to the Standards

This article addresses the following National Science Education Standards (NRC 1996):

Content Standards
Grades K–4
Standard B: Physical Science
Light, Heat, Electricity, and Magnetism (K–4)
- Light travels in a straight line until it strikes an object. Light can be reflected by a mirror, refracted by a lens, or absorbed by the object.

Grades 5–8
Standard B: Physical Science
Transfer of Energy
- Light interacts with matter by transmission (including refraction), absorption, or scattering (including reflection). To see an object, light from that object—emitted by or scattered from it—must enter the eye.

Teaching Standards
Standard A:
Teachers of science plan an inquiry-based science program for students.
Standard B:
Teachers of science guide and facilitate learning.

Building Student Mental Constructs of Particle Theory

By Erin Peters

A fundamental concept in science is particle theory, which states that all matter is made of particles and the particles' behavior and arrangement determine the properties of matter. This concept is a basic idea in chemistry and physics and leads students to understand why solids, liquids, and gases have different properties although they are made of the same materials. Understanding particle theory helps students recognize the differences in the classification of elements, compounds, and mixtures.

One of the biggest challenges in teaching particle theory is the abstract nature of imagining arrangement and behavior of particles. Because abstract thinking is difficult for middle school students, particle theory is not among those concepts covered in the National Science Education Standards for grades 5–8. Even ninth graders can have difficulty grasping this concept, so this activity incorporates many concrete experiences that lead students to evaluate the nature of matter abstractly.

The concept of particle theory, or kinetic theory, requires students to have adequate process skills in observation and inference to arrive at a deep understanding of what is occurring on a molecular level and on a macroscopic level. For instance, if students cannot directly observe that air has volume, they may resort to an everyday experience to gain indirect evidence to show that air has volume, such as air being blown into a balloon. The three-part demonstration that follows is appropriate for ninth graders and any middle-level student capable of abstract thinking, because models of particle theory can be demonstrated that help students transfer the concrete demonstrations to the abstract concept of particle arrangement.

One goal of this activity is to have students draw from their own experiences to explain how matter is made of particles. This is accomplished through a think-pair-share that asks students to share evidence from their daily lives to explain statements about air. The results of this preliminary activity help the teacher discover any

Figure 1.

Statements about air worksheet

Statements about air	Observation or inference	Supporting evidence
Air is invisible		
Air has volume		
Air has mass		
Air can be squeezed into smaller spaces		
Air moves		
There is water in air		

misconceptions students have about particles of a gas. Students complete the chart in Figure 1 by choosing to describe statements about air as either an observation or an inference and defending their choice using evidence. Students are given time to discuss their answers with a partner, and later with a group of four to expand their thinking. Following the small-group discussion, a class discussion is conducted where the teacher chooses several of the statements about air. During this discussion, students and the teacher resolve any confusion students may have about their understandings.

Another goal of the activity is to have students observe four demonstrations of discrepant events and describe in terms of particle theory why the events occurred. Details for the demonstration appear in Figure 2.

Assessment

I check for misconceptions by walking around and reviewing the evidence students present in the Statements About Air activity. After assessing the preliminary activity, I have a baseline from which to begin the class discussions about the various demonstrations. One of the statements about air that is difficult for many students is the statement, "There is water in air." Students present the argument that they can't

see water in air, so it isn't there. The teacher, or sometimes other students, can cause conflict in ideas by asking where the water from condensation comes from. Once the idea that matter cannot mysteriously appear is considered, many of the conflicting ideas resolve themselves. Students who have difficulty understanding the results of a demonstration are helped to form understanding by the statements of their peers. The demonstrations involving mixing sand and water or salt and water produce bubbles as the substances mix. I draw students' attention to the bubbles and ask them to consider how the bubbles form. Students often have the idea that the bubbles are formed from chemical interactions, so I look out for that misconception. The bubbles give a clue to students that there is air trapped between the spaces in the sand or salt, which is helpful in constructing mental models of particles. Along the same lines, the mixture of alcohol and water produces a blur in the clear liquids. I link the appearance of the blur to the appearance of bubbles in the previous mixtures so students can connect the information they are processing.

These activities give students a chance to talk about their experiences with properties of substances, which in turn allows the teacher to gather information about students' prior

Figure 2.
Demonstrations

Coloring water blue

Begin this demonstration by showing students 50 mL of blue water. Remove 25 mL of the blue water and replace it with 25 mL of clear water. Ask students to predict how many additional dilutions you would have to perform until you could no longer detect the blue in the water. (I've found that the blue usually becomes undetectable after eight or nine dilutions.) Relate the results to the idea that particles are so small and dispersed that we may not be able to detect their presence in a very small sample. Have students answer the following questions, which are geared to lead students into thinking about the materials in terms of particles:

1. Is the color spread evenly throughout the water, or are bits of food coloring clumped together?
2. How much of the food coloring do you have in the beaker of water at the end of the demonstration?
3. Do you think there may be some food coloring left in the solution at the end, even though you cannot see any?
4. If matter is made up of particles, what can you infer about the size of the food-coloring particles?
5. Does the demonstration support a particle theory of matter? Why or why not?

Sand and water demonstration

Fill one graduated cylinder with 50 mL of sand and another graduated cylinder with 50 mL of water. Pour 50 mL of water into the graduated cylinder filled with 50 mL of sand and ask students why the resulting volume does not equal 100 mL. Be sure to point out the air bubbles that rise to the surface. Have students answer the following question:

1. Suggest why the combined volume is not 100 mL.

Salt and water demonstration

Pour 25 mL of salt into a graduated cylinder and pour water into the same graduated cylinder until the water meets the 100 mL reading. Put your hand over the top of the cylinder and shake for one minute, turning it upside down as you shake. Ask students to read the resulting volume after shaking. Discuss possible reasons why the mixture has less volume than 100 mL. Ask students if a grain of salt is equal to a formula unit of salt. Have students answer the following question:

1. How do you explain the volume for the combined salt and water after you shook it?

Alcohol and water demonstration

In this demonstration, 50 mL of water are combined with 40 mL of isopropyl alcohol in a graduated cylinder. The level of the solution reaches approximately 88 mL. Students are often surprised by this result because they assume that because both materials are liquids and have similar properties, they will add up to 90 mL. Pour 50 mL of water in one graduated cylinder and 40 mL of isopropyl alcohol in another graduated cylinder. Pour the alcohol into the water and have a student read the resulting volume. Discuss possible arrangements of alcohol and water particles to help them visualize how the particles fit together.

1. Does the combination of 50 mL of water and 40 mL of alcohol equal 90 mL? Why or why not?

Drawing conclusions

At the end of class, have students reflect on the demonstrations and answer the following questions:

1. How does the particle model of matter help to explain the observations you made in these experiments?
2. Do your observations support the idea that matter consists of particles? Why or why not?

knowledge. When students are asked to justify their statements with a reason, they begin to think more deeply about how their ideas are connected. Armed with an understanding of student conceptual frameworks, teachers can scaffold learning from concrete experiences with substances to abstract modeling of molecule arrangements.

Erin Peters is an Albert Einstein Distinguished Educator Fellow for the NASA Exploration Systems Mission Directorate in Washington, DC.

You Can Always Tell a Dancer By Her Feet

By Joan Lindgren and Marcia Cushall

At the front of the class, the instructor stood holding a cup of water directly over the head of a seated volunteer. She then placed an index card over the top of the cup and held it in place with her hand. Finally, she turned her attention to the students and asked: "What will happen if I invert the cup and remove my hand from under the index card?" After noting the students responses and allowing the volunteer to snap open an umbrella, the instructor inverted the cup, removed her hand, and kicked off her unit on integrated science-math methods for preservice teachers.

This discrepant event and the activities that follow examine pressure from a scientific perspective, while applying math to deepen students' understanding of the concept. Although this unit was developed for use with preservice teachers, you can also use the activities with your middle level students to demonstrate the connection between math and science.

Brainstorming About Pressure

After each demonstration, we follow up with a discussion to explore students' understanding of pressure. In the case of the cup and card demonstration, we discuss how the atmospheric pressure pushing up on the index card is greater than the pressure of the water pushing down on the card. The role of surface tension and the cohesive and adhesive properties of water can also be discussed if you have already covered this topic.

Although the word *pressure* is a part of our everyday vocabulary, it is also a foundational concept with special meaning in science. We asked students, "What do you think of when you hear the word *pressure?*"

Student answers included

- high and low pressure areas in weather reports,
- scuba diving and water pressure,
- ear popping sensations in airplanes or on mountain roads,
- inflatable bike tires and basketballs,

- blood pressure, and
- pressure on shoulders from carrying backpacks.

Students may cite peer pressure, or stress, as a type of pressure. Explain that this is not a physical concept, but that it is an excellent example of how words used to describe science concepts are used in our everyday language, sometimes with quite different meanings.

Pressure: A Science Perspective

You can use the activity at the Activity Page, adapted from EQUALS Investigations, Lawrence Hall of Science, to show students that we experience pressure all the time—due to gravity as we stand in place (Equals Investigations 1994).

Divide students into groups of four to six and follow the procedure. List the class pressure calculations on the board or overhead, and have the class discuss the variations in pressure. Your students may be surprised to note the small range of calculated pressures in spite of noticeable and significant differences in weight. Although a person might be very large in terms of his or her weight, that person will most likely have quite large feet as well. This greater surface area supports the greater weight. Therefore, the pressure experienced by a large person might not be much greater than the pressure experienced by a smaller person with correspondingly smaller feet and surface area.

Within the class data set, there are usually one or two outlier measurements with a pressure considerably smaller than the others. Have students hypothesize why. One answer is that these individuals probably have unusually large feet and at the same time are also quite thin. Having less pressure exerted on your body can give anyone a new appreciation for having large feet!

The discussion may turn to the various types of shoes one might wear and how this could change the pressure. Basketball shoes, with their larger surface area, distribute the weight over a wider area than bare feet. If any of the girls are wearing heels, have them calculate their pressure in their stocking feet versus in their shoes. The pressure is noticeably greater when they are wearing shoes with heels where the surface area is much less.

Dancer's Feet

If any of your students take ballet, have them bring in a pair of their ballet toe shoes. With a partner, trace the toe area of the ballet slipper and calculate what the pressure would be if the volunteer stood on one toe like a dancer. In our class, the astounding pressure increase—often 20 to 25 times as great—caused one active dancer to comment, "You can always tell a dancer by her feet." She described the bruised, battered appearance and bleeding toes that were the result of toe dancing. Students now understood why ballet dancers try to stay as lean as possible.

Next pass out snowshoes and/or skis to the groups and have them measure the surface area of one ski or snowshoe. How do these pressures compare to feet measurements? Snowshoes and skis both have large surface areas that distribute the weight of your body over a large area. This reduced pressure prevents sinking into the snow—an advantage when trying to maneuver in deep, light, unpacked snow.

Weight Measurement on Two Scales

As an extension of measurement regarding weight, ask for student volunteers to weigh themselves on two identical scales placed at the front of the room and write their weight for each scale on the chalkboard.

After many "Oh, no!" comments and laughter, usually one male student and one fearless female student will volunteer to weigh themselves for discussion and for further group calculations. Discuss the need to check for discrepancies in the scale readings, and adjust scales so that both register the same weight for each volunteer.

With the volunteers' weight on the board, pose this problem: "What will the two scales show, if that person now stands with one foot on one scale and one foot on the other scale?" (Space scales 3 centimeters apart.) In other words, what value will each scale show when a person divides his or her stance between two scales, rather than the usual way of determining weight with both feet on the same scale?

Use this opportunity to sharpen students' reasoning skills using a modification of Stepans' Conceptual Change Model (see Figure 1, Stepans 1994).

Each student in the group makes a numerical prediction as to what each scale will show when a volunteer stands with one foot on each scale. Give students five minutes to share their predictions with their group and come to a consensus. The reporter should record the group's reasoning and explain the group's decision to the class. Create a chart on the board or overhead and record each group's predicted values and reasoning. After each group has "exposed its belief," allow the class to discuss their thoughts for five more minutes.

Our students came up with four dominant beliefs:

1. Both scales will show the same value as the volunteer's total weight. (If a volunteer weighs 100 pounds, then each scale will show 100 pounds.)
2. Each scale will show approximately half the weight of the person, with slight variations due to uneven stance or slight shifts by the person as they balance between two scales.
3. One scale will show several pounds more weight than the other, but the total weight will be less than the person's original weight by a noticeable amount.

Figure 1.
Challenging conceptions

1. Each group designates a reporter.
2. Within the group, students discuss the different possible outcomes, decide on one, and "commit to an outcome."
3. After each group has made their decision, go around the room and have each reporter "expose the beliefs" of the group to the class.
4. Conduct the activity.
5. Each group's "belief is confronted" via the activity.
6. Discuss what happened during the activity and expand student ideas about how pressure was demonstrated in the activity.

4. One scale will show several pounds more than the other, but the total weight will be more than the person's total weight by a significant amount.

Discuss the variables that might affect the measurements—expect a lively discussion! Examples of variables include the need for identical scales and an even stance, the importance of calibration, and the lack of perfect body symmetry. Several students in our class expressed that some weight would be "lost between the two scales" as volunteers stood with one foot on each scale. Students were eager to find out what the volunteers would weigh on two scales.

The volunteers again weighed themselves, this time standing with one foot on one scale and the other foot on the other scale, balancing themselves as evenly as possible as a partner read the scale and announced the variations.

More than half the students were surprised to see that the weight on each scale was very

Activity page

Materials

Each class needs
- a bathroom scale

Each pair of students needs
- a large sheet of paper marked in square units
- a pencil or pen

Procedure

1. Stand in place for three minutes.
2. How would you feel if you put your backpack on while you are standing?
3. Now stand on one foot only for three additional minutes.
4. Is it is more comfortable to stand on one foot or two? Describe how you feel when you stand on two feet versus one foot.
5. Now try to stand in place on one tiptoe for three minutes.

   What's happening? When you stand, your body pushes down on the floor with a force (your weight) and the floor pushes back on you with an equal and opposite force. These forces are balanced and, therefore, you are able to stand in place. The tired feeling you experience standing in place for a long time is the result of the pressure you experience. The pressure is even greater when you stand on the tip of one foot. How much greater is it?

6. Use your math skills to calculate the increase in pressure under the three conditions—standing normally, on one foot, and on tiptoe. You'll need to know your weight—which is equal to the force you exert—and the surface area of your feet.

7. Find your weight (in pounds) on the bathroom scale.

8. To find the surface area of each of your feet, stand on the large sheet of paper and have a partner trace around one of your feet, then the other. Next, stand on tiptoe on one foot, and have a partner trace around the part of your foot that is touching the paper.

9. Count the number of squares inside the outline of your foot. Include partial squares in your count. The number of squares is equal to the surface area of your foot or feet (in square inches).

10. Pressure is measured in pounds per square inch, or psi. To calculate the pressure your body exerts when you are standing on two feet, use the data you've just collected in the following formula:

$$\text{pressure} = \frac{\text{force (your weight)}}{\text{surface area (both feet)}}$$

11. What do you think the pressure would be if you were standing on only one foot? Use the same equation to calculate the pressure from standing on one foot, then from standing on one tiptoe.

12. Compare these three number values. Which one is highest? Were you surprised?

---

nearly half of the volunteer's total weight. They also saw, as they had predicted, that their ideas about variations due to the way one stood could lead to variations in the numbers on the scales as volunteers shifted their bodies in various ways. Many times, individual students requested that the volunteers stand in a nearly spread-eagle fashion and tell what their weight was then. Several students suggested that there should be a weight loss above the centered point of the two scales. It appears there is a frequently held belief that weight was lost or unmeasured for the middle of the body not directly over the scale.

While interest was high, we encouraged all students to weigh themselves on one and then two scales. Students wishing to hide their weights could do so. However, by this time most students were so curious that they ceased worrying about our cultural conditioning toward thinness and made their measurements openly.

When the discussions were finished, we decided we had achieved our goal of science-math integration when students wondered as they organized their handouts and notes into discrete sections, "Is this science or is this math?"

Assessment

Have students write in their journals each night for homework. Encourage them to reflect on the following questions:

- What did you learn today?
- Describe what was new and what was review for you.
- What was surprising to you about today's topics and investigations?
- What was confusing about today's work? Do you feel uncertain about any aspects of our investigations?
- Is there anything else that you would like to know about this topic?

- How does this mesh with the other things you have learned in this class?

Joan Lindgren is an assistant professor in the College of Education at Florida Atlantic University—MacArthur Campus in Jupiter, Florida. Marcia Cushall is an associate professor in the Educational Professions Department at Frostburg State University in Maryland.

References

EQUALS Investigations. 1994. *Flea-sized surgeons.* University of California, Berkeley: Lawrence Hall of Science.

Stepans, J. 1994. *Targeting students' science misconceptions.* Riverview, FL: Idea Factory, Inc.

Resources

Burns, M. 1987. *A collection of math lessons: Grades 3–6.* New Rochelle, NY: The Math Solution Publications.

Christmann, E. P. 2000. Converting with confidence. *Science Scope* 23 (8): 42–44.

Leyden, M. B. 1993. Teaching science: Expansion and contraction matters. *Teaching K–8* (October): 36–37.

Liem, T. L. 1990. *Invitations to science inquiry.* 2nd ed. Chino Hills, CA: Science Inquiry Enterprises.

Trash or Treasure?

By Donna Kowalczyk

Most children know they should not pollute but have never considered why. I created a lesson for third-through fifth-grade students that makes the connection concrete. In the lesson, students consider the possible effects a trash item would have on an animal and its habitat, identifying ways in which the piece of trash could be helpful or harmful to the animal and its habitat and then communicating their ideas about how people can clean a polluted environment to make it safe for animals. Along the way, students use reading skills to gather information about the animal and its habitat, writing skills to record their ideas on paper, and speaking skills to share their ideas about their animal and piece of trash with the class. Technology can also be integrated if the teacher chooses to use websites for the reading portion of the activity.

Getting Ready

Before the activity, I collect various household trash items: plastic milk containers, paper wrappers from food, cellophane, Styrofoam packing material, cardboard juice containers, aluminum foil, newspaper, plastic bags, paper towel rolls, empty cardboard boxes, and office paper. Make sure you select items that are clean and safe for students to handle—items free of sharp edges, food crumbs, liquids, or jagged metals. Each student will receive one piece of trash along with information on one animal. I use *Wildlife Fact File* cards (CSA 1996), but you could easily assemble your own fact sheets with any animal reference book. These cards contain detailed information about a specific animal's habitat, breeding, food and hunting, lifestyle, and physical features.

For the reading portion of this activity, I select materials focusing on various animal species describing their life cycles, habitats, diet, nutrition, hunting practices, geographic locations, and any other interesting facts about the animal. The online *Zoobooks* magazine and the National Wildlife Federation's Kids and Families web pages provide excellent online reading information for the activity (see Internet). The reading portion of the activity may be conducted in a computer lab, allowing students to select their own websites and gather information about their animals independently. Students may also work in pairs or small groups to find relevant information online or from one of the reading sources.

Creative Thinking in Action

I start with a brief introduction about animals, their habitats, and the role of pollution in the environment. I ask the students to talk about some of their favorite animals. Whales, dolphins, rabbits, deer, foxes, snakes, and fish are among some of the common species my students love to discuss. We usually spend 10 minutes discussing the similarities and differences among the types of species students added to the discussion. The terms *mammal, amphibian, fish, reptile, insect,* and *habitat* emerge from the discussion. I emphasize the fact that an animal's *habitat* is the place where it lives, breeds, feeds, and hunts. Next, I question the students about pollution. "Pollution is caused by people who throw their garbage and waste in the environment" is a common statement given by the students. "Let's think about how pollution affects animals in their habitats" is my response.

As we discuss what we know about the role of pollution in the environment, I explain to my students that they will each be reading about a specific animal and investigating a piece of trash during the activity. Then I assign a different animal to each student and distribute a trash item to each one. Before distributing the material, I pose the following questions to guide students during the activity:

- Where does the animal live?
- What does it eat?
- How does it get its food?
- How would you describe its habitat?

I also ask students to list five interesting facts they learn about the animal as they are reading. Next, I distribute one animal fact card to each student. Allow about 10 minutes for the students to read the cards and list the information.

Next, I ask them to list three to four properties of the trash item on a piece of paper and encourage them to apply the information they read regarding the animal and its habitat. For example, I tell the students that some properties of an empty plastic soda bottle are *soft, plastic, round,* and *narrow* to give them an idea of how they can describe their own trash items. I then encourage them to imagine that the animal they read about encountered that piece of trash in its environment. I ask them to consider two

questions as they handle the trash and imagine this scenario:

- How would this piece of trash be harmful to your animal?
- How would this piece of trash be helpful to your animal?

Following this part of the activity, I invite each student to tell the class about his or her animal, piece of trash, and ideas about the helpful and harmful nature of the trash. Many students generate very creative and humorous ideas and uses for the trash and list appropriate adjectives to describe each trash item and animal. Some examples of student responses are given below:

- Nathan read about the raccoon and received a piece of aluminum foil as his piece of trash. *Shiny, soft, flexible,* and *thin* were properties Nathan listed describing the aluminum foil. He thought that the foil would "hurt the raccoon's stomach" if it was eaten. Nathan concluded that since raccoons wash their food before they eat, they could use the foil to "wrap their food to keep bugs out of it if they didn't want to eat it right away." Students often share unlikely uses for the trash items. Encouraging them to try to think like they believe their animals would think as they encounter the trash is one way I respond to those unusual ideas. I also urge them to imagine what life would be like for the animal living in the habitat described in the fact card. These suggestions sometimes help students to think of more realistic and believable uses for the trash items.
- Renee read about the common mole and imagined that a plastic antacid bottle would act as a good place to hide food from other animals. She also felt that any medicine left inside the bottle when found by the mole could be toxic if ingested by the mole. "I

Figure 1.

Trash or Treasure? activity rubric

	3	2	1
Identifies important information	The student lists all of the main points about the animal and its habitat using the article as a reference.	The student lists three to five main points about the animal and its habitat but uses the article as a reference.	The student can list or name two main points from the article but does not highlight the important points.
Identifies facts	The student accurately locates and identifies three to five specific facts about the animal and its habitat and offers a thorough explanation of the information contained in the article.	The student accurately locates two facts about the animal and its habitat but offers a weak explanation of the information contained in the article.	The student has difficulty locating facts and explaining what was contained in the article.
Identifies details	The student identifies three to five details about the animal, its habitat, and the trash item and does not refer to the article to explain what was read.	The student is able to identify two details about the animal, its habitat, and the trash item but needs to refer to the article to explain what was read.	The student has difficulty identifying details about the animal, its habitat, and the trash item and has difficulty explaining what was read.
Summarizes information	The student uses three to five sentences to describe the helpful and harmful effects of the trash item and can clearly communicate his or her ideas.	The student uses one to two sentences to describe the helpful or harmful effects of the trash item but has some difficulty communicating his or her ideas.	The student has difficulty developing sentences to describe the helpful and harmful effects of the trash item and has great difficulty communicating ideas.

think a large mole might get its head stuck inside the bottle if it tried to crawl or sniff inside," she added. Renee described the bottle as *hard, plastic,* and *small.*

- Neal shared his ideas about the gray fox and an empty cardboard box. *Flexible, sturdy,* and *brown* were the adjectives Neal used to describe the box. He said the cardboard box could be used as insulation for the fox's den during cold winter months and for trapping small animals for food. He also stated that the box could be harmful to newborn cubs that are born blind and helpless if they became trapped inside the box and would be easy prey for predators when the adult foxes are away from the den.

- Christina read about the angelfish and its lifestyle as a reef-dwelling fish. After examining a brightly colored cereal box, she concluded that since the angelfish has colorful markings, it could use the cereal box as camouflage to hide from other reef-dwelling predators. One negative aspect she discovered was the idea that if the angelfish became trapped inside the box it would become easy prey for its predators. She described the cereal box as *bright, colorful,* and *empty* and was surprised to realize that she used some of the same words to describe the angelfish.

- Joey read about the pilot whale. He had no problems generating ideas about the metal soda can and was eager to share his ideas with the class. The *bendable, shiny,* and *sharp* soda can could get caught in the pilot whale's teeth and prevent it from grabbing its prey as it hunts in the North Atlantic waters. He thought the can could help the pilot whale to locate its prey if the can was floating in the water and the whale's echolocation bounced off the can indicating the presence of a large school of fish.

I am always impressed with the students' creative, logical, and reflective thinking abilities as they complete the activity. Not only do they exhibit an understanding of the effects of pollution on animals and their habitats, they also gain additional knowledge about the specific animal species, its habitat, and special features. The concepts of *camouflage, echolocation, prey,* and *predators* were additional concepts typically encountered during the reading segment of the activity and are eagerly shared by the students during the closing discussion.

Extending the Activity

After students share their ideas, I present some additional questions to extend their thinking and spark more interest in reading about animals and their habitats:

- What kinds of litter or trash items have you seen in the environment around your home or school?
- What role do people play in transporting trash into the environment?
- How can people work to clean up the environment for the health and benefit of animals?
- What happens to trash and litter that remain in an environment for a long period of time?
- How do trash and litter affect people?

Another way to extend the learning experience is to take the students on a short field trip around the school building. During the field trip, tell the students to explore the area, looking for animals, insects, living things, and litter that may be in the immediate environment. Encourage them to think about the negative and positive effects of the trash items on the living things they encounter in the outdoor school environment. The field trip helps the students connect the classroom activity to the physical environment surrounding the school.

Final Thoughts

During the activity, the students write their ideas on paper and share them with the class. Figure 1 is a rubric to assess the students' writing, speaking abilities, and formation of ideas regarding the positive and negative uses of the trash. Students may also record their ideas in their science journals, which may be assessed informally or with the use of a rubric.

Following the activity, I ask my students what they learned from the experience. Students invariably say they learned many interesting facts about their animals and that they enjoyed discussing the logical and sometimes silly uses the animals had for the trash items. In my book, that makes this trash-inspired activity a real treasure.

Donna Kowalczyk is an assistant professor at the University of Pittsburgh at Johnstown in Johnstown, Pennsylvania.

Resources

Conservation Society of America (CSA). 1996. *Wildlife fact file*. New York: International Masters Publishers.

National Research Council (NRC). 1996. *National Science Education Standards*. Washington, DC: National Academy Press.

Internet

National Wildlife Federation Kids and Families
www.nwf.org/kids
Zoobooks magazine
www.zoobooks.com

Connecting to the Standards
This article relates to the following National Science Education Standards (NRC 1996):

Content Standards
Grades K–4
Standard C: Physical Science
• The characteristics of organisms
• Organisms and environments

Inquiring Into the Digestive System

By Carlos Schroeder

Teaching science by means of inquiry-based projects has the potential to transform the science lab into a place of debate and discovery, but teachers run the risk of either leaving students to work too independently or forcing them to be too dependent on our guidance. With such issues in mind, I implemented some changes in the way topics are covered and assessment is made. In sixth grade, each new science unit lasts approximately a full quarter (10 weeks, with four weekly lessons of science) and is divided into three major stages: classroom introduction; group (or individual) inquiry projects; and projects, presentations, and discussions. An example of the structure is included based on an inquiry into the digestive system.

Stage 1: Introduction to Themes

Initially, an average of three or four weeks is spent on classroom activities, reading texts from different sources (textbook, magazine articles, websites), and performing laboratory experiments, which introduce the themes covered in the unit. This stage is pretty traditional, with lab report formats and textbook homework. However, when it comes time for experimentation, students don't get a handout with instructions to follow. Instead, the materials to be used are listed on a large board on the wall, along with some simple diagrams that illustrate key steps in the procedure. Students must take the initiative of joining in small groups of three or four, gathering the materials from a resource bench, finding their way through the procedure, and taking notes of the steps followed and results observed, which they'll need for the written report, usually done as homework. Once the activity is done, the groups engage in a final discussion. From this discussion, they are expected to build an explanation for the results. The role of the teacher during the whole process is that of a facilitator, suggesting or reminding students of steps to be followed during the procedure, stressing some of the results, and giving clues or proposing questions for the final discussion. The reports are written individually and must be divided into four illustrated sections:

1. List of materials
2. Steps followed in the procedure
3. Results observed (preferably in charts, tables, graphs)
4. Conclusions drawn from the results

In the first lesson of the human digestive system unit, students were asked to sketch the human digestive system without any previous reference. These initial spontaneous sketches were kept until the end of the unit to be used in the final discussion. The class discussed why food must be digested. Students began to understand that food must be transformed into other substances before the body can use it.

In the first lab experiment, the next day, students compared how fast effervescent pills, both whole and powdered, dissolved in water. The only further instruction given was to stir the water once, soon after the pills were added (sometimes the powdered pill stays afloat and doesn't dissolve). In the next experiment, the day after, students made a simple kind of cheese in the lab, using warm milk and vinegar. The activity began with students collecting the materials from the central bench: chemical-splash goggles, one 500 mL beaker with warm milk, one 50 mL beaker with vinegar, and a spoon. They were instructed to pour the vinegar into the milk, stir it, and observe. Within a few seconds, the milk curds. In this experiment, they could visually detect the effects of adding an acid to milk, similar to what happens when stomach hydrochloric acid is added to food. After this experiment was done, the class engaged in a final discussion about the two activities. The central question in the discussion was "how to relate these two experiments to the theme we're studying." The other questions I proposed to guide them through the discussion were "What kinds of changes happened in the experiments, chemical or physical, and when?" "Why did the reaction in the first experiment happen faster with the ground pills?" "Why do you think we used warm milk rather than cold milk?" and "Why should the food we eat be transformed into other substances by our bodies?" Students were quick to propose that nutrients are needed to keep organisms alive and that food cannot be used by cells before being transformed ("or else we could simply inject, for example, mashed potatoes, into our blood vessels," as one of them said). These questions led students to re-

alize that digestion is separated into a physical change (mechanical digestion) and a chemical change (chemical digestion). In other words, they understood that food can be transformed into other substances by adding chemicals to it and that breaking food into smaller pieces eases the process of chemically changing it.

Once students had agreed on the importance of breaking food into small pieces and transforming it into other substances so our bodies can absorb it, the next step was to discuss what other stages would be necessary to complete the process of digestion. The class debated their initial ideas, which included the existence of different pathways for solids and liquids and the existence of an internal organ that grinds the food (similar to a bird's gizzard). These two ideas were discarded by the class as they realized food, liquid or solid, is swallowed into the same tube (which they couldn't yet name) and that the teeth already do the job of grinding it. The idea I highlighted as important was that blood carries nutrients through the body (deduced from the fact that it circulates through the body). They concluded that the remaining stages are transferring nutrients to the blood and eliminating wastes, mostly from the realization that, in their words, "We eat everyday. If we didn't get rid of wastes, we would burst." Students ended the lesson sketching a map of the needed stages of digestion, similar to Figure 1 (except for the organs). Using this map as reference, students spent the next lesson, a few days after, searching for the names of organs involved and the role of each one, using their textbook as the main reference as well as other books available in the classroom. They also identified the accessory glands responsible for producing substances, such as digestive juices, and their importance. By the end of this lesson, they were capable of sketching a complete map, like the one shown in Figure 1.

Students read a magazine article entitled "In Search of the Perfect French Fry," printed from the online version of *Science News for Kids* (see

Figure 1.

Steps of digestion and the organs involved

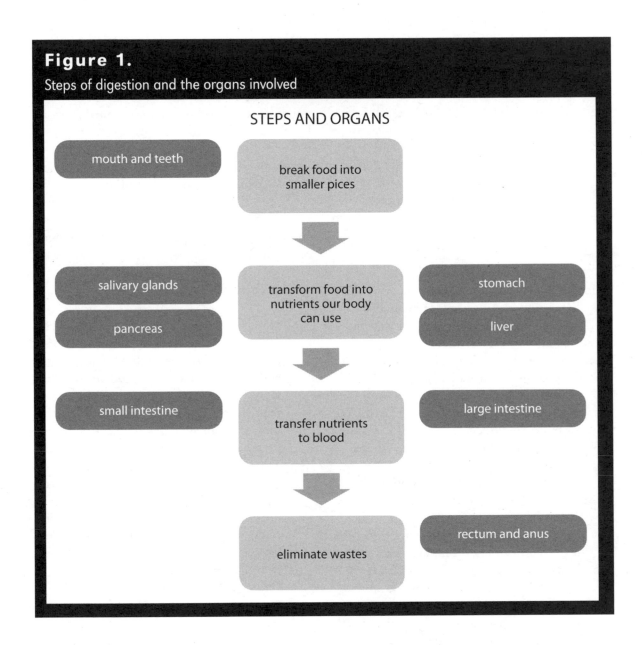

STEPS AND ORGANS

mouth and teeth

break food into smaller pices

salivary glands

pancreas

transform food into nutrients our body can use

stomach

liver

small intestine

transfer nutrients to blood

large intestine

eliminate wastes

rectum and anus

Resources), to introduce nutrition. The lesson ended with students listing food they liked to eat but believed wasn't good for their health and explaining why they thought so. During the next lessons, concepts such as proteins, carbohydrates, vitamins, cholesterol, and fats were introduced, mainly using the textbook. As in other cases when the book was used, students were asked first to browse the pages assigned, gaze at figures, tables, graphs, read the headings, and tell what their impressions were, what the theme of the text was, and what kind of information they expected. After reading and working on section reviews, they were asked to compare their initial impressions of the text with what they actually read, indicating what they expected to find and how satisfied they were with the information provided by the book. With this approach, they began to have ideas for their projects. The next day, a lesson was spent reading different industrialized food wrappers (such as those on cookies, noodles, and sodas) to investigate their contents. The objective was to detect patterns, such as in energy content, amount of carbohydrates, fibers, proteins, percentage of recommended daily diet, that could help distinguish what is normally classified as *junk food* (chips and cookies, for example) from what is called *healthy food* (cereal bars and fruit juices, for example). After these lessons, students were asked to review and refine their list of unhealthy foods.

Stage 2: Inquiry Projects

Students work in pairs in this stage, but occasionally are allowed to work individually or in small groups of three or four. The time allocated for these projects varies from four to six weeks, depending on their level of complexity. The first two weeks are dedicated to planning the projects and gathering information. The next two to four weeks are used for organizing posters, building models, preparing the demonstrations, and giving the final presentations.

There are three mandatory components of these projects:

1. A summary of the topics covered in the introductory weeks. This summary can be in the form of a poster or a PowerPoint (or overhead projector) presentation.
2. A model or an experimental demonstration that helps illustrate the topic.
3. Further research. Students must choose one of the themes covered to enrich or some other theme, provided that it is directly related to the unit topic but not covered during the first weeks; the group researches on the chosen topic and adds their personal interests and discoveries.

In the digestive system unit, students began by gathering in pairs and planning their projects. Elements of this stage included the design of

the poster summarizing topics, research from books or the internet, and teacher-approved experimentation. During each lesson, I would hold a brief meeting with each group (about 10 minutes), as the other ones continued to work. During such meetings, the groups are expected to show their plans, sketches of models, lists of materials for demonstrations, and pieces of information they already gathered. I advise them, mostly suggesting ways to simplify their models. Seldom has a project cost more than about $10, including posters, models, and demonstrations.

Project examples included the following:

- Diseases of the digestive system—This was the most popular topic; many groups researched diseases such as colon cancer and appendicitis. One student, working alone, was curious about finding why so many food wrappings indicate whether their content includes gluten or not and prepared a presentation on celiac disease.
- The job of nutritionists—The article on french fries raised some groups' interest in this occupation. Some students were interested to know where nutritionists work, what kind of degree is needed, and what local institutions (such as universities) offer courses.
- How food is transformed into energy— Two students, working together, expressed their discontentment with the textbook, which never discussed how food was finally transformed into energy, nor where this transformation happened. They were encouraged to search in seventh-grade textbooks and made a presentation on the process of cell respiration using the overhead projector.

The models and demonstrations prepared by the groups made use of a large variety of materials and covered all topics studied. Students were in charge of the design of models and demonstrations, which included the following:

- Models of the digestive system—Two students built models using cloth stuffed with sponges. A group built its model using papier mâché.
- Food pyramid—Students built a model of the food pyramid using wood for the pyramid itself, Styrofoam and papier mâché for the fruits and other kinds of food.
- Demonstrations—A group of three students prepared a demonstration showing all steps of digestion, using trays, plastic bags, food scraps, and several different liquids (water with food colorings) representing substances such as saliva, acids, and bile.

Stage 3: Presentations

A period of approximately one week is allocated for the groups to present their projects to the rest of the class. Each 45-minute lesson is divided into three short presentations in which the groups talk about their projects, and a final lesson is used for general discussions in which the groups express their own impressions of their achievements and contrast them with their expectations. The last week is used to prepare a large one-hour presentation, with bits of each project. A younger grade level is invited to attend. The whole class negotiates, under my supervision, what parts of each project will be added to the final presentation, and all participate in the preparation and presentation to the guest class. This has proved to be an important final step for a series of reasons: Students get a broader perspective of the themes covered, learn more about each other's points of view

(once all projects are condensed into one), and, most of all, even students (or groups) that normally don't volunteer to work together do cooperate during this stage.

Conclusions

Though there are still many aspects to improve, the sequence of these stages followed in each unit of study has facilitated students' initiative. The way laboratory experiments are proposed during the introductory weeks helps them analyze results and build explanations from the information they gather. The fact that no handout is given during these laboratory activities forces them to develop orderly ways of taking notes.

The sketches of the digestive system made by a student before and after the unit of study show strong evidence of how their mental models improved during this period. Assessment is mostly based on "before-after" activities like this, the debates on the projects, and written reports. Tests are a very occasional part of the assessment. Since the adoption of this structure, students' projects, especially their models and demonstrations, have become more and more sophisticated. Given a little teacher input but lots of incentive, they are learning not to fear taking risks, to ask themselves questions and search for their own answers, to express dissatisfaction with ready and simplified explanations, and to work cooperatively in groups.

Carlos Schroeder is a science teacher at the Pan American School in Porto Alegre, Brazil.

Resources

In Search of the Perfect French Fry
www.sciencenewsforkids.org/articles/20030723/Feature1.asp.

Beak Adaptations

By Frank W. Guerrierie

Adaptation—the modification of an organism or its parts—is a basic principle of evolution. The following hands-on simulation helps students understand adaptation by examining the diversity of bird beaks. Students use a variety of household items, such as strainers and pliers, to simulate different types of bird beaks. They then attempt to use their "beaks" to feed on an assortment of simulated bird foods. Students soon discover that, just as in nature, each beak is adapted to gathering and feeding on specific types of food.

Pecking Orders

Before class, set up 12 feeding stations around the room using the food sources listed in Figure 1. During the activity, students will be required to replenish the food source at each station after they are done "eating," so make sure you have a surplus available of each food type. Set out your collection of beaks (see Figure 2) on a lab table.

When class begins, divide students into pairs and provide each with the Bird Buffet activity sheet and a data collection sheet. After selecting a beak, each pair should move to a station. On your signal, the food gathering can begin. The data collection sheet explains how each food

Figure 1.
Food sources

A suitable container should be placed at each station to hold the collected food. As the food items are counted they should be returned to the feeding station for the next group to gather. Items representing snails, flesh, and insects should be discarded after they are counted and replaced with new ones.

- duckweed—green Styrofoam peanuts floating in a container of water
- snails—elbow macaroni in a narrow-mouth jar
- grubs—M&Ms in a bowl of dry oatmeal
- nectar—colored water in a large graduated cylinder
- earthworms—gummy worms hidden in a basket of artificial grass
- small seeds—such as radish seeds, scattered on a tray
- large seeds—such as corn, scattered on a tray
- flesh—staples embedded in a cardboard box
- scale insects—a sheet of small round stickers taped to a desktop
- fish—colored paper clips in a beaker of water
- beetles—raisins hidden in a container of potting soil
- termites—cloves placed in holes (1 cm in diameter, 2 cm deep) drilled into a piece of wood

Figure 2.
Beak simulators

Although the original setup of this lab takes a little time and money, all materials can be stored in a box and reused from year to year. Here are some household items that can simulate beaks:

- slotted spoon
- forceps
- scissors
- probe
- pliers
- plastic spoon
- small strainer
- turkey baster
- tongs
- eye dropper
- chopsticks
- staple remover

Bird buffet

Procedure
1. Select a tool from those provided to use as a bird beak for gathering food.
2. Decide which partner will be the first to gather food and which will record the data.
3. Move to the first feeding station and, at the teacher's signal, see how much food you can gather in 15 seconds.
4. Record the data in the chart provided.
5. Return the food you have gathered and clean up the station.
6. Move to the next station and repeat steps 3 through 5.
7. After you have cycled through all the stations, choose another beak, switch roles, and cycle through the stations again.

After you have completed both cycles, examine the beaks depicted below and answer the following questions:
A. What tool performs a similar function as this beak?
B. What type of food is this beak adapted for gathering?

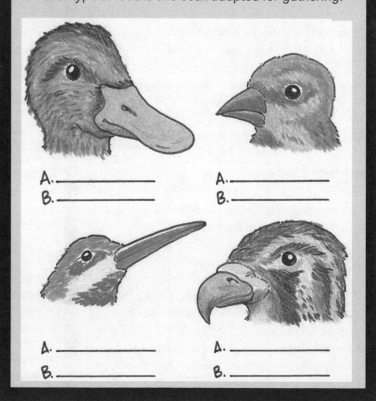

A. _____
B. _____

A. _____
B. _____

A. _____
B. _____

A. _____
B. _____

item should be gathered. After 15 seconds or so, signal students to stop feeding and to record the amount of food gathered. Before students move on to the next station, make sure they clean up after themselves and replenish the food at their present station. When students have cycled through the stations, they should select another beak, switch jobs, and cycle through the stations again. This gives both students a chance to test their food-gathering skills using a beak.

At the end of the second feeding cycle, gather the data for comparison. Finish with a discussion of the four bird

Data collection sheet

Food item	Amount eaten by piece or in mL	
	Tool_____	Tool_____
1. Strain water for duckweed		
2. Pick up snails and break shells		
3. Pick up some grubs		
4. Suck up some nectar		
5. Pick up some earthworms		
6. Pick up some small seeds		
7. Pick up some large seeds		
8. Tear off some flesh		
9. Scrape up some scale insects		
10. Catch some fish		
11. Pick up some beetles		
12. Pick up some termites		

Adaptations worksheet

An adaptation is any characteristic of an organism that makes it better suited for survival in its habitat. Adaptations help organisms move, gather food, reproduce, protect themselves, and carry on other life processes.

Select any organism. Discuss its adaptations by researching the following questions:

1. Common name of organism
2. Scientific name of organism
3. Geographic range
4. Habitat
5. Diet
6. Describe the organism's adaptations to its diet and habitat (in complete sentences):
   a.
   b.
   c.
   d.
   e.

beaks depicted at the bottom of the procedure sheet.

Extensions

As a follow-up, ask students to design an all-purpose beak that can gather each of the food sources used in the lab, or have them research and draw pictures of birds' feet and explain how they are adapted to their environment. I end this activity with a class discussion of two common organisms, such as a barrel cactus and a lion. During the discussion, students list and explain the adaptations the organisms exhibit. Next, they research organisms on their own using the Adaptations worksheet. Their findings can be written up as a report or shared with the class as a presentation.

Frank W. Guerrierie is a science teacher at Eisenhower Middle School in Succasunna, New Jersey.

Choice, Control, and Change

By Pamela Koch, Angela Calabrese Barton, Rabi Whitaker, and Isobel Contento

For the past few weeks, my class has been studying human body systems and learning about how food is digested, metabolized, and used to help their bodies function and grow. Now, students are ready to look at what happens when something goes wrong, by modeling the flow of blood through arteries that have become clogged with plaque. This demonstration sets up students for further exploration of how lifestyle choices can impact the cardiovascular system. (See *www.tc.edu/cfe/choice.html* for the full lesson plan.)

Each pair of students gets two sections of clear plastic tubing (about three-fourths of an inch in diameter), a chunk of yellow modeling dough, and a cup of water that's been dyed red. Students stuff the modeling dough into one of the tubes, push a pencil through to make a narrow hole, and have a model of a clogged artery. One student, holding the clogged tube in front of his eye like a telescope, says, "Whoa, that blood is going to get all stuck up in here!"

After making predictions about what they think will happen when the "blood" travels through each tube, students set about their investigations. As they pour the "blood" through each of the tubes, it's easy to see that the flow is much smoother and faster through the healthy artery. Students use their observations to generate new questions: How much blood can travel through each artery in the same amount of time? What happens if the artery gets completely blocked?

Two students push more modeling clay into one end of their clogged artery until the hole is the size of a pencil point. As one student pours the blood into the artery, her partner observes the trickle falling into the bowl underneath. "It's not getting through—the heart will have to work extra hard to get blood to go through a clogged vessel."

After cleaning up, students discuss how the clogged artery could cause a heart attack or a stroke, depending on its location in the body. One student observes that "high cholesterol is more serious than just being fat." Students are particularly concerned about whether there is a way to unclog a vessel, because, as another student says, "I do not want that stuff in my blood!"

Students refer to a reading on heart-healthy eating habits. One student is dismayed to learn that most donuts can contribute to high cholesterol, but another student is pleased to find that oatmeal, as long as not too much butter and sugar are added, is a heart-friendly food. "My grandma likes oatmeal too," she says. "I'll ask if we could have that at home sometimes."

Childhood obesity and its long-term health implications should be of major concern to science educators. Our team of science educators, nutrition educators, and classroom teachers has been working in this area for several years in support of teachers and youth learning more about this phenomenon and what they can do to support healthy food and activity choices. Prior to this lesson, students had collected data on what kinds of foods are typically available in their neighborhood stores, investigated how humans have a universal liking for fat and sugar, experimented with measuring how much fat and sugar are in food, studied energy balance in the body, and collected data on their own eating and physical activity. All of these activities are part of a larger five-unit, 19-lesson module called Choice, Control, and Change (C3) developed at Teachers College Columbia University (see Resource). C3 is a standards-driven and inquiry-based curriculum that is framed around the driving question, "How can we use scientific evidence to help us make healthy food and activity choices?"

C3 teaches life science through investigating how the human body works; why a state of dynamic equilibrium—balancing energy in and energy out—is important for our bodies to function well; how conditions such as high blood cholesterol and high blood sugar develop and what we can do to prevent them; and how to make food and exercise choices that will promote health and decrease the risk of many lifestyle-related diseases such as heart disease, type 2 diabetes, and some cancers. The curriculum provides teachers and students with rigorous, yet relevant investigations into how an understanding of biology, the environment, and personal behaviors affects weight and health. Classroom activities provide opportunities for students to explore their experiences and feelings and to reflect on them through self-assessment of eating and activity patterns

and learning about consequences. Use of our inquiry-based approach provides students the opportunity and skills to learn about making choices and taking control.

Childhood Obesity: Preventing an Epidemic

The issue of childhood obesity has become a national phenomenon. The rates have been increasing over the past two decades. In fact, the research on childhood obesity indicates that over 50% of the population in the United States is considered to be overweight or obese, with the number of overweight children doubling in the past two decades. Health workers, nutritionists, and social scientists have also shed new light on the long-term health implications of overweight children having increased risk for elevated blood lipids, increased cholesterol levels, type 2 diabetes, and social discrimination that could lead to obesity later in life.

Yet, prevention of childhood obesity is a complex phenomenon, bringing together human biology, environmental factors, and personal choices. The time for this kind of education is now, because the social, physical, and economic environment have dramatically changed our food consumption and exercise habits—energy in and energy out—over the past 25 years. The amount of energy consumed from low nutrient-density snacks and sweetened beverages has doubled, while screen time (watching TV and playing video games) has increased, and physical activities have decreased about 40%. Clearly, youth have to make choices in an environment in which food is ubiquitous, tasty, cheap, and heavily advertised; being sedentary is easily setting them up for a lifetime of being in positive energy balance.

Despite the complexity of the childhood obesity phenomenon, we know that prevention of weight gain is easier, less expensive, and more effective than treatment. The Surgeon General's 2001 Call to Action includes a specific call for obesity prevention activities focused on healthy eating and physical activity in schools. Yet, to date, few projects exist that offer models for schools, and there is little consensus about how to teach kids the challenges associated with childhood obesity or at what grade levels such an intervention would be most effective. There are also questions about how any intervention program might balance between helping youth understand the problem and act on the problem, or what role science education might play in reversing the epidemic.

The Importance of Focusing on the Middle Grades

Although young children mainly make their food choices based on what they like, by middle school, cognitive-motivational processes become important influences on food choice as well. Youth become more able to link cause and effect and to perceive the consequences of their actions. Thus, they can make food choices in light of their perceptions, health and weight concerns, taste, and convenience. In terms of opportunity, adolescents in the United States receive close to $6 billion annually from caretakers in discretionary funds and spend half of it on snacks. Middle school youth have both the capacity and opportunity to practice personal control and mastery in the area of food choices and physical activity.

Behavior, however, is motivated not only by the anticipation that the behavior will bring about desired outcomes, but also by a strong sense of being able to exert personal control over their environment. Youth do have choices and need to learn to take control to create for themselves personal food and activity environments that are conducive to health and body-size regulation. It is important to provide youth the opportunity to achieve a sense of personal control and mastery through understanding the complex systems of biology, the environment, and their behaviors and by learning how to take

action based on their understandings. We call this personal control and mastery over their own behavior and the ability to create personal food and activity environments *competence*. Thus, youth will be able to experience self-determination and to gain personal satisfaction in achieving personal control. With such training, students are creating personal environments that are healthful and reduce the risk of obesity.

A Science-Education Approach to Childhood Obesity

In the past, childhood obesity interventions in schools have focused primarily on specific diet-related behavior, such as fat reduction or fruit and vegetable consumption. Although these interventions play an important role, students can also benefit from having skills to analyze food and exercise and to understand the dramatic changes they have undergone in a short time. This will give students the knowledge and skills they need to be able to maintain a balance of their energy in and energy out despite our current environment. In our work, we have proposed going beyond teaching students which behaviors to enact and the strategies to enact them. We also include how to think about food and their behaviors in ways that help them feel competent in navigating today's food and activity environment. Any program focused on childhood obesity should teach youth about human biology and why they have innate preferences for certain kinds of foods, their ability to learn to eat in particular ways, and how that ability is influenced by social context.

Why Focus on Energy In and Energy Out?

Understanding the body's dynamic equilibrium is central to being able to make smart, scientifically grounded decisions about eating and activity. It is important for students in the middle grades to begin to understand why life depends on an organism's ability to regulate its

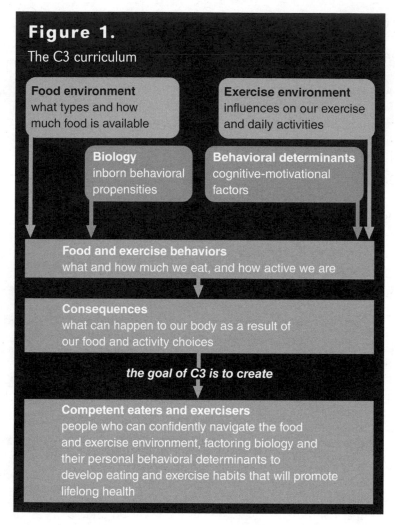

Figure 1.

The C3 curriculum

Food environment
what types and how
much food is available

Exercise environment
influences on our exercise
and daily activities

Biology
inborn behavioral
propensities

Behavioral determinants
cognitive-motivational
factors

Food and exercise behaviors
what and how much we eat, and how active we are

Consequences
what can happen to our body as a result of
our food and activity choices

the goal of C3 is to create

Competent eaters and exercisers
people who can confidently navigate the food
and exercise environment, factoring biology and
their personal behavioral determinants to
develop eating and exercise habits that will promote
lifelong health

Lungs take in oxygen for the combustion of food, and they eliminate the carbon dioxide produced. The urinary system disposes of dissolved waste molecules, the intestinal tract removes solid wastes, and the skin and lungs rid the body of heat energy. The circulatory system moves all these substances to or from cells where they are needed or produced, responding to changing demands (National Science Education Standards, Standard C).

These ideas and others are covered in C3 in a systematic, rigorous exploration of students' personal food and activity choices. Drawing upon Science as Inquiry and Science in Personal and Social Perspectives, in addition to the Content Standards, students explore how they can use scientific evidence to make healthy food and activity choices. To delve into this larger question, students take up smaller investigations into five key questions:

- What influences our food and activity choices?
- How can we make sure we get the right amount of energy to help our bodies do what we want them to do?
- How can we use personal data to help us make healthful food and activity choices?
- Why are healthful food and activity choices important for our body?
- How can I maintain my skills as a competent eater and mover?

As Figure 1 shows, these ideas fit together to help students build a solid understanding of why a state of dynamic equilibrium—balancing energy in and energy out—is important for our bodies to function well.

Conclusion

To prevent childhood obesity, a combined approach must be taken. Youth must have opportunities to investigate and develop deep conceptual understandings of the complex

internal environment (National Science Education Standards, Standard C: Regulation and Behavior). Students need to understand that the amount of food energy (calories) a person requires varies with body weight, age, sex, activity level, and natural body efficiency. Regular exercise is important for maintaining a healthy heart and lung system, good muscle tone, and bone strength. It is also important for students to understand how the body uses food for energy and building materials: The food must first be digested into molecules that are absorbed and transported to cells. To burn food for the release of energy stored in it, oxygen must be supplied to cells and carbon dioxide removed.

relationships among their biology, the environment, and personal behaviors. They also need adequate scaffolding opportunities to develop the scientific skills they need to become competent eaters and exercisers. Whatever one's approach is, one thing is clear: Youth will continue to be bombarded with opportunities to increase their fat and sugar intake cheaply and easily, while remaining sedentary. This is not acceptable. We must find ways to work with individuals both inside and outside of school to help youth gain the understandings and skills they need to competently navigate their worlds to make better and healthier choices.

Pamela Koch is the executive director of the Center for Food and Environment at Teachers College Columbia University in New York. Angela Calabrese Barton is an associate professor of science education at Michigan State University in East Lansing, Michigan. Rabi Whitaker is a research assistant for Choice, Control, and Change, and Isobel Contento is the Mary Schwarz Rose professor of nutrition education at Teachers College, Columbia University, in New York.

Acknowledgment

This project was made possible by Science Education Partnership Award (SEPA) grant number R25 RR020412 from the National Center for Research Resources (NCRR), a component of the National Institutes of Health (NIH). Its contents are solely the responsibility of the authors and do not necessarily represent the official views of NCRR or NIH.

References

Secretary of Health and Human Services and the Secretary of Education. 2000. Promoting better health for young people through physical activity and sports. Report to the President.

U.S. Department of Health and Human Services. 2001. Surgeon General's call to action to prevent and decrease overweight and obesity. U.S. Department of Health and Human Services, Public Health Service, Office of the Surgeon General.

Resource

Teachers College Columbia University. Choice, control, and change (C3)
www.tc.columbia.edu/life/choice.html

Are There Really Tree Frogs Living in the Schoolyard?

By Brooke L. Talley and Melissa A. Henkel

Every schoolyard presents a wealth of opportunities for science exploration. To capitalize on this resource, we developed an activity in which students assessed whether our schoolyard could provide a viable habitat for tree frogs. This inquiry-based module was composed of three lessons: A Hoppin' Tree Frog Adventure, Field Research Means Having Fun in the Field, and All These Data! The actual sampling for tree frogs occurred over a period of time with several sampling events. There is no specific minimum number of sampling events necessary, but there should be enough to determine if trends in the population exist.

Sampling for tree frogs is accomplished by temporarily installing vertical PVC pipes around the schoolyard, pounding one end into the ground. Tree frogs are commonly monitored by herpetologists (scientists that study amphibians and reptiles) using frog calls and PVC pipes. Tree frogs are attracted to these pipes for protection from the elements, as well as from predators. Being in a pipe does not en-

danger or trap the animal, so this is a safe and cost-effective way to perform large-scale studies for novice and expert herpetologists alike (Boughton 1997; Moulton et al. 1996; Staiger and Boughton 1999).

After a series of sampling events, students assessed their results to make conclusions about the schoolyard habitat. In our case, the number of tree frogs was very limited, so students determined the schoolyard habitat was not conducive to supporting a large population. The students were able to make suggestions for habitat and sampling regimen improvements. Results will vary depending on the schoolyard habitat and sampling effort.

Education Standards

The introductory lesson and inquiry-based labs on surveying tree frogs meet the following specific middle grades standards outlined in the National Science Education Standards: Content Standard A, Science as Inquiry; Content Standard C, Life Science (structure and function in living systems, regulation and behavior; populations and ecosystems, diversity and adaptations of organisms); Content Standard E, Science and Technology; and Content Standard F, Science in Personal and Social Perspectives (populations, resources, and environments; natural hazards) (NRC 1996).

Science and Ecology Background

Tree frogs typically live in trees—but may be found on other vertical surfaces, including outdoor school walls—clinging to the surface with enlarged adhesive toe pads. As bioindicators (biological indicators), tree frogs may become fewer in number when the environment is degraded (i.e., if the environment surrounding their habitat has been disturbed too extensively, then the tree frogs will either become locally extinct or move to more suitable areas).

Tree frogs are considered bioindicators because (1) they have permeable skin that directly absorbs toxins from the water and air; (2) they have two life phases consisting of an aquatic larval phase (tadpole) susceptible to change in water systems and an adult terrestrial phase (the adult frog) susceptible to change in terrestrial systems; and (3) they have a relatively low physiologic threshold for extreme change in temperature and moisture. Typically, tree frogs are negatively affected by habitat destruction, chemical pollution (water, land, and air), and increased UVB radiation.

A Hoppin' Tree-Frog Adventure (50 minutes)

Through a teacher-facilitated discussion (in congruence with a computer-generated PowerPoint presentation) the first part of the lesson introduces students to the importance of bioindicators. The presentation, including notes and lesson plan, is available online free-of-charge at the SPICE website (see Internet). Before beginning, teachers should familiarize themselves with the presentation so that they can anticipate student questions and responses. Specific notes are included on each slide for reference. The species list used in the presentation may need to be altered for different parts of the United States, because the online version is for Central Florida distributions. To have a better idea of what species may be present in the schoolyard, teachers should search the internet for their region's tree-frog species list. The entire presentation should take approximately 35 minutes. During the presentation, student participation is encouraged by asking probing questions, such as What are tree frogs? Why study them? If you could, how would you study tree frogs? The presentation is designed to get students interested in the subject matter and to have teachers gain a better understanding of their students' current understandings.

In this specific presentation, the tree-frog species covered are common to the southeastern United States: spring peeper *(Pseudacris crucifer)*, gray tree frog *(Hyla chrysoscelis)*, green tree frog *(H. cinerea)*, pinewood tree frog *(H. femoralis)*, and squirrel tree frog *(H. squirella)*. Photos and common names of all the species are included in the presentation. Scientific names can easily be substituted if the teacher desires. Many other tree-frog species exist throughout the United States (and the world). For more information about what species may be found in your area, look in a field guide or visit the U.S. Department of the Interior, Checklist of Amphibian Species and Identification Guide website (see Internet).

The second part of the lesson is an activity labeling individual PVC pipes for subsequent installation during the following class day. Some advanced preparation is needed for this portion, including cutting PVC pipes to the appropriate length (2.5 to 3 ft. segments). The total number and size of the pipes can be altered to fit your classroom needs. However, pipe diameter should not exceed two inches to prohibit occupancy by large exotic tree frogs (such as the Cuban tree frog). The same online lesson plan outlines instructions for six PVC pipes per class, for five classes (30 total pipes). Pipes can be purchased at any hardware store, where they can also be cut to length free of charge. Total purchase costs should not exceed $30. Teachers may also consider using various lengths and diameters so that students can interpret effectiveness of different variables for frog detection.

Student instructions for pipe preparation include details about how to label the PVC pipes so that each one is unique. Permanent markers should be made available for student use. PVC pipe preparation instructions can be laminated and reused for each lab group (Figure 1). Students should work in lab groups of three to four people. Once students finish labeling the pipes, they should set them aside for installation during the following class. The activity should take approximately 15 minutes. If students finish early, encourage them to begin thinking about the habitat where they want to install their pipes—for example, near buildings, in grassy areas, and near retention ponds.

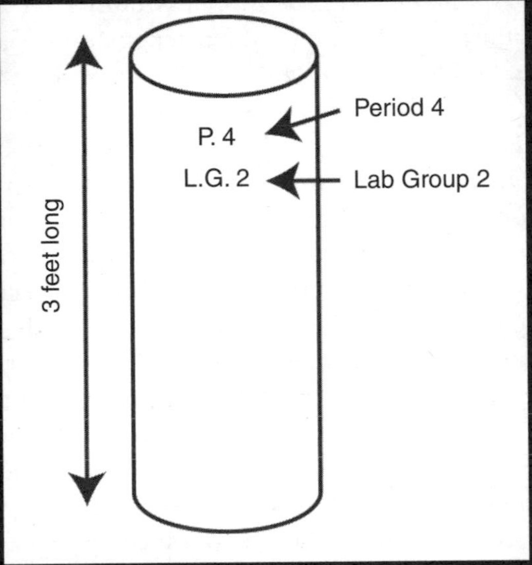

Field Research Means Having Fun in the Field (50 minutes)

The first part of the lesson begins with installation of the PVC pipes, followed by a data integrity discussion and practice using students' field notebooks. Before taking students outside to install PVC pipes, teachers should speak with relevant faculty and staff to locate potential survey areas where they have seen tree frogs. Once PVC pipes are installed, they should not be removed until the study is over. Therefore, pipes should not be placed in grassy areas where mowing occurs frequently, where heavy foot traffic could damage pipes, or in areas that should remain free from clutter for fire safety procedures. Students should decide where to install PVC pipes according to where they think frogs would occur naturally. Through discussion with one another, students will prob-

Figure 1.

PVC prep

Procedure (complete as a lab group)
1. Obtain one PVC pipe and a permanent marker from your teacher.
2. As a group, decide which end of the pipe will be the "top" and "bottom." On the top of the pipe, label the pipe with your period number (P. #), and lab group number (L.G. #).

ably decide to put pipes near buildings because tree frogs are known to "stick" to walls. They also may decide to put pipes near light sources because frogs could be drawn to eat bugs that surround the light at night.

PVC pipe installation is simple and easy. Once a site is selected, the pipe should be held vertically by one student at midheight. Another student should hammer on the top of the pipe with a rubber mallet until placement feels firm in the ground. The teacher should supervise the installation process and may need to assist in hammering. When done in one class period, pipe installation should take no longer than 25 minutes.

Sampling for tree frogs is as simple as looking down the vertical pipe to see if a frog is present. The first tree-frog sampling day should not occur until the two weeks following the installation. From that point, pipes can be checked as frequently as the class and teacher decide is warranted. Checking pipes one time per week is an adequate frequency that can easily be rotated through class periods to accommodate regular lessons. Checking the pipes for tree frogs only takes a few minutes, unless several frogs are detected that need identification.

Upon returning to the classroom after installing the PVC pipes, the teacher should pass out student field notebooks (one per student) and brief students on aspects of the notebook. Field notebooks can be printed from the SPICE website free of charge (see Internet). Inside the front cover, field notebooks have photocopies of tree-frog pictures and written characteristics (Conant and Collins 1998) to aid in species identification. When a frog is found, students must determine what species it is and write down additional data (period/group, date, time, area condition, weather, and notes) in their field notebooks. While explaining how the field notebook is used, discussion about scientific integrity should also be pursued. Emphasis must be placed on keeping accurate records that correctly identify what was observed.

Students must also understand that, when a tree frog is encountered, it should be left in place for the safety of the students themselves and of the tree frog. Even lotion on human skin can be toxic to the animal. Furthermore, tree frogs have fragile leg bones that could be broken if handled improperly. Tree frogs can be identified by size, shape, and color while they are inside the PVC pipe.

The last portion of the lesson is dedicated to practicing identification. As a lab group, students use their field notebooks to identify tree frogs seen in photos. These photos and an accompanying worksheet are also available on the SPICE website (see Internet). Teachers may choose to print and laminate photos for re-use, or students may look at them online if enough computers are available. The introduction to field notebooks and identification practice should also take 25 minutes.

All These Data! (50 minutes)

After completing several sampling events to look for tree frogs, the data must be compiled and analyzed. The exact number of sampling events is not as important as making sure that a clear trend is present before the study is terminated. The teacher should create a spreadsheet with all of the results to be manipulated by students. The lesson plan, available on the SPICE website (see Internet), gives specific instructions for using Microsoft Excel. Nonetheless, the teacher should become familiar with the program so that he or she can help students when they encounter problems. If computers are unavailable for student use, hand-written graphs can be created in place of those that are computer-generated.

The first graph to be created by each student plots sampling date against number of tree frogs detected. Once the graphs are completed, students independently respond to questions assessing the suitability of the schoolyard as a tree-frog habitat. Worksheets are available on the SPICE website (see Internet) free of charge. Next, students independently choose two variables to graph, either sampling event versus average temperature or relative humidity. These data are available online (historic weather data) or can be documented by students while looking for tree frogs. Students gain abiotic factors to see if there is a relationship with the presence or absence of tree frogs. Average temperature and relative humidity were chosen to be graphed because students understand what temperature and humidity changes feel like, relating personal experiences to what's being studied.

Following data manipulation, students assess their results and draw conclusions regarding how their schoolyard habitat performed, as well as how they would improve the study in the future. For example, we asked students, "If your school principal asked you about the results of our tree-frog study, what would you tell him about the habitat our schoolyard provides?" Their replies included:

- "I would tell him when the cold months come the frogs just want to be in something warm."
- "That are [sic] schoolyard is not really a habitat in warm weather, but in cold."
- "That the habitat does have frogs, but not many."

Assessment and Extensions

Student participation was heavily weighted by grading field notebooks and assessing general participation while outside. Were the students interested and engaged? Did they ask questions about what they did or did not see? Additionally, laboratory and computer activities were graded based on student responses and participation.

Extensions

- A lesson designed to help students practice classification focusing on tree-frog species is available on the SPICE website. Students create a binary classification system and dichotomous key that can be used when identifying individuals.
- The final lesson can be followed with discussion about amphibian declines. Additional information on amphibian decline can be found online or through the following student readings:

Brownlee, C. 2006. The case of the croaking frogs. *Science World* 62 (13): 14–17.

Hamilton, G. 2004. *Frog rescue: Changing the future for endangered wildlife.* New York: Firefly Books.

Conclusions

The tree-frog monitoring module is an easy way to get students out of the classroom and into the outdoors, while examining real organisms living in their immediate environment. Our students looked forward to sampling days, questioning whether they got to go outside as soon as they walked through the classroom door. While excited to get "out of class" by going outside, students were enthusiastic to write down data in their field notebooks and to correctly identify any tree frog seen. Even those students who typically kept to themselves during class became much more communicative and excited about science when out looking for tree frogs in small groups.

Brooke L. Talley is a graduate student in the Department of Environmental Engineering Sciences at the University of Florida in Gainesville, Florida. Melissa A. Henkel is a sixth- and seventh-grade science teacher at Westwood Middle School in Gainesville, Florida.

Acknowledgments

Special thanks to the SPICE program and Westwood Middle School for encouraging and implementing this education activity. Sara Charbonnet and Gabriela Blohm offered helpful insight into implementation of this module. The National Science Foundation provided funding for the SPICE program.

References

Boughton, R. G. 1997. *The use of PVC refugia as trapping technique for hylid tree frogs.* Master's thesis, University of Florida, Gainesville.

Conant, R., and J. T. Collins. 1998. *A field guide to reptiles and amphibians of Central and North America.* 3rd ed. New York: Houghton Mifflin Company.

Moulton, C. A., W. J. Fleming, and B. R. Nerney. 1996. The use of PVC pipes to capture hylid frogs. *Herpetological Review* 27: 186–87.

National Research Council (NRC). 1996. *National Science Education Standards.* Washington, DC:

National Academy Press.

Staiger, J. S., and R. G. Boughton. 1999. *Factors affecting hylid tree frog use of PVC refugia in north central Florida.* Poster presentation at the Joint meeting of the American Society of Ichthyologists and Herpetologists, American Elasmobranch Society, Herpetologists' League, and Society for the Study of Amphibians and Reptiles, Penn State University, State College, Pennsylvania. Available online at *http://cars. er.usgs.gov/posters/Herpetology/PVC_Refugia/ pvc_refugia.html.*

Internet

SPICE website
  http://www.spice.centers.ufl.edu
U.S. Department of the Interior, Checklist of Amphibian Species and Identification Guide
  www.npwrc.usgs.gov/resource/herps/amphibid/ index.htm

The Alien Lab: A Study in Genetics

By Nancy Cowdin

For the past several years, my seventh-grade life science classes have been building a population of aliens. But no need to worry about invasion. These aliens are friendly—and educational. They are part of a lesson I've developed to introduce my students to the fundamentals of genetics. The purpose of this alien invasion is to give students some basic information about genetics. It also has fantastic integration possibilities with language arts, art, and mathematics.

Teaching genetics to seventh graders is both fun and challenging. With a plethora of new information on the human genome, the study of genetics now has new relevance. Newspapers and magazines cite the findings of researchers with increasing frequency. It is our task as educators to provide fundamental information that will allow students to understand the principles of genetics and to be able to approach more complex genetics-related topics with increased facility.

The lesson begins with a history of Gregor Mendel and his classic study of heredity in pea plants. We go on to discuss and define vocabulary such as *dominant, recessive, gene, trait, incomplete dominance, purebred, hybrid, genotypes*, and *phenotypes*. Next, we identify certain dominant and recessive traits in our student population. Students enjoy the opportunity to stick out their tongues at me to display tongue-rolling ability (a dominant trait) and debate what constitutes a "free" versus "attached" earlobe in their classmates. The class takes a survey to look at the ratios within our student population of known dominant and recessive traits, and then hypothesize as to whether or not they think the ratios might hold true within the student body or community. We also discuss patterns of traits that may exist within the students' families. Students are encouraged to test family members to identify common traits.

Having already completed a thorough study of mitosis, a discussion of meiosis is necessary to provide understanding as to how sex cells (*gametes*) receive the information that is passed on during fertilization. Understanding this process also helps students understand how several phenotypic outcomes can be possible from the potential selection of genes donated by each parent. This is followed up by exercises with *Punnett squares* to examine possible genotypic and phenotypic ratios of a given set of parent traits. A Punnett square is a tool used to predict all possible combinations of genotypes and resulting phenotypes for a given trait as might be expressed in the offspring (see Figure 1). The gene pair for a particular trait of one parent is written on the outside of the square on the left and the other parent's gene pair is written at the top. In an orderly fashion, gene pairs are created using one gene from each parent until all possibilities are shown.

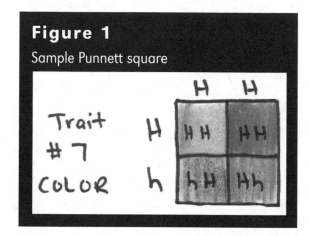

Figure 1
Sample Punnett square

Data Collection

After becoming comfortable with the vocabulary, students begin the data collection phase. Each student pairs with another, and each student is given a penny and a data grid. Working together, student partners flip the coins and record the results as follows: Heads=H, Tails=h. Each grid contains space to record 12 sets of data that give the information for one alien. You may want students to fill out additional data sheets to create several aliens.

Each student in the pair flips the coin, and together they record the results. For example, Joe and Sue flip their coins. Joe gets heads, and Sue gets tails. They each record results on the first line of their first data sheet. The students continue this process until all spaces on all grids are filled. We then have a discussion of alien characteristics and develop a list of traits necessary to build our aliens. Some examples include body and head shapes, antennae, wings, tails, scales, number of legs and arms, etc. The only limitations are their imaginations. But in the end the class must have the same key to the alien traits in order to build their population. A key is created that is used to translate the data into specific traits (see Figure 2).

Although the key could be determined in advance of the coin flipping, there is an advantage to doing it after because it makes the flipping process entirely random. Knowing the key to the traits in advance could cause some data manipulation by the students if they happen to like certain traits more than others. Some students are disappointed when they begin construction of their aliens once they find that they have no aliens with wings, for example, but this lends well to a discussion of diversity.

Figure 2.
Sample trait key

#	Trait	Homozygous dominance HH	Heterozygous dominant or incomplete dominance Hh	Homozygous recessive hh	Other Influences
1	Body shape	peanut	peanut	hersey kiss	
2	Head shape	octagon	octagon	twinkie	
3	Legs	4 tentacles	4 tentacles	3 chicken	
4	Wings/tail	wings	wings	tails	
5	Eyes on stalks	3 on stalks	3 on stalks	3 no stalks	
6	Mouth	with fangs	with fangs	w/o fangs	
7	Color	blue	green	yellow	✓
8	Hair	afros	dreds	braid	
9	Suction cups	s.c.	s.c.	none	
10	Nose	small	small	slits	
11	Ears	average	average	Dumbo	
12	Gender	female ♀	male ♂	female ♀	

While traits are typically shown by different capital and lower case letters, such as B=brown hair, b=blond hair, we do not translate the "H" and "h" into other letters. Rather, we focus on whether the genotypes resulting from our coin flips represent the *homozygous dominant*, *heterozygous dominant*, *heterozygous with incomplete dominance*, or *homozygous recessive* conditions.

Alien Construction Zone

My classes use sketchbooks throughout the year to illustrate cell and anatomic structures, as well as physiologic processes. These sketchbooks are used to draw the alien population. Each grid contains the information needed to construct an alien. Next to each gene pair is a space to translate the genotypes, using the key, into their phenotypes. Students cut out and place the grids on the sketchbook page, allowing space to draw the alien next to it.

While students are guided by the information on each grid to construct their aliens, there is still room for genetic variation. If a triangle head is required, the type of triangle drawn is the student's decision. Questions such as, "Is it okay to use a different shade of blue?" or "Does the mouth have to look identical to my partner's alien mouth?" give the opportunity to discuss the variety of traits we see in our human, animal, or plant populations. It is important to relay that other factors contribute to variations in traits found in a species and to help students understand that in real life some traits are *multifactorial*, or affected by environmental and genetic factors. A return to the topic of meiosis will remind students that recombination and mutations contribute to the amazing genetic variability we find in our world. We create an opportunity in our alien population for certain traits to be altered by an additional factor consisting of a roll of a die. For example, some students wanted to include spots or stripes on their aliens. To try for this outcome, each student was allowed to roll the die only once per alien. A student who rolled a

"1" could include spots for that alien; if a "6" was rolled, that alien could have stripes.

The symbol for male or female is added next to each drawing to show the results of the gender genotype on each grid. The students then name their aliens. There is an incredible amount of excitement in the room as the aliens take shape. In the days that follow, students are excited about "how cute" or "how cool" the aliens are. Even students who are not artistically inclined seem to love this exercise. Now the fun begins!

The Dating Game

The students are asked to pick one alien from their collection to go in search of a mate. To this end, each student creates a tasteful personals ad, such as one would find in the classified section of the newspaper. The students take turns reading them aloud and then get a chance (this is not a quiet activity) to shop around for a suitable mate. Students are allowed to choose alien mates. Some students look for particular traits in their potential mates. For example, if they are hoping to have wings in their baby alien offspring, they might look for an alien mate that has this characteristic.

To create the offspring, the parents share the data (copy the "spouse" genotypes) given on the grids for their respective aliens. Once shared, each student creates 12 Punnett squares using the information for each trait (see Figure 1 for an example). Students color code each of the four squares in order to identify the genotypes for each "baby." For example, the first baby would be drawn using data given in the upper left-hand corner of each Punnett square. When the 12 Punnett squares are completed and the four alien babies are created, the students have a chance to share their first generation.

Mutations

Scenario: A radical ion storm of cosmic radiation has bombarded the aliens' planet. The result is a mutation affecting the gametes of one of the original parents. Create a mutation in one of the alien babies.

After our alien babies are created, we spend some time discussing how mutations can occur, both through transcription errors in the DNA or by potential mutagens. We also discuss how mutations, or changes in the information of a gene, can be neutral (have no observed effect), helpful, or harmful and give examples of each possibility. I tell the students that we are going to rewrite the script of one of their alien babies to include a mutation. I let the students determine the type of mutation and whether or not its outcome is neutral, helpful, or harmful to the offspring. Then each student creates a story about the alien family to explain what happened as a result of the mutation. Students often want to share these stories, often giving the baby "super" powers.

Back on Earth

The last part of the alien lab is a set of discussion questions used to review terms and to evaluate what was learned (see Figure 3). The exercise could stand alone as an evaluation tool as students display their understanding of dominant, recessive, and hybrid traits in the drawing of their aliens and the use of the Punnett squares.

If time allows, the class data could be used to examine predicted ratios for the given traits. Or, when given an unknown set of alien offspring, students could try to predict the traits of the parents. As students generally don't want this activity to end, the babies could grow up and be parents of the next generation.

Nancy Cowdin is a science coordinator at Holy Trinity School in Washington, DC.

Figure 3.
Discussion questions

1. What is a *genotype*? Explain using an example from your alien data.
2. What is a *phenotype*? Explain using an example from your alien data.
3. List the traits that showed *incomplete dominance* in your aliens.
4. Distinguish between the terms *hybrid* and *incomplete dominance*. Use examples in your alien population to explain.
5. List the traits that were either dominant or recessive only (purebred or homozygous) and explain how this is evident in our alien population.
6. List three traits that showed up often (high frequency) in your aliens.
7. Define *mutation*. Then explain how mutations can occur.
8. How could a mutation be considered good? Give an example.
9. How could a mutation be passed on to future generations?
10. List several things that you learned in doing this lab.

References

Alford, R. L. 1999. *Genetics & your health: A Guide for the 21st century family.* Medford, NJ: Medford Press.

Bloom, M., M. Cutter, R. Davidson et al. 2000. *Genes, environment, and human behavior.* Colorado Springs, CO: Biological Sciences Curriculum Study 7–11.

DiSpezio, M., M. Linner-Luebe, M. Lisowski et al. 1996. *Science insights: Exploring living things.* New York: Addison-Wesley.

Alien lab activity sheet

Purposes

To learn about dominant, recessive, and hybrid traits and how they affect the traits of an organism. To distinguish between genotypes and phenotypes.

Materials

- colored pencils
- sketchbook
- pennies

Procedure

1. Flip pennies and record your results in sets of 12 on your data sheets (Heads=H, Tails=h). Each data sheet will create one alien.
2. As a class, create a key for each of the 12 genotypes (see Figure 2).
3. Label the specific trait represented by each numbered line on your data sheets (according to the key).
4. Based on the information from one data sheet, draw your alien.
5. Choose a mate for your alien(s) and create offspring using Punnet squares to gather the information.
6. Draw the offspring, accounting for mutations.

#	Trait	First coin toss	Second coin toss
1			
2			
3			
4			
5			
6			
7			
8			
9			
10			
11			
12			

Glossary of terms

- *Dominant:* term given to an allele (a form of a gene) that is always expressed when present
- *Recessive:* an allele that is usually only expressed when a dominant gene is not present
- *Gene:* instructions found on the chromosome for a particular characteristic
- *Trait:* another name for a characteristic
- *Purebred:* a gene pair composed of either two dominant or two recessive genes (homozygous dominant or homozygous recessive)
- *Hybrid:* a gene pair composed of one dominant and one recessive gene
- *Genotype:* the gene pair for a given trait
- *Phenotype:* the physical expression of the genotype
- *Incomplete dominance:* a gene pair that results in a trait somewhere between the traits of the two parents
- *Homozygous dominant:* HH genotype
- *Homozygous recessive:* hh genotype
- *Heterozygous dominant:* Hh genotype; dominant gene is expressed

Light Foundations

By Peggy Ashbrook

Day and night, day and night—the lives of young children are governed by this cycle—the classic refrain, "Why do I have to go to bed?" is no doubt commonly heard around the world by many parents every night.

The day-and-night cycle forms the basis for understanding many other natural cycles in plants, animals, and Earth processes, as well as later learning about the solar system, and it is part of the National Science Education Content Standard D, Earth and Space Science, for grades K–4. Learning about light is part of Content Standard B: Physical Science Light, Heat, Electricity, and Magnetism.

When asked to consider the difference between day and night, most children comment that "in the day the Sun makes it light" or "the Sun is bright" and "it's dark at night," but they do not understand the details about how the solar system works, even though they may tell you that Earth goes around the Sun.

When studying this topic in early childhood, it is appropriate to focus children's attention on the Sun and its movement across the sky through discussion and observation (AAAS 1993). The observations are indirect evidence of the Earth's movement, a concept the children will become ready to understand in later years.

A good starting point for helping children understand our observations of the Sun is the understanding that light travels in a straight path, which is explored in the hands-on activity that follows.

Peggy Ashbrook is the author of Science Is Simple: Over 250 Activities for Preschoolers *and teaches preschool science in Alexandria, Virginia.*

Resources

American Association for the Advancement of Science (AAAS). 1993. *Project 2061: Benchmarks for science literacy.* New York: Oxford Press.

National Research Council (NRC). 1996. *National Science Education Standards.* Washington, DC: National Academy Press.

Observing Light's Path

Objective:
To observe that light travels in a straight line.

Materials:
A darkened area in the classroom, such as a space underneath a table covered with a tablecloth, or a box large enough to fit both a child's head and a flashlight.

For each pair of students:
- 1 flashlight
- 1 m of flexible opaque pipe, 5–10 cm in diameter, such as corrugated black plastic pipe used for draining water (check your local hardware store) or a discarded vacuum-cleaner hose (well cleaned). Note: store the tube coiled up in a bag so that it maintains a curved shape.
- Paper and pencil for recording observations

Procedure:
1. As an introduction to describing the path of light, set up a center with a darkened area and a flashlight for students to use independently. Allowing independent play before asking the students to work with the tubes will help them become comfortable using the flashlight, and since it will no longer be a novelty, they can focus on recording their observations.
2. Have the students work in pairs, one at each end of the pipe. One student will shine a flashlight into one end of the pipe while the other looks in the other end to see if the light is visible.
3. With each trial, the students should draw or describe the shape of the pipe length (flat, curved, wavy, straight) and say whether or not the light was visible. Then have them switch roles, and the shape of the pipe, and shine the light through the pipe again.

   Allow enough time for the students to discover by themselves how to straighten out the pipe to make the light visible, or the reverse. If they are becoming frustrated, ask, "What can you see if you hold the pipe so it is in a straight line (is curved)?"

4. If the students have not noticed that light does not travel in curved lines, have the students put their hand through the pipe to touch their partner's while you remark, "Your arm can go through a bent tube but the light did not. What can your arm do that light cannot?"

   Keep discussions about light and the Sun simple and relate them to children's direct experience. The next time you are outside with the children, point to a patch of sunlight and say, "This comes to us straight from the Sun!" Always tell children that they should never look directly at the Sun or they will damage their eyes. If the Sun is not directly overhead, you can rotate your body so your face rotates toward and away from the Sun and in and out of shadow. Tell the children, "As I turn, part of me is in the light, and part of me is not. If I were the Earth, the side toward the light would have daytime and the side away from the Sun would have night."

They're M-e-e-elting! An Investigation of Glacial Retreat in Antarctica

By Samuel R. Bugg IV, Juanita Constible, Marianne Kaput, and Richard E. Lee Jr.

Our laboratory studies cryobiology, or life at low temperatures. One of our research subjects, a wingless fly called *Belgica antarctica,* is found on islands near Palmer Station, a U.S. research base on the Antarctic Peninsula. An ancient glacier that has dwarfed the station buildings huddled on the coastline is wasting away. This glacier, which is 130 m tall, has receded by approximately 300 m since 1981. Why has this melting occurred? What happens when that much freshwater enters the ocean? Will this melting continue? These questions inspired us to design a directed inquiry in which middle school students simulate glacial retreat in Antarctica. Students melt glaciers, change the water level and salinity of the Southern Ocean, and examine alterations to the Antarctic food web—all without leaving the classroom.

Background

Average air temperatures along the Antarctic Peninsula have increased 2° to 3°C in less than 50 years—10 times faster than the global trend (Kaiser 2003). Nearly 90% of the Antarctic Peninsula's glaciers, which are composed of freshwater, have retreated in the past 50 years due to increases in air and water temperatures (Cook et al. 2005). If this trend continues, there will be an increase in coastal meltwater zones and a global rise in sea level (Dierssen et al. 2002).

Scientists have observed that the salinity of coastal water decreases as glaciers rapidly melt, causing a shift in the Antarctic phytoplankton community from diatoms (which prefer a high-salinity environment) to cryptophytes (which favor a low-salinity environment) (Moline et al. 2004). The shift from diatoms to cryptophytes

Figure 1.

Effect of glacial retreat on the marine food web of the Antarctic Peninsula

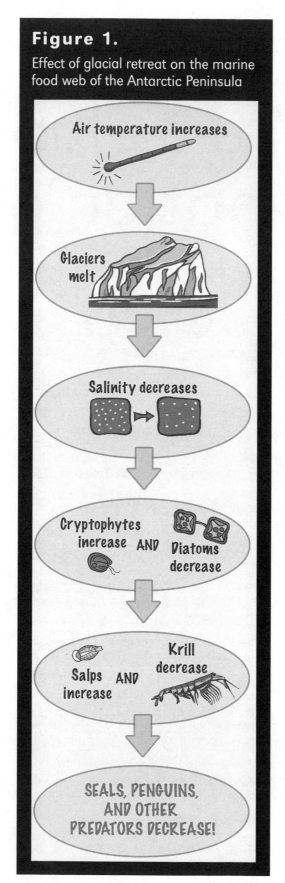

Air temperature increases

Glaciers melt

Salinity decreases

Cryptophytes increase AND Diatoms decrease

Salps increase AND Krill decrease

SEALS, PENGUINS, AND OTHER PREDATORS DECREASE!

is unfavorable for Antarctic krill *(Euphausia superba),* a shrimplike crustacean that is a keystone species of the Antarctic food web. Cryptophytes are a low-quality food source for krill; they are too small for krill to feed on efficiently and may be of low nutritional value (Haberman et al. 2003). An additional threat to krill is competition from a nutrient-poor, gelatinous tunicate called salp *(Salpa thompsoni).* Salps are effective competitors because they rapidly proliferate via asexual reproduction, eat a wider range of prey items than krill, and prefer low-salinity environments (Moline et al. 2004; Loeb et al. 1997). Due to overharvesting by commercial fishermen, a decrease in salinity, an increase in competition, and the loss of sea ice, krill populations have declined by as much as 80% in some areas in the past 30 years (Gross 2005). Predators such as seals, penguins, and albatrosses depend on krill for their survival; recent declines in Adélie penguin *(Pygoscelis adeliae)* populations near Palmer Station have been attributed in part to declines in krill populations (Smith et al. 2003). Salps, unfortunately, have few nutrients and cannot replace krill in the Antarctic food web (Loeb et al. 1997). Figure 1 summarizes the relationship between salinity, krill, and vertebrate predators.

Salinity Think Tank

To prepare for They're M-e-e-elting!, students need to understand the concept of salinity and why it is important to aquatic plants and animals. We have developed a discussion guide (see Figure 2) to help students understand these ideas before they proceed.

They're M-e-e-elting!

This hands-on activity simulates the past, present, and future of the Antarctic Peninsula (Figure 3). The Past Environment models conditions before climate change (at least 50 years ago), the Present Environment models current conditions (2° to 3°C warmer than historical

Figure 2.

Salinity think tank discussion guide

1. Define salinity.
2. Ask students to identify freshwater and saltwater habitats.
3. Have students create a list of plants and animals that live in saltwater and freshwater.
4. Ask students: What would happen if you put saltwater animals directly into freshwater? What would happen to saltwater animals if you slowly decreased the salinity of their water?
5. Introduce the topic of climate change in Antarctica. Stimulate prior knowledge by discussing what students know about the geographic location and geology of Antarctica, and how Antarctica compares and contrasts with the Arctic. Discuss how and why the temperature at Palmer Station differs from that at the South Pole. Explain that, on average, the atmosphere over the Peninsula is 2–3°C warmer now than it was 50 years ago. Tell students that scientists predict a further increase of 5–8°C in the next 50 years.
6. Introduce the topic of glacial retreat with this diagram of an aerial view of Palmer Station. Explain that the glacier, which is about 130 m tall, has receded 300 m since 1981. The glacier is currently retreating at a rate of 10 m/year. Point out that buildings have been constructed where the glacier used to stand.

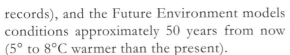

Edge of glacier in 2005

Edge of glacier in 1981

Palmer Station

records), and the Future Environment models conditions approximately 50 years from now (5° to 8°C warmer than the present).

Preparation of materials must start at least two days before the main activity. The simulation itself takes 40 to 45 minutes from setup to cleanup. To ensure effective use of time, teachers should split the class into cooperative groups that stay together from initial preparation to the end of the simulation. Each student should be assigned a responsibility, such as

- task master: keeps group focused and on task;
- materials manager—setup: makes sure all materials are functional and readily available;
- materials manager—cleanup: makes sure all materials are put back in their proper

place, reports any malfunctioning equipment to the teacher;
- quality control manager: makes sure all the appropriate data are collected and that the group is getting consistent results; and
- speaker: asks the teacher questions for the entire group and reports results to the class.

Each group of students should work with only one environment (past, present, or future) to reduce setup and cleanup time. Data can be pooled and discussed before the web quest starts. By the end of the simulation, students should be able to

- make predictions about the kinds of physical changes that will occur in the ocean, glaciers, and atmosphere of Antarctica as

Figure 3.
Materials and methods for They're M-e-e-elting!

Summary of procedures:

	Teachers	Students
Day 1—Preparation (15 minutes)	Form student groups. Assign a responsibility to each student. Assign one environment (Past, Present, or Future) to each group. Review procedures for Days 1 and 2.	Start making miniglaciers.
Day 2—Preparation (15 minutes)	Review procedures for Day 3.	Finish making miniglaciers.
Day 3—Simulation (40–45 minutes)	Facilitate simulation and discussion.	Make initial observations. Set up light fixtures. Make intermediate observations. Make final observations. Pool data with the class. Clean up.
Day 4—Discussion (15 minutes)	Facilitate class discussion about pooled data.	

Day 1—Preparation (two days before simulation)

Materials (Makes one miniglacier)
- Round plastic container, approximately 8 cm deep and 10–12 cm in diameter (500–1,200 mL; one container per group). (Teaching tip: The plastic pint containers in the deli section of the grocery store work well for this step. Ensure that every group has identical containers.)
- 300 mL beaker (one per group)
- Blue Kool-Aid (300 mL per group) (Teaching tip: Before class, teachers should dissolve one packet of Berry Blue Kool-Aid in 1,500 mL of water to make blue "freshwater." This brand, flavor, and concentration of Kool-Aid must be used to achieve desired visual results.)
- Freezer space (Teaching tip: A class of 30 students [six groups, one environment per group] will need about 10 × 15 cm of freezer space. The school's cafeteria staff may be able to help with this.)

Procedure
Pour 300 mL of blue Kool-Aid in the round plastic container and freeze overnight. (Safety note: Teachers should remind students that the Kool-Aid is a science material and should not be consumed.)

Day 2—Preparation (one day before simulation)

Materials (Makes one miniglacier and the ocean for one environment)

- Partially finished miniglacier from previous day
- Rock, slightly less than 10–12 cm in diameter (one per group) that can fit in the bottom of the plastic container. (Teaching tip: Rocks can be found by students or purchased at a gardening supply store. We used rocks to ensure that the miniglaciers would not float. Make sure groups have similar-sized rocks.)
- 300 mL and 1,000 mL beaker (one of each size per group)
- Blue Kool-Aid (100 mL per group)

Figure 3. (continued)

- Freezer space
- Tap water
- Iodized or plain table salt (30 mg per group)
- Refrigerator space

Procedure
1. Place one rock inside the plastic container on top of the blue ice that has formed.
2. Pour 100 mL of blue Kool-Aid over the rock. Freeze overnight so that the initial layer of blue ice, the rock, and the new layer of blue water will freeze together.
3. Prepare 1,000 mL of saltwater to simulate the actual salinity of the Southern Ocean by mixing 30 mg of table salt with 1,000 mL of water. Cool the saltwater overnight in a refrigerator. Do not add Kool-Aid to the saltwater.

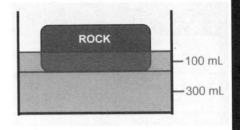

Day 3—Simulation (two days after initial preparation)
Safety Note: Be careful when using water near electrical outlets and fixtures. Students must wear chemical-splash goggles.

Materials
- Plastic shoebox-type container approximately 34.5 cm × 20.5 cm × 10 cm (4.5 L) (one per group)
- Piece of white paper (one per group)
- Cooled, colorless saltwater (1,000 mL per group)
- Miniglacier (one per group)
- 75-watt lightbulbs with fixtures and stands (one per group observing the Present or Future environments) (Safety note: Teachers should ensure that light fixtures can safely accommodate 75-watt bulbs.)
- Paper towels
- Metric ruler (one per group)
- Timer or wristwatch (one per group)
- Graphing paper (one sheet per student) or a computer with a spreadsheet program (one per group)
- Pencils or pens

Procedure
(Teaching tip: The most dramatic color changes in the ocean environment occur after miniglaciers have been melting for 30 minutes or more. If class periods are 45 minutes or less, setting out the miniglaciers at room temperature for 5–10 minutes before class begins will improve results.)

1. Put your plastic shoebox container on a piece of white paper.
2. Pour 1,000 mL of cooled, colorless saltwater into the container. Label your shoebox "Past," "Present," or "Future," depending on which environment you are working with.
3. Remove your miniglacier from its round plastic container. If your miniglacier doesn't pop out easily, run warm water over the bottom of the container to free the ice (make sure the ice is facing down).
4. Once the miniglacier is free from the container, wipe the ice and rock with a paper towel to remove any excess blue color on the surface of the miniglacier.
5. Place one miniglacier in your shoebox container (make sure the ice is facing up). When all the groups are ready, your teacher will set a timer for 30 minutes. (Teaching tip: Five minutes before each set of observations, teachers should use a bell or other signal to warn students that a new task is approaching. If class periods are 45 minutes or less, teachers may need to shorten the time between observations to allow sufficient time for the entire lab. If class periods are longer, teachers may wish to lengthen the time between observations to improve the results.)

Figure 3. (continued)

6. Use the data sheet below to record winter measurements for each environment (the salinity index is already filled in for you). Measure the water level by placing one end of a ruler on the inside bottom corner of your shoebox container.

Complete the data sheet at the start, middle, and end of your experiment.

	Past environment	Present environment	Future environment
Winter (0 min)			
Salinity index (scale 0–7)	7	7	7
Water level (mm)	mm	mm	mm
Spring (15 min)			
Salinity index (scale 0–7)			
Water level (mm)	mm	mm	mm
Summer (30 min)			
Salinity index (scale 0–7)			
Water level (mm)	mm	mm	mm

Salinity index

Use the salinity index at right to match the color of the liquid (not frozen) water in each shoebox container on a scale of 1 to 7. If the water has no color at all, you will enter 7 in your data table. If the color of the water is between two values (e.g., somewhere between 1 and 2), enter the closest value in your table.

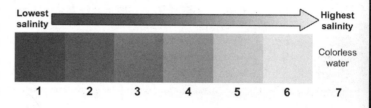

7. Set up your light fixture.
   (Safety note: Be careful when using electrical fixtures near water. Also, do not handle the lightbulbs or light shade—they will be hot!)
   a. If your group is responsible for the Past Environment, do not add an external heat source to your simulated environment.
   b. If your group is responsible for the Present Environment, stand a 75-watt lightbulb and fixture directly over the shoebox container so the tip of the bulb is 45 cm from the bottom of the container. Measure distance from tip of lightbulb to bottom of saltwater container. Turn on the light.
   c. If your group is responsible for the Future Environment, stand a 75-watt lightbulb and fixture directly over the shoebox container so that the lightbulb is about 30 cm from the bottom of the container. Measure distance from tip of lightbulb to bottom of saltwater container. Turn on the light.
8. While you are waiting for spring to arrive, answer the following questions.
   a. On the back of this paper make a diagram of your experimental environment and label the following parts. (Hint: You will find each part in your experimental setup.)
   • Antarctic Peninsula   • Southern Ocean
   • Atmosphere   • Glacier
   b. Predict what physical changes and evidence of these predicted changes might be observed in each of the experimental environments (Past, Present, and Future). Why do you think those changes will occur? How will the Future Environment differ from the Present Environment? How will the Present differ from the Past?

Figure 3. (continued)

9. After 15 minutes, go back to the data sheet in Step 6 and record spring measurements.
10. While you are waiting for summer to arrive, finish the questions in Step 8.
11. After 30 minutes, go back to the data sheet in Step 6 and record summer measurements.
12. Pool your data with the rest of the class.
13. Using the pooled summer data from the class results, create line graphs to compare changes in water level and salinity between the Past, Present, and Future Environments. In the salinity graph, place the salinity level on the vertical axis and the time periods/environments on the bottom. In the water-level graph, put the water-level scale on the vertical axis and the time periods/environments on the bottom.
14. Go back to the diagram you made in Step 8a. Add labels that describe the physical changes that occurred in each environment from winter to summer.
15. Answer the following questions:
    a. According to your graphs and your diagram, how has the level of the ocean changed from the Past to the Present Environment? How will it change in the Future?
    b. According to your graphs and your diagram, how has the salinity of the ocean changed from the Past to the Present Environment? How will it change in the Future?
    c. Did your results support the predictions you made in Step 8B? Why or why not?
    d. Predict how changes in water level and salinity will affect the plants and animals that live along the coast of Antarctica. (Teaching tip: If time is short, these questions can form the basis of a future class discussion.)

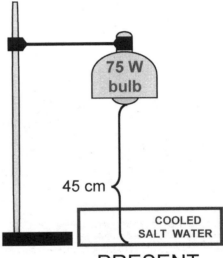

No light fixture

PAST

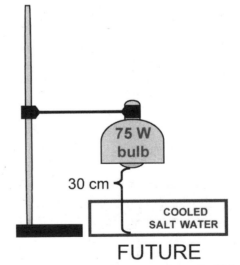

PRESENT
(Air temperature 2–3°C warmer than PAST)

FUTURE
(Air temperature 5–8°C warmer than PRESENT)

Figure 4.

Sample data from They're M-e-e-elting!
Simulated effect of glacial retreat on water level
and salinity near Palmer Station

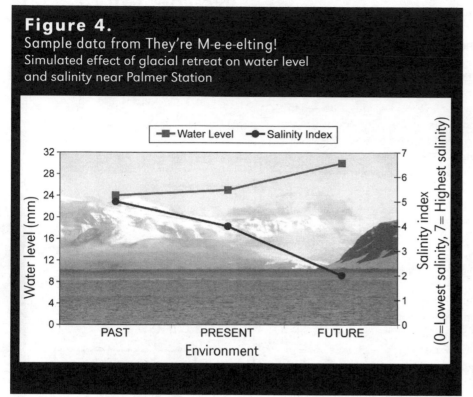

Conclusions

Many students are familiar with the idea that global sea level will rise as glaciers and polar ice caps melt. However, dramatic changes in sea level are not expected for several decades and therefore may not seem important in the present. This inquiry illustrates how a seemingly small change of a few degrees in air temperature can have important consequences for entire food webs. Perhaps more important, it reminds students that life on the planet is already feeling the heat of climate change.

Samuel R. Bugg IV is a graduate student in the Institute of Environmental Sciences and Juanita Constible is an outreach coordinator and science writer in the Department of Zoology at Miami University in Oxford, Ohio. Marianne Kaput is a sixth-grade math and science teacher at Troy Intermediate School in Avon Lake, Ohio. Richard E. Lee Jr. is a distinguished professor of zoology at Miami University in Oxford, Ohio.

Acknowledgments

This project was supported by National Science Foundation grants numbers NSF OPP-0413786 and NSF IOB-0416720. We thank Michael Elnitsky for photographs and Marianne Kaput's sixth-grade science class for piloting this activity.

a result of climate change;

• use appropriate tools to measure salinity and sea level;

• clearly summarize the results of the experiment using graphs and a scientific diagram; and

• relate their data summaries to their predictions in a critical and logical manner.

Sample data from our class are shown in Figure 4.

Antarctic Food-Web Quest

In the last section of the inquiry, students use the internet to research changes in krill populations and Antarctic food webs (see Resources). This activity, in which students conduct research and complete a work sheet (Figure 5) that has been modified from Figure 1, will take 25 to 35 minutes.

References

Cook, A. J., A. J. Fox, D. G. Vaughan, and J. G. Ferrigno. 2005. Retreating glacier fronts on the Antarctic Peninsula over the past half-century. *Science* 308 (5721): 541–44.

Dierssen, H. M., R. C. Smith, and M. Vernet. 2002. Glacial meltwater dynamics in coastal waters west of the Antarctic Peninsula. *Proceedings of the National Academy of Sciences of the United States of America* 99 (4): 1790–95.

Figure 5.

Antarctic food-web quest

Use this flowchart to describe some of the effects of climate change on the Antarctic Peninsula. Fill in the missing word(s) and/or pictures in each bubble using the results of They're M-e-e-elting!, your internet research, and the hints on the left side of this page. If you find interesting information or alternative explanations during your research, you may add notes, extra bubbles, or arrows to the right side of the page.

Hints and questions		Notes and additional bubbles
	Air temperature	
How does climate change affect air temperature?		
What is the name of a massive accumulation of compressed snow? (Hint: These structures are found high in the mountains and at both poles.) How are these structures affected by the previous step?		
You explored this property of water during the Salinity Think Tank. How does the previous step affect this property?		
These are species of phytoplankton (microscopic plants). How are the populations of these organisms changing?	AND	
This step includes two animals: One is a tunicate and one is a crustacean. How are they interacting or changing? Think about what these two organisms eat.	Salps AND	
These are the best-known animals in Antarctica. How are they affected by the previous changes? (Hint: You might need to write some extra notes if your answer doesn't fit in the bubble.)		

Final question: Think back to the predictions you made about how changes in water level and salinity might affect plants and animals in Antarctica. Did your research support your predictions? Were you surprised by anything you learned today?

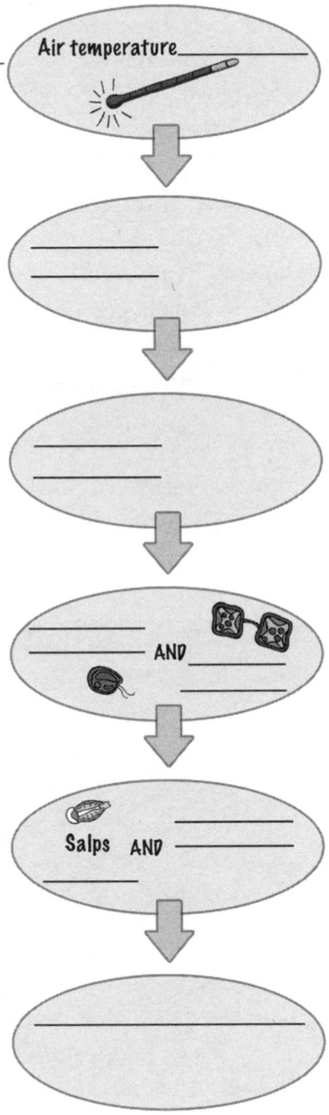

Extension

As an enrichment activity, have students consider the following question: Now you understand the potential effects of climate change on the Antarctic food web. How do you think those changes might affect us? Can you think of ways climate change might affect food webs in your area of the country?

Gross, L. 2005. As the Antarctic ice pack recedes, a fragile ecosystem hangs in the balance. *Public Library of Science Biology* 3 (4): 557–61.

Haberman, K. L., R. M. Ross, and L. B. Quetin. 2003. Diet of the Antarctic krill (*Euphausia superba* Dana): II. Selective grazing in mixed phytoplankton assemblages. *Journal of Experimental Marine Biology and Ecology* 283 (1–2): 97–113.

Kaiser, J. 2003. Warmer oceans could threaten Antarctic ice shelves. *Science* 302 (5646): 759.

Loeb, V., V. Siegel, O. Holm-Hansen, R. Hewitt, W. Fraser, W. Trivelpiece, and S. Trivelpiece. 1997. Effects of sea-ice extent and krill or salp dominance on the Antarctic food web. *Nature* 387 (6636): 897–900.

Moline, M. A., H. Claustre, T. K. Frazer, O. Schofields, and M. Vernet. 2004. Alteration of the food web along the Antarctic Peninsula in response to a regional warming trend. *Global Change Biology* 10 (12): 1973–80.

Smith, R. C., W. R. Fraser, and S. E. Stammerjohn. 2003. Climate variability and ecological response of the marine ecosystem in the Western Antarctic Peninsula (WAP) region. In *Climate variability and ecosystem response at long-term ecological research (LTER) sites*, eds. D. Greenland, D. Goodin, and R. C. Smith, 158–73. New York: Oxford Press.

Resources

Krill

www.enchantedlearning.com/subjects/invertebrates/crustacean/krillprintout.shtml.

Physical factors and the Antarctic food web

www.botos.com/marine/antarctic01.html#body_1.

The Dimensions of the Solar System

By Stephen E. Schneider and Kathleen S. Davis

We have added a few new wrinkles to the popular activity of building a scale model of the solar system. The new activity takes advantage of some of the special features of Google Earth. Our goal was to create an activity that would give a much more powerful sense of the enormity and emptiness of the solar system and, at the same time, provide an opportunity to make connections with the community.

Traditional Models

Historically, solar-system models are built by choosing objects of the appropriate relative sizes of the Sun and planets, and then laying them out along a line from the Sun outward. Unfortunately, the sizes of the Sun and planets often need to be exaggerated relative to their distances to make them visible. This may seem inevitable given the huge difference in the distances versus the sizes, but we see this as an obstacle to students gaining a deeper insight into the scale of the solar system. The problem can be solved if we expand our model sufficiently, so that we can have realistic separations between the solar-system bodies and still have an Earth that is not microscopic.

The second problem with traditional models is the practice of laying out the planets along a straight line. Again, this is understandable as a convenience, but what if we could make a scale model that reflected the essentially two-dimensional character of the solar system? When everything is placed along a line, it is not hard to find even small objects. However, imagine trying to find a grain of rice somewhere in the outskirts of your community. That gives a clearer idea of the challenge facing astronomers who are hunting for dwarf planets in the Kuiper belt.

Middle school students are expected to have some understanding of the solar system, the Sun, and planets and may even be able to name them in their order from the Sun (NRC 1996). However, as one middle school teacher stated, "I have learned over the years that middle schoolers have zero concept of distance." In addition, at the middle level, students' attention needs to shift from the properties of particular

Figure 1.

GIF overlays showing the orbital paths of planets in the inner solar system and outer solar system. The digital files are available at *www.umass.edu/seo*.

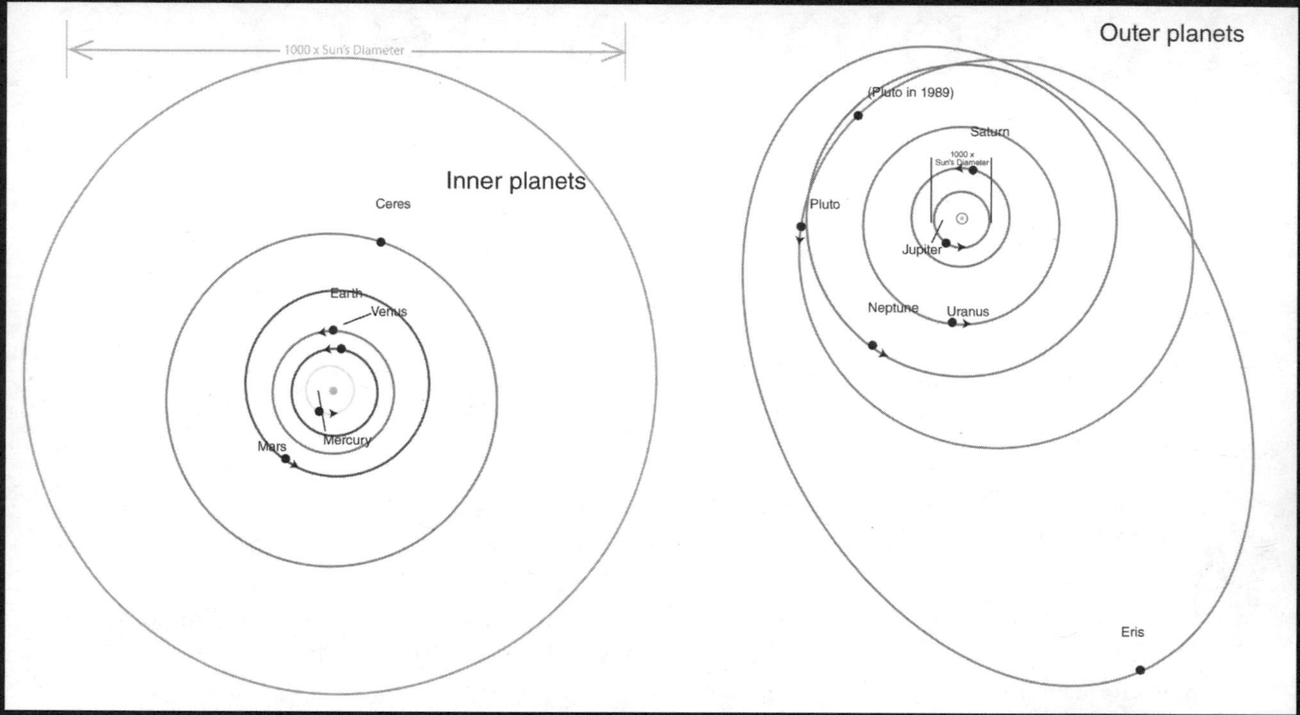

celestial objects toward an understanding of the place of the Earth in the solar system (Massachusetts Department of Education 2006). Thus, building an accurate model helps students grasp the size of the solar system.

We have found a fun way to design a more-realistic 2-D model of the solar system where students can learn about maps and scaling using easily accessible online resources that include satellite images. This activity also invites reaching out to a school's community in a way that will engage and educate.

Using Google Earth

Google Earth is a wonderful, free resource for looking at our planet (see Internet). Once installed, play with the program to learn how to zoom in and out, select layers to show different information on top of the images, and tilt the landscape to see it in 3-D. Under Tools/Options you can change to metric units.

For this project, we suggest using Google Earth to focus on the landscape around your school. Type in your school address and Google Earth will take you there. Now "back out" using the zoom controls until the image encompasses the community surrounding your school. This article is based on a scale in which the Sun is 1 meter in diameter, but you might decide to rescale the numbers we provide so you can make the solar system reach to local landmarks and stores that students are familiar with.

An Overlay of the Solar System

The next thing we want to do is to lay a map of the solar system on top of the bird's-eye view of your community. To do this, we created two transparent GIF images (Figure 1) that you can download to your computer from *www.umass.edu/seo*. These diagrams show the orbits of the planets (and dwarf planets) in the inner and the outer solar systems—it is almost impossible to show both on the same map because of the huge difference in distances.

To incorporate these images in Google Earth, adjust the zoom until you are at an "Eye Alt[itude]" of about 1.5 k (this is displayed in the lower-right corner). This gives you a field of view of a little under 2 km across in your viewing window. In the "Add" menu, select "Image Overlay" then click "Browse" and select the copy of "solsys-inner.gif" that you downloaded to your computer.

You will now see the orbit diagram on top of your map, something like Figure 2. You might name this new overlay "Inner Solar System." The green "handles" let you adjust the size, position, and rotation of the overlay. To adjust the position, grab the central green cross so the Sun is on top of your school. To change the size, first press shift then grab a corner marker to maintain the proportions of the figure.

Setting the Scale

Next use the ruler (under the "Tool" menu in Google Earth) to help set the overlay to the scale you want. For our example, we wanted the Sun to be 1 m in diameter, so we used the ruler tool to draw a horizontal bar on the figure that is 1 km across (yellow bar in Figure 3). You can choose other sizes, but our scale is about the smallest you might want to use because the Earth is about the size of a pea.

Along the top of the inner-solar-system overlay is a bar that shows the diameter of the Sun multiplied by 1,000. (Incidentally, this is approximately the size of Jupiter's orbit.)

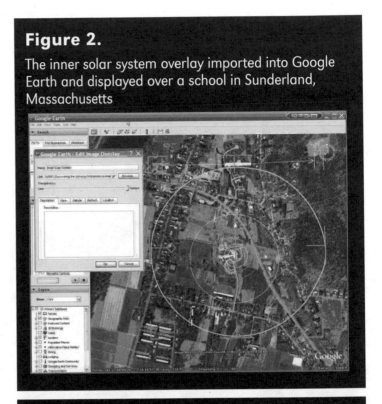

Figure 2.

The inner solar system overlay imported into Google Earth and displayed over a school in Sunderland, Massachusetts

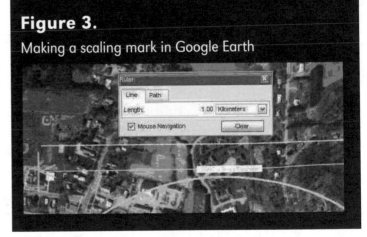

Figure 3.

Making a scaling mark in Google Earth

Figure 4.

Outer-solar-system orbits shown to same scale over Sunderland, Massachusetts

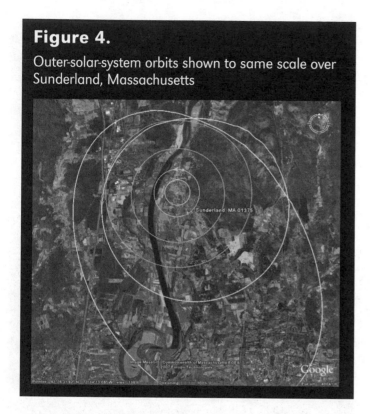

Because we decided to make the Sun 1 m across for our example, we adjusted the size of our overlay so that the bar was 1,000 m (1 km) long. (Note: If your green overlay adjustment handles are gone, you can get them back by right-clicking on your inner-solar-system overlay under "Places" on the left side of the window, then selecting "Properties.")

Once you've resized the overlay so that the "1,000 × Sun's Diameter" bar is the length you want, realign the overlay so the Sun is over your school in a location you'd like. The images in Google Earth are often clear enough to position the Sun right over your own classroom! You can save a copy of your image by going to the "File" menu, clicking "Save," and then "Save Image."

Next, you can add the outer solar system over your surrounding community. Zoom out until your "Eye Alt" is about 15 km. Now load the "solsys-outer.gif" overlay onto this image. To get it so that it has the same scale as the first

overlay, you can adjust the size until Jupiter's orbit and the 1,000 × Sun bar match those shown on the inner-solar-system overlay. You can save another image showing your outer-solar-system map over your community (Figure 4). Note that you can turn the layers you have created on and off by clicking the boxes next to them on the "Places" menu in Google Earth. These overlays will remain linked to the program even after you exit, so you can come back to them at a later time.

Putting It All Together

The next step requires a little math. What would be the diameter of the Earth, Jupiter, and other planets on a scale where the Sun is 1 m across? This might be a good project for students to carry out using the first two columns of Figure 5. We have listed objects, mostly with a food theme, that could be used to match these sizes. You can find other objects or use clay to make any of these—although the Sun, at a meter across, is a challenge.

Now that you have the solar system mapped to scale in your community and have some objects that may serve as scale models of the planets, you can begin to set up your model in reality. You might build the Sun out of papier-mâché to the correct scale and place it in the school. In our example, we can get only the Sun and three inner planets to fit within the school, because the distances really are very large compared to the sizes. To add more planets, you might choose a spot where an orbit crosses a street or other accessible spot, and place the accurately scaled model of the planet there. Because the planets are so small, you might want to make larger signs to indicate each planet's location. You might also want to extend the activity by having students add the Moon and set it at its distance (about 28 cm) from the Earth, or have them figure out where the Earth will be in your model a month later.

Even if you do not put grains of rice several kilometers away to represent some of the outer dwarf planets, working with Google Earth will

Figure 5.

The sizes of the Sun and planets, and their scaled sizes in a model where the Sun is 1 m across

Celestial body	Diameter (km)	Rescaled size	Possible object
Sun	1,392,000	1 m	Large beach ball
Mercury	4,878	3.5 mm	Peppercorn
Venus	12,102	8.7 mm	Pea
Earth	12,756	9.2 mm	Pea
Mars	6,794	4.9 mm	Caper
Ceres	940	0.7 mm	Salt grain
Jupiter	142,984	10.3 cm	Grapefruit
Saturn	120,536	8.7 cm	Large orange
Uranus	51,118	3.7 cm	Small lime
Neptune	49,528	3.6 cm	Small lime
Pluto	2,300	1.6 mm	Small grain of rice
Eris	2,400	1.7 mm	Small grain of rice

give your students a better grasp of the size and distances involved. Even finding a 9 mm Earth somewhere along its orbit around the entire school grounds would be quite a challenge. That might even make for a fun challenge—but you had better give students plenty of hints if they are to have much chance of finding it!

Inside Students' Heads

You can get a sense of what students think about planetary size and the scope of the solar system both before and after this activity. Provide them with a model of the Sun made from clay. Ask them to form a model of the Earth made to the same scale. How far would they place the Earth from the Sun? Can they think of analogous objects from everyday life to represent these celestial bodies? Asking middle school students to express what they think

about these questions again after the activity should illuminate a new sense of distance.

Stephen E. Schneider is a professor of astronomy at the University of Massachusetts-Amherst. Kathleen S. Davis is an associate professor of science education at the University of Massachusetts-Amherst.

Acknowledgments

This activity was developed for an online course titled "Discovering the Universe: Astronomy for Teachers," which was funded as part of National Science Foundation ESI #0243536—"Science Education Online" *(www.umass.edu/seo).*

Internet

Google Earth—*http://earth.google.com*
Solar-system overlay maps—*www.umass.edu/seo*

References

Massachusetts Department of Education. 2006. Massachusetts science and technology frameworks. Available at *www.doe.mass.edu/frameworks/current.html.*

National Council of Teachers of Mathematics. 2000, 2004. Principles and standards for school mathematics. Available at *http://standards.nctm.org.*

National Research Council (NRC). 1996. National science education standards. Available at *www.nap.edu/catalog.php?record_id=4962.*

Conclusion

CONCLUSION

This book opened with the lines:

> There's more to teaching science than stuffing kids with facts—
> 'cause unconnected data flows like rain right off their backs.
> Help kids discover nature, stars and waves, and tracks,
> dinosaurs, and temperature, and killer bee attacks.
>
> They have to learn to question, to observe, and to explore—
> to seek the basic causes, to measure, count, and more.
> So shelve that fault-line lecture; it'll bore them to the core.
> Active kid engagement is the key to learning's door. (Ronsberg 2006)

The importance of memorizing discrete science facts has decreased as access to information provided by computer networks and cell phones increases. Instead, importance needs to be placed on concepts and process. NSTA President John Whitsett wrote, "To succeed in the 21st century, students have to learn how to be creative problem solvers who can work in collaborative groups. These new-world students must have the ability to think critically, use technology efficiently, and communicate effectively" (Whitsett 2007).

As a teacher, you have a passion for working with children. The biggest rewards come when you see your students eyes light up in excitement or when the "lightbulb" of understanding comes on. Few things are as enjoyable as watching a child engaged in asking questions, actively learning, and discovering. As a teacher (current or future), you know this and have a passion for working with children. Science is unique in its potential for fostering this on a daily basis. The articles in this book have provided you with strategies and examples for science teaching that supports the development of a learning community that supports inquiry. Science teaching should be fun, not fun as entertainment, but fun through enlightenment and discovery.

Good teachers do not work alone. Good teachers collaborate with colleagues, participate in professional organizations, and continually learn about what they teach and how they teach. The final article in this compilation, "Forces at Work: The Top 5 Reasons for Belonging to a Professional Organization," explains how professional organizations like the National Science Teachers Association can help your professional growth. The American Association for the Advancement of Science also provides fantastic resources for science teaching through its NetLinks initiatives *(www.sciencenetlinks.com/)*. Internet-based social networks provide a way to connect with informal networks of educators from around the world. You can join these networks for free at *www.classroom20.com* or the recently launched *www.teachingscience20.com*.

I hope this compilation has given you a glimpse of what teaching science can be. A good education is the greatest gift that we can give to our children. Christa McAuliffe, NASA's first Teacher in Space and a crew member on the *Challenger* space shuttle when it exploded in 1986, summarized the importance of teachers. "I touch the future. I teach," she said.

References

Ronsberg, D. 2006. There's more to teaching science. *Science and Children* 44 (6): 24–25.

Whitsett, P. J. 2007. Meeting the needs of the new world student (A message from the NSTA President). *Science and Children* 45 (6): 8.

Forces at Work

By Christine Anne Royce and Judi Hechtman

The word *dynamics* relates to energy or force in motion at work in any field. A physics text defines dynamics as the study explaining why objects act as they do. Therefore, to be a dynamic teacher requires an exchange of energy between the teacher and something else. Although we all interact within our classrooms and with our students all of the time, we also need the dynamic of peer interaction. This article describes the benefits of participating in a professional organization for science teachers, whether it be a state, regional, or national one. The forces at work in this context are teachers allowing a professional organization to be the energizing or re-energizing source in their professional life.

The Forces at Work

Every state has a dedicated science association or organization whose main goal is to promote current trends in science education among teachers. Membership is available in these state organizations; in regional educational groups, such as local Eisenhower Consortiums; in subject-specific groups, such as the American Association of Physics Teachers (AAPT) and the National Association of Biology Teachers (NABT); and in other national groups, such as the Association of Presidential Awardees in Science Teaching (APAST) and, of course, the National Science Teachers Association

(NSTA). Your state organization likely seeks to further science education within your geographic area, whereas specialty organizations strive to expand subject content understanding and methodology, disseminate grade-level strategies, or maintain a network of colleagues with common interests. They all provide opportunities for teachers to stay informed, get involved, and be active. Professional organizations offer new teachers opportunities to interact and network with more experienced educators. At the same time, experienced educators get the opportunity to continue their professional growth by being mentor teachers and gaining a perspective different from that within their local school or district.

Just how do these forces, or groups, work? Most have a board of directors, advisory boards, executive committees, or some type of assembly that is elected or appointed to set policy, plan events, and serve as the body that disseminates information about the organization. As teachers who have been part of these affiliations and introduced to these benefits at different points within our careers, we can offer our own experiences as evidence of personal growth and of becoming more dynamic teachers as a result of our involvement in these organizations.

The question then becomes, "Why should I get involved in a professional organization?" Each organization has a specific purpose. Your selection of an organization will be directly related to your own personal goals and philosophy. As you consider any of the possibilities mentioned in this article, think about how an organization can help you expand your knowledge about your content area, interact with colleagues outside your own school, develop a network of resources, and remain a lifelong learner. The top five reasons to be involved in a professional organization are listed below.

It Places You on the Information Highway

Professional organizations offer their members many opportunities to be placed in the mainstream of information exchanges. You receive current news related to your field. Being in the know is one of the first steps to being active. Professional organizations place you on the information highway.

One way teachers enter this information highway is through Listservs. A Listserv is the equivalent of a mass mailing done electronically to disseminate general information to a wide audience. To find out about getting on an organization's Listserv, check its website. Many association websites provide links to their own Listserv. Information on a Listserv is distributed to members and provides timely information on topics, such as legislative issues in science education. Keeping up with the latest trends—such as topics relating to the U.S. House of Representative's bills that focus on funding science and mathematics education; statewide standards, assessments, and systemic initiatives; and the need for political activity in contacting local representatives—are critical to being active. Additionally, many state organizations find that Listservs are an excellent vehicle for disseminating information and are the fastest way to contact members and apprise them of inservice opportunities, award programs, and other timely news. To find out if your state organization provides such a benefit, simply search the internet for your local organization or contact one of its officers.

A second way you merge onto the information highway is through searching the internet for topical websites. The web pages cite information right at your fingertips. Each state association website is informational: Some provide activities, important links to other science education sites, and science lesson plans and activities.

You Can Expand Your Horizons Through Conference Opportunities

As a member of a professional organization, you are made aware of upcoming conferences and conventions. Whether it is a state, regional, or national conference, you can find just about any subject-related topic of interest at a convention. Conferences offer various sessions that can provide new teaching strategies and opportunities to increase content knowledge and recharge your passion for teaching. If attending a conference could be summarized by one word, it would be *energizing*. To find out where and when your state association conference is, contact a member of the convention committee or check *NSTA Reports*, which lists many of the state conference dates. If your state does not hold an annual conference, try to attend an NSTA regional conference in the fall or the NSTA's national one in the spring of each year. Attending a conference can expand your horizons not only in terms of content or pedagogical knowledge, but also in terms of professional connections.

Educators agree that one of the single most important reasons for attending conferences is networking. When you network, you make initial contacts and start a series of connections. These connections are important in an educator's professional world. Educators often spend the majority of their day in isolation with students and may interact only with the other teachers in their own building. Often those teachers are not even teaching the same subjects. Although ideas are shared and discussions happen, there often is no new, content-specific material discussed. The *National Science Education Standards* states "the challenge of professional development is to create optimal collaborative learning situations in which the best sources of expertise are linked with the experiences and current needs of the teachers" (NRC 1996, p. 58). Teachers feel validated when they can hear other teachers describing what they are already doing in their own classrooms. Conferences provide these kinds of learning situations and the teachers who attend reap the benefits.

You Can Read All About It

Every professional organization provides some type of publication for its members. Whether they are professional refereed journals or newsletters, the publications provide an avenue for the exchange of new information. Many of these publications offer a mix of activities for classroom use, regular features, technology information, announcements about free or new materials, and upcoming events calendars. Members usually receive two types of publications. The first is informational, contains time-sensitive material, and is distributed more frequently. The second type is activity- or content-based and provides activities or knowledge background for educators to use within their classrooms. The articles are a helpful way to get to know other members. When you attend a conference, you can check the conference program and attend a session being conducted by someone whom you met in print. This is a wonderful way to hear the expanded version of a topic that has caught your interest.

All the World Is a Stage

In addition to increasing your knowledge and strategies at conferences, you have the chance to reciprocate and share your own ideas by presenting a session or workshop yourself. Don't be shy. Choose your favorite activity, unit, or series of lessons developed around a central theme, and share them with your colleagues. Giving a presentation challenges the presenter in several ways. First, it requires you to develop or assemble a sequence of materials that is logically organized for presentation. To do this, you delve into your own files, reexamine activities you have used throughout your career, and investigate what's available in the current literature. Next, you spend some time thinking about how to present these activities to fellow educators. This often requires thought processes different from those you use with students. Finally, you generate discussion during the presentation that is beneficial and challenges people to think in various ways. Often there are additional pieces offered by the participating educators. The result: You actually learn as you share. If you are interested in presenting, the first step is to obtain and submit a session proposal form from the convention you are interested in attending. It is important to note that deadline submission dates differ from organization to organization and often are months in advance of when the actual presentation will occur.

It Challenges You

Every organization has some type of board of directors or advisory committee that needs volunteers to become involved in some aspect of the group's mission. Elected or appointed positions allow you to become professionally active and influential in developing standards, policies, and future goals for a particular organization. However, leadership roles do not necessarily mean holding an office. Minor, but important, jobs range from serving on a convention-planning committee to volunteering your knowledge to coordinate a teacher-development opportunity. Serving in such a role not only develops friendships and networking opportunities, but also it allows you to grow as a leader. Direct involvement in a professional organization is recognized by administrators in your district. Your efforts reflect back directly to the district. Your successes become their successes.

Some General Suggestions for Becoming Involved

Begin by finding out if your state organization has a website. If so, it will contain many links to the topics mentioned above. NSTA's website (*www.nsta.org*) has links to many of the state association sites. Remember, websites provide information about upcoming conferences, sponsored programs, grant opportunities, and award programs. Contact NSTA to purchase a copy of the *NSTA Handbook*, which lists contact information for state and specialty organizations that may interest you. Find out if your state association has open board meetings, and, if possible, attend one to learn about committees and appointments.

Becoming a Dynamic Force

Teaching can be a rewarding profession. Involvement in professional organizations will increase the reward many times over. If you are a lifelong learner, have some untapped talents, or enjoy social interaction, a professional organization may be just what you have been missing in your life. You will never know for sure until you become involved.

Christine Anne Royce is an academic dean and science teacher at Bishop Hannan High School in Scranton, Pennsylvania. Judi Hechtman is the director and chairperson for the University School of IUP at Indiana University in Indiana, Pennsylvania.

Reference

National Research Council (NRC). 1996. *National Science Education Standards*. Washington, DC: National Academy Press.

Appendixes

Unit Planning

Unit planning is a much more deliberative process than just identifying and sequencing activities. To design an effective unit, you must have a clear idea of what you expect your students to be able to understand and do. This appendix outlines a "Backwards Design" (Wiggins and McTighe 2005) process that begins with an understanding of where you want your students to end. The process involves the following steps:

- Identify the appropriate **content**
- Develop learning **objectives**
- Create **assessments** to measure student progress toward objectives
- Identify an **instructional sequence**

Content

Content can be described in terms of basic understandings (vocabulary and simple concepts), more difficult concepts (including application of basic ideas), real-world applications (including opportunities for students to synthesize information and evaluate an issue), and pro-cess skills (including opportunities for science inquiry).

Do this: Use national or state standards documents, the internet, textbooks, and library resources to identify the appropriate content for your topic and grade level. Consider the following:

- Unit vocabulary
- Basic concepts
- Difficult concepts (and applications of basic concepts)
- Real-world connections (Why should kids care? Think about, for example, uses, controversies, and ethical issues.)
- Possible student initial ideas and misconceptions
- Science process skills and science inquiry concepts you would like to emphasize

Objectives

Learning objectives specify what a learner should know, understand, and be able to do as a result of instruction. Objectives should be observable and measurable and should often describe an action that a learner should be able to do. Objectives should use action verbs that reflect Bloom's Taxonomy.

"Students will understand the life cycle of a plant" and "Students will understand the concept of heat" are examples of poorly worded objectives. The first objective could be improved by using these two objectives:

- Students will illustrate at least four stages in the life cycle of a plant.

- Students will explain how the parts of the flower are used in reproduction.

The second objective could be improved as follows:

- Students will compare and contrast heat and temperature.

Do this: Write four or five learning objectives for this unit. Include both knowledge and skill outcomes.

Table 1.
Assessing in the 5E Model

"E"	Purpose	Example Assessments
Engage	Initiate, introduce, and engage Identify prior knowledge Motivate and focus	KWL, concept map, card sort task, memoir, brainstorming, interview, questionnaire, Venn diagram, science notebook, predicting, "scientists' meeting," observation
Explore	Test prior knowledge Provide common experiences Actively explore environment	Science notebook, conceptual cartoon, think-pair-share, drawing completion, predicting, demo memo, "scientists' meeting," chart, observation, performance assessment
Explain	Student-developed explanations Introduce formal terms and content Help students describe prior knowledge in terms of actual scientific concepts	Exit sheet, exit ticket, minute paper, discrepant event, concept test, making a model, making a claim, theory choice, meaningful paragraph, science notebook, KWL, labeled drawing, predicting, letter to the teacher (or other audience)
Elaborate	Apply or extend concepts to new contexts Develop deeper or broader understanding	Application problem, pair problem solving, thought experiment, debate, writing and analyzing fiction, design activity, science notebook, identification game, team report, data table and graph, predicting
Evaluate	Assess understanding as students apply what they know/have learned to solve problems	Poster, constructed response, presentation, comparison essay, final reflection, one-page memo, self-evaluation, scenario exam, concept mapping, Venn diagram, science notebook

Source: Adapted from Abell and Volkmann 2006.

Assessments

Once the content and learning outcomes are defined, you should determine how you will identify students' initial ideas *(preassessment)*, monitor student progress *(formative assessment)*, and evaluate mastery of the learning outcomes *(summative assessment)*. It is important to develop initial ideas on how to assess students before you begin thinking about actual instructional activities. You can refine your assessment plan as you work on your instructional sequence.

Abell and Volkmann (2006) describe how to embed assessment throughout the 5E instructional model. Table 1 describes the purpose of assessments in each phase and gives example assessments. The articles selected for section two also provide a variety of assessment strategies.

Do this: Describe your initial ideas for each component of the 5E model for your assessment plan.

Instructional Sequence

Finally, the fun part of unit planning! This is where your creativity really shines. How can you engage students, provide them with a variety of learning experiences, and help them learn content? An example unit plan and instructional calendar is provided in Figure 1.

Your students do not enter the classroom as blank slates. They have created naive conceptions of phenomena through a variety of experiences. Your job as an educator is to identify these ideas and help them move toward a more scientific understanding. At the core, constructivism contains these three components:

- **A**ctivating prior knowledge
- **B**uilding new knowledge
- **C**onnecting new knowledge to prior knowledge (metacongition: how do your ideas change?)

The BSCS 5E Model exemplifies these components of constructivism. Students identify their initial knowledge (Engage), participate in a common experience (Explore), build scientific knowledge (Explain), and apply this knowledge (Elaborate). Students also demonstrate their new knowledge (Evaluate). The 5E Model can be used to develop lessons around a single concept. It can also be expanded to facilitate unit planning in a constructivist manner. Engage and Explore components should always be positioned before specific science content is addressed (Explain).

Do this: Create an instructional calendar using the 5E Model.

- *Engage:* Introduce the unit by providing an activity to help students identify their previous knowledge. This should also motivate them to participate in the unit.

- *Explore:* Provide all students with a common foundational experience. This is a great place for guided or structured inquiry. Students should not be formally introduced to scientific content at this stage. Instead, this activity should allow students to work with manipulatives and play with ideas. This can be a short (one- or two-day) activity or a long-term exploration.

- *Explain:* This is the bulk of your unit. This component includes a variety of activities and assignments to build scientific content knowledge and process skills. Include a variety of modalities as appropriate (Table 2).

- *Elaborate:* This component may also include multiple activities. Students work with more complicated concepts. Students should apply the basic knowledge from the Explain component. This is great place for guided or open inquiry!

- *Evaluate:* Students demonstrate their knowledge. Opportunities should be provided to show mastery of the objectives. NOTE: This is the place for *summative assessment.* It should not be the only time for assessment in your unit. *Formative assessment* should be integrated into each component. Students should be challenged to think critically about content. This can be accomplished by having students respond to *synthesis questions.* These questions should be designed to allow students to conduct research and judge the value of ideas and should require original, creative thinking.

References

Abell, S. K., and M. K. Volkmann. 2006. *Seamless assessment in science: A guide for elementary and middle school teachers.* Arlington, VA: NSTA Press.

Wiggins, G., and J. McTighe. 2005. *Understanding by design.* Exp. 2nd edition. Alexandria, VA: Association for Supervision and Curriculum Development.

Figure 1.
Example 5E unit plan

Topic: Electric Circuits

Grade: Middle School

Author: Eric Brunsell

Objectives

At the end of this unit students will be able to:

- Identify conductors and insulators
- Explain the characteristics of a complete circuit
- Create an analogy for voltage and current
- Compare and contrast series and parallel circuits
- Calculate resistance, voltage, and current using Ohm's Law

Assessments

Engage: Students will be pre-assessed by trying to light a bulb with a battery and single wire. Students will also begin a KWL chart.

Explore: Students will be assessed on how they complete the redundant circuits activity sheet. As a class, students will also add to their KWL chart.

Explain 1: Students will be assessed in multiple ways.

- oral defense of vocabulary. They will be asked to define three random vocabulary terms from the list of vocabulary.
- Students will explain how a water "system" is an analogy for an electric circuit and then create their own analogy.
- Students will add to their KWL chart.

Elaborate 1: Teacher will observe students, specifically looking for how they use parallel and series circuits in their model house/rooms. Teacher will informally interview students by asking for examples of when it would be best to use a series or parallel circuit.

Explain 2: Students will accurately complete the activity worksheet to show that they understand how to use a voltmeter and ammeter.

Elaborate 2: Students will create a poster to describe how they investigated current and voltage in series and parallel circuits. Students will revisit either their analogy or the water analogy and expand it to include new knowledge from this activity. Students will add to the class KWL chart.

Evaluate: Students will take a unit test. The test will include multiple-choice (or true/false or matching) questions related to vocabulary, scenario recognition (in which circuits will the bulb light?), Ohm's Law questions, and a writing piece to compare and contrast series and parallel circuits.

This electric circuit unit has two synthesis questions. These will be given as a take-home essay assignment. Students are required to complete a certain number of synthesis questions each grading period.

Is wind energy a viable alternative to producing electricity from coal?

What is a "plug-in hybrid" car? Does it really save energy?

Figure 1. *(continued)*

Example 5E unit plan—unit calendar

Day 1	Day 2	Day 3	Day 4	Day 5
Engage: Battery & Wire, Begin KWL	Explore: Redundant circuits—in this activity, students create different types of circuits to provide redundancy in case of faulty switches. Students are able to discover parallel and series circuits without being formally introduced to the concepts.	Explain: Watch the Bill Nye electric circuit video (from *www. unitedstreaming. com*) HW: Introduce water analogy & have students create their own analogy.	Explain: Activity to identify conductors and insulators. Use a compass to indicate direction of current flow in a simple circuit. Add to KWL. HW: Read text section on electric circuits and answer summary questions.	Elaborate: Wire a model of a house to show an understanding of complete circuits and parallel vs. series circuits. Describe situations where you would use a series or parallel circuit. Explain the difference between conductors and insulators and how they are used in a house.

Day 6	Day 7	Day 8	Day 9	Day 10
Explain: Activity—how do you measure voltage and current in a simple circuit? HW: Read text section on Ohm's Law and complete Ohm's Law worksheet.	Explain: Student groups "whiteboard" and present Ohm's Law worksheet. Add to KWL. Student groups expand water or original analogy to include Ohm's Law. HW: Design the investigation for Day 8.	Elaborate: Develop and conduct an investigation to discover how voltage and current "work" in series and parallel circuits. HW: Read text section on parallel and series circuits. Expand water or original analogy to include voltage and current in series and parallel circuits.	Elaborate: Create a poster to describe their investigation (poster presentation/gallery walk). Review for unit test by revisiting and completing the KWL chart.	Evaluate: Unit test includes a performance assessment to create a parallel circuit and measure the current at a specific point.

Table 2.

Strategies for incorporating multiple modalities

Visual	Aural	Read/Write	Kinesthetic
Bulletin boards	Books on tape	Book reports	Building models
Graphs	Brainstorming	Case studies	Collections
Diagrams and pictures	Debates	Collecting and reading magazines	Creating exhibits
Dioramas	Explaining ideas to other students	Composing and studying sentences that use rich language and contain a lot of information in few words	Cultural dances
Displays	Group discussion		Demonstrations
Flannel boards	Group study sessions	Creating books	Drama
Flashcards	Guest speakers	Editing	Drawing or doodling as a mnemonic aid
Flow charts	Interviews	Essay	Hands-on activities
Graphic organizer	Lecture	Flashcards	Having students teach a lesson
Graphs	Listening to yourself	Internet	Highlighting while reading
Picture books	Listening to a podcast	Investigation notebooks	Manipulatives
Imagining information with eyes closed—visualizations	Mnemonics	Journals	Outdoor games
Maps	Oral exams	Learning definitions of words	Puppets
Mind maps	Oral response	Library research	Role-playing
Models	Playing music	Lists	Simulations
Outlines	Producing a jingle/song	Notes	Skits/plays
PowerPoint	Reading aloud	Outlining	Teaching students actions to go along with new vocabulary words
Time lines	Reading summarized notes aloud	Pen pals	Using all senses
Underlining and highlighting	Retelling	PowerPoint	Walking field trips
Videos	Rhythm & rhyme	Quotes	Working in a standing position
	Teacher-read stories	Reading books, essays, or newspapers	
	Singing	Rewriting notes or vocabulary	
	Videos	Writing a persuasive letter	

Note: List created by University of Wisconsin–LaCrosse students, fall 2007.

Safety in the Middle School

This reprint of the 2004 NSTA Press publication *Safety in the Middle School Science Classroom* is available in flip-chart form from the Science Store at *www.nsta.org*. The *Safety in the Elementary School Classroom* flip chart, which contains all the safety information pertinent to elementary grades, was published in 2003 and is also available through the Science Store.

NSTA is committed to publishing quality materials that promote the best in inquiry-based science education. However, conditions of actual use may vary, and the safety procedures and practices described in this publication are intended to serve only as a guide. Additional precautionary measures may be required. NSTA does not warrant or represent that the procedures and practices in this publication meet any safety code or standard or federal, state, or local regulations. NSTA and the author(s) disclaim any liability for personal injury or damage to property arising out of or relating to the use of this publication including any of the recommendations, instructions, or materials contained therein.

Introduction

Safety is not just a set of rules. It is a state of mind. This flip chart is just one tool to help you form good judgments every day in your science classroom. First form a mindset. Then:

- Read this guide from cover to cover.
- Survey your facility to see possible hazards from different points of view.
- Complete the safety checklist in the last section of this guide.
- Meet with your principal, science supervisor, and school nurse to review your findings.
- With your school team, develop an emergency plan. Put it in writing. List emergency telephone numbers, evacuation routes, and locations of key materials. Post the plan in a prominent place.
- Check your inventory. Make sure you have material safety data sheets (MSDS) for

every chemical, and that everyone knows the location of the MSDS file.

- Ask the administration to contact a disposal firm to properly dispose of old or unnecessary chemicals.
- Review first aid procedures. Make sure all staff, students, and other occupants of your science facility know what to do in an emergency.
- Review individual sections of this guide. Create your own plan for safe science.
- Check your lesson plans each week. Identify potential hazards, and revise your methods to reduce risk.
- Post this guide in a convenient place, so that it will be there when you need it.
- Post a list of telephone numbers for Emergency (911 or other); Fire Department; Police Department; Poison Control; School Nurse; School Principal; School Safety Officer; School Science Supervisor; School Address; and School Phone.

In Case of Accident

Before an accident occurs, obtain a written copy of your district's emergency plans and instructions, correlate it with the advice below, and modify this guide to conform with your district's policy. Then:

- Make sure emergency cards are on file for every student, and that they include parental releases for emergency medical treatment.
- For every chemical you have, keep on file a material safety data sheet (MSDS). Your MSDS file should be kept near the chemicals and in full view. Make sure the main office has a master file of all MSDSs that includes the location of the chemicals.
- Check and keep a written inventory and record of all safety equipment (e.g., ANSI-compliant eye protection, aprons, fire extinguishers, fire blankets, shower, eyewash) to ensure they are present, function

properly, and have up-to-date inspections.
- Make sure all exits and access to emergency equipment are clear and unobstructed.
- Have emergency numbers and evacuation plans posted prominently.
- Make sure you have kits for spills and body fluids, impermeable nonlatex gloves, and bandages.
- Demonstrate the use of emergency equipment to students so they can help in an emergency. Keep a record of your demonstrations.

In case of an uncontained emergency, FIRST evacuate the area and activate the nearest alarm.

For flames on persons or clothing, SHOUT "Stop, Drop, Roll," and apply fire blanket or running water.

In the event of contained emergency, take the following steps immediately:

1. Use all appropriate emergency equipment (e.g., eyewash, shower, fire blanket).

2. Call the main office and follow building emergency procedures.

3. If there is a possibility of serious injury:

- Summon school medical personnel immediately. Otherwise notify main office to summon emergency help (911 or local equivalent).
- Keep the injured person quiet and protected.
- Maintain Standard (Universal) Precautions for all body fluids.
- If you are trained in first aid, apply first aid according to your school district's policy. Do not administer medication unless specifically directed on the student's emergency card.
- Contact the physician or emergency service identified on the student's emergency card if the office staff or nurse does not do this.

- Contact the parent, guardian, or other designated contact.
- When the student is safely in the hands of professionals, prepare a thorough written report of the incident for the record. Collect independent recollections of other witnesses as appropriate.

After any incident, meet with your school team to create plans to avoid similar accidents.

If these recommendations conflict with local policy, FOLLOW YOUR DISTRICT'S PROCEDURES.

Reference

Learning by Accident (vols. I, II, III). 1997, 2000, 2003. Laboratory Safety Institute, 192 Worcester Road, Natick, MA 01760. *www.labsafety.org.*

Eye Protection

Several types of eye safety devices exist:

Chemical splash goggles are indirectly ventilated, fit the face around the eyes, seal to the face, and have side panels and vents; they are needed whenever students use chemicals or heat.

Impact goggles can be indirectly ventilated, fit the face around the eyes, seal to the face, and are ANSI Z87.1-compliant to indicate that they are impact-resistant. They are always needed with material that could break, fly, or shatter.

We strongly recommend that you buy ANSI Z87.1-compliant chemical splash goggles. They will also protect against impact.

A face shield is used in addition to goggles and protects the face and throat against impact and splashes.

A safety shield provides splash and impact protection for the viewing group, but not for the demonstrator.

Even though safety shields may add protection for demonstrations, we do not recommend conducting any demonstrations at the middle school level that require the use of safety shields.

Eye protection is necessary but not sufficient. Begin by selecting an investigation method that reduces the possibility of damage to the eye. That can include low heat, unbreakable containers, appropriate equipment, and small quantities of chemicals.

Then, to establish an effective eye safety program, you should:

- Become fully aware of all state and local eye protection equipment requirements and comply with them.
- Be certain that you have the right kind of eye protection for the activity.
- Establish consistent rules about eye protection; goggles belong on for the entire activity, until everyone is finished, whenever an activity involves heat, chemicals, impact, or the potential of projectiles.
- If the teacher is wearing goggles, then every student also should be wearing goggles—even for demonstrations.
- Establish a system for distributing, storing, and sanitizing goggles. If students cannot be assigned their own goggles, goggles should be sanitized after each use. If you use a sanitizer, the goggles must be placed carefully. (Tip: See if your PTA/PTO would consider purchasing a pair of safety goggles for each student upon entry to your middle school.)
- Check to see if your state has statutes or laws about using goggles.
- Make sure that teachers, paraprofessionals, and visitors model best eye protection practices.
- Be conscious of other activities that use equipment that can spread eye infections—microscopes, binoculars, blindfolds, or sunscreen eyewear. Monitor each of these activities to make sure that bacterial or viral conjunctivitis can't be spread on the equipment.

References

ANSI Z87.1. 2003. *Occupational and Educational Eye and Face Protection.* American National

Standards Institute, Inc., 1430 Broadway, New York 10018.

Occupational Safety and Health Administration. (OSHA) Regulation 29CFR1910.132 and Regulation 29CFR1910.133. Washington, DC: OSHA.

Plants, Fungi, and Bacteria in the Classroom

A classroom where students can observe, compare, and classify organisms enhances their understanding of the natural world. But only introduce organisms you know well, and maintain them in safe conditions.

Precautions for dealing with plants:

1 Do not place any part of a plant in your mouth.
2 Do not allow any sap or fruit juice to penetrate your skin.
3 Do not inhale or expose your skin or eyes to the smoke of any burning plant.
4 Do not pick any unknown wildflowers, seeds, berries, mushrooms, or cultivated plants.
5 Do not eat food after handling plants without first scrubbing your hands with soap and water.
6 Do not transport plants across state lines or release non-native plants into the wild.

A Plants poisonous to the touch due to exuded oils are:

1 Poison ivy (*T. radicans; R. diversiloba*)
2 Poison oak (*R. quercifolia; T. diversilobum*)
3 Poison sumac (*R. vernix*)
4 Oleander (*N. oleander*)(often found on school grounds)
5 Yew (*T. baccata*)
6 Other_____

B Plants poisonous when eaten include:

1 Many fungi (*mushrooms*)
2 Aconite (*A. napellus*)
3 Belladonna (*A. belladonna*)
4 Wake robin (genus *Trillium*)

5 Henbane (*H. niger*)
6 Pokeweed (*P. americana*)
7 Tansy (genus *Tanacetum*)
8 Foxglove (*D. purpurea*)
9 Indian tobacco (*L. inflata*)
10 Jimson weed (*D. stramonium*)
11 Poinsettia (*E. pulcherrima*)
12 Mistletoe (*V. album*)
13 Other_____

C The saps of the following plants are toxic:

1 Oleander (*N. oleander*)
2 Poinsettia (*E. pulcherrima*)
3 Trumpet vine (*C. radicans*)
4 Other _____

D Be aware that many common houseplants are toxic.

1 Poinsettia (*E. pulcherrima*)
2 Dieffenbachia (*D. maculata*)
3 Castor bean (*R. communis*)
4 Mistletoe (*V. album*)
5 Lantana
6 Other _____

Avoid Molds and Mildew:

1 Many people are allergic to mold, mildew, and other fungi. Use only commercial potting soils. Discard moldy soil, and maintain plants with only the minimal water necessary for growth.
2 Do not grow molds in open containers. For observational purposes, grow molds in sealed containers, and sterilize with 10% chlorine bleach solution before disposal. Be aware of the possible accumulation of molds in heating, cooling, and ventilation systems. Report dirty filters, leaks from ductwork, and persistent allergies to the appropriate administrator.

Bacterial Cultures:

1 Environmental bacteria can be extremely dangerous when cultured. Middle schoolers

should never culture bacteria in systems that can be opened. (Safer commercial systems that remain sealed are available from vendors.)

2 Ensure that any bacterial culture is treated with aseptic techniques. Observational cultures should be sterilized with 10% household chlorine bleach solution before disposal.

3 Never attempt to develop antibiotic-resistant cultures or genetically modified cultures in middle school programs.

References

AMA Handbook of Poisonous and Injurious Plants. 1985. Kenneth F. Lampe and Mary Ann McCann, AMA, distributed by Chicago Review Press, Chicago, IL.

CDC/NIH. 1999. Biosafety in Microbiological and Biomedical Laboratories. See *cdc.gov/od/ohs*.

First Aid

First aid is the immediate care given to someone who has been injured or suddenly taken ill. It is used in emergencies where medical assistance is not immediately available, and its purpose is to protect rather than to treat. Each teacher carries the responsibility for knowing what to do if a victim becomes ill or injured in the classroom. We recommend that science teachers take American Red Cross first aid training and Standard (Universal) Precautions training and follow up with review courses as recommended by the Red Cross.

Obtain medical aid for injuries and sudden illness, in every case of injury to the eye, and whenever the seriousness of the injury or illness is unknown. School employees should not diagnose, treat, or prescribe or offer medication, but they may give first aid if properly trained. Remember that there should be an emergency card for every student. Find out where they are kept, and take duplicate copies on field trips. Check your local policy on administering first aid and using first aid kits.

1 Protect the victim. Get victims to the fire blanket, the shower, or the eyewash as appropriate. For falls and impact injuries, keep the victim flat and protected. In case of chemical splash in the eye, continue flushing with clean water for a minimum of 15 minutes—do not stop while waiting for emergency or medical personnel.

2 REMAIN CALM and keep crowds away from the victim.

3 Call the main office, school medical personnel, or emergency services (911 or local alternative) as prescribed by district policy.

4 Handle the victim as little as possible before professionals evaluate the injury. Cover the victim if appropriate. Do nothing else unless you are certain of the correct procedure.

5 Minimize the damage from a burn that has not broken the skin by flushing with clean cold water until appropriate assistance arrives.

6 Minimize bleeding while using Standard (Universal) Precautions to prevent infection. There are designated personnel and procedures to deal with body fluids and spills. Do not allow untrained persons to help clean up blood or other body fluids.

- Always wear impermeable nonlatex gloves when handling blood or body fluids.
- Severe bleeding can be slowed by applying a large compress with direct pressure.
- For a small wound, check for embedded foreign objects. Wash, rinse, and apply a dressing.
- Use labeled, designated containers to dispose of any material that might be contaminated by body fluids and clean the premises following approved Standard (Universal) Precautions.

7 If a victim is not breathing, a trained person may try to restore breathing using one of these methods:

- Mouth-to-mouth (mouth-to-nose) method
- Cardiopulmonary resuscitation (CPR)
- Techniques for clearing obstruction of the airway (including the upward thrust, commonly known as the Heimlich maneuver)

8 For severe injuries, shock may be a risk. While waiting for first responders, minimize the chance of shock by
  - Placing the victim in a reclining position with the head lower than the body, unless the victim is having difficulty breathing.
  - Controlling any bleeding by applying direct pressure.
  - Wrapping the victim with blankets, coats, paper, etc.
  - Keeping the victim's airway open.

After the victim has been placed in the care of appropriate medical personnel, write a report of the incident.

References

American Red Cross. *Community First Aid and Safety.* 2002. Staywell, San Bruno, CA.

American Red Cross. *The American Red Cross First Aid and Safety Handbook.* 1992. Little Brown & Co., Boston.

American Red Cross. *American Red Cross First Aid: Responding to Emergencies.* 2001. Staywell, San Bruno, CA.

Roy, Kenneth R. 2004. What is your first-aid policy? *Science Scope* 27(4): 38–39 and 27(5): 14–15.

Animals in the Classroom

Organisms put the "life" in life science. But before you introduce animals and protists to your classroom, check the possible hazards and your district's policy.

Animals that should not be permitted in classrooms:

1 Wild animals (dead or alive). They can spread zoonotic diseases and/or injure students.
2 Poisonous or venomous animals.
3 Exotic mammals, no matter what the source.
4 Diseased animals or any animals infested with ticks, mites, and other parasites.
5 Animals with high dander levels (e.g., rabbits and guinea pigs) should not be permitted in carpeted classrooms and generally should be avoided, because they produce allergens that persist in the environment despite regular cleaning.

Discourage students from bringing personal pets to school. The health and temperament of personal pets are too frequently incompatible with classroom situations including large numbers of strangers.

Handling and Maintaining Animals:

1 Obtain all animals from a reputable source. Make sure that fish are healthy, and check with the dealer about their behavior and maximum size.
2 Provide animals with properly sized living quarters. Animals must be kept clean and free from contamination and remain in closed, well-ventilated cages.
3 Make provisions for care of classroom animals on weekends, holidays, and over the summer and other long school breaks.
4 Make provisions for professional veterinary care for classroom animals. Have animals checked if there is any question of illness or disease.
5 Use gloves for handling animals, and have students wash their hands with soap before and after they handle animals.
6 Caution students never to tease animals or to insert their fingers or objects into cages. Report animal bites and scratches immediately to the office. Provide basic first aid.
7 Pick up rats, hamsters, and mice by the scruff of the neck, with a hand placed under the body for support. If young are to be handled, remove the mother to another cage—by nature she will be fiercely protective.
8 Before you bring an animal into the classroom, make plans for its future following its use in the classroom. Never release nonnative or tamed animals into the wild.
9 On field trips, tell students to avoid picking up, feeding, or touching unfamiliar animals.

Protists and Microinvertebrates:
Protists and microinvertebrates can be used in studies of water quality and biodiversity. But remember that the water in which they live can be polluted. Students should always wash their hands with soap and hot water after handling cultures (purchased or collected).

Some protists and microinvertebrates can cause disease. Flush faucets and eyewashes regularly, and make sure that students never work in polluted water.

Reference

Classroom Creature Culture: Algae to Anoles. 1997. National Science Teachers Association, Arlington, VA: NSTA Press.

Field Trips

Field trips are valuable, positive additions to the middle school science program. A good field trip is well planned, with educational objectives identified and activities planned to reach those objectives. With careful organization, the possibility of accidents is greatly reduced. But expect the unexpected. A few relatively simple precautions can improve safety.

Before you go:

1 Preview and thoroughly check the site before bringing students. Ask owners and facilities staff about specific hazards. Make sure you tell them about students with special physical needs.
2 Prepare specific permission slips for the trip including a description of the site and activities planned. Ask that parents review the information and let you and the student know what specific accommodations or precautions might be needed for their child to participate.
3 Bring along complete information on your students, including permission slips and copies of emergency cards. Make sure you have material safety data sheet (MSDS) information on all chemicals to be used in the field.

4 A second knowledgeable adult is always necessary on a field trip. Additional trained chaperones will depend on the site, the maturity of the students, and the complexity of the tasks you will expect students to perform. The chaperone/student ratio should be no greater than 1:10. Hazardous sites such as water bodies or sites that involve climbing and sampling require lower ratios. Special education students should have additional assistants to ensure that they can participate fully and safely.
5 Make sure you have contact numbers along for emergencies and late returns. If you bring a cell phone, be sure that there is reception and that you do not engage in any activity that would be imprudent if there were not a cell phone.
6 Prepare your chaperones before the trip. Ask them to practice the skills, review the map, and discuss emergency procedures. Siblings should not be included on field trips.
7 Require appropriate dress for the trip. That may include hard shoes, long pants, and clothing appropriate for anticipated temperature and weather.
8 Pair students with buddies for organization, discipline, and accounting for everyone's presence.
9 Divide responsibilities before the trip and arrange for periodic attendance and equipment checks.
10 Plan for insect protection in advance including designating appropriate clothing to reduce exposure. Ask students to bring their own insect repellent along with written parental permission for using the repellent.
11 Check first aid kits to ascertain that they contain the appropriate items for the site and activity.
12 Carry a change of clothes—sweatshirts and pants work well—in case of accident.
13 On a water-related field trip, at least one trained lifeguard is required. Special needs

students may need individual supervision in addition to class chaperones. Life jackets must always be worn on water trips.

14 Warn students about the organisms they might encounter. Tell them not to pick plants and not to feed or touch animals.

15 Plan in advance for good discipline. Discuss the rules and consequences. Inform parents.

16 Make sure trips to factories and laboratories are well supervised and that an experienced representative conducts the tour. Make sure safety equipment, such as hard hats or eye protection, is available when appropriate. Remember that tour guides may not be used to middle school students, so they need advance preparation.

17 Notify parents when you will return. Never leave students unsupervised back at the school; wait until all have found their transportation home.

Fire Prevention and Control

The first step to fire safety is prevention. Check your room regularly:

- Get rid of clutter. Don't accumulate anything flammable or combustible, including extra paper.
- Make sure that all aisles and escape routes are clear and accessible.
- Do not store flammable liquids in a classroom or use them near heat sources.
- Check the electrical system for frayed wires, overloaded circuits, hanging wires, and make sure that all plugs have all three prongs intact.
- Use only laboratory-certified hot plates and short, thick candles as heat sources in middle school. Avoid using open flame (including gas burners) whenever possible. Never use alcohol burners in the middle school.
- Enforce a dress code (e.g., no loose clothing, hair tied back) that minimizes the risk of fire.

Prepare for the Worst
- Have a plan for fires, and post it.
- Practice fire drills repeatedly during the year.
- A/B/C extinguishers and fire blankets should be in every room.

Teachers are responsible for acting deliberately and intelligently in a classroom fire. You must know the location of the firefighting aids—the blanket, the extinguishers, and the fire alarm box—and also how to use them. Make sure fire alarms are installed and checked regularly.

The following classification of fires is based on the type of material being consumed:

Class A—*Fires in wood, textiles, paper, and other ordinary combustibles.* Extinguish this type of fire with water or a solution containing water (loaded steam) that wets down the material and prevents glowing embers from rekindling. A general purpose dry chemical extinguisher is also effective.

Class B—*Fires in gasoline, oil, paint, or other flammable liquids that gasify when heated.* Extinguish this type of fire by smothering—shutting off the air supply. Carbon dioxide, dry chemicals, and foam extinguishers are effective. To use a dry chemical or carbon dioxide extinguisher, follow PASS: **P**ull the pin, **A**im the nozzle at the flame, **S**queeze the handle, and **S**weep across the fire. Do not hold the horn of the carbon dioxide extinguisher with your hands; use the handle, because the carbon dioxide causes supercooling of the horn. To use a foam extinguisher, invert the extinguisher and point the nozzle so the foam floats over the fire; do not point the stream at the flame. This extinguisher does not have a cutoff valve and must be completely expelled.

Class C—*Fires in live electrical equipment.* Extinguish this type of fire by using a nonconductive agent. A carbon dioxide extinguisher smothers the flame without damaging the equipment. A dry chemical extinguisher is also

effective. Whenever possible, cut off the source of power to the burning equipment.

Class D—*Fires in combustible materials such as magnesium, titanium, zirconium, sodium, potassium, and others.* This new and somewhat specialized classification is extinguished by a special extinguisher powder, which is applied by a scoop. Dry sand can also extinguish small Class D fires. Apply by scoop.

If the Worst Occurs

For a fire in a room, evacuation is the first priority. Take only a grade book or class list (to check that everyone has been accounted for).

- If a student's hair catches fire, smother the fire with hands or a lab coat.
- If a student's clothing catches fire, a fire blanket can be used.
- Practice "Stop, Drop, and Roll" with students.
- Never use a CO_2 fire extinguisher on a person. It can cause frostbite and sometimes spread a fire.

Reference

Fire Protection Handbook, NFPA, 18th edition. 1997. National Fire Protection Association, Quincy, MA.

Storage and Labeling

Poor storage invites accidents. Adequate, efficient storage is essential for safety in the classroom. Provide at least 10 square feet per student of separate, secure storage and preparation space. Keep in mind the following when storing equipment and materials:

Chemical Storage Areas

- Keep storeroom doors and storage cabinets locked.
- Do not store chemicals in classrooms or in preparation/equipment rooms.
- Store chemicals no more than two deep on

a shelf with enough space to reach in without knocking anything over. Provide a lip or dowel fence on the shelf edge to help prevent items from falling off.

- Separate flammables, corrosives, and reactive and toxic chemicals. Store each type in approved cabinets.
- Ventilate chemical storage areas at all times (not just when the facility is occupied).
- Providing both smoke and heat detectors is recommended.

Quantities

- Maintain only a select group of chemicals and only in small quantities (a one-year supply is recommended). Don't store anything you don't need or anything that is not appropriate for your own curriculum.
- Never accept excess chemicals from another school or an industrial or laboratory source.
- Never bring stock bottles of chemicals into the classroom. Dispense daily quantities into smaller, labeled, secure containers for classroom use.
- Mark stock bottles with date of purchase.
- Make sure you have material safety data sheets (MSDS) for every chemical, with duplicate copies in the classroom laboratory and in the office.
- Use alternatives to dangerous or highly concentrated chemicals: vinegar for acid, baking soda for base, etc.
- Following school district, state, and federal regulations, carefully remove substances if they have lost their labels or if there is any confusion about their identity. They should never be used in experiments.

Transfer and Control

Ideally, the chemical storeroom should be as close as possible to point of use. If chemicals must be transported through a hallway, a lockable rolling cart can be used, but only small (classroom) quantities should be removed from the storeroom. Hazardous materials should be transported, in a suitable secondary container, through the halls only under the direct supervision of a teacher wearing safety equipment and when few or no students or other people are in the halls. Maintain a method for checking in and checking out materials and supplies.

Reference

Fisher Science Education Catalog/Manual. 2003-4. 4500 Turnberry Drive, Hanover Park, IL 60133.

Safe Use of Equipment and Materials

Tools and equipment represent significant hazards in a science classroom. Never allow students to operate equipment and tools except under your direct supervision. The following is a list of the more common equipment and materials with suggestions for their safest and most efficient use.

Electrical Devices

- Check all devices before you bring them to the classroom. Make sure your circuits can handle the equipment, that the power connections are safe (not frayed, cracked, or broken), and that all plugs have three prongs intact.
- Make sure that electrical equipment can be plugged in safely. Cords should not hang or stretch across work areas or sinks. In the rare occasion that a cord must extend across a floor it must be taped securely to avoid tripping.
- Show students how to plug in and disconnect electrical devices—pull the plug, never the cord.
- Never grasp any electrical device that has just been used. Most electrical devices remain hot after use, and serious burns may result.
- Do not short circuit (directly connect the terminals of) dry cells or storage batteries. High temperatures in the connecting wire can cause serious burns or fires. Rechargeable batteries can have dangerously high voltage.

- Do not use socket multipliers to increase the number of items that can be put on a single receptacle.
- Use only devices with grounded, three-wire connections.
- Do not remove the ground connector on a plug or use an adapter to bypass the ground connection.
- Every electrical outlet in a classroom laboratory should be protected by a ground fault interrupter (GFI). An emergency classroom shutoff should also be available.
- Never open an electrical device unless the plug has been removed. Never open a computer monitor or television, even if it has no plug, because these devices can maintain significant charges.

Glassware

- Prevent student injuries from sharp edges on mirrors, prisms, and glass plates. Remove sharp edges by grinding or by using an emery cloth or carborundum stone, or by having the edges painted with quick-drying enamel or nail polish.
- Glass rods or tubing should not be bent in middle school classrooms. Only trained teachers (wearing gloves) should insert tubing or thermometers into rubber stoppers.
- Use plastic containers instead of glass whenever possible. When glass is necessary, use heat-resistant borosilicate equipment. Never reuse a chipped or broken item of glassware. Never use glassware that is not thoroughly dry.
- You should have one container for disposal of broken glass that was used for chemicals. Clean the glass before disposal. You should have a second container for disposal of other sharps potentially contaminated with biological materials.

Equipment

A variety of small power tools, appliances, or equipment may be found in classrooms. Three-prong plugs should be used on all power tools and other equipment to reduce the chance for electrical shock. Extension cords should not be used. Special care should be taken to avoid contact with moving parts or heating elements of any equipment. The following items should be used with caution: heating elements for fish tanks, small motors, soldering irons, hot plates, and electrical fans. Power tools (saws, drills, and sanders) should not be used.

Hand Tools.
Many hand tools are used in science activities. Provide a workbench with a suitable work surface and storage facilities for tools. Hand tools are designed for specific purposes and should be used only for those purposes. Earth science activities require rock hammers, not building hammers. In all cases, use appropriate eye protection.

Pencil Sharpeners.
Students have suffered eye damage inadvertently from the point of an extra pencil in the hand turning the crank. Locate the pencil sharpener below eye level, preferably at tabletop level, to reduce the occurrence of such accidents.

Balances.
Balances are among the most frequently stolen articles from science facilities. If possible, avoid storing them in the classroom or out in the open. If this is impractical, secure the instruments to counters or work surfaces with bolts or chains. Before you drill, be sure counters do not contain asbestos.

Electronic Equipment.
Avoid placement of electronic equipment where water or other liquids are likely to be spilled or splashed. Provide extra security (double locks or bolts) for small electronic equipment.

References
Flinn Chemical Catalog/Reference Manual. 2000. Flinn Scientific Inc., P.O. Box 219, Batavia, IL 60510.

Handbook of Laboratory Safety, A.K. Furr, 5th edition. 2000. CRC Press, Boca Raton, FL 53545.

Safety Checklist
Safety Every Day
- Know your federal, state, and local regulations, your school's policies, and best practices.
- Know your students. Choose activities and materials that match their developmental level.
- Know yourself. Choose activities that match your training, protective equipment, and facilities.
- Check your facilities regularly, using a checklist from a good organization.
- Make sure that you have enough space for safety. Clear out excess furniture and reduce class sizes or modify the curriculum to ensure safety.
- Maintain your fire equipment and practice fire safety drills regularly.
- Check your equipment before use. Make sure it is operating correctly.
- Check your inventory. Keep it current. Don't store what you don't need, and store everything in appropriate, secure cabinets or shelves.
- Start the year with a safety lesson, and begin each lesson with a review of safety procedures required for the activity.
- Make sure you have a system to teach those who are absent the appropriate precautions.
- Schedule carefully; make sure there is enough time for preparation and cleanup, but not too much time to allow for nonsense. Break complex procedures into smaller units with a check and safety review midway.
- Create a system that works every time for distributing and returning safety equipment (such as eye protection).
- Do not ask substitute teachers to conduct laboratory activities. Keep plans for nonlab activities available for use by substitute teachers.

When Working With Chemicals

- Instill a sense of caution with chemicals.
- Keep stock bottles in a locked storeroom; bring only the minimum to class in labeled containers.
- Never taste a chemical.
- Tell students to touch chemicals only when instructed.
- Use chemical splash goggles all of the time that chemicals are in use.
- Never use chemicals that are stronger than needed, or in greater quantities.
- Keep MSDS available at all times. Review the sheets with students before using the chemical. Know the hazards, spill cleanup, and waste disposal before using the chemical.

Glassware

- Use plastic containers whenever possible. If glass is needed, use heat-resistant borosilicate.
- Tell students to report sharp edges, cracks, or chips.
- Keep available a whisk broom and dustpan for sweeping up broken glass, and place broken glass in a separate disposal container.
- Warn students not to eat or drink from glassware used for science experiments.
- Use thermometers filled with alcohol, not mercury.

Electrical Safety

- Check all electrical equipment and cords for safety before use.
- Have ground fault interrupters on every receptacle.
- Never open electrical equipment.
- Keep cords away from water.
- Never overload your circuits.
- Use only grounded equipment.

Fire Safety

- Make sure your fire equipment is in good condition.
- Practice fire prevention and escape routines regularly.
- Avoid using open flame if possible.
- Never use alcohol burners in middle school.
- Never allow flammable liquids near sources of heat.

References

Laboratory Safety Guidelines. Laboratory Safety Institute, 192 Worcester Road, Natick, MA 01760. Copies free. *www.labsafety.org*.

Science Teachers' Association of Ontario. Safety articles from *Crucible*, STAO's professional journal for science teachers. *http://www.stao.org/safartcl.htm*. Accessed Sept. 15, 2003.

"Safety and School Science Instruction." 2000. NSTA Position Statement. See *www.nsta.org/position#list*.

Index

Note: Page numbers in *italics* refer to tables or illustrations.